Thriving on Adaptability

Best Practices for Knowledge Workers

Foreword by

Surendra Reddy

Excellence in Practice Series

Published in association with

Workflow Management Coalition

W f M C

22 Years of Thought-Process Leadership

Edited by

Layna Fischer

Future Strategies Inc., Book Division

Lighthouse Point, Florida

Thriving on Adaptability:
Best Practices for Knowledge Workers
Copyright © 2015 by Future Strategies Inc.
ISBN-13: 978-0-9863214-0-5

Published by Future Strategies Inc., Book Division

3640-B3 North Federal Highway #421
Lighthouse Point FL 33064 USA
954.782.3376 fax 954.719.3746
www.FutStrat.com; books@FutStrat.com

Publisher's Cataloging-in-Publication Data

Library of Congress Catalog Card LCCN No. 2014959387

© 2015 ISBN 9780986321405

Thriving on Adaptability: Best Practices for Knowledge Workers

/Layna Fischer (editor)

p. cm.

Includes bibliographical references, glossary, appendices and index.

1. Adaptive Case Management. 2. Intelligent Systems. 3. Knowledge Work 4. Business Intelligence. 5. Business Process Technology. 6. Production Case Management. 7. Productivity Improvement 8. Predictive Analytics 9. Business Process Technology. 10. Process Mining

Reddy, Surendra; Swenson, Keith; Palmer, Nathaniel; *et al* (authors)

Fischer, Layna (editor)

Thriving on Adaptability

Table of Contents

Section 2: Appendices

Foreword

ACM 2.0: Decoding the Business Genome

The power of Data-Driven Adaptive Process Management, Contextual Intelligence, Case-Based Reasoning, and Machine Learning

Surendra Reddy, Quantiply Corporation

"As far as the laws of mathematics refer to reality, they are not certain, and as far as they are certain, they do not refer to reality." Albert Einstein.

The future is about rapidly dealing with change. Competitive intensity is rising all over the world. Customers are the single biggest factor in any company's long-term growth and profitability. Global competition and digital transformation have given customers more choices and access to information than ever before. This means that customers are able to choose from an overwhelming selection.

Customers are demanding services in real-time. Business processes need to be executed in real-time in response to customer demands. Managers and employees need to work collaboratively, share knowledge, and prepare to make instant decisions. The demand pull of the fast competitive global business landscape, the tectonic shifts caused by digital transformation, and instant connectivity to everything are disrupting the rigid process-oriented operating system. At the same time, customers, competitors and even cooperating partners continually change the way business is done and thus are altering the overall business landscape itself. These changes and shifts in customer behavior have turned *every* industry into a service industry. Service businesses know they must incorporate customer-focused adaptive processes into their business operations; which can create increased complexity, variability, and constant change to deal with new realities.

Business Process can be simply defined as a way of doing business. It is the central nervous system of the 21st century enterprise. The rise of a new generation of knowledge workers, the emergence of networks of experts, and the fast diffusion of knowledge are also changing the way business processes are conducted.

Modeling business processes is not an easy task as it is very difficult to capture all the relevant conditions and facts beforehand. Real-time situations are frequently unpredictable and ambiguous, and cannot be described precisely. Furthermore, complete characterization of a real system requires high fidelity data and real-time contextual insights to realize fully automated, adaptive, and reflexive business processes. Most of the conventional tools for formal modeling, reasoning, and computing are hard, deterministic, and precise. Companies have invested heavily in business process management systems and static dashboards to optimize their operations for a perfect one-way stream; the line of production. Over time, business processes have been standardized, outsourced, off-shored, in-sourced, shared, re-outsourced, and even sometimes ignored, primarily to reduce costs.

Enterprises immensely benefited from optimized processes within command-and-control structures. Today, however, the challenge is to coordinate and orchestrate sharing of knowledge and expertise both inside and outside of the organization. Enterprises need to continuously innovate and reinvent new processes and business models by harnessing enterprise and business ecosystem-wide knowledge and expertise.

Command-and-control structures are becoming obsolete, if they are not already. Enterprises are transforming into self-organizing, self-learning, distributed and collaborative expert or knowledge worker-centric networks to engage and draw knowledge and resources from inside and outside the enterprise. Enterprises are decoding their *business genome* to create their unique differentiation. Business genomes provide valuable insights into the critical success factors of total customer experience, velocity, and operational efficiencies, for example, enabling enterprises to learn and adapt their operating processes or systems delivering instant customer value; every time and all the time.

Welcome to the age of intelligent machines and connected everything. It is the world of consumerism. Processes now travel at the speed of light. Adaptive processes do, in fact, provide huge competitive advantages. It is not enough to design processes that are efficient. These processes, at the core of the digital transformation, also need to help us rapidly predict and act. Enterprises should be able to uniquely construct and map their business process genome so that enterprise is able to create unique identities, and hence deliver continual competitive differentiation for their customers. Today's market dynamics offer virtually every business a channel to constantly redefine or reimagine their processes. Every step of the customer experience—from marketing and sales, to order fulfillment and customer support—offers opportunities to optimize business processes and identify new markers and sequences to enable creation of new products and services.

Unpredictability and variety are the new reality. Unpredictability can be found in every area of our daily lives. The driving forces for fuzziness or unpredictability are rapidly changing new knowledge or insights, human judgment, analysis, elasticity, and the half-life of decisions and intellectual property. Hardly any business processes in today's business context are fixed or predictable. Moreover, human knowledge or subject matter expertise is key to optimal performance of these business processes. Augmenting business process with the human insights or knowledge to refine and optimize these so-called non-predictable case scenarios is extremely critical for the next generation enterprise to be able to continually create and re-create their optimal competitive advantage. Change is not only constant but it is disrupting the way of doing business and impacting every part of the organization. Enterprises need to collaboratively map and remap their business genome to understand their unique differentiation and build an adaptive data-driven operating environment.

While business process modeling (like BPMN) tools helped organizations improve workflow, newer technologies—social media, mobile, analytics, and cloud, etc., —are driving a new era of business process innovation. Technology drives many effects: it reduces the friction of distance, it increases the variety of options and possibilities, it increases the velocity of just about everything. It also increases complexity and interdependency. New technological innovations in machine learning, real-time analytics, contextual intelligence, mobility, and cloud are now enabling Adaptive Case Management (ACM) as a strategic tool for transforming organizations into customer focused organizations. These tools and technologies enable real-time, collaborative decision-making by creating networks of subject matter experts (knowledge workers) and providing them the needed insights, information, next best actions, and recommendations, creating an optimal operating environment.

The sequence of human or customer actions is not knowable in advance, and this course may vary greatly from case-to-case. The course—I call it *customer journey* —will depend greatly on the details of the situation itself, and the details of how the business is conducted (i.e. business process) may change before the customer interaction is complete.

Prediction of the course of events is no longer based on a statically defined set of rules. It must be based on new and relevant information that the organization has about the customers, products, and competition at the time. Most of the real-world business processes are always tentative, contingent upon the next piece of knowledge/insight discovered. This style of business process patterns is becoming the new normal in modern enterprise. Sensing, Reasoning and Predicting the next best action (NBA), or next best recommendations (NBR) to the business process step, is becoming a critical requirement. I clearly see and envision how ACM fits into transforming organizations from static silos to dynamic, continuously learning, adapting organizations, enabled through ACM into next generation, customer-focused, adaptive organizations.

Collaboratively discovering and dynamically adapting to the real-world and even real-time situation is the key for 21st century organizations to deal with unpredictability. There will be rapid advancements in technology, as well as, the human interaction and or response to these technological changes. Soon, human and machine conversations will be an integral part of our daily lives. Though it may take little longer to realize singularity, there will be an intersection of time where human intelligence symbiotically augments machine intelligence to move us closer to singularity.

Organizations should become more creative and innovative. We don't need to reinvent more acronyms. A combination of BPM and ACM gives us the needed framework to deliver social casebooks to drive customer focused and socially responsible organizations. Enterprises can view ACM as a strategy to simultaneously increase customer experience and drive business innovation. It is not *either* BPM *or* ACM, it is the combination of these two that enables integration and automation of processes and analytics to improve information and collaboration and to incorporate best practices through a network of subject matter experts and organizational knowledge.

Imagine a fully integrated ACM system layered into the value stream of an enterprise. The customer support team is able to focus on customer needs, with easy access to the entire company's repertoire of knowledge, similar cases, information, and expertise, as if it were a service. To truly accommodate customers, companies must vest real power and authority in the people and systems that interact directly with customers, at the edge of the organization and beyond. ACM augments business processes to deliver true data driven process infrastructure entering enterprises into the age of intelligent machines and intelligent processes. ACM empowers the knowledge worker to collaborate, derive new insights, and fine tune the way of doing business by placing customers right in the center where they belong, to drive innovation and organizational efficiencies across the global enterprise.

ACM also helps organizations focus on improving or optimizing the line of interaction where our people and systems come into direct contact with customers. It's a whole different thing; a new way of doing business that enables organizations to literally become one living-breathing entity via collaboration and adaptive data-driven biological-like operating systems. ACM is not just another acronym or business fad. ACM is the process, strategy, framework, and set of tools that enables this evolution and maturity.

ACM, in my opinion, is the future blueprint for the way of doing business. Business leaders should incorporate ACM thinking as a way to radicalize, disrupt and sharpen their business processes to better anticipate an increasingly unpredictable future and to better prepare for resulting emerging opportunities.

Surendra Reddy

Surendra Reddy is the founder and CEO of Quantiply Corporation, an emerging technology venture being incubated at PARC to deliver a platform for real-time high-performance analytics. Prior to Quantiply, he was the CTO of Cloud & Big Data Futures at Palo Alto Research Center (PARC), a Xerox Company.

Thriving on Adaptability

Introduction and Overview
Layna Fischer, Future Strategies Inc.

Adaptive Case Management is ultimately about allowing knowledge workers to work the way that they want to work and to provide them with the tools and information they need to do so effectively.

As Surendra Reddy points out in his foreword:

"Imagine a fully integrated ACM system layered into the value stream of an enterprise. The customer support team is able to focus on customer needs, with easy access to the entire company's repertoire of knowledge, similar cases, information, and expertise, as if it were a service. To truly accommodate customers, companies must vest real power and authority in the people and systems that interact directly with customers, at the edge of the organization and beyond. ACM augments business processes to deliver true data-driven process infrastructure entering enterprises into the age of intelligent machines and intelligent processes. ACM empowers the knowledge worker to collaborate, derive new insights, and fine tune the way of doing business by placing customers right in the center where they belong, to drive innovation and organizational efficiencies across the global enterprise.

"ACM also helps organizations focus on improving or optimizing the line of interaction where our people and systems come into direct contact with customers. It's a whole different thing; a new way of doing business that enables organizations to literally become one living-breathing entity via collaboration and adaptive data-driven biological-like operating systems. ACM is not just another acronym or business fad. ACM is the process, strategy, framework, and set of tools that enables this evolution and maturity.

"ACM, in my opinion, is the future blueprint for the way of doing business."

Thriving on Adaptability describes the work of managers, decision makers, executives, doctors, lawyers, campaign managers, emergency responders, strategists, and many others who have to think for a living. These are people who figure out what needs to be done, at the same time that they do it.

In award-winning case studies covering industries as a diverse as law enforcement, transportation, insurance, banking, state services, and healthcare, you will find instructive examples for how to transform your own organization.

This important book follows the ground-breaking best-sellers, *Empowering Knowledge Workers*, *Taming the Unpredictable, How Knowledge Workers Get Things Done*, and *Mastering the Unpredictable* and provides important papers by thought-leaders in this field, together with practical examples, detailed ACM case studies and product reviews.

Part 1: About Case Management

MY SANDBOX, YOUR SANDBOX
Keith D Swenson, Fujitsu America

Case management helps support knowledge workers when the work to be done is not predictable in advance. Not all knowledge workers use the same case management system, which means that, to collaborate, a given knowledge worker might be required to use many different systems. Different systems will naturally allow different operations with different capabilities, and this is a significant usability challenge.

The proposed solution is to allow a knowledge worker to copy a case to the system with which they are familiar, and to maintain synchronization of the copied contents with the original, so that a knowledge worker can perform the work supported by a system with which they are familiar. This paper presents a scheme for accomplishing this kind of federated case management system, and introduces the personal assistant as an important element in making this federation work.

UNDERSTANDING AND EVALUATING CASE MANAGEMENT SOFTWARE

Nathaniel G Palmer, WfMC and Business Process Management, Inc. And Lloyd Dugan, Business Process Management, Inc.

Case Management is an approach to both process and information management that exposes structured and unstructured business information (business data and content) and allows collaborative teams to execute work in a secure but transparent manner. It is sometimes incorrectly regarded as a separate management discipline from Business Process Management (BPM). Yet just as often it also struggles to be understood on its own terms as helping to further expand BPM with new concepts.

This inherent confusion which still surrounds the "BPM vs Case Management" discussion is exacerbated by the leading analysts groups who have been unwilling to standardize on terms. *Forrester*, for example, has fairly consistently talked about "*Dynamic Case Management*" software products, without directly addressing the overlap between their list of these and their list of BPM products. While *Gartner* has yet acknowledge case management as a distinct category of software and sought to pigeon-hole products as "*Case Management Frameworks*" or "CMF's" using phrases such as "*...a CMF and the BPMS it runs on*" to make the concept of case management intractable from BPM or BPMS.

Both competing approaches have elements of truth and inaccuracy. The fact is, Case Management software is a distinct category and is not simply a use case or implementation pattern for traditional BPMS. Yet Case Management is an important part of the broader BPM landscape and fundamental to the redefinition of BPM in recent years. This chapter provides a perspective for understanding and evaluating the most advanced platforms for delivering case management – specifically *Adaptive Case Management (ACM)* – as a specific category of BPM software, distinct from the more traditional, integration-centric BPM. The material presented here is meant to inform those seeking to acquire or use case management software, and to provide help in finding the correct solution as opposed to selecting from the correct "magic quadrant" or other arbitrary round-up.

ONTOLOGY-BASED ACM - THE NEED FOR TRULY ADAPTIVE SYSTEMS

Jürgen Kress, Clemens Utschig-Utschig, Hajo Normann, Torsten Winterberg

After seven months of traveling Curiosity lands on Mars. The engineers in NASA mission control are excited to start scientific research. These scientists have a special challenge; the Mars rover is so far away and the signal takes so long, that they need to rely on automation in order to maintain control in the wildest scenarios. There are many decisions that must be made on a daily, and even on a minute-to-minute basis. Involving the scientist in every possible decision, given the round trip time to consult and answer, would slow the research to – literally – a crawl.

The scientists who operate the rover are knowledge workers. Just like knowledge workers in a business setting, they must figure out how to accomplish goals, as they uncover new information that affects their goals. The automation that they use built into Curiosity is very much like the business processes that businesses use to achieve their goals: the process works fine as long as the situation matches what was expected. But what happens to a business process when confronted with something unexpected?

This chapter takes us on an exploration of how to adapt to the unexpected--including a Little Green Man--using the Mars Curiosity as an entertaining, but highly enlightening example.

COMBINING COMPLIANCE WITH FLEXIBILITY; REAL LIFE EXPERIENCES FROM NORWEGIAN PUBLIC SECTOR

Helle Frisak Sem, Steinar Carlsen, Gunnar John Coll, Computas AS, Norway

Modern, civilized societies depend on law and structured relations, providing a substrate for organizations and individuals to collaborate and compete. Both businesses and public sector must behave in compliance with such rules, and at the same time need sufficient flexibility to perform their tasks according to the situations at hand and in a constantly changing world. IT tools supporting businesses and public sector organizations must aid the users with compliance as well as flexibility. Traditional IT systems have laid the burden of compliance on the users, whereas BPM-systems attain compliance at the expense of flexibility.

This paper describes a set of means to providing compliance with flexibility, based on real life experiences from widely used and long running ACM systems in the Norwegian Public sector. In the highly regulated Scandinavian societies, the public sector takes on responsibilities that may, in other jurisdictions, be covered by private corporations. The experiences should therefore be equally relevant for the private sector.

JUSTICE IS SERVED THROUGH PRODUCTION CASE MANAGEMENT

John T. Matthias, National Center for State Courts, United States

Most efforts to develop requirements for court case management systems are inadequate to capture the intricacies of production case management. But a methodology relating capabilities (the "what" and "why") and processes (the "how") successfully describes what court case workers want.

Practitioners may debate the definitions and relationship of capabilities and processes, but this approach to development of case management requirements is purely a practical one, for use in identifying best commercial off-the-shelf candidates and for implementing in highly-configurable systems such as BPM suites.

Business needs drive the requirements for a system, so interactively identifying with case managers a hierarchy of capabilities, usually decomposed three levels, generates a large tree structure that describes what case managers do. Developing each detailed capability leads to identifying demonstration scenarios, business rules, reports/ displays, application capabilities, data exchanges, data needs, and technology infrastructure which support each capability. Processes identified at this detailed level contain reusable tasks, overlapping the content of detailed capabilities. With system functions specified with this amount of detail, case workers are able to exercise capabilities in any order as needed – just what they want.

The author explores the court world where many organizational aspects of case management are generally agreed-upon, including roles and responsibilities of case managers, the goal of disposing cases as quickly (and fairly) as possible, and the force of statutes and court rules specifying many business rules.

USING PROCESS MINING TO IMPROVE ADAPTIVE CASE MANAGEMENT PROCESSES

Dr. William A. Brantley, University of Maryland United States of America

Big data and data mining have revolutionized how organizations improve their services and products. Companies such as Amazon.com, Target, and grocery stores use transactional data to serve customers better with specific offerings and even predicting what customers are most likely to buy next. Social networking applications such as Twitter and Facebook collect enormous amounts of data from users tweeting each other and posting Facebook statuses. Social networking data is also mined to create detailed user profiles and track trending news events.

Processes also create data that can be mined and use to create models of processes that show how tasks and information flow through the process. Process mining can also map the social networks of the workers involved in the processes. In this chapter, the author explains how adaptive case management (ACM) can benefit from using process mining methods. Process mining is designed to discover, inspect, and enhance routine, repeatable business processes.

Increasing the efficiency of routine processes increases the overall effectiveness of ACM processes. Further, process mining can be used to improve ACM processes by discovering hidden routine processes and helping knowledge workers reflect on and improve their case management methods.

ANALYZING COMMUNICATION CAPABILITIES OF CM/ACM SYSTEMS, WITH THE HELP OF LANGUAGE/ACTION PERSPECTIVE

Ilia Bider, Stockholm University/IbisSoft, Sweden

Case Management (CM) and Adaptive CM (ACM) systems are aimed at supporting knowledge workers to run their knowledge intensive processes (Swenson, 2010). An essential part of such support is providing the process participants (i.e. knowledge workers) with the effective means of communication between them in the frame of each process instance/case. The implementation of means for communication/collaboration can differ from one CM/ACM system to another. Some systems may use the traditional message exchange means, others can exploit more modern means; the ones that are already widely employed in social software. To these means belong forums, bulletin boards, and other implementation of the concept of shared spaces. An example of using shared spaces in ACM systems can be found in the chapter "Means to Support Compliance and Flexibility" of this book.

To improve the communication means in the existing CM/ACM systems or design them for new systems, there is a need to have a framework that helps with conducting analysis of existing means and designing requirements on the new ones. Such framework should take the variety of possibilities that exist and could appear in the future for arranging communication between the instance/case participants. It should not, for example, assume that all communication is conducted through the messages in a natural language, written, or oral.

The paper presents a draft of a framework for analysis of communication capabilities in CM/ACM systems based on so-called Language/Action Perspective (LAP) introduced by Flores and Winograd and their associates in 1980s. This perspective, which is based on the speech act theory (Searle, 1969), has been originally suggested as guidelines for designing communication parts of business information systems (Winograd, 1987).

ENTERPRISE AS A SYSTEM OF PROCESSES

Alexander SAMARIN, SAMARIN.BIZ

Both classic BPM and classic ACM are about coordination of business activities to achieve particular results. But both of them use different coordination techniques.

This chapter discusses coordination as a potential base for a common view on BPM and ACM. It is an updated version of my paper on how to understand how separate processes work together as one functional whole (i.e. a System Of Processes -- SOP) at the scale of an enterprise. Use of processes (and constructions related to them) will reduce the undesired complexity of an enterprise, improve understanding of its structure and behavior which thus facilitates the management and evolution of the enterprise.

Real-World Award-Winning Case Studies

COGNOCARE, AN ACM-BASED SYSTEM FOR ONCOLOGY

Nominated by IActive US Corp, US

Cognocare is an ACM-based Clinical Decision Support System for Oncology that interprets clinical guidelines and expert knowledge, enabling a true dynamic and knowledge-based process generation based on Artificial Intelligence, where these processes are personalized treatments, adapted to each single patient condition. Physicians use it as an assistant to design, follow-up, modify and update fully detailed treatment processes in a very flexible environment.

CRAWFORD & COMPANY, UNITED STATES
Nominated by Appian Corporation, United States

With 700 offices in more than 70 countries, Crawford & Company provides claims management services used by the largest insurance providers in the world. A core part of Crawford's business is Global Disaster Response for incidents such as hurricanes in the U.S or tsunamis in Japan. Crawford must deploy small armies of claims adjusters to the world's most devastated regions so life – and business – can begin to return to normal in the quickest time possible. These adjusters are not Crawford employees, they are contractors who are unschooled in Crawford business processes.

Using a modern work platform, Crawford built a series of Business Process Management (BPM)-based mobile and social business applications to streamline the management and execution of Case Management across all catastrophe-related resources and claims, from the assignment of insurance adjusters to the management of claims and final claim resolution. Applications include Claim Portal, Global Claim Intake, Claim Assignment & Scheduling (CAT Connection), Contractor Extranet (repairStream), Automated Claim Report Review/Approval, GTS Large Loss Management, Customer Billing, Employee On-Boarding, and more, all via a single platform.

INFOSYS McCAMISH SYSTEMS, USA
Nominated by PegaSystems, USA

The life insurance industry is complex – multitudes of products, different markets, each with their own unique set of processing rules, many policy owners holding multiple policies, spread across broad geographic regions – and each expecting the same customer care they experience when interacting with companies such as Apple, Amazon, etc. As a service provider, supporting call center and back office operations for 36 insurance carriers, this complexity increases exponentially. Call center and operational processes were carrier specific and the outdated/legacy system limitations acted as a bottle neck to consolidate and unify these processes. For every new client/carrier addition, we had to proportionately increase the team size to support the additional volume. Employee satisfaction and motivation levels were low since they had to refer to data from multiple systems to service a call. This was not a sustainable model.

We established a customer service optimization strategy (case management and workflow solution) with the main objective of providing the highest level of service possible for each individual customer, while still maintaining the carrier specific processes. Case management and workflow solution developed by leveraging the technical capabilities of BPM software and proprietary insurance industry specific framework of our vendor with our insurance industry expertise in call center and back office operations integrates with any backend systems, thereby providing a unified desktop to our customer service and operational teams.

JURISHARE - CONTRACT GENERATION SYSTEM
Nominated by Camargo Correa Engineering and Construction, Brazil

The Contract Generation System, named JuriShare, designed for contracts, was developed on a Sharepoint platform and consists in creating documents based on templates that are part of a workflow solution. This solution automates the analysis processes and establishes a workflow for internal approvals, enabling lawyers to focus on the document's legal aspect.

The system is designed for contracts with suppliers and with the Company's public or private Clients. The Company refers to the first type of documents as "non-strategic" and the second type as "strategic". For both types of documents, a distinguished workflow was established by the legal department of the Company through which the users may either generate a contract using the system or it may use the system to store the document and to control its status.

The system had a significant impact which resulted in cost and time savings, work transparency and quality, as well as monitoring management of documents. Additionally, it enabled control of potential risks, centralized access to documents and decentralized its usability, since some users are remotely established. Overall, the tool stimulates a collaborative and integrated environment among all areas, including the many construction sites which are located throughout Brazil, Headquarters and back office. It also allows all the lawyers spread throughout Brazil and in other Latin American countries to have access to all of the documents included in the system, being an integrative tool which allows the Company to have a better management of all of its contracts.

THE NATIONAL POLICE IMMIGRATION SERVICE, NORWAY
Nominated by Computas AS, Norway

An asylum seeker's first encounter with Norwegian authorities is through the National Police Immigration Service (NPIS). The NPIS collects information about each immigration case, prior to application handling by the Norwegian immigration authorities. A large percentage of asylum seekers have no passport or valid ID, and many provide inaccurate information, adding to the complexity of identity determination and case investigation tasks.

UTSYS is the NPIS' ACM solution. Used by all operational personnel, UTSYS supports registration, identity analysis, interviews and forcible return, as well as managing Norway's asylum seeker detention center. UTSYS helps NPIS monitor every pending asylum case, continually updating and completing case information. Case managers are responsible for a portfolio of cases that they own throughout the case lifecycle. Using case context, UTSYS offers the case manager suitable functionality for resolving the case effectively.

THE OFFICE OF SECRETARY TO THE GOVERNMENT OF FEDERATION OF NIGERIA
Nominated by Newgen Software Technologies Limited, India

The Office of Secretary to the Government of the Federation (OSGF) of Nigeria is responsible for effective coordination and monitoring of the implementation of Government policies. The Cabinet Secretariat office of OSGF collates, vets and disseminates memoranda and associated documents from various Council Members, Ministries, Departments and Agencies (MDAs) of the Government. These memoranda and documents form the basis of agenda setting and discussions at the Federal Executive Council (FEC) of the Nigerian government. The FEC comprises of ministers handpicked by the President of Nigeria to spearhead different ministries and businesses of the Nigerian government.

The memoranda and documents have dynamic lifecycles undergoing several levels of checks, iterations and annotations. This was largely handled manually, causing problems such as slower processes, manual errors and high operational costs. Maintaining security of information was a challenge too. To overcome these impediments, the Government delegated Galaxy Backbone Limited, its wholly owned ICT subsidiary to create the right solution to this challenge. Galaxy Backbone launched its *1-Gov.net program*, which would create a common Information and Communication Technology (ICT) platform for all Ministries, Departments and Agencies of the Federal Government.

PERSHING LLC, A BNY MELLON COMPANY, USA
Nominated by Pershing LLC, a BNY Mellon company, USA

Prior to implementing its Task Management solution for onboarding new clients to Pershing LLC, a BNY Mellon company, the Client Transition (conversion) team relied on a highly manual, paper-intensive project planning system to track the conversion process and manage multiple tasks. This required frequent in-person meetings, e-mails and phone calls among departments. Administration was difficult and time consuming as project plans had to be printed and shared prior to each meeting and updates were restricted to a single team member from each department. The new automated task management solution allows the conversion team to access and adapt up to 1,100 steps within the master conversion plan for the new client and distribute the plan to more than 150 impacted team members.

STATE OF HAWAII, DEPARTMENT OF HUMAN SERVICES, U.S.
Nominated by Imagine Solutions, U.S.

Who: Citizens of Hawaii seeking services and support for food, shelter, childcare assistance, employment support and work training, and dependency diversion and prevention.

What: State of Hawaii, Department of Human Services (DHS), Benefit, Employment and Support Services Division (BESSD). BESSD is the largest division in the Department of Human Services and provides services through nine programs that serve different populations. There are 14 processing centers statewide with a total of 34 physical locations.

Why: A common theme with Health and Human Service agencies is tackling an increasing need for citizen support by leveraging case management solutions (CMS). For Hawaii's BESSD, did so their objective was to improve data quality, eliminate errors, and manage more efficiently an increasing number of cases, without increasing staff, as well as to eliminate the restriction for citizen documentation to only be accessible at one location, on any island.

STATE OF MAINE, USA
Nominated by Pegasystems, USA

Under the directive of its CIO, Jim Smith, the State of Maine launched a transformation into a digital enterprise built on top of a BPM solution. The goal – create an organization with the agility to adapt to market changes and provide superior customer services, replicating the operations of market-leading commercial organizations. This philosophy is unique to state government. Supporting the State of Maine's emergence as a BPM thought leader, is the establishment of an Enterprise BPM Center of Excellence, to ensure the state continually evolves and expands its operations through the use of BPM.

The State of Maine's successful first rollout was an application to bridge the State's unemployment insurance benefits and tax systems. The state then began to deploy this model into other internal functions, operations and initiatives including licensing. This was all built to increase efficiency using BPM, CRM, and case management combined in a single platform.

Key to Maine's decision was the ability to deploy via a secure and reliable cloud platform including the ability to easily and safely move applications and/or data to and from the cloud while maintaining security, privacy, regulatory and compliance requirements. Maine's visionary approach sets the standard for government and private sector alike.

THE ANTWERP PORT AUTHORITY, BELGIUM
Award: Judges' Choice, Best Entry

This personal story is written with a holistic perspective in mind: it's not just about case management, it's a case on knowledge management, information management, lean work organisation, performance management, internal communications, team management. Adaptive case management has shown itself as a major supportive methodology - or even better: philosophy for the organisation of our work. I strongly believe that adaptive case management is one of the pieces of the puzzle that forms our 21st century way of working, though, we do not see the whole yet.

We suspect adaptive case management thinking to be a revolution for today's knowledge company. At least, it made us conscious that in fact any problem-solving act can be perceived as a case, where intuition, trial and error is necessary to bring it to a good end. To see the agile process being developed around the information in a dialectic way, was for us the discovery of the natural, intuitive way that completely fits knowledge work; mirroring how knowledge production works.

This chapter, explains that it is not about the introduction of case management in one particular business unit, supporting one specific process. It is about the central Information Management department that takes the initiative to introduce case management thinking with knowledge workers in the whole company, and the externalisation of this will differ from team to team. We promote tools, practices, habits and help teams to fit these into their daily practices.

TIAA-CREF, USA
Nominated by IBM, USA

TIAA was the vision of the philanthropist Andrew Carnegie and founded in 1918 (nearly 100 years ago) through his Carnegie Corporation of New York and the Carnegie Foundation with the goal of supporting the financial well-being of college teachers through a pioneering system of annuities and low-cost life insurance. CREF was established in 1952. The organization now employs 9,000 employees in more than 90 local offices with $564 billion assets under the management as of May 2014. TIAA-CREF is currently serving 4.8 million individuals overall. TIAA-CREF has diversified product portfolio offerings, including retirement, IRA, brokerage, insurance, mutual funds, management of 529 college savings plans, trust and banking services, which, by virtue of their complexity, require a great deal of synergy and collaboration within and across the business lines. TIAA-CREF has implemented solutions to their stakeholders across diversified businesses, empowering them to collaborate and achieve a highly efficient and low-cost business model, mitigating operational risks, adhering to regulatory controls and enhancing customer satisfaction and case worker competence. With the case management end-to-end solution, TIAA-CREF case processes can now be consistent across all channels (web, phone and paper), achieving and optimizing a 360-degree case view. The solution enables all correspondence from all channels to be stored within the case folder and available to all necessary parties.

WESTMED PRACTICE PARTNERS, USA

Nominated by Hyland, creator of OnBase®, USA

Providing high-quality services through cutting-edge technology is the longtime mission of WESTMED Practice Partners (WPP). However, with thousands of policies and procedures supporting its multispecialty practice facility clients, WPP was challenged to effectively manage all processes.

Searching for a solution to these challenges, Dr. Simeon Schwartz, WPP's Chairman and CEO, found inspiration in a checklist approach to healthcare – as well-documented in Atul Gawande's book *The Checklist Manifesto.* This led WPP to look for a software solution that would help WPP build checklist-style applications to improve process quality, consistency and outcomes, both for the organization itself and its hospital system clients.

WPP partnered with its enterprise content management (ECM) vendor to implement these applications using its comprehensive case management platform. WPP used the flexible platform to design and deploy a wide variety of applications supporting processes enterprise-wide. These range from more standard case-based applications to unique checklist-driven applications for process control in areas like IT help desk, labs and medical testing, front desk, patient billing, new site openings, human resources and physician compensation.

HOW TO WIN AN AWARD FOR YOUR CASE MANAGEMENT PROJECT

The WfMC Awards for Case Management are the ideal way to be recognized by the industry worldwide, to publicly acknowledge and recognize the efforts of your team and to inject passion into your case management projects.

Read 2014 winners' highlights here: http://adaptivecasemanagement.org/awards/2014/index.htm

Get recognized for your vision and your team's superb efforts by entering the Global Excellence Awards

Co-sponsored by WfMC and BPM.com, these prestigious awards recognize user organizations worldwide that have demonstrably excelled in implementing innovative Case Management solutions.

These awards are designed to highlight the best examples of technology to support knowledge workers. In 2014 fourteen teams were awarded top honors at the ACM Live Gala Event in June, and are featured in the new book, "Thriving on Adaptability."

Previous winning submissions were published in "How Knowledge Workers Get Things Done" and "Empowering Knowledge Workers."

We work with leading industry analysts Forrester and Gartner who use these case studies to analyze ACM technology suppliers, illustrate trends, industry growth, ROI and more.

Enter the Awards here: http://adaptivecasemanagement.org/

Knowledge Work and Case Management

My Sandbox, Your Sandbox

Keith D Swenson, Fujitsu America

ABSTRACT

Case management helps support knowledge workers when the work to be done is not predictable in advance. Not all knowledge workers use the same case management system, which means that, to collaborate, a given knowledge worker might be required to use many different systems. Different systems will naturally allow different operations with different capabilities, and this is a significant usability challenge.

The proposed solution is to allow a knowledge worker to copy a case to the system with which they are familiar, and to maintain synchronization of the copied contents with the original, so that a knowledge worker can perform the work supported by a system with which they are familiar. This paper presents a scheme for accomplishing this kind of federated case management system, and introduces the personal assistant as an important element in making this federation work.

1. INTRODUCTION

Most research has been on implementing work processes within a single environment with homogenous support for a process, particularly processes that are predictable. When you assume a single type of system, you fall prey to the invalid assumption that all users will have a consistent model paradigm and a consistent set of capabilities. It is much simpler to think about a single system and the set of capabilities that would allow people to interact, but in reality people have to deal with multiple different systems that need to interact. Processes now regularly cross organizational boundaries, and it is entirely unreasonable to assume that both organizations use the same system.

This paper presents a canonical example of how case work can be shared across organizational boundaries between people who typically use different case management systems. Using that example, we will compare several different approaches in order to show that a federated case architecture is the most realistic. Then comes an explanation of how a federated case system would need to work, including the concept of a personal assistant. The paper concludes with a description of the requirements for a case interchange protocol.

2. A CANONICAL SCENARIO

To demonstrate and discuss the necessary capabilities of widespread case management we can use the following medical care scenario which outlines how four different people, working within four different organizations, might be expected to interact.

The story starts with a patient, *Alex*. Alex has an unexpected pain in his back. Alex starts by conferring with his primary care physician, *Betty*, a general practitioner who can identify the most common things, and advise about next steps.

Before making a preliminary diagnosis, Betty will order some routine tests and measurements. Based on those, and based on what Alex said about the symptoms, she determines that Alex probably has a back problem. Alex resists the urge to say "that is what I told you" while Betty makes a referral to a back specialist *Charles*.

Alex then makes an appointment with Charles, and during Alex's visit, Charles is going to want to see the results of earlier tests. Charles works in a completely different company and so integration with Betty's system of storing these results is minimal if at all. The scenario will focus on how Betty and Charles share information in the course of providing health care for Alex. While Charles would have loved to perform surgery, he determines that this problem can probably be addressed by a good round of physical therapy, and refers Alex to *Dennis,* a physical therapist

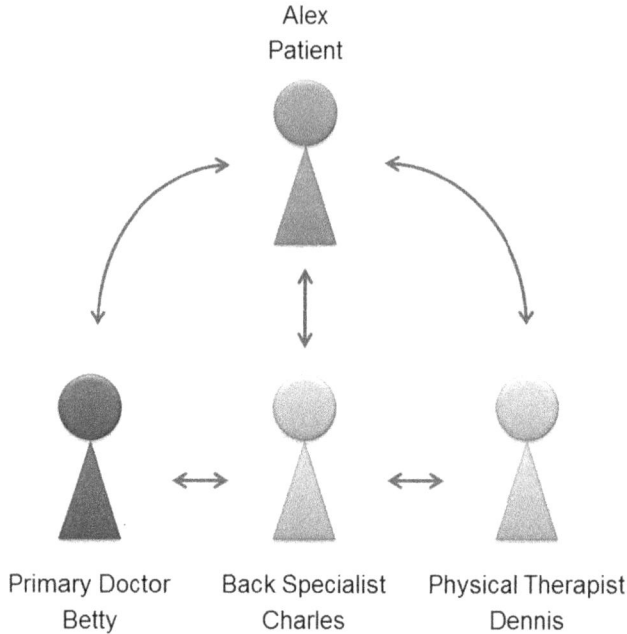

Figure 1: Roles and Interaction Diagram

Alex sets up a schedule to meet with Dennis weekly and work through a set of stretches and exercises. While this is going on, status and results need to be reported back to Charles and Betty. This scenario has a happy ending: after 4 months Alex is feeling completely cured, decides to work out more, and fills out a daunting pile of paperwork for the insurance company.

There are four reasons why this is a good scenario for discussing personal assistants:

1. Health care is an important field and rapidly expanding field. You will never find one doctor who knows everything, and so you will always need to consult experts outside of the immediate organizations.
2. Neither Betty, Charles, nor Dennis own the entire process. They all work for different organizations and we cannot assume that there is one IT department setting up a single system. We have to assume that these requests transfer across systems; that those systems were not designed by the same people; that each system has some characteristics unique to that organization.
3. Still, they have to work together to provide coordinated and consistent care for Alex. Somehow, the difference between the systems must be bridged.

4. Finally, medical information can potentially be very sensitive. The information must be carefully guarded, and shared on a need to see only basis.

The information flows both ways in this scenario: it will be to Alex's benefit that the early tests are available to the others, but it also is important to communicate the status as Alex improves back to the earlier doctors as well. The circle will be closed the next time Alex visits Betty for another checkup and Betty is able to see how the treatment was concluded.

3. MULTI-PARTY CROSS-SYSTEM INTERACTION

Most discussions of work support system focus on a single unified system. This unified system supports a single designed business process in a uniform way from start to finish. Every user has sufficient access to the system, and is assumed to be sufficiently familiar with that single unified system. These assumptions, which underlie almost all of the discussion of group support systems, are overly simplistic.

Most real-world situations do not have the luxury of encompassing the entire business process in a single unified system. There are many systems already resident in organizations which users are familiar with and comfortable with using. As we envision processes that extend beyond the boundaries of a single organization, we need to consider how the systems-in-residence will interact. We must consider technical, fiscal, political, and usability issues.

The medical care scenario is constructed explicitly to expose the issue that these people are using different systems. This scenario has four people potentially using four different systems, but the number of systems that must interact is far larger than that. Alex, the patient, might be using a health record system that is used by thousands of other patients as well, and there are surely other health records systems available to the public. There are many primary care physicians at several different institutions. Each institution needs to work with the health record system of the patient. There could be hundreds of back specialists, and each one needs to work with any of the primary care physicians. There also could be hundreds of independent physical therapists, each one needing to interact with hundreds of other doctors and specialists. While the scenario outlines four specific systems for interacting, in the real-world situation there are hundreds of systems that need to interact.

We should compare five basic approaches:

- **Unified Process** -a business process is designed that includes all four participants, distributing tasks to each from a single unified work support system.
- **Email Exchange** -each party has their own system, and they interact only by exchanging documents by email.
- **Deep Integration** -each party has their own system for their own part of the process, and specific application programming interfaces (APIs) are provided to pass information back and forth.
- **Remote Access** -each party has their own system for their own part of the process, and the other participants access those other systems through the web.
- **Federated Cases** -each party have their own system, but the case folders from one system are linked to case folders on the other systems for two directional synchronization of information.

3.1 Unified is Unrealistic

The unified process can be eliminated without much consideration. It would be technically easy to design a process within a single system to support this specific scenario. It is technically easy to run a process support system in the cloud that is accessible to all participants. It is politically unreasonable to expect that all doctors, all specialists, all patients, and all physical therapists will be using a single system. Who would own and take responsibility for the system? In the scenario, Betty, Charles, and Dennis need to have the capabilities to customize their parts of the process for their own purposes. Who is going to control those changes? These changes require developer-level access to the system. The developer for Charles will have complete access to all the same things that the developer for Betty has, and that the developer for Dennis has. There is no practical means to enforce access control of data between different *developers* in the same development environment. Betty handles some information that she is not allowed to share with the others. There is essentially no way for Betty to guarantee that the information is properly handled, if the developer for Charles is working in the same system.[1]

If one was going to provide a single system for all participants to use, it would need to be very general purpose. It would probably focus on those features that all participants have in common, to the exclusion of features that might make a lot of sense for one given participant. It is unlikely that Betty, Charles, or Dennis want to hire a developer to design their own part of a common system anyway. It is far more likely that they would purchase an off the shelf system for their particular specialization. Alex uses a "personal medical record management system" much like Microsoft HealthVault. Over his life Alex may work with many different doctors, possibly in different cities, and the increasing trend is for patients to take charge of their own records independently from the care providers. Betty might use a general purpose "clinical business support system" such as something a typical clinic or hospital might use. Dennis might use a system that is pre-built to have all the things that a physical therapist normally needs. Charles may be in a small clinic and make use of a software package designed for small clinics. Betty might be in a large medical center, which uses software which has all the features that a larger, general practice might need.

Requiring all of these participants to use the same centralized system would significantly increase the cost to each of them. Consider also that there is no natural boundary: medical people often have to help in detective cases, and detective often need to help in legal cases, etc. A single unified system would need to encompass all workers in all field, and that is simply unrealistic.

3.2 Email is Unsafe

The other four approaches assume that each party has their own work support system. The first of these is the approach where email, physical mail, or hand carried disks, are used to transport the information between the parties. This is the approach that is in use today. A doctor refers a patient to a specialist using a paper

---

[1] It is theoretically possible to create a system that provides for strict access control to information to different parties within a single development environment. This would add a tremendous complexity to the development of applications, as well as a large performance penalty at run time. Such complexity is not needed for most programming environments, so it is not commonly available, and would be very expensive if it was available. In practice, if you have different pieces of code that need controlled access to data, the tested approach is to provide different development environments, and then at runtime control the information that flows through the interfaces. This is essentially the same as each party having their own runtime.

referral slip. The patient either carries the documents, or the doctor and specialist exchange document using email or a document sending service. Email might be OK for non-sensitive documents, but it should be clear that email is not secure enough for even moderately sensitive information.

There are secure document sending services, and we might assume that hand carried can be securely guarded, however there is a security flaw in all of these approaches. Sending a document by any means requires that the person receiving the document handle it properly and put it in a suitably secure location. This is actually prone to error. Setting up a folder that can only be read by the people actually working on that patient presents so much difficulty that it is essentially never done. Instead, documents are stored in common, medium security holding area, which all of the office personnel have access to. Security is maintained by the diligence of workers to avoid looking at documents they are not supposed to have access to. Access to the system can then not be made available to anyone who is not properly trained and willing to enforce the security. Clearly, people outside the office cannot be allowed to participate directly on the work, which is an impediment to getting the best people directly involved.

The following approaches both offer significant improvements in being able to manage a case, by offering a way to being external parties directly into the work, giving them secure access to only the things they should have access to, and yet are still significantly safer than email or any approach that distributes documents outside of the system.

3.3 Deep Integration Untenable

Deep integration comes from the point of view that there are many separate systems, but a single, unified process can still be deployed across them by fashioning specific web services at the right places in the process. Custom APIs are created to pass information back and forth between the systems. This approach has most of the same problems that the single unified approach has: all of the parties (thousands of them) have to agree on the basic process. Deep integration requires that common data structures be used in all parts of the process, and that every system support the same kinds of process diagrams and programming constructs.

Some believe that a health record standard, such as HL7, will resolve all issue with such deep integration. HL7 is an important step, but it only represents part of the story. All human action takes place within context, and HL7 is not designed to represent the context within with a particular request is being made. Once again the need for interoperability at this level of detail would prevent parties from using of the shelf packages for their particular field, and would raise the overall cost. The fact that there is no clear boundary that limits the people who might have overlapping cases, means that such standards would need to nation-wide or possibly global.

This approach has a significant deficiency when you need to change to the process or data structures; you have to propagate this changed potentially everywhere at the same time. A solution to this, Interface versioning, greatly complicates the system, and does not always work when changes are coming from multiple parties simultaneously. Deep integration requires too much coordination, would require the parties to give up too much autonomy, and would be too costly to be a practical solution in the real world.

3.4 Remote Access Leaves Burden on User

The remote access approach is a viable approach which is in use in some places today. The way this works is that one party, like Betty, creates a case folder for all of Alex's things. After referring the patient to Charles, and after both the patient and Charles agree to work together, Betty gives Charles a limited access to the case folder. Charles uses a web browser to access that case folder, all the appropriate information and tasks in there. The idea is that Charles does his work there, meaning that he marks tasks as complete, in that remote system.

Usability is an important consideration. Each system works a little differently. Charles may be familiar with one system, and has learned to be proficient in it, but if Betty's system is just one of ten different systems from ten different organizations that refer to him, it is a significant usability problem. Using an unfamiliar UI can lead to mistakes. Doctors live to help patients, not to learn different user interfaces. It would be far more comfortable, and reliable, if he could use the same UI for all of his patients.

When he takes Alex on as a patient, he need to perform specific tasks which Betty's system may not know about. Charles may want things done by his staff members who Betty's system does not know about. He is not likely to be able to make these task assignment in Betty's system. These are task assignment that he will have to do in his own system specialized for his work.

One consideration trumps all: if he adds document and information the remote system, he will not be able to control who has access to that information. He is not going to keep his own notes in the private system if he needs those notes to be private.

With the remote system approach he is still able to (and must!) use his own system to coordinate care for Alex. He creates a case folder in his system, which has all the advantages that his custom system has for him: prebuilt procedures for his way of working, all the people in his office already entered into the system, roles set up for people in his office associated with the tasks they normally do. Most importantly, he has control (shared with others in his office) of the information, and can guard its privacy from others outside the office. His notes will remain private.

The main problem with this approach is that he needs to manually download and upload files between the remote system and his own system. This is a manual task that is tedious. It does not require particular skill, so the moving of documents could be delegated to another office worker, but it still, like the documents received from the patient or by email, requires care and handling to make sure it is done right.

4.   THE ADVANTAGES OF A FEDERATED APPROACH

The federated approach essentially starts with the former model where a particular patient episode may be represented in multiple case management systems for each of the various professional involved, and adds one simple capability: to be able to link these cases together and to synchronize information directly between them. From Charles' point of view, Betty already has a case folder, but Betty's folder is not sufficient for his own work, so Charles is going to have to make a local case folder, and put all the stuff in it, so Charles starts by cloning the case folder from Betty as the starting point for his own copy of that. Charles will have an ability to "pull" a copy of the case to his own system. This has a number of distinct benefits: the invitee can use their own system they are familiar with to access and update the case information; they can extend the case with commands and capabilities that they are used to; they have sufficient access to their own system to extend the case; they have greater control over accessibility of the case instead of being excluded at some point.

It is the best of all worlds. Each user is using the system that they are most familiar with. For example, Charles does not need to learn how Betty's or Alex's systems work. Charles can leverage all the features of his own system, including customizations his organization might have made, as well as having all the people from his office already set up properly. Charles is not dependent upon the time that the foreign systems are available, because his own system works completely independently.

The idea of using a *sandbox* for doing work independently, later to be merged with work from others, is a common approach in the software development world. Source management systems do exactly this; they give each developer a copy of the entire source for the project. That copy can be modified and tested independently of everyone else. Only when the work is completed are the final tested changes pushed back to the shared repository, and ultimately to the other developers. This idea of a federated case is quite similar; each organization gets a copy of the documents to work on, and completed change can be pushed or pulled between organizations. The difference between federated case management and a source management system is that in a source management system every developer gets a copy of *all* of the source, while for the case management system each organization will have their own view and have some documents which they keep to themselves which are not shared with others, and different sets of documents might be shared to different partnering organizations.

5. PERSONAL ASSISTANT

The federated approach becomes a step more powerful with the concept of personal assistants. A personal assistant is a set of rules and actions that are designed to work to access the foreign systems. The assistant accesses the remote system on your behalf through web services calls to pre-filter things. You might make a rule for an assistant to automatically accept particular tasks, and to automatically replicate the project. Or to automatically reject certain tasks.

Personal assistant are different from the traditional rules that you find in a BPM system in that they are designed to work not within a particular process, but on case folders on remote systems. You can see the assistant as the glue that integrates the two systems together: the remote system offers a task to you, and the personal assistant has the rules that links that remote task to your local system. In a sense, this personal assistant forms an integrating bridge between the systems, automating in some ways the tedious tasks of copying information around.

The personal assistant is under the control of one person, while the process it interacts with is under the control of other people. Considered all together, it appears like a distributed design system, with some people providing process-like aspects, and others providing a collection of agent-like aspects that all need to work together to complete the process.

Is this realistic? Will it be possible to create an assistant that is really helpful? This paper presents a conceptual framework within which personal assistants could be trained to work to the benefit of users, without requiring that the systems be implemented with an unreasonable amount of agreement. Personal assistants become the glue that links work in one organization, to work in another organization.

After defining what a personal assistant is, a specific concrete scenario is presented to be used in assessing various assistant proposals. Some of the requirements of a personal assistant are fleshed out, and some conclusions about the workings are made.

Start with a dictionary definitions of an agent:
- person who acts on behalf of another
- person or company that provides a particular service organizing transactions between two other parties.
- person or thing that takes an active role or produces a specified effect.

Taken literally, any software program would fit the definition of an agent, in the sense that a software program always performs a service for the person running it. Some of the terms are nuanced, and mean more than just automation in service of a person. Instead consider that the agent needs to ``act'' and ``take an active role''. Software agent are not actually intelligent or conscious and act only on things they are programmed to respond to, however lets define a Personal Assistant as a style of agent that can be trained to provide an illusion of acting on the user's behalf. A personal assistant might need the following qualities:
- **asynchrony** - personal assistants are specialized do their work for the user at a time when the user is not available.
- **responsive** - a personal assistant is programmed to receive events, recognize their significance, and respond to them.
- **autonomy** - the need to in some way behave and to act on its own' in some sense of the phrase.
- **rules** - it is natural for a user to express desired responses is as rules which stand independent of each other, yet can be used to deduce an appropriate response to a situation.
- **negotiation** - imperative programming often depends upon inputs being in a specific predefined format, but that leads to fragility. A personal assistant might be prepared to handle a variety of formats, and one might expect a back and forth interchange to determine the best format for further exchange.
- **semantic matching** - we can't expect all information to be structured in a single universal way, so there has to be a way to automatically map from an external format to an internal one.
- **personal** - the personal assistant is something that each person trains for their own patterns of use. It is not an agent provided by the organization for uniform use across an organization.
- **trained, not programmed** - because it is personal, we cannot expect everyone to be programmers, so it has to pick up the necessary behaviours without requiring programming skills. A training approach implied some capability that allows a personal assistant to do something again the right way, having failed the first time.

6. INTERACTION PATTERNS

It is not the purpose of this paper to define how Betty does work in a clinic to any level of detail. Instead, the purpose is to show how different systems might interact to allow for coordinated care to emerge from the combined systems. For this reason, an extremely simplified, unrealistic process is depicted below.

Betty's care process might be symbolized by the following diagram showing a couple of steps performed by Betty followed by a selection of potential treatments, one of which is assigned to the back specialist, Charles.

In Figure 2, the rectangles represent activities, and the dotted lines represent a user interface that a user might use to interaction with the system, either to pick up an assignment, or to input the results of completing a task. All of this is hosted in the clinical support system that Betty uses, and it allows a user interface to Charles.

We know that Charles has his own system that he uses to manage his work in a way appropriate to his own work patterns. At the very minimum, Charles must access the task from Betty, copy the information, and then create a new case instance in his own system.

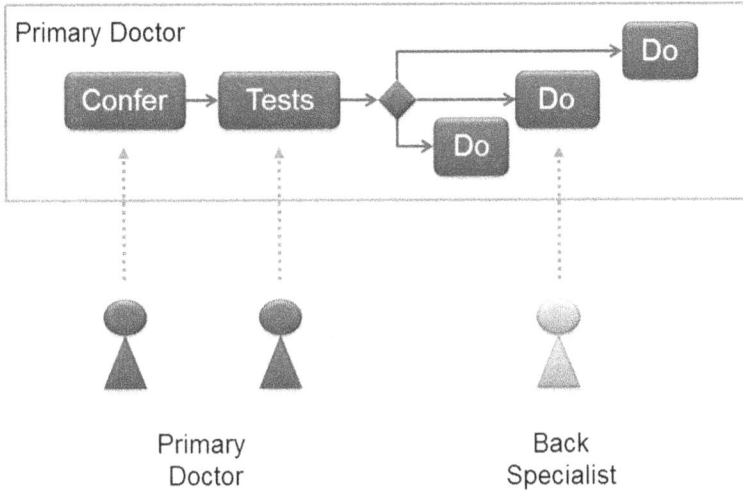

Figure 2: Simplistic Top Level Process for Doctor

This discussion on personal assistants proposes that we can do better than this!

The personal assistant can access the remote system (the system is remote to Charles) pick up the necessary information, possibly act based on some rules, and start a local process in Charles' system.

In the diagram below, the personal assistant steps in to help Charles. We assume that Charles would receive some form of notification of that task in Betty's system (probably an email message) but the personal assistant intercepts that notification. It accesses the remote system, and through the use of a few simple rules determines that it is appropriate to pick this task up for Charles. It creates a "clone" instance in the local system, and it copies whatever documents and information into the local system. Then, based on rules, it starts a specific local process with tasks assigned to Charles.

This provides a place where Charles can do his work, potentially assigning an activity to Dennis, and letting Dennis' personal assistant do the same sort of thing.

The job of the personal assistant is not done when the local case instance is created. As documents and data are modified, the personal assistant will need to continually synchronize the contents of the two systems. In this way, the personal assistant forms a communications channel between the systems.

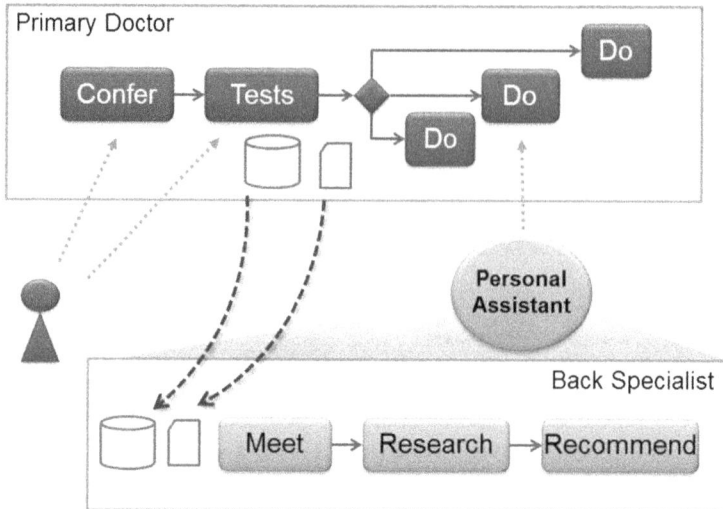

Figure 3: Personal Assistant links the Sites

This pattern looks like a standard subprocess. It *would* be a standard subprocess if this was designed and implemented within a single system. Because we need to bridge the gap between two systems, the personal assistant performs an important integrating role.

The system as described above has been implemented and tested. Called "Cognoscenti" it is an open source case management system available for research usage. This assistant was demonstrated in March 2014 at the BPMNext conference, in Asilomar, California.

7. DATA TRANSFORMATION

The representation of integration in the above section is overly simplistic because it assumes that information can be conveyed by simply copying the data files. Given that these are different systems implemented separately, it is unlikely that they all have the same way to represent things. Take something basic, like patient info, and you will find that the kinds of information that Betty needs to keep on the patient are different from the kinds of information that Charles needs, and probably different still from what Dennis needs.

The best example today is the way that US publicly-traded companies exchange information with the Securities Exchange Commission (SEC). The company sends an Extensible Business Reporting Language (XBRL) document which can be read by the SEC and automatically integrated into their control system. XBRL has a relatively small instance document, along with relatively large, shared taxonomy documents. The basic shared taxonomy for all US accounting can be extended into industry specific and even company specific ways. The important aspect for this discussion is that financial information is complex, and this solution is in place and working on a large scale today.

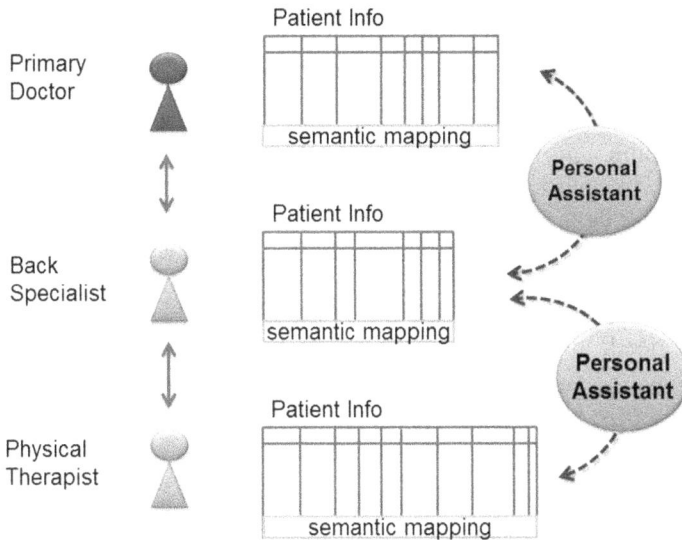

Figure 4: Semantic Mapping between Sites

It is reasonable to expect that a similar approach will work in many other fields, including the medical field. The basic instance information will be accompanied by some form of semantic information which will allow for automated mapping of information from one system to another. This job of mapping could be done by the personal assistant. It must be done while the personal assistant accesses the remote system before attempting to apply any rules.

8. PERSONAL ASSISTANT REQUIREMENTS

One unanswered question is: how do these personal assistants learn to do what they do? It is unreasonable to expect that Betty and Charles program them directly because they are not programmers.

There might be preconfigured assistants provided by companies that specialize in a particular job function. Charles will shop around to find a personal assistant that works the way he wants to work, possibly trying out a couple before settling on one that has the right habits.

It also might be that the personal assistant can learn by observing what Charles does. Charles activates learn mode, and the assistant watches what he does. Then, after asking a number of clarifying questions, the assistant starts doing things autonomously for Charles, perhaps in a ``monitored assist'' mode at first, but once Charles is comfortable with it, letting it act on its own.

The job of a personal assistant is to really act on a user's behalf, to interact with another system as if it was the user, and to relieve the user from tedious, repetitive actions associated with linking the separate systems. It does all of these:

- **Receiving and screening notification** --filter the spam for relevant notifications.
- **Task Introduction** --find offered tasks, gather additional information about the task to evaluate using a set of rules to determine interest.
- **Task Acceptance** --sending a notice back to the sender that the offer is interesting and going to be considered by a human.

- **Clone Project** --based again on rules it may automatically retrieve all the accessible information in the project, and put it safely in a local place for access.
- **Determine the Right Template** --again based on rules, and start the process if necessary.
- **Transform** --access the taxonomies that give the semantic meaning of the data, to transform the data to a form that you are used to, and to transform back again when responding.
- **Synchronize** --in both directions: pull down new documents and information that appear at the original site, and to push back modified information, or new documents, to the originating doctor's site, in anticipation of the need.

Spelled out this way, personal assistants are less magical than the marketing rhetoric builds them up to be. At the same time, this outlines a clear and important mode of use for personal assistants for cooperating knowledge workers. This may be the model for personal assistants in future systems.

9. SUMMARY

Given that knowledge worker need the support of IT systems, and need to work across organizations, we have presented reasoning that a federated approach is the best workable way to provide for this. With a federated system, organizations can get the system that supports their own specialty, while at the same time providing robust secure way to transport and guard the associated documents. Each organization sets up their own sandbox to work in, and information is replicated between them. Personal assistants are a way to help automate these interactions, linking the system, and allowing knowledge workers to cooperate across organizations in the real world.

10. ACKNOWLEDGMENT

Many thanks to Fujitsu for supporting this work on the open source project. Significant contributions to the development of Cognoscenti came from Shamim Quader, Sameer Pradhan, Kumar Raja, Todd Palmer, Jim Farris, Sandia Yang, CY Chen, Rajiv Onat, Neal Wang, Dennis Tam, Shikha Srivastava, Anamika Chaudhari, Ajay Kakkar, Rajeev Rastogi, and many more people at Fujitsu around the world.

Understanding and Evaluating Case Management Software

Nathaniel G Palmer, WfMC and Business Process Management, Inc., Lloyd Dugan, Business Process Management, Inc.

1. INTRODUCTION

Case Management is an approach to both process and information management that exposes structured and unstructured business information (business data and content) and allows collaborative teams to execute work in a secure but transparent manner. It is sometimes incorrectly regarded as a separate management discipline from Business Process Management (BPM). Yet just as often it also struggles to be understood on its own terms as helping to further expand BPM with new concepts.

This inherent confusion which still surrounds the "BPM vs Case Management" discussion is exacerbated by the leading analysts groups who have been unwilling to standardize on terms. *Forrester*, for example, has fairly consistently talked about *"Dynamic Case Management"* software products, without directly addressing the overlap between their list of these and their list of BPM products. While *Gartner* has yet acknowledge case management as a distinct category of software and sought to pigeon-hole products as *"Case Management Frameworks"* or "CMF's" using phrases such as *"...a CMF and the BPMS it runs on"* to make the concept of case management intractable from BPM or BPMS.

Both competing approaches have elements of truth and inaccuracy. The fact is, Case Management software is a distinct category and is not simply as a use case or implementation pattern for traditional BPMS. Yet Case Management is an important part of the broader BPM landscape and fundamental to the redefinition of BPM in recent years. This chapter provides a perspective for understanding and evaluating the most advanced platforms for delivering case management – specifically *Adaptive Case Management (ACM)* – as a specific category of BPM software, distinct from the more traditional, integration-centric BPM. The material presented here is meant to inform those seeking to acquire or use case management software, and to provide help in finding the correct solution as opposed to selecting from the correct "magic quadrant" or other arbitrary round-up.

2. CASE MANAGEMENT AND ACM OVERVIEW

As its own term of art apart from what is thought of as traditional BPM, case management is the fortunate and necessary byproduct of a growing understanding, as well as epiphanous revelation, that many of an organization's process spaces involve "cases" and not "transactions." In such situations, the knowledge worker needs help in making decisions and otherwise managing the case in ways that go beyond the straightforward automation of routine and largely procedural activities. Hence, the optimal software solution may not turn out to be what a traditional BPMS does or aspires to offer, but rather a new class of software solutions that more directly address the needs of the knowledge worker performing case management.

Case management inevitably involves content-intensive and data-driven processes, such as the creation of supporting documentation that surrounds a process or other operations, such as an investigation. It likely involves the creation of checklists, delivery of user guidance, and the associate tracking and reporting. Specifically, cases would represent a master system of record for all projects and other process-related activity through the project lifecycle, capturing the "what" (data, files, email, messages, etc.) and the "how" (an audit trail and activity log of decisions made, rules applied, actions taken, etc.) within a virtual case folder. In this way, the new case management system will facilitate effective collaboration around projects as well as better data and records management through the ability to identify, organize, and share critical information.

Case management systems by their very nature are dynamic, adjusting the workflow based on changes in the informational context and events driving the case forward in a manner that the system can understand. Some case management systems can also be said to be "adaptive" (in the ACM sense). This refers to the characteristic that such systems are not explicated, programmed, or hand-coded by specialists as in the past, but instead can be dynamically modified by ordinary users in the course of their work.

This orientation frames the definition of ACM systems as those that are not simply ad hoc and devoid of any manageability, but are able to support decision-making and data capture, while giving users the freedom to apply their own subject matter expertise to respond to unique or changing circumstances within the business environment. A core quality of ACM is support for collaborative, goal-driven processes, where goals can be modified "in flight" by users with appropriate authority. Similarly, knowledge captured during the performance of the case can support the identification and creation of new processes or case rules, without requiring IT/developer involvement.

For example, consider how an ACM system would address the space of a project. An ACM system will enable predefined tasks and role-based processes such as "Request Review" and "Approve Project" as well as generate a project checklist and track project status using core BPM capabilities. Yet the larger focus of this type of system will be centered on managing the entire project life cycle, from planning and submission, reviewing acceptance, performance and eventually closure and archiving. This larger scope demands the broader functionality offered through an ACM framework, which is not available through alternative approaches.

Throughout the project life cycle, the project and related work will be subject to defined policies and business rules. It will require guidance to the user on standard operating procedures. At various points, the achievement of milestones may involve specific tasks occurring within the system, such as a fillable form, or other checklist item required to be performed by a user. This may even involve a purely human task occurring entirely outside of this system. In each situation, the "case flow" involves a series of activities that have known outcomes or goals associated with them. What isn't known is the exact combination and sequence in which the activities must be performed. Often, the next required activity or task cannot be determined until the current activity has been completed.

This pattern fits well with ACM, but not traditional or integration-centric BPM, where the process must be scripted in advance such that the sequence of each activity is predetermined. Other software categories face similar limitations; they address a portion of the requirements, yet leave significant gaps, particularly in comparison with the ease with which the capabilities can be implemented through ACM.

Figure 1 below offers a comparison of four related software product types (*ACM, ECM, CRM,* and *traditional BPM)* with respect to how well they address the requirements aligned with the typical problem set which ACM targets.

	ACM	ECM	CRM	BPM
Support for one or more collaboration patterns, such as integration with external/third-party Instant Messaging platforms, to facilitate real-time discussions within a case (where this interaction is added to the case record and audit trail).	●	○	◐	○
Enable automation of both tasks and workflows, able to be launched at any pointed within the case folder.	●	◐	○	●
Provide a *Virtual Case Folder* and authoritative record of information (both structured and unstructured) from external Systems of Record (SORs) using standard integration (Web services, CMIS, RSS, WSRP, et al.) as the ability to populate the same repositories through similar methods.	●	●	○	◐
Allow fine-grain tracking of status and activities according to roles, rules and context captured within the case folder (rather than solely predefined scripts).	●	○	◐	◐
Facilitate planning and user guidance according to business rules and the context or data within the case folder.	●	○	●	○
Support a context-aware knowledgebase populated with case histories as well as supporting data and documents.	●	◐	◐	○
Allow role-based routing of the Virtual Case Folder based on inherited permissions and access privileges.	●	◐	○	●
Incorporate Business Rules Engine (BRE) for policy enforcement and decision support.	●	○	○	●
Leverage existing channels (email, IM, SMS, et al.) for alerts and notifications (where this is not necessarily added to the case record or audit trial).	●	◐	●	◐
Apply governance to managing the specific configuration of policies, business rules, business processes models, and other artifacts defining how cases are managed.	●	◐	○	◐
Systematically identify non-compliance within cases, as well as enable procedure for overriding of defined policies	●	◐	◐	●
Provide Business Activity Monitoring (BAM) dashboard.	●	◐	◐	●
Identify/present "Next Best Action" based on case context, business rules, and/or process optimization calculations.	●	○	◐	◐
Generate context-specific preformatted forms and response letters using case data and business rules.	●	●	◐	◐

Figure1: Comparison of ACM, ECM, CRM, BPM

3. CASE MANAGEMENT PRODUCT CLASSIFICATION

To properly understand and evaluate case management software, one must first define how it is similar to and/or different from other, traditional BPMSs. The standard (and still valid) way of achieving this result is to first see full-bodied BPM as covering both structured and unstructured process spaces, with traditional BPM addressing the former and case management addressing the latter. The next step is to overlay on top of this spectrum of process types the characteristics that dominate at each end of the spectrum, and to call out the transitions that occur as one moves across it. This approach is illustrated in **Figure 2** below.

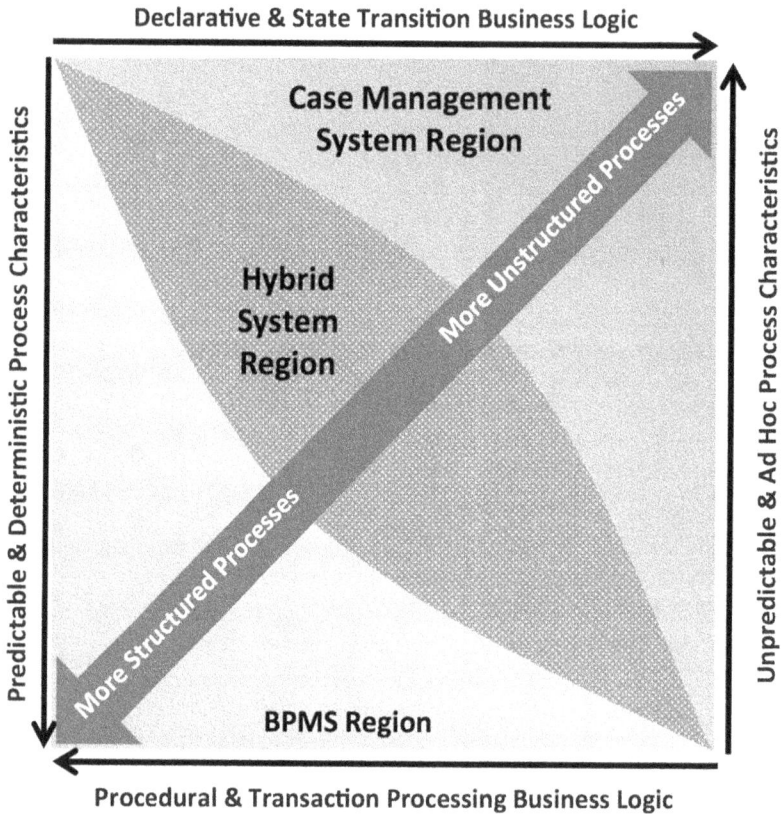

Figure 2 – Spectrum of Process Types in BPM

It is not just the characteristics of the automated processes that distinguish one pole from the other. The nature of the business problems being solved is also different at each end of the spectrum. However, just as was the case with process type, the differences are more distinctions of degree or emphasis: traditional BPMS solutions tend to be focused on optimizing cost and time, while true case management solutions tend to be focused on quality and value of the case outcomes. This leads to overlapping areas of focus, as shown in **Figure 3** on the next page.

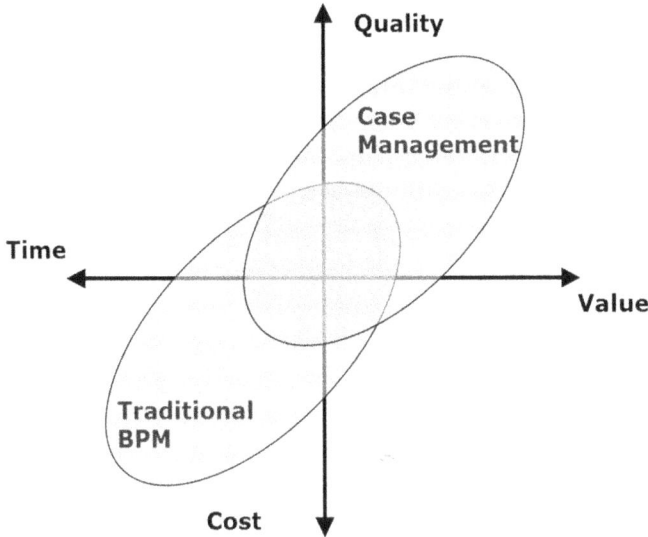

Figure 3 – Business Problems Addressed by Different BPM Solutions

Traditional BPMS Region

These are the dominant features of software in the traditional BPMS region:

- Nodes in the process workflow are predefined, including exception handling, pre-ordered in sequence of execution for both the main path of execution and any exception paths
- Generally must use an application server for traditional integrity because the work item is viewed and managed as a transaction.

The workflow will look something like what is illustrated in **Figure 4** below, which is an a priori statement about what the process will do.

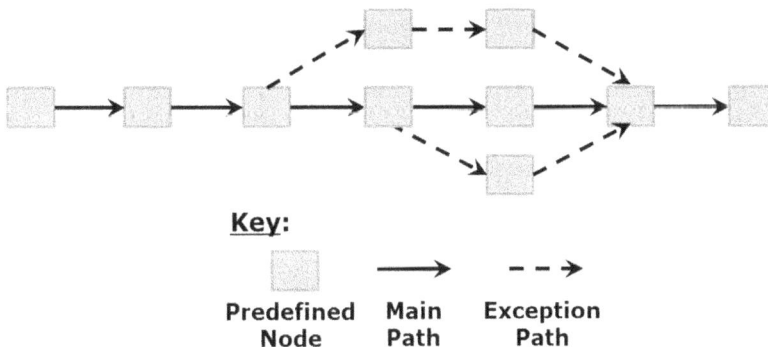

Key:

Predefined   Main   Exception
Node   Path   Path

Figure 4 –Workflow in Traditional BPMS Region

Though not shown here, the Business Process Model and Notation (BPMN) process modeling language from the Object Management Group (OMG) is well-suited as the procedural language for describing such deterministic behaviors and serving as the basis for executing the process.

Hybrid System Region

These are the dominant features of software in the hybrid system region:
- Nodes in the process workflow are predefined and designated as either mandatory or discretionary, and are not pre-ordered in sequence of execution since multiple permutations of possible paths exist
- May or may not use an application server for traditional integrity, depending upon whether the work item is viewed and managed as a transaction or as a case.

The workflow will look something like what is illustrated in **Figure 5** below, which is both an a priori statement about what is possible for the process to do and an a posteriori statement about what the process ended up doing.

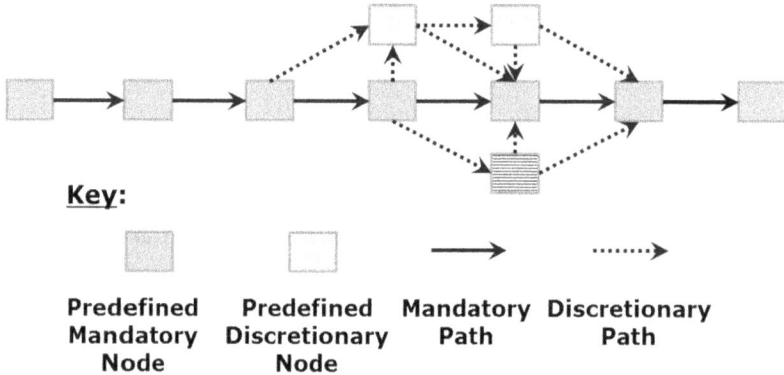

Key:

Predefined	Predefined	Mandatory	Discretionary
Mandatory	Discretionary	Path	Path
Node	Node		

Figure 5 – Workflow in Hybrid System Region

Though not shown here, BPMN (following a state-machine design pattern) or Case Management Modeling Notation (CMMN), also from the OMG, can be used as the modeling language for describing such behaviors.

True Case Management System Region

These are the dominant features of software in the true case management system region:
- Nodes in the process workflow are neither predefined nor pre-ordered, but can be added as needed, and are best considered as eligible to occur until enabled to occur as a result of the changing state of the case and enacted as having occurred as the case advances through the workflow through one of many permutations of possible paths exist
- Do not typically use an application server for traditional integrity, because the work item is viewed and managed as a case and not a transaction.

The enacted workflow will look something like what is illustrated in **Figure 6** below, which is only an a posteriori statement about what the process ended up doing.

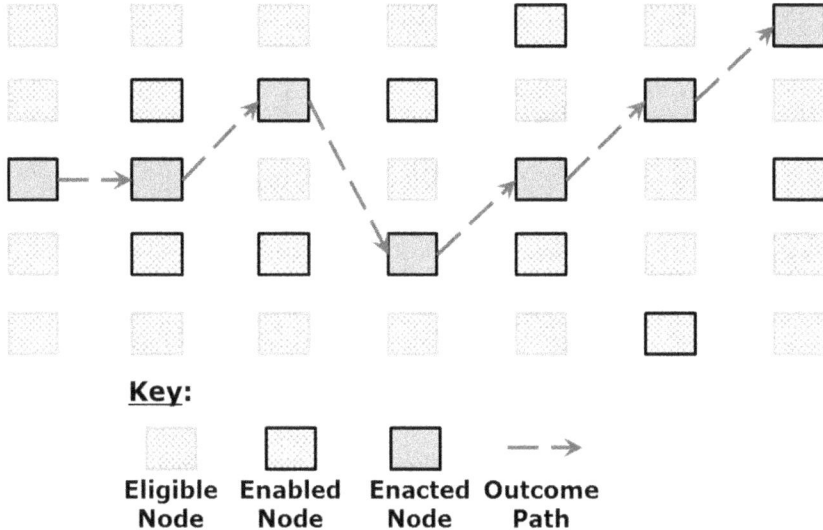

Key:

| Eligible Node | Enabled Node | Enacted Node | Outcome Path |

Figure 6 – Workflow in True Case Management System Region

Though not shown here, CMMN is can be used for describing such complex behaviors, but true process knowledge is only revealed through an after-the-fact examination

A product that is pitched as more of a case management system offering than a traditional BPMS one can automate simple structured, non-traditional processes (e.g., correspondence tracking) that require little in the way of predefined exception handling and only nominal systems integration outside of typical document management technologies (for document capture, storage, retrieval, routing, etc.), but this would be leveraging only a fraction of the true power of such a solution. Its true power lies in being able to incorporate ad hoc moments and reconfigure the workflow adaptively.

Reconfiguration of the case workflow is rather easy to do for this class of software, and since there is no need for the traditional integrity that an application server would otherwise provide, deployment of changes to the automated business process are quick and straightforward to accomplish. Such changes alter the running process rather than extend it for the new exception, but appropriate and rich audit trail information is being captured throughout process execution both before and after any such change.

The key is to associate all of the related threads, using the case ID common to each thread. Such audit data, as is shown in **Figure 7** (see next page) is virtually indistinguishable from the type of data that is typically used in process mining to generate a visualization of the process as a map and to support the analysis process performance using the map.

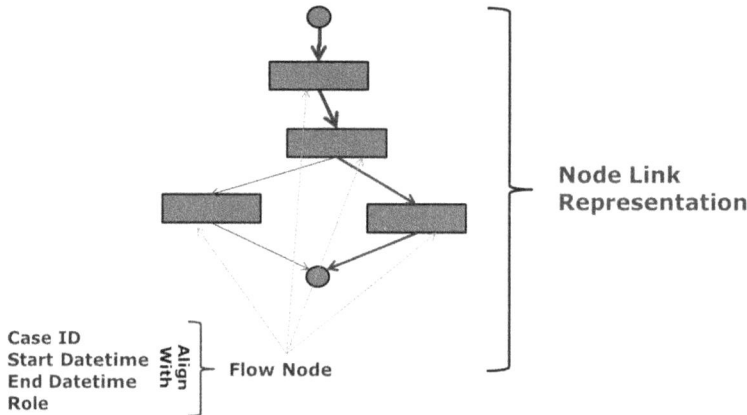

Figure 7 – Case Management System Audit Data

4.   WHAT DOES IT MEAN TO STABILIZE A PROCESS DESIGN DEPLOYED FOR EXECUTION?

"Stabilizing" in this context means whether the executing process is accomplishing its intended objectives in the expected manner. Let us compare how it is determined for a modeled process that is executed by a traditional BPMS with one that is executed by a true ACM system.

In a traditional BPMS, the model is more of an a priori statement (that is prescriptive), so stability will be measured to determine if the ongoing and completed processing indicates whether normative corrections are needed in the design of the process. This will be achieved via changes in control flow and the business logic executing at the flow nodes.

A traditional BPMS platform will be focused on the transaction processing aspects of the workflow, and BAM process instance reporting will provide workflow statistics on that while KPIs attached to the flow nodes in the process sequence will also be reported via BAM. Orientation of this data is mostly towards measuring efficiency of the process (e.g., time-in-system for the work, cycle time of work at a flow node, whether or not QoS/SLA expectations are met during the workflow, etc.).

Stress in the stability of this type of system would be understood in terms similar to what is understood as stress in most IT systems – namely, system latency, system resource contention, user backlogs, etc. Addressing such stresses would be pursued as a redesign of the system (or process).

In a true ACM system, the model is more of an a posteriori statement (that is descriptive), so stability will be measured to determine if the ongoing and completed processing indicates whether normative corrections are needed in the understanding of the process, which will be achieved via changes in the informational context for decision-making and the rules that affect decision-making.

A true ACM system will be focused on the state of the case aspects of the workflow, including outcomes, and the BAM-equivalent will generate and report on audit data for the case as it advances through the workflow. Orientation of this data is mostly towards measuring effectiveness - e.g., how many cases were closed, how many cases were approved vs. rejected, who made what decision, etc.

Stress in the stability of this type of system would be understood in terms similar to what is understood as stress to the knowledge worker – namely, information overload, resource contention over routine vs. value-add work, user backlogs, etc. Addressing such stresses would be pursued as a redesign of the informational and decision-making contexts.

Keep in mind that these two poles describe positions on a continuum of different types of business processes. Thus, the distinctions called out here are more of differences of degree of emphasis than mutually exclusive characteristics. For example, effectiveness might be defined for a health care delivery process as minimizing wait times between doctor examinations as well as the realization of positive medical outcomes, just as efficiency might reverse these in order of importance.

5. WHAT ARE THE IMPLICATIONS OF DIFFERENT DESIGN APPROACHES FOR MODELING EXECUTABLE PROCESSES?

Different design approaches are applicable for different types or different aspects of processes. For example, the structured and unstructured aspects of a process typically require different approaches. However, all approaches have in common the removal of ambiguity about intended behaviors in the design because the system platform cannot execute it otherwise. Let us examine these differences for a modeled process that is executed by a traditional BPMS vs. one that is executed by a true ACM system

A traditional BPMS application or a true ACM system application is (or should be) predicated on a process design/reengineering project, having first created a reasonably stable model to hand off for deployment as the pilot. This is really a question of how much of the application design has to be correct for the pilot, and if one assumes the 80-20 rule, then 80% of the design should be correct before deploying.

Let us further assume that the design delta (the gap between the actual design and the correct design) for the structured portion of a process is with respect to the procedural logic that is understood at design time (i.e., the business logic, control flow logic, etc.), while the design delta for the unstructured portion of the process is with respect to the declarative logic that is understood at design time (i.e., state transition logic, informational context, fuzzy decision-making rules, etc.). Thus, the 20% that is not correct is some mix of these deltas, with the mix depending on the makeup of the modeled process.

A process that is automated by a traditional BPMS will typically be one that consists of far more structured elements than unstructured ones (e.g., 75% vs. 25% of the process). This means the process is well-suited for being designed with a procedural language. A good pilot design would be one where (within the timeframe of the pilot) a large proportion of the overall design is known with respect to the structured elements (e.g., 60% calculated as 80% of 75%) and a small proportion of the overall design is known with respect to the unstructured elements (e.g., 20% calculated as 80% of 25%). Addressing the design delta would be addressed through new releases.

Support for the integration phase of work in deployment has to be supplied by the power of the modeler/IDE being used. In this case, it should support redesign that can really be tested BEFORE deployment, which makes this more like a standard software release management context. Such logic typically cannot be changed on the fly (as in a hot deployment), although abstracted logic, like a rules engine invocation, can change internally without consequence if I/O is the same.

A traditional BPMS platform typically comes as a complete set, with the only variation being the type or make of the application server on which it runs (and thus the various extensions to same it makes available). The skill set needed for development and deployment is heavily biased in favor of the BPMS platform, but also the application server on which it typically runs. This may create some common competencies due to the standardized nature of application server features. For example, a software engineer knowledgeable about one traditional BPMS platform that runs on Java-based application servers is likely to be able to quickly become knowledgeable about another traditional BPMS platform that also runs on such servers.

A process that is automated by a true ACM system will typically be one that consists of far more unstructured elements than structured ones (e.g., 75% vs. 25% of the process). This means the process is well-suited for being designed with a declarative language. A good pilot design would be one where (within the timeframe of the pilot) a large proportion of the overall design is known with respect to the unstructured elements (e.g., 60% calculated as 80% of 75%) and a small proportion of the overall design is known with respect to the structured elements (e.g., 20% calculated as 80% of 25%). Addressing the design delta would be addressed through new releases.

Support for the integration phase of work in deployment has to be supplied by the power of the modeler/IDE being used. In this case, it should support redesign that can really be tested AFTER deployment, which makes this less like a standard software release management context. Such logic typically can be changed on the fly (as in a hot deployment), though connecting the audit data across affected process threads can prove problematic.

A true ACM system platform generally comes as a lightweight software component, and typically without reliance on an application server. The skill set needed for development and deployment is heavily biased in favor of the ACM system platform, which may not create common competencies due the platform's own idiosyncratic design concepts and vocabulary. For example, a software engineer knowledgeable about one true ACM system platform is not necessarily likely to be able to quickly become knowledgeable about another true ACM system platform.

Traditional BPMS platforms have been around for long time and have long been the purview of large system integrators, as VARs and/or (presumably) trusted sources for needed technical skill sets, but true ACM system platforms are still emerging and have yet to become so aligned. For the time being, this gives the true ACM system vendor community the edge over system integrators because they do know the platforms. However, this edge may ebb away as case management concepts and vocabulary become more standardized through evolution of the technology and associated standards (such as CMMN).

Ontology-based ACM - The Need for Truly Adaptive Systems

Jürgen Kress, Clemens Utschig-Utschig, Hajo Normann, Torsten Winterberg

ADAPTIVITY ON MARS

After seven months of traveling Curiosity lands on Mars. The engineers in NASA mission control are excited to start scientific research. These scientists have a special challenge; the Mars rover is so far away and the signal takes so long, that they need to rely on automation in order to maintain control in the wildest scenarios. There are many decisions that must be made on a daily, and even on a minute-to-minute basis. Involving the scientist in every possible decision, given the round trip time to consult and answer, would slow the research to – literally – a crawl.

The scientists who operate the rover are knowledge workers. Just like knowledge workers in a business setting, they must figure out how to accomplish goals, as they uncover new information that affects their goals. The automation that they use built into Curiosity is very much like the business processes that businesses use to achieve their goals: the process works fine as long as the situation matches what was expected. But what happens to a business process when confronted with something unexpected?

Like business, the mission to Mars was well-planned. The scientific team chose the landing site based on satellite images. They prepared a research plan as best they could, given that they really had no way to know exactly what would be encountered. They anticipated the various roadblocks that might appear while Curiosity would explore the planet and program reactions through a set of well-defined processes and activities. These activities include navigating in an environment with rocks of various sizes and shapes and – who knows - maybe even lakes, taking pictures and measuring the outside world.

The team breaks down the planning ahead into cases such as *navigate and discover in rocky environment*. These cases contain *islands of predefined flow* for contexts in which all parameters of the robot and its environment indicate that it is safe to apply it. And these cases contain *islands of adaptive decisions and activities* when decisions must be made based on data in flux -- data that needs human interpretation. For example the robot sends a thermal graphic image that deviates from the ones sent an hour ago in curious ways. The engineers are challenged to come up with a creative solutions ad-hoc, defining a new process and activities for additional scientific research that was not planned at all.

Therefore they gather information from Mars and reason on it. This data gets continuously fed by multiple sensors like cameras, lasers, x-ray and radiation detectors, chemistry and mineralogy diffraction and multiple environment sensors - forming a *data lake of living knowledge* which is constantly morphing and refining. It supplies the NASA agent (the knowledge-worker), millions of miles away in the control center, with plenty of unstructured and maybe unexpected data-points.

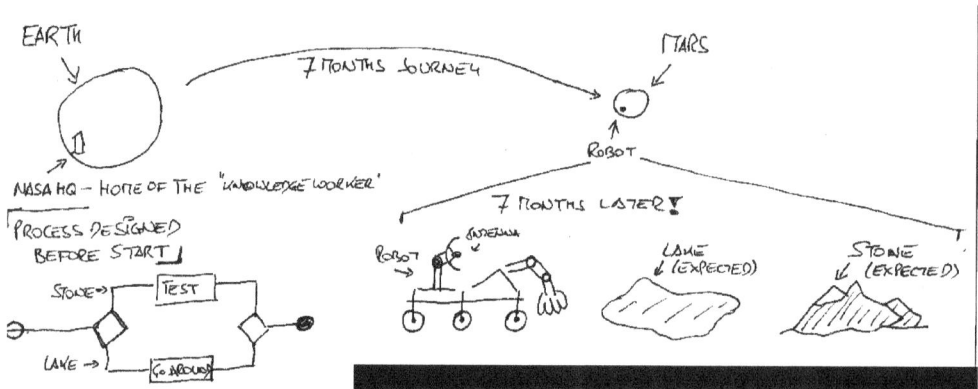

Figure 1: NASA's knowledge workers, Mars and the Robot

ADAPTIVE SYSTEMS ARE SYSTEMS IN CONSTANT FLUX (EVOLUTION)

Managing a robot on Mars is an extreme example for the challenges that knowledge workers encounter every day.

Knowledge workers in business need a new set of IT tooling and systems that continuously explore new situations while aiding and guiding in tough decision making based on past experience. This mega-trend shapes the future of IT-enabled knowledge work. It is reflected in the evolution of software we observe in this series of books: New tools that address various needs for adapting to unforeseen contexts gather under the - vague - umbrella term Adaptive Case Management (ACM).

ACM tools reflect the reality of situations in work in which many things are known – and standard processes exist, but unknowns occur, and sometimes radically change the approach to solutions. Typical use cases for adaptive systems include first aid for patients, fraud detection, criminal investigation, compliance, crisis management, high value / high risk proposals or credit-checks.

In contrast the traditional approach to manage repeating problems to outcomes has been through business process automation. Business owners first define the exact business process, its activities and sequence flow, including all possible optional branches, and then to strive for stability by controlling the process and making limited, carefully planned releases of process changes. When a new situation is encountered, a programmer (or business analyst of some sort) must get involved, design a proper response, and release it to the business users. This works well if the environment does not change very often, but if it does, this becomes a barrier to adapting the process to new situations, particularly when the use case inherently is unpredictable.

Yet unpredictable use cases greatly benefit from truly adaptive systems which continuously morph and evolve through recognizing new data and adding new activities. In their essence they thrive intrinsically less towards stable forms of activity graphs - a classical flowchart as we see it in typical BPM tools - but embrace constant intermediate forms – such as the next steps in a process suggested by an ACM tool. If you would visualize several paths taken for the same business process in an ACM tool you would recognize less stability and common structure compared to the paths taken in a flowcharting tool. In this chapter we present the idea of process support systems that automatically change and evolve to help the knowledge worker cope with environmental changes. Great care must be taken so that the system changes only when it should, and an ontological approach is the key to this.

THE EVOLUTION AND RISE OF ADAPTIVE SYSTEMS

Current ACM tools; Gartner refers to them as iBPMS (intelligent Business Process Management Suites)[1] are just the first wave of tools that strive to support truly adaptive systems. These systems are characterized by working on a mix of structured and unstructured process *and* data.

The evolution of ACM and BPM tools will evolve towards not mandating a choice to approach business process modeling and design either rigid or adaptive, thus forcing an organization to choose either a classic BPM tool or a new ACM tool. This is an arbitrary choice which currently still dominates discussions in the BPM and ACM communities.

Rather it will be a set of tools that allow for working in a continuum of different levels of structure: From rigid flowcharts, over semi-structured lists of activities and rules to tools that allow the knowledge worker in the field to add activities ad hoc while the intelligence in the ACM tool on the server learns whether these new activities are successful and should be suggested in similar contexts in the future.

Today ACM focusses on processes. Yet, the same continuum of structure is needed and will apply for data. Here the goal is a constantly evolving vocabulary that needs to be governed in order to become the one shared language spoken by everybody participating and owning a business process.

Thus, adaptive systems evolve their knowledge embracing the cumulative experience of process participants in the field, process owners and business departments while new situations occur and new data is gathered.

Seeing and experiencing the enormous amounts of data generated, these systems will attempt to make sense of knowledge, beyond being aids to knowledge workers, to eventually predicting, based on advanced statistical models and social collaboration, the most efficient, scalable, cost-effective way to achieve a desired outcome – and not stupidly following process and sequence flows.

DYNAMIC BPM – A FIRST STEP FORWARD TOWARDS ADAPTIVITY

It is interesting that often, while the way to reach the goal is less known beforehand, the business results of the related use cases that are supported by such adaptive systems are clearly structured and unambiguous. So in fraud detection the only possible outcomes are *no fraud detected* or *fraud detected*, in criminal investigation: *guilty* or *not guilty*, in patient care: *sick* or *healed* or in high value/high risk proposals or credit-checks: *approved* or *rejected*.

The unpredictable part lies in determining the path that leads to such a decision. The data structure, the data and lastly the workflow(s) leading to these results is in many of these use cases very complicated. Activities and their order cannot be predicted at modeling and design time. Therefore in old times, before the advent of ACM tools, the knowledge worker had to find his path through these use cases with

---

[1] *"Intelligent Business Process Management Suite (iBPMS) addresses the increasing need of business managers to react quickly to events that impact their business. By gaining better insight into business operations, managers can quickly take the right corrective action."* – Gartner iBPMS Magic Quadrant 2014 (Research Document: G00255421)
See also--iBPMS: Intelligent BPM Systems: Impact and Opportunity published by Future Strategies Inc. http://futstrat.com/books/iBPMS_Handbook.php

limited or no IT software support based on his knowledge, experience and gut feeling. The result often was that it is impossible to understand the rationale behind a decision if the person who has made it is not available any more.

With the emergence of more adaptive systems the knowledge worker of today greatly benefits in terms of transparency and productivity from an adaptive system to make his simple decision.

On the road to adaptivity, we have seen an evolved type of tools--*dynamic* BPM engines, often branded *ACM tools*. Many of these tools have a strong history of *BPMN/workflow engines*.

BPMN based tools are more rigidly structured than ACM tools. These tools still impose some structure that defines what happens next. The difference is that the flow is not determined in a visual graph, while visual elements can be used to depict and group feasible activities in a subsection of a case. What is by nature missing in less structured ACM workflows is the connection between activities. This connection depicts for each step the next step in a visual manner. In BPMN this relationship between process steps is a direct line or a gateway that indicate the flow between activities. An excellent trigger to consider embarking on the less structured ACM approach is when the sheer number of lines and gateways in a BPMN model that depict all these variances and exceptions becomes excessive and unmanageable.

The focus of those ACM tools is the support of the knowledge worker by *guiding information* that aims to aid in decision-making. This information includes business intelligence information like decision dashboards and potentially social information. An example would be a dashboard that shows that in a similar case situation 80% of the other knowledge workers used certain activities what led to an optimal solution. Adapted concepts from social networks can be used to rate or like data and activities that proved successful reaching a business goal in a similar situation. For example, a case step taken by a very skilled and experienced knowledge worker is rated by his peers with 4 out of 4 stars, showing that it provided value towards reaching the desired outcome of a step. However this is based on aggregated single occurrences (80 out of 100 used this activity) – while in the adaptive world the context (and any pre-work) of the current user is used by the engine to suggest the best next step.

Type (level of Adaptivity)	Systems / languages / means	Example
Adaptive	Ontologies, Semantic models, ObACM ('ontology based ACM')	Learning knowledge, inference of results rather than static queries, changes on the fly to activities, addition of new activities, changes to data structures, one (NON IT centric) vocabulary
Guiding	Analytics in ACM decision dashboard, integration of statistical means (e.g. R), Collaborative	Others have done ABC in your current context, rules bases reasoning, sharing of knowledge across contexts. ACM engine suggest best next steps; user picks one, rules

	Decision Making (CDM), Social BPM	/ statistic framework integration. Still finite set of a priori defined activities (known already at design time).
Dynamic	BPMN / workflow engine / ACM	More dynamic workflows. Typically using features like events in BPMN or like business rules for gateway logic. Often list of possible steps is dynamically read from external places, like Excel sheet. First ACM engines address this. Finite set of a priori defined activities (known already at design time),
Predefined	BPMN / workflow engine	Static workflows – a priori defined activities (all known during process design), static, changeable through IT only.

Table 1: Overview of adaptivity levels, building blocks and examples

LIMITATIONS OF DYNAMIC BPM ENGINES ON MARS

More and more engines reflect the level of *guiding*, characterized through offering only a finite and a priori defined set of activities. This means, all possible activities are thought and modeled by the design team. It is not possible to add completely new steps during runtime, because somebody has to implement them. Such an ACM engine is not adaptive in the sense of this chapter, but e.g. it is able to suggest *best next steps*. The user picks one of the (predefined) suggested next steps. The intelligence and strategies that lead to these suggested next steps are often based on rules in a business rule engine, maybe adding integration to a statistic framework.

The level of engine adaptivity can be easily verified through a simple question: "Can new activities and steps (beyond a notification) be added at runtime while one works within a process / case instance?"

Back to our mars mission example: In the NASA Robot use case, Curiosity is roving the surface of Mars, and encounters something nobody, even in their most exotic serious scenarios, expected to see: a Little Green Man (LGM). Since nobody expected this, there is no automation to deal with it. How does Curiosity react to this situation? How does it *adapt*?

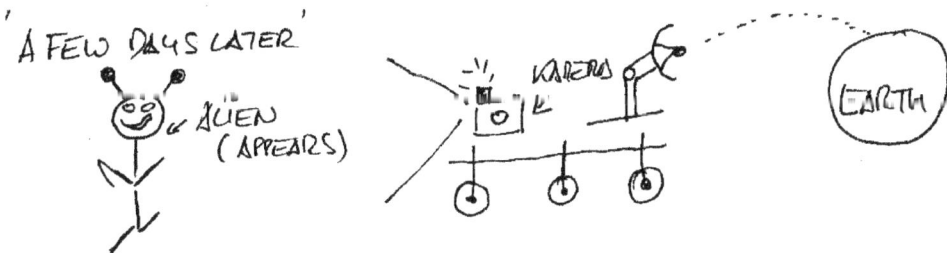

Figure 2: An "Alien" (the Little Green Man) appears - information is relayed to earth

In the classic *dynamic* or *guiding BPM* world, Curiosity, the robot is now stuck; because the program logic, the activities currently provided by the software, have no "react to an alien" options – the unpredictable wasn't foreseen and therefore not implemented.

Now the IT department needs to be involved to implement the "react on an alien" – activities, change processes, data structures, etc., while critical time may be lost, or even worse, when applying the new release of the workflow and data structures, data of the Alien occurrence may be lost, or needs to be migrated – preventing knowledge sharing.

Figure 3: The knowledge worker and Dynamic BPM

TRULY ADAPTIVE PROCESSES ON MARS

In contrast to the rather *dynamic* or *guiding* BPM tools currently marketed as ACM tools, a truly adaptive engine allows the knowledge worker to change the behavior and data structures of the system at runtime and add new behavior(s) on his own without the need to consult the IT department or re-deploy components of the system after a software change.

For a process engine to truly reach the *adaptive* level, it needs to let the knowledge worker access information in a *business vocabulary,* a language he relates to, that he can browse and understand without detailed IT knowledge, while being able to enhance and add structures on the fly.

Back to Mars; in the *adaptive world,* Mission Control not only can add the alien as a new data structure and also new activities to search for aliens, based on data from different sensors, but more importantly, all that could be done instantly by the knowledge worker without the interaction with the IT department.

Many business critical use cases that highly paid knowledge workers need to find a solution for under stress, greatly benefit from truly adaptive systems which continuously morph and evolve through new data and new activities being added.

Such a level of adaptation can be achieved by a new type of adaptive engine that supports *adaptivity* on all its technology layers (storage, orchestration, user interface and business processes). Table 2 puts these characteristics of an adaptive engine that is built based on ontology into perspective.

Layer	Rigid; Declarative	Adaptive-Ontology-based
Business Process	BPMN, rigid graph with a-priori defined activities	Loosely coupled activities, constrained by knowledge rules and knowledge-relationships
Page Flow / User Interface	Page-Flows, Java Server Faces	Page flows are only defined on use-case level, and they are the result of information objects and their linkages in the ontology, and hence assembled dynamically
Orchestration	BPEL / SCA	Information Objects are backed by services, "orchestration" is expressed through relationship between use-cases or between entities within the ontology
Integration / Storage	Graphical Mappings within Integration Infrastructure (e.g. ESB)	Semantical mappings based on micro annotations within data structures allow the engine to map data at runtime.

Table 2: Architecture layers and implementations in adaptive and rigid engines

ONTOLOGY-BASED ACM ENGINES TACKLE BOTH PROCESS AND DATA IN NEW WAYS

The key component that enables an adaptive approach to business processes is an engine that transforms data into inferable knowledge. As it stands today, ontologies are the most promising concept to materialize such a type of emerging knowledge. A toolset that is based on ontology allows organizations to constantly apply learning. Ontologies are the key to changing the lifecycle of software away from rigid design-test-deploy cycles towards constantly evolving software. This new lifecycle recognizes and embraces constant flux. It is a fundamental new paradigm to software development, changing the modes of operation and collaboration for requirements gathering, design and governance of an organization where it is applied. It will also impact sourcing and vendor strategies since *ontology-based middleware* is a characteristic that ripples through the execution architecture, requiring middleware components to collaborate in new ways.

What is an ontology?

"To support the sharing and reuse of formally represented knowledge among AI systems, it is useful to define the common vocabulary in which shared knowledge is represented. A specification of a representational vocabulary for a shared domain of discourse — definitions of classes, relations, functions, and other objects – is called an ontology"[2].

---

[2] A Translation Approach to Portable Ontology Specifications - Thomas R. Gruber, Stanford University, 1993

In short, an ontology formally describes, clusters and relates knowledge, through defining classes, and the relationships between those – very theoretic indeed.

For Curiosity, NASA's robot, a small ontology describing known objects and actions (classes) as well as their relationships can be found below, bringing theory to practice.

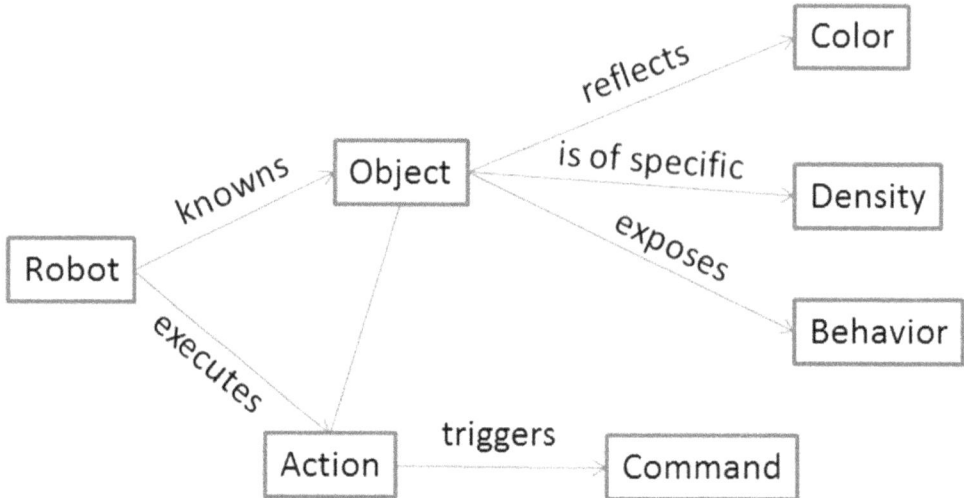

Figure 4: The ontology describing objects and their relationship in the context of the NASA Robot

The robot *knows* a stone (*object*). The stone is red *(reflects a color)*, is hard *(is of specific density)* and is immobile, not moving *(is exposing a behavior)*.

What can be inferred by reading the above example ontology is that something that is red, hard and not moving is a stone. In reverse something neither red, standing still or hard, cannot be a stone.

Of course a look into (real) nature proves this ontology wrong! Many things are red, hard, and immobile yet are not stones – true - but the above ontology describes the robot's knowledge, and not nature.

Beyond describing (to the robot) known objects – the above ontology can be used to configure actions (expressed through the *executes* relationship), the robot shall fulfill upon known objects.

For example the robot shall move around *(execute action)* the stone *(object and relationship)*. This action triggers to move its wheels 300 revolutions to the right and then forward *(command)*.

When the robot encounters the LGM (Little Green Man), its programs recognize that this object does not resemble in its *lake of knowledge* something it has a concept of. LGM surely is not standing still, it's green, and is waving with its arms. As no known object can be inferred - it's a new piece of information the robot has no action for. This is the time of the knowledge-worker back on Earth. He can act upon this new information – providing / creating more knowledge through *defining* what the new object is, and deciding *what to do* with it (e.g. have the robot say hello, or run away – which are new *actions* with new *commands*).

The Mars ontology is an example to proof that business users can read, understand and manipulate the information within an ontology. Compared to systems based on binary data format (XML) the knowledge worker does not require to interact with IT to understand and manipulate the information.

Using Ontologies to build adaptive systems

Let's consider a more advanced example showing the difference between data and information: the data structure of a sales order. It contains e.g. a customer record with attributes such as *who ordered, whom to ship to, whom to bill*. Further, the sales order consists of multiple order lines, each with a reference to a specific material and a quantity. Conventional engines often store this kind of sales order as one object, most of times in binary format.

Now let's consider what it takes for the owner of the sales order process to understand, among not one, but many sales orders what material is the most ordered one in order to focus on the right aspect in purchasing. Therefore queries need to be written that extract sales orders, parse each order for its order lines, and aggregate on referenced materials. The starting point is the entire sales order object.

In contrast, an ontology based engine *contains* the semantic model of a sales order. It stores a sales order as *resolved* data points. We refer to this as *information*. The query to get the most ordered materials is here based on inference (through natural relationships), starting at the material, referenced by the most order lines, aggregated over its quantities.

Reversely, this allows inference: based on those relationships, materials that are not ordered at all can be extracted (all materials without a relationship to an order line).

- Using this concept as foundation for an engine allows instant access to knowledge, rather than to stored data entities.
- Having access to certain information will allow the knowledge workers to make better decisions, and an engine to use this vocabulary and its relationships for configuration.

In the NASA sample the knowledge worker who controls the path of the rover contacts a colleague to get details on the current battery status before to start a movement. The combined knowledge of all knowledge workers who use the engine is the *living knowledge base*. All this information must be stored in the ontology and can then be accessed, read and browsed by all knowledge workers.

AN ADAPTIVE APPROACH TO BEHAVIOR

In the Mars rover example the knowledge worker has to decide to turn left or right. Based on the information of previous turns e.g. inclination angle of the site, he might turn right. In truly adaptive systems the knowledge worker might change the structure of the flow within the use case in real-time. Our mission control knowledge worker is changing the flow of activity to the case. E.g. as the left rover wheel is damaged he always checks the wheel status with the camera while he is driving and not only before he drives.

Engine architecture requirements

The knowledge worker needs to be able to have "hot" access to instance and service data. User interfaces need to be hot deployed at runtime or need to be data-based, self-configurable interfaces. If the knowledge worker changes data structures, the engine needs to support this on the fly without re-deployment or re-start including post conditions and events. At the same time the engine, behavior and data needs to be audit proof and secure.

In a second scenario the knowledge worker not only changes the behavior of the system by using predefined functionality in a certain order to reach his goal. Now he is even adding new activities or functionality to extend the system behavior to match new and unforeseen requirements. This might include new approval steps or new automated enrichment steps. Because the wheel of our rover is damaged, every time before the rover starts, a second knowledge worker needs to approve to move, as to not damage the rover wheel further.

Engine architecture requirements

The engine needs to support the addition of new activities, while an instance is running and hence the reevaluation of the knowledge base while preserving audit proof and security.

AN ADAPTIVE APPROACH TO DATA

What applies to behavior also applies to data and data-structures: knowledge workers will want to change / enhance them in an adaptive system. Today's Business Intelligence systems allow users to extract aggregated information from IT systems. Often users can create reports by themselves and export the data to Microsoft Excel to do further calculations. To change the underlying data and the data structure in the systems, the interaction with the IT department is required. With the growing amount of data which might be well structured and even more data which is unstructured it becomes more and more a challenge for the knowledge worker to get the right data to make his decision.

Big data systems like Hadoop allow us to store unstructured data in one repository. The knowledge worker needs to find the right information based on his current context to decide on the activities - based on the data, through making it meaningful. In traditional system architectures (including those based on service oriented design) data is rigidly determined on all its layers (from the user interface to the storage layers). IT experts are required to support the knowledge worker to get access to the required information, chunk it into relationships, and help translate the information into business language.

Engine architecture requirements

The rigidly-structured master data is stored as a *statum* in the ontology. The unstructured more volatile contextual data and the data in motion which changes are stored as a *factum* in ontologies. Factum data can be adopted and changed easily by the knowledge worker in a business user friendly way. Secondly the ontology structure (backing the instance data) can be amended w/o the need of IT interaction. These changes need to be reflected by a flexible, annotated user interface.

In the NASA Robot use case, the mission control's knowledge worker has to make a decision if the rover should drive over or around a specific kind of ground consistency (modeled by different color findings in the sample later on). As there are now several rovers on Mars they decide to learn from previous decisions. How did mission control act when the much older Mars rover "Opportunity" was faced with a similar problem? Can this information help us to make a decision also in this case? Technically this data lies very often outside the current occurrence (instance). An ontology based adaptive engine is not tied to instances, as those cannot be easily accessed by other running (process) instances, but rather stores relationships open for everyone.

The knowledge worker can query the whole knowledge base in a language he understands immediately at the moment he requires the information. So the knowledge worker finds that "Opportunity" already had found this type of ground consistency and that it is save to drive over this kind of ground. This information is now persistent in the ontology – the system learned. From now on, the rover will *know* that future findings of this kind of ground are save to drive over.

In the second use case of data adaptivity, mission control wants to add a new at-

> **Engine architecture requirements**
>
> Technically this requires a different solution to instance/data management. In simple terms it's built upon linked knowledge: using an ontology, rather than creating an instance of a process as container for data changes occurring in this process instance.

tribute or change an attribute type. As mission control found an alien (the famous LGM) on Mars it needs to come with a way to search for aliens going forward. Therefore they add the data structure with all the attributes to describe the alien to the ontology. The next time a context appears, it is obvious for all of the mission control employees that an Alien is found again and eventually the engine could trigger the right follow up actions / activities. In a stable transaction oriented system this would require major changes in the data structure (relational data) and in the semantic data. Re-design to adapt to the change and re-deployment by IT experts would be necessary. A truly adaptive system allows these kinds of data structure and data value changes without breaking the running system.

> **Engine architecture requirements**
>
> In an ontology-based system where structure is decoupled from data instance, the new attribute is added at runtime, and data can be accessed through the modified structure. This requires strict separation of the type system from the data, and even more fault tolerant access to data, ensuring that existing data is not corrupted based on structural changes.

PROOF OF CONCEPT "A2X" - AN ONTOLOGY BASED ACM ENGINE

Let's consider *Adaptive Activity Execution (A2X)*[3], a *proof of concept* engine - not about cases, processes, graphs and instances – but about data and activities.

Would an ontology based approach really work and how would it work beyond theory? Would it perform, or would inference just be way to slow to react in real time scenarios? And last but not least, would it be sufficient generic to be capable of supporting more than one business domain?

We asked ourselves these questions and decided to implement an engine that reflects all the ideas we described so far with the goal of gathering more knowledge and to proof the discussed concepts.

To make the things more real and interesting, we constructed a toy Mars rover using Lego Mindstorms technology that would serve as executor for decisions a knowledge-worker makes and as creator of new information for the knowledge-worker. With both, the Lego Mars rover and the A2X engine we challenged the engine using a real Mars rover adventure of "Curiosity" as example.

---

[3] More information about A2X can be found at http://www.acmcommunity.com

Of course our toy rover has no real sensors, e.g. to analyze ground consistency. So we used a color sensor instead and several different colors on the ground simulating different kinds of terrain. Our rover reacts on the color findings depending on the knowledge it finds in the A2X ontology base. The knowledge worker in our scenario is Mission Control, also using the A2X system to reach the goals of the Mars mission – the knowledge worker uses A2X to react on the unpredictable things that happen to the rover.

Architecture of A2X

We agreed on these key (technology) design cornerstones to build an adaptive engine in general and subsequently implemented them in A2X:

- A meta-model configurable at runtime (aka an ontology), mapable to CMMN[4] (an emerging standard to model cases)
- No domain specific but generic support of use-cases
- An Information object layer that models business data relationships and information objects
- An (internal) type system decoupled from data, including fault tolerant de-/serialization and changes to it on the fly without restart etc.
- A living knowledgebase, supporting external services as well as internal caching, based on the above type system
- An evaluation engine bound to the knowledgebase, able to suggest next steps, influence able through ratings from outside (e.g. social)
- A multi-tenant security and lifecycle concept going through all building blocks enabling changes on the fly, from identity configuration, through sharing of artefacts
- A really generic user interface, derived from types and micro annotations
- Extension points for security, shell rating, suggestions and the Service Framework to integrate with the external world
- Hot direct access to knowledge, components and their configurations – deployment only creates a tenant, nothing more
- A no-instance, no-case concept – all knowledge lives audit proof and can be reused and linked without any limitations

---

[4] http://www.omg.org/spec/CMMN/1.0/PDF - CMMN Specification 1.0, The Object Management Group, last accessed Aug 2nd 2014

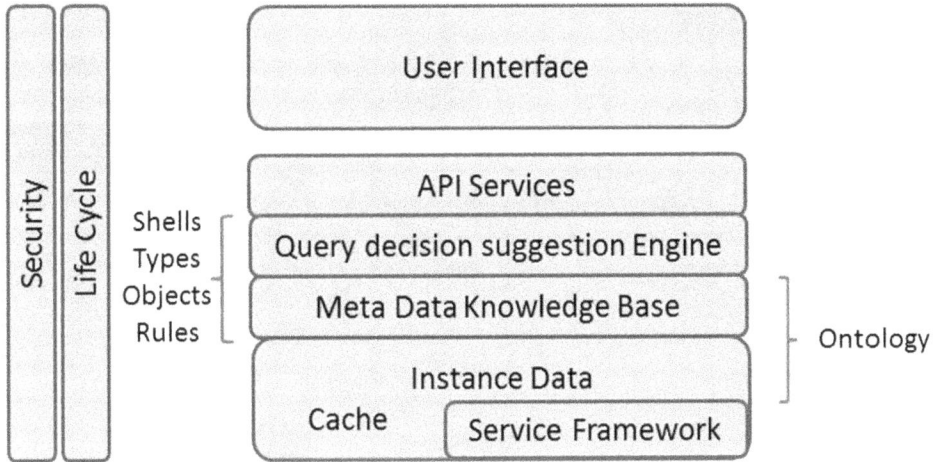

Figure 5: Architecture blocks of A2X

We used Protégé (by Stanford University) to model and configure the ontology. The common Java framework Spring was leveraged for bootstrapping a microkernel. For the runtime we used the lightweight Jetty Webserver to host the user interface based on JavaScript/HTML5. The Apache CXF framework is the foundation for the A2X Service Framework, and lastly SDO (Service Data Object) is used to have access to data and for de-/serialization. .

Introduction to the main ontology

The key component of the A2X engine is the configurable meta-model (*Meta Data Knowledge Base*), shown in detail below. All components, the *API Services* providing access to it, the *suggestion engine*, as well as the *Instance Data Cache* and the *Service Framework* are configured through this ontology. Any changes to this ontology (to relationships, to instances) will immediately cause those components to reconfigure themselves to changes (e.g. type systems, etc.).

At its core an *Activity Shell* represents a use-case. A use case could be the sample described above, to decide what to do, when the Mars rover detects a new kind of ground consistency. In A2X we map this scenario to the decision what to do with an unknown color finding of our Lego Mindstorms robot. A use case (automated or humanly driven) can be fulfilled / closed through events (*Event*) which cause certain actions or post-conditions (*Condition*) to trigger. These in-turn call services, java classes, modify instance data, trigger other use-cases, etc.

Furthermore the ontology relates, which actor (*Role*) can perform a use case, to which information objects (*Entity*) a use-case (*Activity Shell*) is bound and lastly when it becomes applicable (through *Conditions*) to a certain context.

Lastly - in order to integrate seamlessly with external systems, a service framework (*Entity Service*) can back any information object defined through the ontology.

An information object (*Entity*) is defined through a data structure, in the prototype implementation this is done through XSD (XML Schema definition), but can be easily enhanced to other means, such as JAVA Beans, or a type ontology.

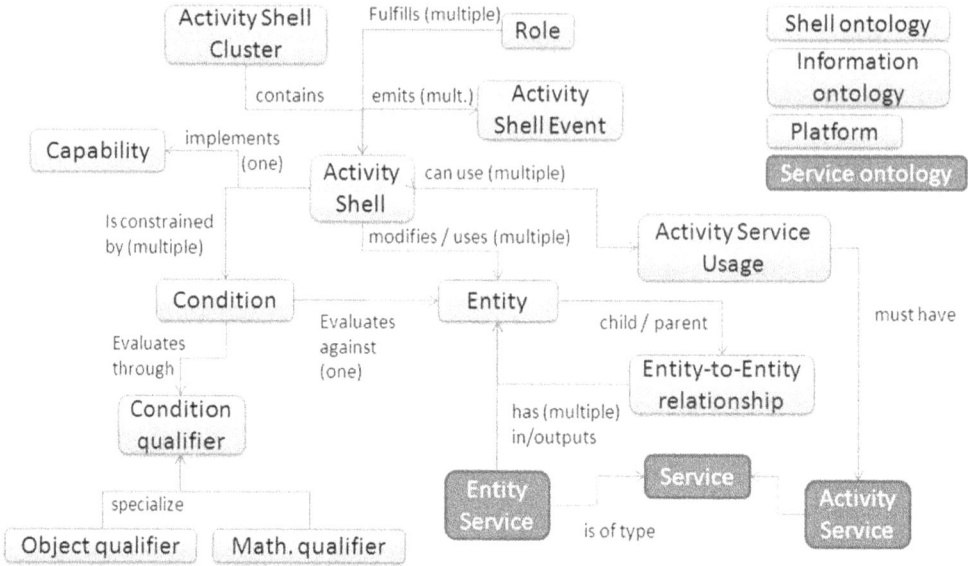

Figure 6: The internal meta-model of A2X

A concrete use-case – the robot found a new color – Mission Control needs to decide what happens next

Before the NASA robot went on its seven-month journey, NASA's scientists foresaw that it would find different terrains with different ground consistencies (simulated by certain different colors). This is the implemented data and behavior for the foreseeable things that might happen. But what shall happen when unpredictable things occur? Like a new color (ground consistency) is detected by the rover, that was not expected and therefore no relating action is built into the system? Then the system must be adaptive to allow reactions on the new situation.

In a knowledge worker's day-to-day job in arbitrary companies, situations like this happen all the time: new information is coming through, from new channels, or new insights being generated. A well understood example might be disease management: while trying to confine or cure a decease outbreak (such as Ebola, currently making its way through Western Africa), all kinds of unpredictability might happen.

In the following we will walk through the example of our Lego Mindstorms rover (or the real rover on Mars) handling an unpredicted situation: An *Unknown color finding event* occurs. Is it safe to drive over this new color? Do this only once or also for future findings of this color? Better drive around the new color? Or is it so dangerous that the rover should retreat as fast as possible?

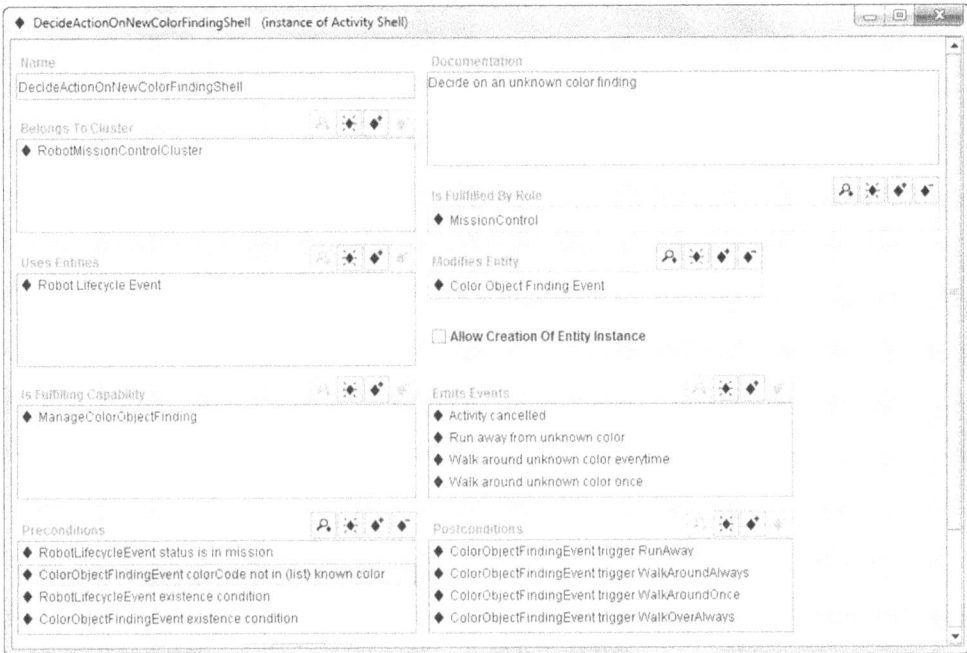

Figure 7: The meta-model for the use-case. Decide on new color finding

In figure 8 we see a part of the meta-model coping with the New-Color-Finding use case in the Protégé modelling tool. The use-case of deciding what to do can be executed by the role *Mission Control*, and allows for four actions (Events) to be triggered:

1. *Activity cancelled* – cancel the activity, and leave the knowledge as is
2. *Run away from unknown color* – this will trigger an action to send a message to the robot to run away from the found object
3. *Walk around unknown color every time* – this will trigger the robot to walk around the object every time, here the ontology will be modified to ensure the next time a similar occurrence happens, this action will trigger automatically
4. *Walk around color once.* This triggers a call to the robot to walk around the color on time only.

This meta-model is rendered in the generic user interface of the A2X system, which allows somebody in the role *Mission Control* to decide what should happen in this use case. As described earlier, use-cases are constrained by conditions (the status of the knowledge base, its instances and relationships) as well as the executing identity.

In the use-case to decide on new color finding, the NASA robot found an unknown color, hence the pre-condition models not every possible color, but rather the known ones. When a new color is found – after the decision was made - this color will be added to the known ones (through new relationships), and hence extending/modifying the knowledge-base.

The next time the same color comes along, the engine can infer based upon the modified knowledge that this color is now a known one, and eventually react accordingly (and trigger actions predefined).

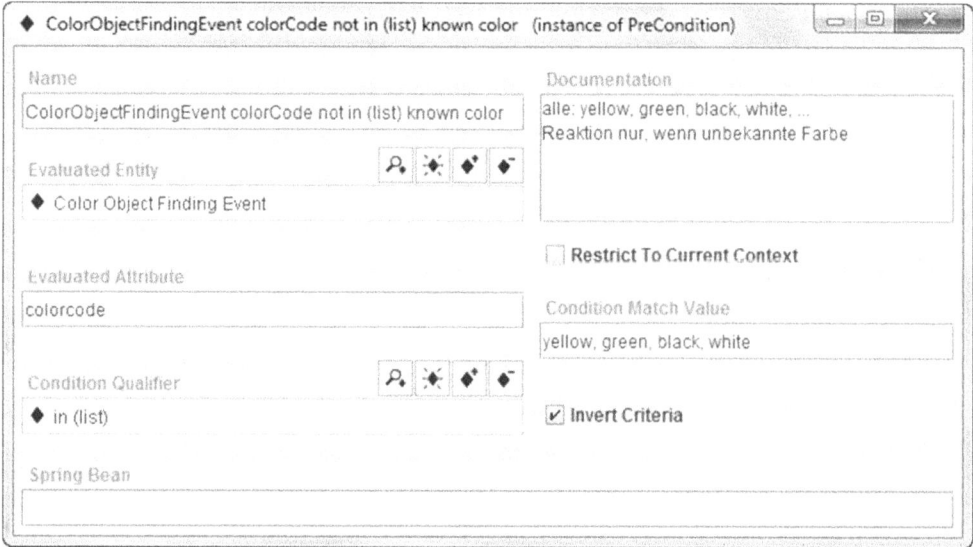

Figure 8: Precondition for colors - model the expected

The User Interface is driven by the ontology and the type system. It shows all shells that are available to the current identity (configured through *Role*), yet some are applicable (*DecideActionOnNewColorFindingShell*), while others aren't (*StartMissionShell*): see Figure 11.

Furthermore the user interface shows what has happened before the *DecideActionOnNewColorFindingShell* became applicable: The NASA robot sent a signal to the Mission Control, notifying it of being *alive*. Through multiple conditions this triggered Mission Control to be able to start the mission (sending a message to the Robot to start its engine and move forward). Shortly thereafter the robot ran into an unknown color (*red*) which caused it to stop, and wait for further instruction, based on the new finding (History Shells: *CreateUnknownFindingShell*).

Given the relationships between information objects in the ontology, the User Interface also allows the knowledge worker to retrieve linked information and history data (*Available Entities*), showing the current status and location of the robot, and so forth.

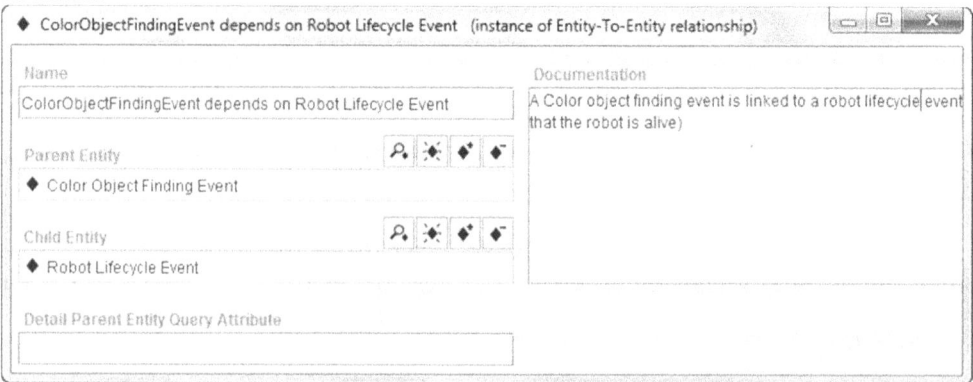

Figure 9: Relationships between Entities

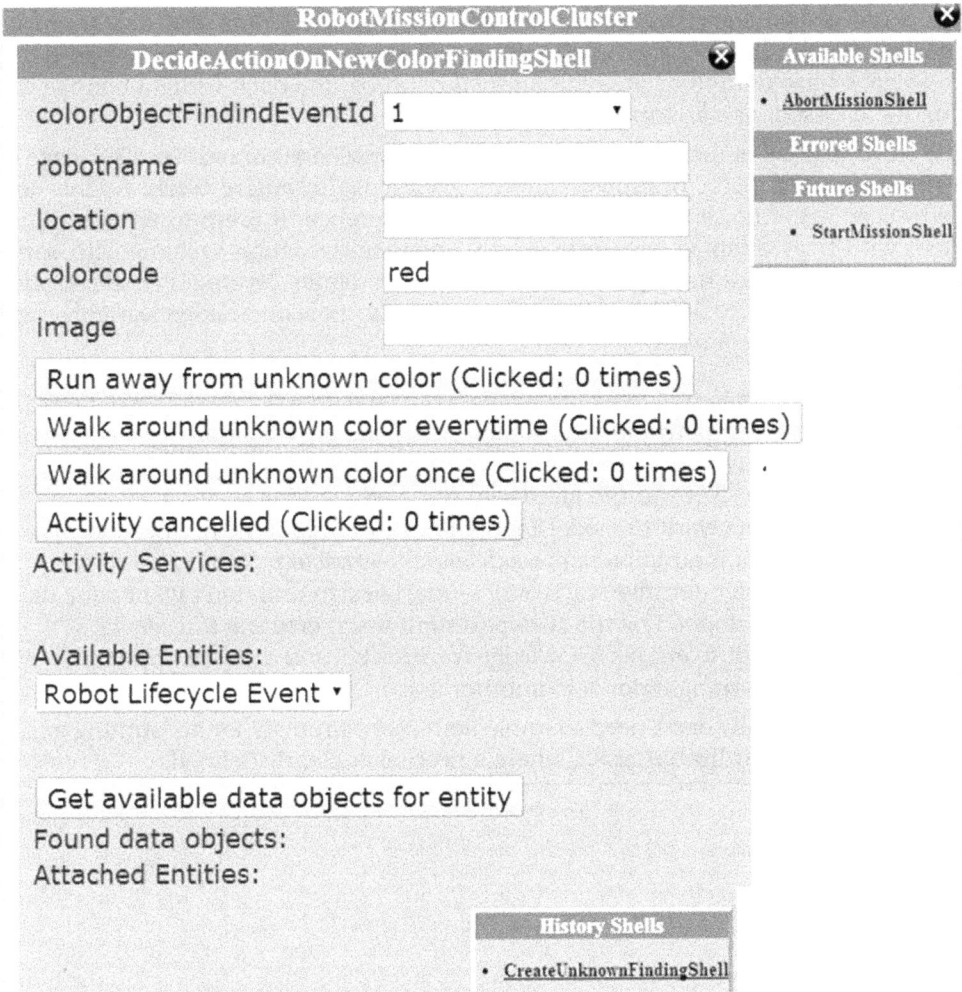

RobotMissionControlCluster ✗

DecideActionOnNewColorFindingShell ✗

colorObjectFindindEventId 1 ▾

robotname

location

colorcode   red

image

Run away from unknown color (Clicked: 0 times)

Walk around unknown color everytime (Clicked: 0 times)

Walk around unknown color once (Clicked: 0 times)

Activity cancelled (Clicked: 0 times)

Activity Services:

Available Entities:
Robot Lifecycle Event ▾

Get available data objects for entity
Found data objects:
Attached Entities:

Available Shells
• AbortMissionShell

Errored Shells

Future Shells
• StartMissionShell

History Shells
• CreateUnknownFindingShell

Figure 10: The user-interface generated real time from the information available and metadata from the ontology

Of course it is hard to envision this walkthrough without seeing a live demo. For us, this prototype implementation and use case delivered a lot of insights on how it feels to have an ontology-based system with a fully generic user interface running. The prototype implementation showed us, that adaptivity needs different concepts, different building blocks – far away from those of conventional BPM and ACM engines, which are based on state machines, instance data and process graphs. Yet it also showed us, that we had to rethink most we've learned through the many years, in order to wrap our heads around these new concepts.

CONCLUSION

We have entered the era of the knowledge worker. Like on Mars, knowledge workers discover unknown territory. Based on their experience they make decisions. ACM systems can support them to make better decisions and to train new knowledge workers. With the outbreak of diseases like Ebola doctors are faced with new situations in first aid patient care.

Similar to mission control on Mars, unknown territory like an Ebola outbreak has to be discovered with a variety of unstructured data sources, such as where are the patients located, how they got infected, should more persons be isolated, what was the route of transmission. Based on this unstructured data the doctor might change his behavior. Like on Mars our rover changed directions based on knowledge base data from an additional Mars probe, the doctor might change the treatment based on additional similar cases.

The same applies to many similar use cases in knowledge companies. The class of ACM systems is here to support today's knowledge intensive work. In the new knowledge age, knowledge workers make the difference. It is up to us to support them with truly adaptive systems: simply enhancing existing systems with some dynamic aspects is a jump going far too short. Companies leveraging real adaptive system capabilities to deliver optimal IT support for their knowledge workforce will make the difference – soon.

When should a company employ adaptive methods and tooling?
- If you don't know what your knowledge workers need to solve their problems – yet want to give them value add tooling
- If you don't want to model each and every exception case (because it's simply not maintainable) : *modelling the expected*
- If you prefer iterative work over a-priori design and don't want your users to be stopped by the IT department when creating knowledge
- If you want to enable knowledge transfer beyond a single occurrence without writing it down in another tool

However, you really don't need to implement real adaptivity for accounting and other very standardizable tasks, where a process is clearly defined.

Combining Compliance with Flexibility

Real life experiences from Norwegian Public Sector

Helle Frisak Sem, Steinar Carlsen, Gunnar John Coll, Computas AS, Norway

1. ABSTRACT

Modern, civilized societies depend on law and structured relations, providing a substrate for organizations and individuals to collaborate and compete. Both businesses and public sector must behave in compliance with such rules, and at the same time need sufficient flexibility to perform their tasks according to the situations at hand and in a constantly changing world. IT tools supporting businesses and public sector organizations must aid the users with compliance as well as flexibility. Traditional IT systems have laid the burden of compliance on the users, whereas BPM-systems attain compliance at the expense of flexibility.

This paper describes a set of means to providing compliance with flexibility, based on real life experiences from widely used and long running ACM systems in the Norwegian Public sector. In the highly regulated Scandinavian societies, the public sector takes on responsibilities that may, in other jurisdictions, be covered by private corporations. The experiences should therefore be equally relevant for the private sector.

2. MOTIVATION

The need for compliance

Most organizations, be it in the public sector or in private business, are regulated by law. Legislation may apply to the organization of the business, to security matters, to the business relationships with external actors or to its economic practices and accounting. In addition, the company or organization will normally have internal policies regulating how its employees shall perform their tasks, as well as a set of best practices or guidelines.

To stay within the law and adhere to internal policies and practice requires consistently compliant behavior throughout the organization. There is a general wish to treat similar cases in the same way, in order to provide adequate customer satisfaction and maintain a good reputation.

The need for flexibility

In knowledge-based operations, however, context can make a big difference. Each situation must be handled with due concern for the particular details of the case. To operate in a constantly-changing world, the knowledge worker must therefore have sufficient flexibility to handle new situations in order for the organization to meet demands in an effective way. Within their area of empowerment, competent employees should be able to make decisions and act according to their professional judgment of the situation at hand.

Compliance means conforming to rules, and this puts the judgments in the hands of those making the rules. As far as laws and national regulations go, this is unavoidable, but when it comes to policies and company internal practices, it is a matter of choice how far the leaders want to detail the rules and make the judgments, and how far they trust their employees to decide actions themselves. This also addresses questions regarding methods of leadership. Flexibility in the operational work requires leading by confidence – confidence that the employees conducting the operative work are capable and knowledgeable and can be trusted and empowered to use their good judgment within given bounds.

Flexibility in changing the definition of how the system behaves at runtime without programming – also called configuration of the system – enhances the possibility to micromanage, whereas flexibility in the way the system behaves may enable empowered employees able to make their own judgments.

Flexibility in legacy systems

Traditional IT systems, with navigation-oriented screens to register and modify data, burden the employee with finding their way through the system, manually ensuring compliance with rules and guidelines as they work. In this sense, such tools are actually quite flexible, and it is mainly up to the user to ensure that work is correctly performed. As a consequence, however, in a large organization, particularly if it is geographically dispersed, different cultures may emerge in terms of how tasks are performed, and compliance will vary accordingly. Such unbounded flexibility may impact reputation and customer satisfaction negatively, and may even develop into behavior that is in conflict with the law.

Compliance in BPM solutions

By contrast, BPM systems, with predefined end-to-end processes, are excellent in providing support for a uniform practice across an organization and ensuring adherence to regulations and guidelines. This comes at a cost, however, as there is limited flexibility for handling situations that fall outside the set of pre-designed alternative paths. In such systems, these deviant cases are generally seen as «exceptions», and the need for exception handling can be significant. Having to stall work in unexpected situations is not an efficient way of operating. Worse still, if the system fails to mobilize the best of employee competence in such situations, this can be detrimental to operational effectiveness, in terms of the achieved result.

Combining compliance and flexibility

For organizations that base their operations on empowered knowledge workers, there is a real need for tools that provide maximum freedom to act in accordance with the best of knowledge – within the bounds of regulations. Must they choose between flexible but task- and regulation-ignorant registration tools, and the compliance-enhancing but rigid BPM approach? We argue that this is a spurious dilemma, and that ACM-systems for knowledge work may indeed be both highly flexible and strongly supportive of compliant practices. Adaptive systems must be devised to handle unexpected cases not as exceptions, but as business as usual.

It may perhaps seem odd to treat flexibility and compliance as complementary rather than contradictory aspects, but we think this is a fruitful view. The unifying keyword is confidence. We believe that the professional who is unsure of his ground, will stick to the middle of the road and hesitate to apply own best knowledge to the full. In a highly-undetermined situation, it can easily become more important *not* to make mistakes than to do something eminent. Flexibility is dangerous unless you know what is actually allowed and what is not, and this can cause rational actors understandably to prefer over-conservative practices.

For less predictable tasks demanding flexibility, a non-flexible BPM system will fail to release the potentials of the competent employee, who is in effect reduced to a frustrated system operator. The more knowledgeable the employee, the worse the experience of a rigid tool which lacks freedom to solve the tasks really well.

Hence, a tool for knowledge workers must provide flexibility to act with justified confidence that the system has reliable mechanisms to fulfil compliance requirements. Confidence that, whenever challenged, the employee will be able to answer and defend the decisions made.

This paper shows how a series of ACM-systems for the Norwegian Public sector have come a long way in reconciling these aspects. These systems have been in use for several years, the first one in production as early as 1995. The systems all build on the same core mechanisms, evolved to fit a diversity of domain needs. But first, we need to indicate where and how in the work cycle compliance support can be addressed.

3. A CLOSER LOOK AT THE COMPLIANCE ASPECT

We argue that compliance support should be applied selectively to fit a wide range of tasks. It is useful to make some distinctions between different strategies to obtain this, used in the systems described later in this paper.

Although we are ultimately concerned with *operational* compliance support during actual work performance, essential aspects must be covered long before any work is started. This concerns interpretation of legislation, establishing procedural requirements and implementing executable business logic. This predesigned support, shown as (1) in the diagram in Figure 1 below, is the basic mechanism of a "classic" BPM solution, and also remains a significant part of an ACM solution, for those aspects of work that are truly predictable.

Being able to show proof of compliance after the actual work performance (3), is often important. Systems can be configured to leave traces of automated compliance proof (3a) because the IT solution can log what tasks and steps have actually been performed and verify changes to the domain. Thus, automated compliance proof may be subdivided into procedural proof and domain requirements proof.

Offset from the work context, compliance professionals deal with compliance as its own discipline (4), which may address all or none of the former. This may e.g. include analysis of the extent to which an application can generally be expected to support compliant practices.

Our main aim in the following is to show how compliance can be satisfied during execution of work, using partly predesigned, flexible support mechanisms. Real time complex work will benefit from a well-considered mix of rigid and flexible support. This includes guardrails against violation (2a) as well as assistance (2b) in presenting, interpreting and operationalizing laws and regulations but leaving the decision to the knowledge worker.

Compliance support

(1) Before work: Predesigned, rigid support

(2) During work: Partly predesigned, flexible support

(3) After work: Documentation of proof

(4) As a decoupled service

(2a) Guardrails   (2b) Supportive

(3a) Automatic audit trail   (3b) Manual trace

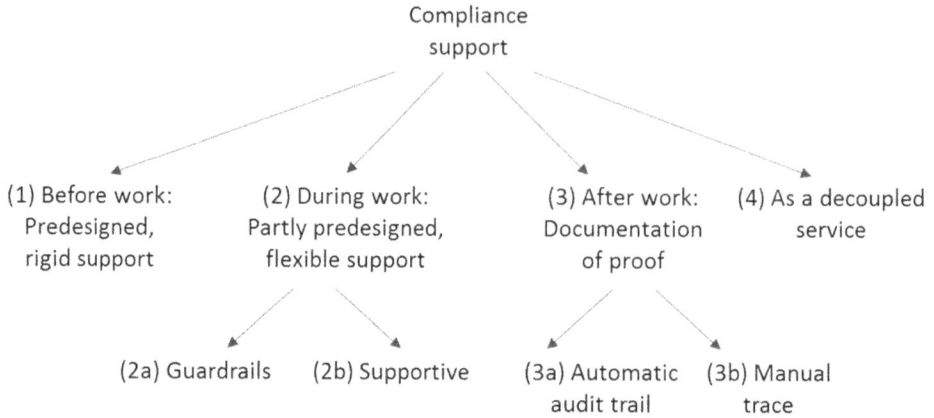

Figure 1: Variants of compliance support

The need for compliance is not the only motivation for restricting or guiding the employee in performing his tasks. As long as there is sufficient flexibility, and the guidance and restrictions are adjusted to how the work is performed, this may boost efficiency, reduce the need for training, and improve the employee's work situation.

In the public sector, we often see a pattern where there is rigid support regarding case handling procedures (within a particular domain, like the juridical procedural law) combined with flexible compliance support regarding subject matter handling (like the particular juridical decisions according to the Criminal Code).

4. MEANS TO COMBINING COMPLIANCE WITH FLEXIBILITY

The sections below describe specific means for how an ACM solution can be made to reconcile the needs for flexibility and compliance. Each section is related to an operative solution in Norwegian public administration, to show how each feature addresses the needs of practical knowledge work. It should be noted that all the examples contain many of the described features, in different combinations.

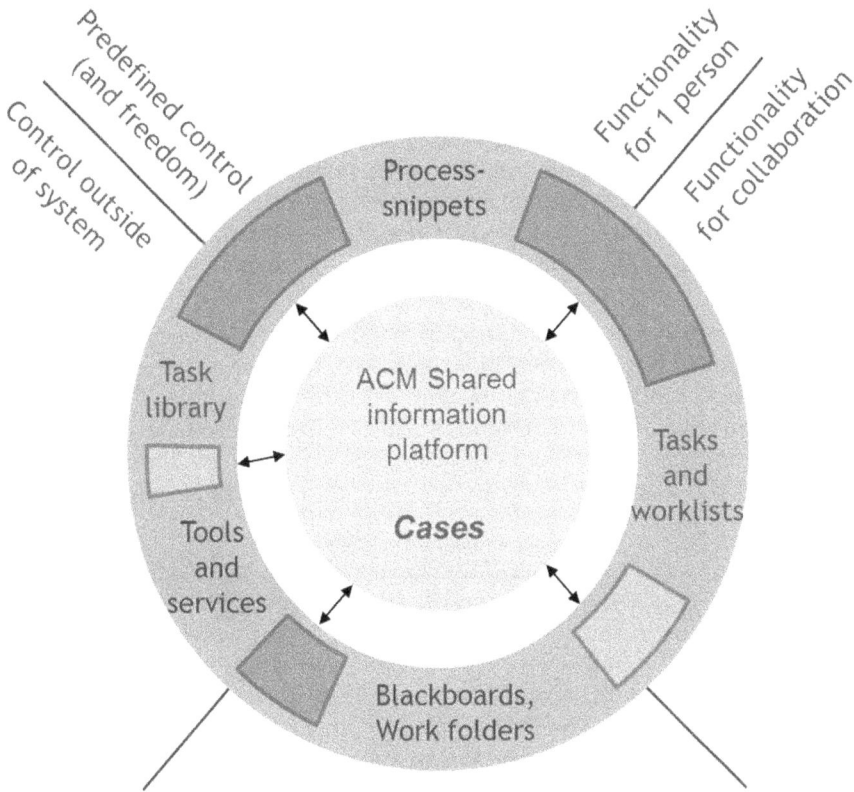

Figure 2: Shared information platform

Several of the example solutions are documented elsewhere. MATS is described in (Sem 2012a) and (Sem 2012b). LOVISA is described in (Pettersen 2013), and UTSYS is described in (Sem 2014a) and (Sem 2014b).

The concepts described below all depend on a system architecture that places the information at the center. In this way, heterogeneous services can operate as and when required, leaning on the shared information platform as an integrating medium providing coherence over time. With regard to the surrounding services, we distinguish between collaborative and individual support mechanisms, as well as between rigid (predefined) and flexible (not restrained by the system) mechanisms.

Information-centric architecture

Core to an information-centric architecture is a shared, rich domain model for cases with a set of services operating on the data. One advantage in having modelled data is the possibility to use the data in rules and tests, and add and change the data through tools and supported user-driven tasks. Having and working with a case model and its services enables information to flow between different tools independent of business processes.

Example: MATS – The Norwegian Food Safety Authority (NFSA) – 2009-Ongoing

The overall objective of the NFSA is to ensure safe food and animal welfare. The NFSA's area of responsibility comprises plant health, food and fodder production and handling, water supply plants, cosmetics, animal health and welfare for production animals and pets. MATS is their ACM solution. About 1000 of NFSA's knowledge workers (veterinarians, biologists, engineers, other professionals) use MATS actively as a work environment and decision support system for the main bulk of their professional work; to plan, conduct and register audits. The system also has around 40.000 external users; farmers, farmers' representatives, restaurants etc.

MATS provides rigid compliance support regarding the Norwegian Public Administration Act, combined with flexible compliance support regarding national and EU Food safety regulations. The system provides situational flexibility, and is open for knowledge workers' judgment. MATS assists providing juridically correct justification and formulation of decisions, and assures these have a statutory basis. MATS also may assist in ensuring that the right set of regulations is applied in the specific case.

An example of a rich-information model, the control objects of NFSA range from reindeer farms to restaurants. These objects need to be followed-up over time spanning decades, with different scopes of work coming up at unpredictable intervals, often triggering new work during execution. Coherence over time is essential. In our architecture, each such control object is represented as a case, maintained and accessed in a shared MATS information platform. The case concept is the kingpin of the NFSA's ACM solution, accumulating a complete track of each NFSA control object. It is the case data that keep the flows of events together, rather than a particular predefined process. The work is driven by real-world events, each task supported by tool modules fit for the particular purpose.

Tasks and worklists

A task is a definite purpose that needs to be fulfilled, and a worklist is a set of such tasks. A worklist may represent all of the tasks of a responsible person or unit, or it may represent all the tasks pertaining to one common object of interest. In the MATS example, this object can be a farm or a restaurant. In LOVISA, below, this object is a court case. The movement of tasks between responsibles and the flow from one task to the next constitutes a workflow. The task is the relay baton and the worklist for the responsible represents the person holding the baton.

Example: LOVISA - Norwegian Courts Administration (NCA) 2005-Ongoing

LOVISA is the ACM solution for the Norwegian first and second instance courts in their case handling and court management.

All court employees are LOVISA users, including judges, clerks and other staff. LOVISA supports juridical case management and court management. Case handling is a highly collaborative process, and LOVISA facilitates the complex interchange between court staff and external stakeholders.

LOVISA is a hub for "business to business" collaboration in Norway's judicial system with integrations to police authorities, prosecuting authorities, tax authorities, public registries and correctional services.

LOVISA provides rigid compliance support regarding the Norwegian Procedural law across a multitude of case types, combined with flexible support regarding Criminal Code and other legislation. LOVISA ensures that cases are handled correctly for a wide range of case types.

Supporting the complete value chain of the courts, LOVISA focuses on the active participants' decision-related parts of the juridical case handling. For each case, a work folder provides a shared work environment for the case manager (normally the judge) and other participants. These work folders provide access to worklists, case data and documents, giving users active and adaptive task support, ensuring high-quality uniform case handling in accordance with Norwegian procedural law, while leaving the specific legal contents of the case for professional judgment.

Process snippets – adaptive task support

Adaptive task support may be viewed as partially defined process snippets, each capturing a smaller part of the overall process, while leaving to the user relevant choices about what to do in which sequence and how to continue. Where appropriate, the flow from one task to the next may be defined, combining several tasks into a longer process segment.

We do not aim at a total definition of the behavioral possibilities, but at a partial definition imposing restrictions on the employee only where and when it is necessary. At the same time, we try to support their work in the best way possible, offering exactly the functionality they need in the current state of work and with regard to the current state-of-affairs.

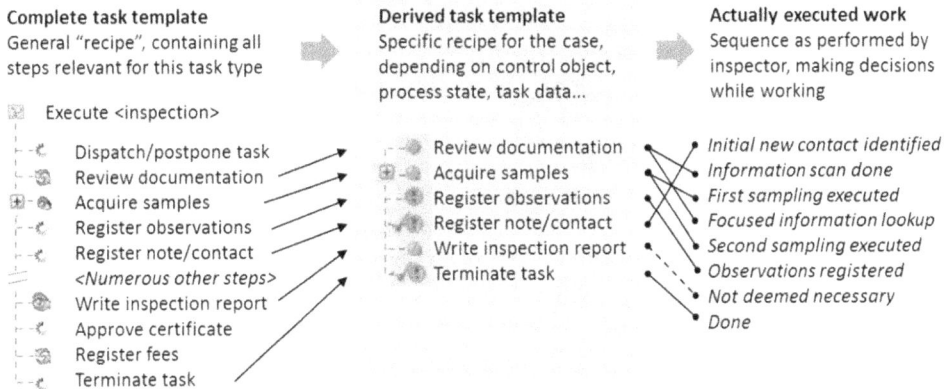

Figure 3: Adaptive task support – context- and user-driven

The declarative task definition gives a general recipe for a task type. Each step may be supplied with an include condition (under which circumstances it is to be displayed) a pre-condition (when it may be performed), making the derived task template presented to the user adapted to the circumstances – the case data, other data in the system, and the earlier performance of the user. In addition, each step may be marked as mandatory, whether it can be executed more than once, or whether it relies on some of the other steps to be performed first.

How to perform a task is declaratively defined in a task template. The balance between controlling the behavior and giving flexibility is obtained by imposing restrictions on these definitions only where necessary, and giving the user full freedom in all other respects. Sometimes, a particular work sequence may actually be necessary, and only then will other possibilities be barred. As a general rule, the user is in charge, and the system presents all relevant possibilities.

Example: BL – The Norwegian Police – 1996-Ongoing

BL is the main case management solution for the Norwegian Police and Prosecution authorities, which supports police knowledge work with the correct application of the Criminal Procedure Act together with flexible operationalization of the Police instruction and the Prosecution instruction. BL assists in the correct use of coercive measures, supporting the organization of cases with respect to defendants and counts, allowing for splitting and merging these cases and maintaining relations across cases, filing petitions and bringing cases to court.

In all judicial and police work, there are sets of tasks that the employees need to perform, in order to produce something, such as documents, or to update data or give an analysis and decide further work on the basis of some state of affairs. The focus is on granular tasks and task support rather than on end-to-end processes. The employees are highly-skilled knowledge workers who need to be in control of the overall workflow. BL offers support for each task, in the form of pre-specified step sets. Each step represents collaboration between the system and the user, with the user in charge.

LOVISA uses a rich variety of case type templates with specific case handling functionality, ranging from simple types with short lifespans to complex types spanning several years. The system has integrated multilingual document handling, including generating/merging documents from case data, using hundreds of document templates maintained by the NCA. LOVISA assists with delegation, deadlines, reminders and escalations—also based on task support. To assist in planning and follow-up, case folders have a generated timeline view contrasting the current state with the desired state, independently of all concurrent partial workflows operating on the case.

Goal-oriented task library

All the task types a user may opt to start are organized in a runtime task library. In order to achieve a particular goal, the knowledge worker can select to create a new task instance. Access to the task types is controlled by permissions linked to actively managed user roles. The knowledge worker may start any task available to him in the runtime task library, whenever he wants.

Example: Helene – Parental debt recovery – 1995-2005

Helene supported case clerks in the forced recovery of parental contributions, ensuring that the regulations of the Enforcement Act, the Creditors Security Act, and the Contributions Collection Act were followed. Helene provided a rich repertory of means for the seizure of assets, forced sale of assets and coercive measures. A major challenge in this domain is taking action within the short time-spans when it is possible to do so, respecting applicable deadlines. Many of Helene's case clerks were local laid-off iron mine workers. They were retrained as clerks, and through Helene, were empowered to perform debt recovery swiftly in accordance with Norwegian legislation, operating from an office in Kirkenes in the far north of Norway.

Goals may also be identified by the system, triggered by events. Such events may be the arrival of a new document, the submission of an application, the execution of a step in another task, or an event pattern. A typical event pattern is an expected reply from an external source not having arrived in time, giving rise to the need for some other action. When the system identifies a need for action, it must be able to instantiate and dispatch new tasks to be solved by the knowledge worker. Tasks that are created automatically may or may not be manually accessible from the runtime task library.

In Helene, the task support is strict with respect to step sequence execution, giving strong guardrails to case clerks inexperienced in the legal particulars of cash collection and seizure of assets. A relatively strict task definition was provided for each legally different coercive measure, providing a task library with a choice for each type. However, the circumstances of each debtor are different, and the case clerk was free to choose the means fit to the situation of the debtor.

Work folders

A task is normally about a particular case. In case management, the data of a case is collected in a *case folder*. Generally relevant data for a case include its history, what is happening to it right now, and what the plans are regarding the case. The case folders in the systems presented above are equipped with a worklist for each case, listing all tasks that concern the particular case, with appropriate task execution tools. We call a case folder with a worklist, task support and task execution log for a *work folder* for the case, which constitutes a collaborative environment for all personnel working on the case.

The work folder gives an overview of all tasks pertaining to the case, across responsibilities, whereas the worklist for a responsible person or unit gives an overview of all tasks that the person or unit is responsible for, across cases.

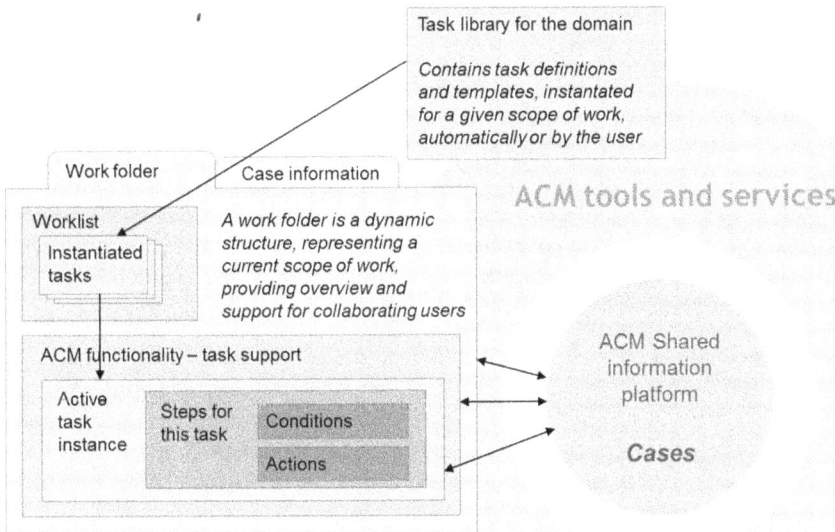

Figure 4: Work folders as a collaborative environment

In this way, the case folder is made actionable, as an environment where all of the case participants get an overview and may choose to contribute to each other's tasks. For the user, the work folder represents a window on a case spanning perhaps 30 years. The work folder contains the current scope of work to be addressed, to which the user may add new tasks, or delete those not considered necessary.

Blackboards

The blackboard metaphor is designed for collaboration and coordination between several knowledge workers or teams mutually adapting to the results of each other's work. Rather than waiting for a relay baton, the participants get inspired by information and ideas posted to the blackboard. At their own initiative, they perform additional activities and use the blackboard to communicate plans, articulate further work and post results. The blackboard provides a current presentation – a snapshot – of the case folder with visualization of case state, goal achievement and central case information.

Example: UTSYS - National Police Immigration Service (NPIS) 2012-Ongoing

An asylum seeker's first encounter with Norwegian authorities is through the NPIS, which collects information about each immigration case prior to application processing by Norwegian authorities, and manages the case until it is eventually resolved. A large percentage of asylum seekers have no passport or valid ID, and many provide inaccurate information, adding to the complexity of identity determination and case investigation tasks.

UTSYS is the ACM solution that helps the NPIS monitor and manage every pending asylum case. Case managers collaborate extensively with regional police authorities, identity analysts, legal experts, and experts on the state of affairs in receiving countries. A rejected asylum application triggers a process that may take any number of directions, all with the ultimate goal of returning the unsuccessful applicant to the country that will rightly accept the return. This is a highly unpredictable process, depending on a wealth of information from national and international authorities and agencies.

UTSYS provides one blackboard per case, subdivided into areas for different lines of work (Sem 2014a), (Sem 2014b). The UTSYS process required to return an illegal alien successfully is goal-seeking. The overall goal is to get the subject transported out of the country. To achieve this goal implies several subgoals, such as establishing the identity of the subject, making sure the receiving country will accept the subject, producing necessary travel documents etc.

In the real world, goal structures are often non-monotonic, in the sense that an achieved subgoal may get undone by new events. To ensure sustained compliance, the system must therefore keep track of the actual conditions as they unfold. Failing a subgoal must cause change of case state, triggering new work to re-establish the subgoal. In UTSYS, receiving countries may change their policies and need for travel documents, it may be impossible to effectuate a planned travel, causing the creation of a new traveling plan etc. Where achievement of goals is non-monotonic, such a snapshot case view is particularly useful for coordination.

The division of the blackboard into one area for each line of work allows for the use of other work support tools as described above. Each line of work may have a task library in its blackboard area; a dedicated repertory of process snippets for structured as well as unstructured work. In this way, the blackboard combines action orientation with information orientation, allowing for a broad range of work support mechanisms. These may range from full process- and workflow support, through process snippets and emergent workflow, to emergent coordination through pattern recognition and distributed initiative on the basis of available shared information.

Using the blackboard metaphor for visualization of data in the case folder is useful for contexts where different lines of work have their own goals, with autonomous agents acting at their own initiative. Action is instigated based on the current situation across lines of work rather than as a result of participants receiving tasks. The blackboard thus serves as a coordination mechanism across lines of work, where the coordination is allowed to emerge through mutual adjustment, pattern recognition and response.

Model-based representation of regulations

In some of our solutions we have needed to explicitly represent acts and regulations with their interpretations, to make these available and accessible for the knowledge workers.

Example: Representing operational requirements in MATS

In the MATS example, all sections of the acts and regulations that the NFSA is responsible for are automatically coded into a hierarchical code set. Each section is then interpreted into operational requirements, and each operational requirement is annotated with a reference to its origin in the legislation.

This ensures that every observation recorded by an inspector is also connected to an operational requirement, and by means of that, to a specific section in an act or regulation. Every decision made will be based on a set of observations, and the decision is encoded with the relevant section in that act or regulation.

Expert groups can build one or more requirement set templates for each type of control object, representing the specific items that the control worker should typically check in an inspection or audit of a given type. In such a requirement set template, items included may be marked out as mandatory.

The control activity worker first decides the scope of an inspection or audit by deciding the control object(s), and next selects the regulations that he wants to base the inspection or audit on, that is, the legal basis for the control activity. The system presents him only with the regulations that are relevant for the control object type(s) in the scope.

He then proceeds to select a requirement set template for each type of control object in the scope. The system filters the requirements set template, and presents the control activity worker with all the operational requirements from the selected template that are also in the legal basis. Mandatory requirements in a template cannot be deselected, but for the rest of the requirements, he can choose as many as he considers relevant. He may also add more requirements from the requirements base.

The wide variation of control object types in MATS has been handled through alternative ways of modeling. We have combined traditional information models and object types with declarative modeling of reference data in xml (codes, combined code sets by means of code relations). We have also used declarative models for extending base types with additional attributes and view definitions.

Example: Balancing flexibility and control in MATS

NFSA management and centers of expertise are responsible for uniform work practices, and need flexibility to continually improve and roll out new practices. The inspector in the field needs a somewhat different kind of flexibility, to meet the unique requirements and events of each case. To accomplish this, the generic mechanisms of the underlying ACM platform play in close harmony with specific custom-built mechanisms in the MATS application.

The NFSA felt that this would sometimes be too flexible. Some situations would require more standardized and uniform inspections or audits. There was also a need for an easier way for the control worker to set up the control activity plans. MATS therefore contains compound templates, containing preselected legal basis, preselected requirements set templates and also preselected mandatory tests and analyses. These control activity templates may be marked as strict or flexible. In both cases, the control activity worker may add more requirements and tests. In the flexible ones, he may also remove requirements and tests that he finds unnecessary.

The strict control activity templates are particularly useful in the surveillance functions of the NFSA, where NFSA inspectors run standardized control activities and tests in order to monitor food safety or plant and animal health. The flexible control activity templates are useful as a quicker starting point for the control workers as well as to more uniform control activities throughout the country.

Declaratively modelled tasks, rules, code sets and code relations are all represented in xml, as important business logic. These xml definitions may be hot-deployed into the system. This makes it possible to define a new type of control object, connect it to the legal basis relevant for it, to the correct tasks for registering or apply for approval in the self-service web client, and so forth, in xml. The definitions may then be hot-deployed into MATS, becoming operational on-the-fly.

5. CONCLUSION

The application examples shown in this paper demonstrate how an ACM tool can acquire the qualities of an operational quality system, constituting a flexible work environment for the knowledge worker. The means and mechanisms described provide rich and varied ways to promote uniform practice in professional work, without sacrificing the headroom required to meet the uniqueness of each case.

The difficult part is discovering the ideal harmony between compliance and flexibility in each new application context. Determining the appropriateness of exactly where and how to apply the different mechanisms requires close and committed involvement of both management and professionals during all phases of system development. This calls for the participation of established domain experts as well as visionary managers and dedicated functional architects.

We do believe that the information-centric architecture with active task support is perhaps the one a priori principle needed, in order eventually to arrive at a good harmony between compliance and flexibility. Having information rather than process at the center means that tools and services can be modular and independent, leaving selection and implementation of more specific means until project insights and needs have matured sufficiently.

6. REFERENCES

(Sem 2012a) Helle Frisak Sem, Steinar Carlsen and Gunnar Coll. Norwegian Food Safety Authority, Nominated by Computas AS, Norway. In Fischer, L. (ed): How Knowledge Workers Get Things Done - Real-world Adaptive Case Management, Future Strategies Inc, Florida, 2012

(Sem 2012b) Helle Frisak Sem, Steinar Carlsen and Gunnar Coll. On Two Approaches to ACM. ACM 2012 1st International Workshop on Adaptive Case Management and other non-workflow approaches to BPM, Tallinn, Estonia, 2012

(Sem 2013a) Helle Frisak Sem, Steinar Carlsen, Gunnar Coll and Thomas Bech Pettersen. ACM for railway freight operations, in Intelligent BPMS, BPM and Workflow Handbook series, Future Strategies Inc, Florida (2013)

(Sem 2013b) Helle Frisak Sem, Steinar Carlsen, Gunnar Coll, Håvard Holje, Eli Landro, Heidi Mork and Thomas Bech Pettersen. GTS - Cargonet AS Norway, http://adaptivecasemanagement.org/awards_2013_winners.html. Empowering Knowledge Workers, page 115, Future Strategies Inc, Florida, 2013

(Pettersen 2013) Thomas Bech Pettersen, Helle Frisak Sem, Steinar Carlsen, Gunnar Coll, Margit Matras and Tove Moen. LOVISA - Norwegian Courts Administration (NCA), http://adaptivecasemanagement.org/awards_2013_winners.html. Empowering Knowledge Workers, page 163, Future Strategies Inc, Florida, 2013

(Sem 2013c) Helle Frisak Sem, Thomas Bech Pettersen, Steinar Carlsen and Gunnar Coll. Patterns boosting Adaptivity in ACM. 2nd International Workshop on Adaptive Case Management and other non-workflow approaches to BPM, OTM 2013, Graz, Austria.

(Sem 2014a) Helle Frisak Sem, Steinar Carlsen, Gunnar Coll, Geir Borgi, Steinar A. Kindingstad. UTSYS The National Police Immigration Service, Norway, http://adaptivecasemanagement.org/awards/2014/index.htm

(Sem 2014b) Helle Frisak Sem, Steinar Carlsen and Gunnar Coll. How can the blackboard metaphor enrich collaborative ACM systems? 3rd International Workshop on Adaptive Case Management and other non-workflow approaches to BPM, EDOC 2014, Ulm, Germany.

Justice is Served through Production Case Management

John T. Matthias, National Center for State Courts, United States

1. INTRODUCTION

Most efforts to develop requirements for court case management systems are inadequate to capture the intricacies of production case management. But a methodology relating capabilities (the "what" and "why") and processes (the "how") successfully describes what court case workers want.

Practitioners may debate the definitions and relationship of capabilities and processes, but this approach to development of case management requirements is purely a practical one, for use in identifying best commercial off-the-shelf candidates and for implementing in highly-configurable systems such as BPM suites.

Business needs drive the requirements for a system, so interactively identifying with case managers a hierarchy of capabilities, usually decomposed three levels, generates a large tree structure that describes what case managers do. Developing each detailed capability leads to identifying demonstration scenarios, business rules, reports/ displays, application capabilities, data exchanges, data needs, and technology infrastructure which support each capability. Processes identified at this detailed level contain reusable tasks, overlapping the content of detailed capabilities. With system functions specified with this amount of detail, case workers are able to exercise capabilities in any order as needed – just what they want.

In the court world many organizational aspects of case management are generally agreed-upon, including roles and responsibilities of case managers, the goal of disposing cases as quickly (and fairly) as possible, and the force of statutes and court rules specifying many business rules. There is still much variation in practice and leeway in specifying inputs and outputs, flow within work units, dependencies among units, timing of work, artifacts of the work, awareness of progress toward business goals and customer outcomes, and measurement of performance.[1] These are among the elements that need to be specified as case management system requirements.

One of the conundrums of requirement development is, "Should I gather requirements of the as-is work situation, or the to-be environment I want to create?" Work patterns have formed around the kinds and amounts of legacy technology available, and work will likely need to change substantially with new technology. One approach is to figure out how processes must change to work optimally with a new system, and specify a requirement to hit the target that you visualize. When you procure a system, the task is to determine the extent to which commercial off-the-shelf candidates meet specified requirements. The wild card in this game of cards

---

[1] Roger Burlton, "The Burlton Hexagon Segment Definitions," www.enjourney.com.br/cie/images/stories/site/Extra/hexagondescription.pdf

is guessing the limits of configuration or customization that any system can successfully incorporate – pushing the limits may create problems. A BPM suite may offer more flexibility.

2. WHAT IS WRONG WITH MANY SETS OF REQUIREMENTS?

Accurate and complete requirements are difficult to write. Despite best efforts at clarity by the court case management community and the industry segment that provides systems, there are still inadequacies in specifying requirements:

1. **Ambiguous wording** of many functional requirements, capable of being interpreted in subjective ways;
2. **Multiple parts** of many functional requirements, so providers indicate they "Comply" if any part of the requirement is partially satisfied;
3. Judging from the **workarounds** in implemented systems, court case workers often don't get what they need, partly because requirements are inadequate to specify what they need.

Court case management is a domain of Production Case Management, as defined by Keith Swenson and illustrated in the diagram below.[2]

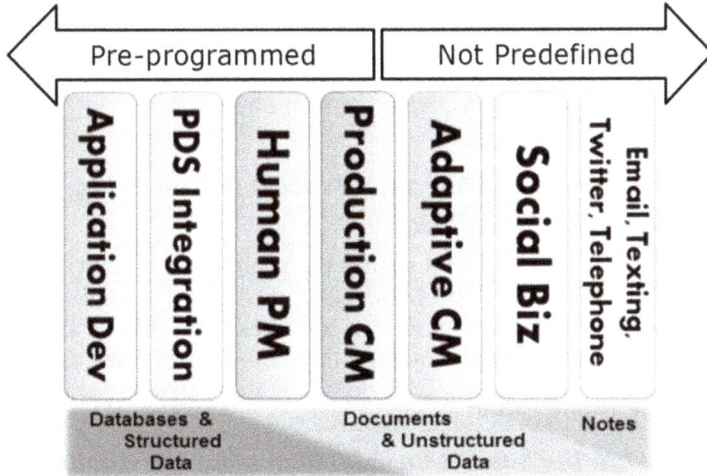

Figure 1: Spectrum of Case Management

Cases in courts follow well-worn paths toward disposition, and it may be asserted that all pathways can be predefined, but there are likely some undefined pathways possible because judges tend to be creative in dispensing justice. Whether court case management is merely complicated (and can be completely pre-programmed) or whether it has emergent complexity (and is susceptible to adaptive case management) is not known. In any event, it is certain that most sets of requirements are inadequate. The proposed methodology is intended to remedy that defect.

3. HOW BEST TO FORMULATE REQUIREMENTS IDENTIFYING WHAT COURT CASE WORKERS WANT?

Either relying entirely on identifying capabilities, or relying entirely on identifying processes, does not provide a complete and accurate set of court case management system requirements. A composite of the two produces better requirements.

---

[2] Keith D. Swenson, "Innovative Organizations Act Like Systems, Not Machines," *Empowering Knowledge Workers* (Future Strategies Inc., 2014), p. 39.

In Case Management, How do you Fit Together Opposite Orientations?

The history of science and philosophy contains many examples of opposite orientations, possibly resulting from the structure of the brain as left and right hemispheres.

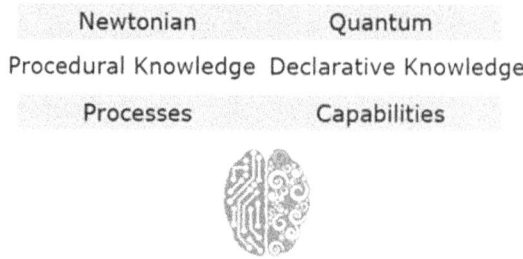

Newtonian	Quantum
Procedural Knowledge	Declarative Knowledge
Processes	Capabilities

Figure 2: Opposite but Complementary Orientations

This approach positions processes as different from but complementary with capabilities. The practical effect of this is illustrated by asking the following question in court case management:

Is **Issuing a Warrant** a

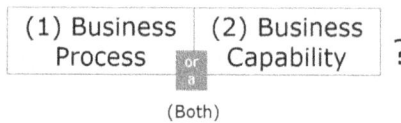

(1) Business Process	or a	(2) Business Capability	?

(Both)

Figure 3: Is Issuing a Warrant a Process or Capability, or Both?

What are Business Capabilities?

Business capabilities describe what courts do in all areas of activity, including the goals and performance objectives of courts, and their organizational and cultural dynamics. One capability contains sub-capabilities which describe in more detail as each is decomposed, to describe what a business (court) does, but without identifying how this is accomplished or who does it. A full analysis contains a hierarchy of capabilities with layers of detail or abstraction.

Start with what the business needs, then what the application does

Inspired by the Court Technology Framework, an enterprise architecture, system requirements are related to four layers of the framework.

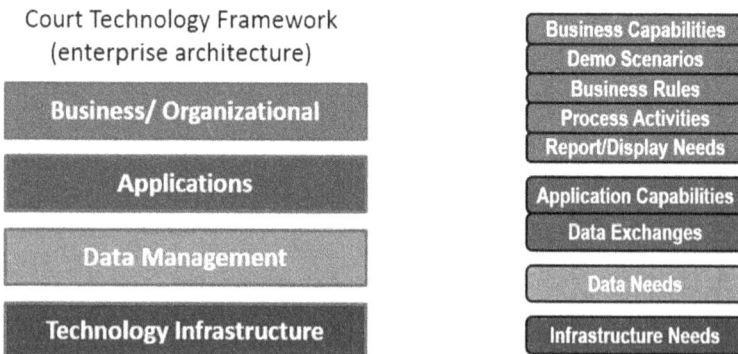

Court Technology Framework (enterprise architecture)

Business/ Organizational

Applications

Data Management

Technology Infrastructure

Business Capabilities
Demo Scenarios
Business Rules
Process Activities
Report/Display Needs

Application Capabilities
Data Exchanges

Data Needs

Infrastructure Needs

Figure 4: Requirement Types Inspired by Court Technology Framework

A software requirement specification (SRS) is a collection of functional and non-functional requirements for a software product. The following SRS template includes all of the kinds of requirements needed in the proposed methodology.

Business/ Organizational	
Business Capabilities	Business Capabilities are high-level business functions. Requirements supporting detailed business capabilities describe the application, data management and technology needed to perform the business capabilities.
Demonstration Scenarios	A demonstration scenario is a sequence of events that a judge, clerk, or judicial staff will experience when performing a high-level business process. Participant scenarios notify software vendors what activities their CMS should be able to support, and will serve as a script for vendor demos and for product acceptance testing.
Business Rules	A business rule is a criterion used to guide day-to-day business activity or calculation, and it specifies decision criteria for carrying out a business process. A jurisdiction's policies are embodied in local or state court rules or statutes, which are its business rules.
Process Activities	Process Activities are the steps or activities of a detailed business capability. For some detailed business capabilities, the sequence of Application Capabilities describes the process activities.
Reports/ Displays	These requirements are called "Reports/Displays" because they can be printed on paper or displayed on a screen, at the option of the user. Almost all reports are specified for a given date range, and need to be exportable to Excel and other formats.
Applications	
Application Capabilities	Application capabilities are functions that an application must perform during a business process – how a business capability is accomplished. Vendors will be required to state whether their case management solution has an application capability built into it through configuration, or whether it must be customized.
Data Exchanges	Data exchanges mean data and document content imported to and exported from the CMS.
Data Management	
Data Needs	Data elements required by other requirements are identified as data management needs, such as indicator flags, drop-down lists of values, and other kinds of data used by business rules and for reports/ displays.
Technology Infrastructure	
Technology Infrastructure Needs	Infrastructure needs include requirements related to hardware, systems software, network capabilities and facilities.
Nonfunctional Requirements	A nonfunctional requirement describes a property or characteristic that a system must exhibit or constraint that it must respect.

Figure 5: Software Requirement Specification Template

4. CAPABILITY EXAMPLE

Identifying capabilities requires a fresh approach to thinking about what the goals ("whys") of the business are, and what the business needs to be able to do to achieve the "whats." The list of capabilities may include more than a dozen items. A free-thinking and collegial group of high- and mid-level practitioners able to brainstorm their business' capabilities can capture the results in a mind-mapping tool like xMind.[3] The capabilities for courts were identified in this manner.

---

[3] xMind.net

1.	Enable E-filing	10.	Obtain Contract Services
2.	Initiate Cases	11.	Manage Records of Charges and Criminal Judgments
3.	Maintain Data on Parties and Participants	12.	Manage Civil Judgments
4.	Maintain Case History	13.	Control Access to Court Records
5.	Schedule Events and Resources	14.	Manage Court Records
6.	Manage Warrants	15.	Measure Performance
7.	Conduct Hearings	16.	Adapt to Changing Business Environment
8.	Manage Finances (Fines, Costs, Fees)		
9.	Manage Assets in Trust	17.	Manage Jurors

Figure 6: Capabilities of Courts

After the main capabilities are identified, further analysis identifies more detailed capabilities. In the example below, drilling down on the "5. Schedule Events and Resources" capability reveals four more-detailed capabilities (including 5.2 "Search/ Assign Case Events to Calendars," and further drilling-down reveals still more, including 5.2.5 "Comply with Legal Deadlines."

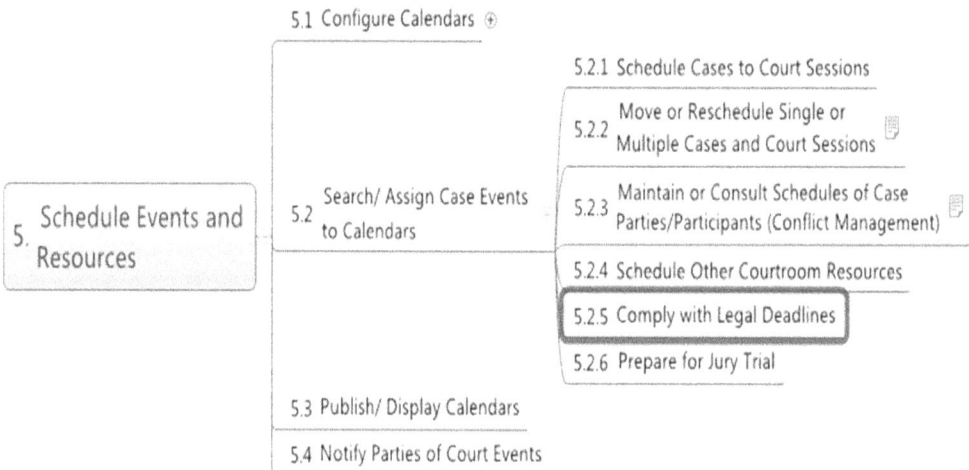

Figure 7: Capability Hierarchy of "5. Schedule Events and Resources"

Software requirements supporting these capabilities include the following:

Capability Description	Courts comply with deadlines and case disposition time standards imposed by law or court rule. Also see **5.2.1 Schedule Cases to Court Sessions** related to Speedy Trial.
Business Rules	**BR 5.2.5-1 Speedy Trial Clock** (Detail of statute, and additional Business Rules)
Report/ Display Needs	**RD 5.2.5-1 Speedy Trial Data Display** For a case, listing of cases by type which are near or have exceeded time standards for such cases. (Additional Report/ Display Needs)

Application Capabilities	**AC 5.2.5-1 Start Speedy Trial Clock**
	Automatically populate the start date of the speedy trial clock when a plea is entered, or at arraignment, with the number of days on the speedy trial clock and on what date the speedy trial clock will be exhausted (End Date).
	(Additional Application Capabilities)
Data Needs	**DN 5.2.5-2 Clock Events History**
	This history of a case is updated automatically by event codes affecting the Speedy Trial Clock (see **BR 5.2.5-1 Speedy Trial Clock**), or manually when a judge orders the case clock to be stopped, started or restarted, showing Start Date, Reason, Stop Date, Reason, Days Used, Days Stop.
	(Additional Data Needs)

Figure 8: SRS for Capability 5.2.5 "Comply with Legal Deadlines"

During procurement, vendors and software developers are asked if their product or software complies with these specific requirements.

5. BUSINESS PROCESS HIERARCHY

What is the Best Method of Process Diagramming?

Identifying processes appears deceptively easy because everyone knows that a process is a sequence of activities performed for a particular purpose, and flowcharting software makes it easy to diagram. This much is routine but it is easy to lose one's way between the forest and the trees; the difficulty is finding the right level of granularity to represent levels of abstraction of processes within processes.

Process diagramming is harder than it looks and many kinds of mistakes are possible. One mistake is packing too much into a process: the author's Traffic Initiation process below, for instance, actually contains six sub-processes connected by decision shapes; the human decision-making element needs to be represented differently.

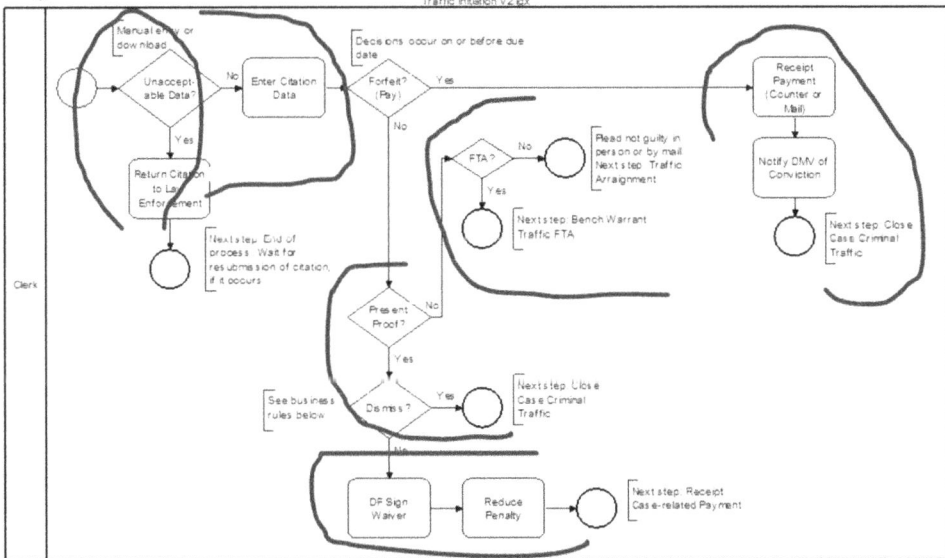

Figure 9: Overloaded Process Diagram

Experience shows that process diagrams may be "true but useless" because each piece is correct but, as a whole, the diagram does not provide insights helpful for specifying requirements to automate the process.

Given the pitfalls of process diagramming, an abstraction-based, levels-oriented approach was needed.

Abstraction is a hierarchical grouping principle, where a process with a higher level of abstraction encompasses multiple process steps at the next level down. A more abstract process level has fewer details available so that one can focus on the process steps included in it. Each process level has more detailed processes within it than the level above it. This approach is similar to Paul Harmon's decomposition of a hierarchy of processes.[4]

Court case management has four distinct levels in its business process hierarchy:

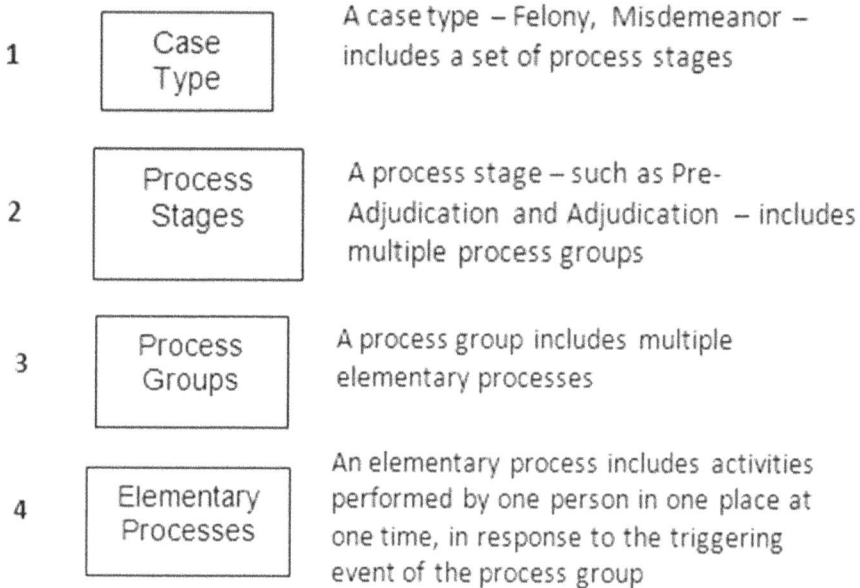

1	Case Type	A case type – Felony, Misdemeanor – includes a set of process stages
2	Process Stages	A process stage – such as Pre-Adjudication and Adjudication – includes multiple process groups
3	Process Groups	A process group includes multiple elementary processes
4	Elementary Processes	An elementary process includes activities performed by one person in one place at one time, in response to the triggering event of the process group

Figure 10: Case Management Business Process Hierarchy

Trial court ①Case Types include Criminal, Civil, Domestic Relations, Juvenile, and Traffic/Parking/Ordinance Violations. There are numerous sub-types, but cases within a case type generally share the same characteristics.

The next level of abstraction below ①Case Type is ②Process Stage. A Criminal Felony/ Misdemeanor case type has five Process Stages: Arrest/ Detention/ Release, Charging, Pre-Adjudication, Disposition, and Post-Disposition. Case types have similar process stages relating to case initiation, disposing of the case and the aftermath of disposition.

A ②Process Stage such as Arrest/ Detention/ Release contains, at the next level down, multiple ③Process Groups, such as Warrantless Arrest. Each process stage has a set of process groups unique to it. There are also process groups that may be invoked during more than one process stage (labeled "Any Stage"). For instance, a bench warrant can be issued or recalled at any time during a case.

---

[4] Paul Harmon, "Working at Different Levels," BPTrends Vol. 11 No. 5, March 12, 2013, www.bptrends.com/bpt/wp-content/publicationfiles/advisor20130312.pdf

2 Process Stage: Arrest/ Detention/ Release of Criminal Case Type

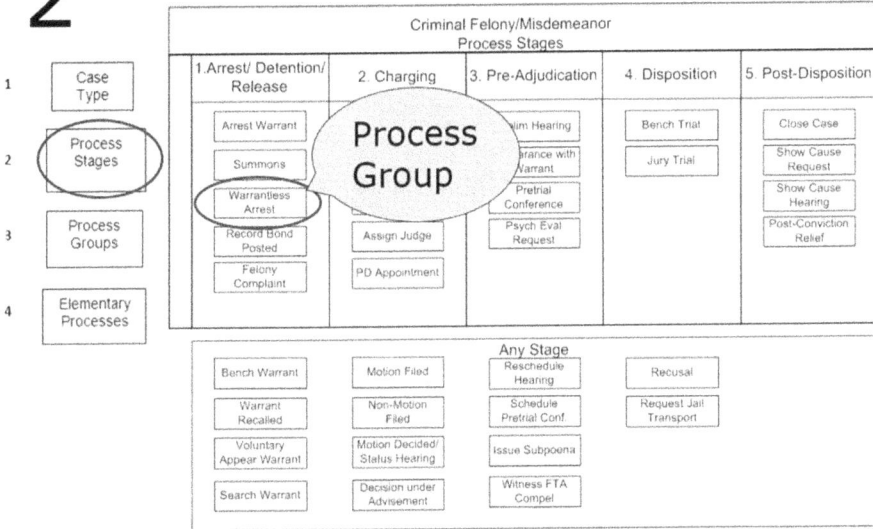

Figure 11: Process Stage Arrest/ Detention/ Release Contains MultipleProcess Groups

A ③Process Group involve handoffs between case workers, using familiar swim lane notation. The ③Process Group Warrantless Arrest in turn contains, at the next level down, a number of ④Elementary Processes, including Issue Order Appointing Public Defender, as shown in Figure 10 below.

3 Process Group: Warrantless Arrest

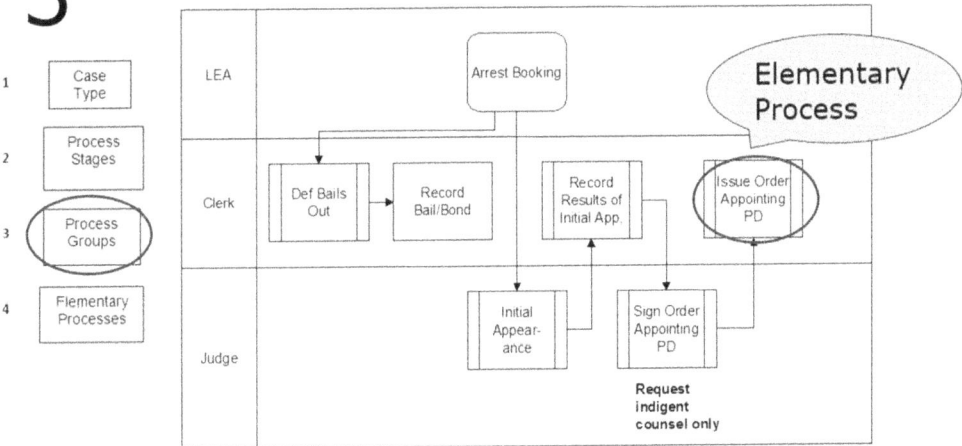

Figure 10: Process Group Warrantless Arrest Contains Multiple Elementary Processes

The ④Elementary Process Issue Order Appointing Public Defender contains event-driven process fragments, which can often be fully automated via workflow and business rules, as shown in Figure 11 below.

4 Elementary Process: Issue Order Appointing Public Defender

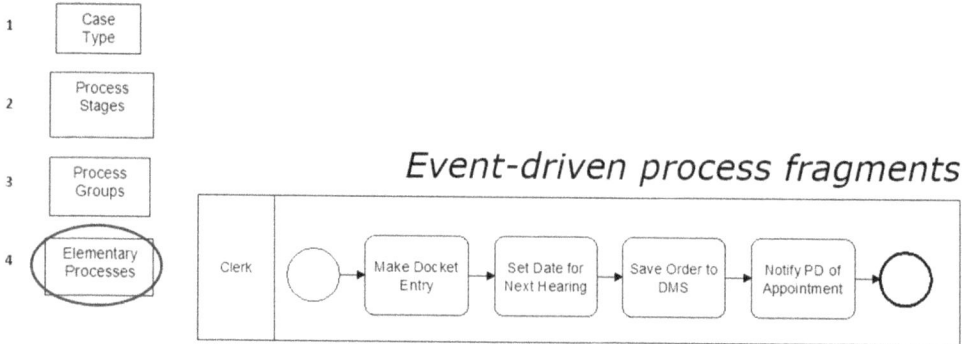

Figure 11: Elementary Processes Contain Automatable Process Fragments

An ④Elementary Process consists of activities performed by one person in one place at one time, in response to the triggering event of the ③Process Group. The Elementary Process level also corresponds most closely with a detailed capability, and the elements of the software requirement specification template described above (demonstration scenarios, business rules, reports/ displays, application capabilities, data exchanges, data needs and technology infrastructure needs) can be developed for it.

6. RELATIONSHIP OF CAPABILITIES AND PROCESSES

Going back to the rhetorical question: Is issuing a warrant a business process or a capability, or both? The answer is "both."

There is a many-to-many relationship between capabilities and processes. "Issuing a Warrant" as a capability is fulfilled through multiple processes, such as generating, signing and issuing a warrant, as illustrated above in Figure 12 below. It is also true that "Issuing a Warrant" as a business process is used in a number of capabilities, including Investigation of Probable Cause (PC), Grand Jury, Failure to Appear, and Failure to Comply.

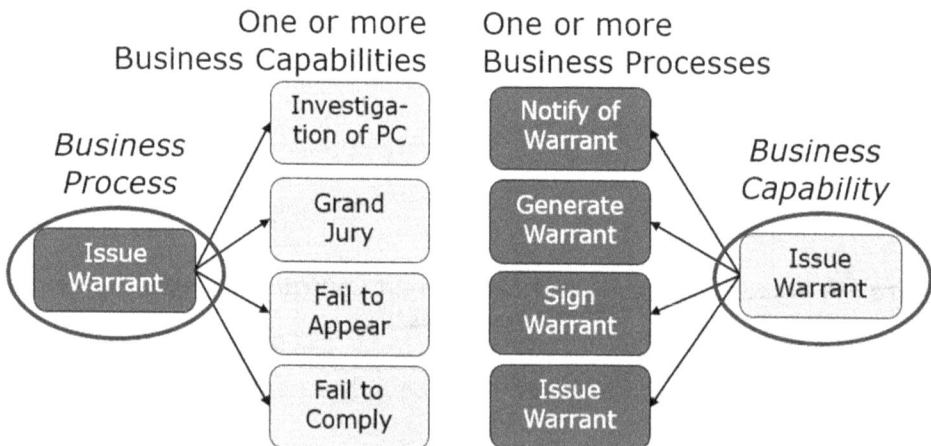

Figure 12: Many-to-Many Relationships between Capabilities and Processes

Capabilities and processes complement each other, and are incomplete without the other. They address similar things but from a different approach; identifying capabilities enables developing software requirement specifications, and identifying processes enables developing workflows for implementation, including collaborative hand-offs between case workers.

7. Summary: Integrate Knowledge and Process

This approach to developing court case management requirements starts with business needs to drive development of requirements for a system.

1. Interactively identify **capabilities** with case managers

   - Decompose several levels of capabilities (using xMind mind mapping software), to generate a tree structure that describes what case managers do.
   - Identify and develop demonstration scenarios, business rules, report/ display needs, application capabilities, data exchanges, data needs and technology infrastructure needs.

2. Develop the **process hierarchy** for the target domain

   - Identify successive levels of process from the general to the detailed. Identify ①Case Types, ②Case Stages, ③Process Groups and ④Elementary Processes.
   - Identify the internal and external events that determine where the case goes next
   - Look for reusable elements that are used in different sequences of related processes in Level ③ and Level ④.

Process fragments (③Process Groups and ④Elementary Processes) may emerge when describing a detailed capability and when identifying processes when moving down the process hierarchy. Some processes should be specified as a capability, and others are more useful during implementation. The relationship of capabilities and processes will become evident.

What Should Case Management Requirements Look Like?

During procurement, case management system requirements are typically formulated in a matrix for vendors or developers to respond to, indicating compliance with the requirements, supported by explanation. The recommended matrix will include reports/ displays, application capabilities, data exchanges, data needs, and technology infrastructure which support each capability. The matrix will be supplemented by demonstration scenarios that inform the system provider of typical interactions with the system that must be demonstrated during procurement and later during system acceptance.

At specification time (design-time) we define the purpose and logic behind tasks and activities. At run-time the system evaluates the logic after every change in the case and, based on the results, helps the user select an appropriate step from the set of tasks/ activities available to the user. This use of capabilities and processes is depicted in Figure 13 below.

Business Processes
Use During Implementation

Business Capabilities
Use During Procurement

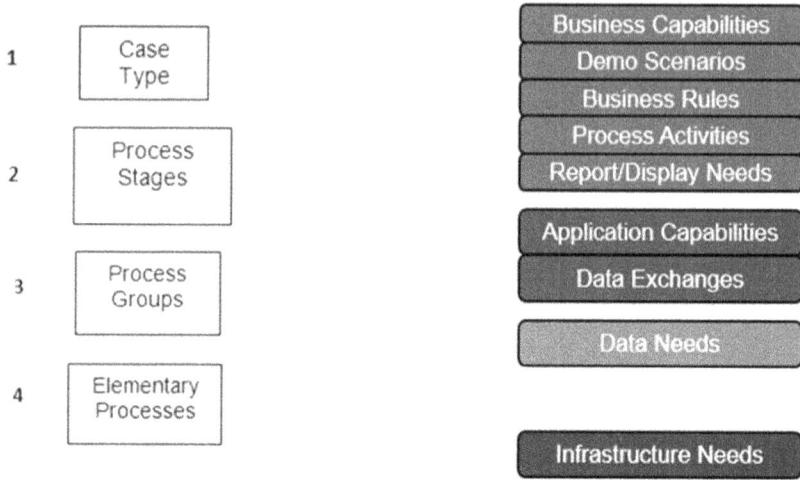

1 — Case Type

2 — Process Stages

3 — Process Groups

4 — Elementary Processes

Business Capabilities
Demo Scenarios
Business Rules
Process Activities
Report/Display Needs

Application Capabilities
Data Exchanges

Data Needs

Infrastructure Needs

Figure 13: Use of Capabilities and Processes

Production Case Management Capabilities to be "Built to Change"

Many case management solutions are unable to keep up with users' increasing demands for efficiency and flexibility, forcing users to use workarounds to accomplish what needs to be done. PCM does not require the run-time agility of ACM but, if well-specified, provides a large but finite number of alternatives from which the user can choose a task/ activity after a court event. A PCM system supporting court case management should have the following capabilities to enable case managers (following orderly governance procedures) to configure tasks and activities to be available when needed:

1. Awareness of timeliness and progress toward case disposition and litigant outcomes
2. Availability through navigation to tasks appropriate to respond to changes in the case in any order as needed
3. Notification of and collaboration with litigants and participants to achieve timely disposition
4. Configurability
   - Add new case type templates as they arise
   - Drag-and-drop configuration, adjustable parameters
   - Identify and codify regular patterns and responses to events
   - Reuse basic capabilities and processes
   - Change access to tasks and documents
   - Change collaboration, who does what
   - Change natural language business rules
   - Add data fields to screens, tables and reports
5. Ability to monitor and then manage the workload with available resources
6. Application integration – in-bound and out-bound data exchanges
7. Co-innovation – enable both buyer and provider to innovate simultaneously and independently

PCM assumes a large measure of routine work that can be identified up front, but court case management requires agility to adapt to changes mandated in particular cases and in the justice environment as the law and rules change.

8. CONCLUSIONS

This requirement-development methodology relates capabilities (the "what" and "why") and processes (the "how"), seeking to describe what court case workers want.

What PCM Case Workers Want, and What the Application Should Do

Drilling down into the capabilities numbered in the previous section creates a "wish list" for case workers.[5]

1. Search for any combination of data appropriate to the context, and use the results in case activities and as ad hoc reports
2. Select from actions available based on case status, to reach the next step or the case or its disposition
3. Navigate easily to all information needed, including the context of linked cases
4. Track case progress to disposition with a progress graphic, using a checklist based on time standards to fuel time-awareness
5. Provide alerts, ticklers, notifications based on status of a case
6. Enable updates to multiple cases and multiple elements of a case at once with the same transaction

Better requirements do not produce better systems, because the limiting factor is the range of configuration or customization that a system or BPM platform will accommodate before it reaches its technical or supportability limits. But a fuller understanding of requirements will enable courts to make better decisions about what changes are available within the system framework, and what the targets of optimization are. There will always be workarounds.

Useful books are available to guide development of software requirements.[6] Experience confirms lessons taught in such textbooks: a requirement analyst needs to interview and observe case workers as they work, and validate what one finds. This much is routine; the difficulty – and where it is easy to lose one's way - is finding the right level of granularity. It is tempting to go too deeply into things, and one may lose the context for a requirement.

The key questions to keep asking are, "What would you like to see/ be able to do? What capabilities and processes are important to you?"

9. REFERENCES

(Harmon 2013) Paul Harmon, "Working at Different Levels," BPTrends Vol. 11 No. 5, (March 12, 2013). www.bptrends.com/bpt/wp-content/publication-files/advisor20130312.pdf.

(Swenson 2014) Keith D. Swenson. "Innovative Organizations Act Like Systems, Not Machines," Empowering Knowledge Workers. Lighthouse Point, Florida: Future Strategies Inc., 2014. www.FutStrat.com

---

[5] See additional PCM requirements in John T. Matthias "Case Management Forecast: Mostly PCM with a Chance of ACM," How Knowledge Workers Get Things Done, (Future Strategies Inc., 2012.

[6] *Software Requirements Third Edition*, Karl Wiegers and Joy Beatty (Microsoft Press, 2013).

Using Process Mining to Improve Adaptive Case Management Processes

Dr. William A. Brantley, University of Maryland United States of America

1. Introduction

Big data and data mining have revolutionized how organizations improve their services and products. Companies such as Amazon.com, Target, and grocery stores use transactional data to serve customers better with specific offerings and even predicting what customers are most likely to buy next. Social networking applications such as Twitter and Facebook collect enormous amounts of data from users tweeting each other and posting Facebook statuses. Social networking data is also mined to create detailed user profiles and track trending news events.

Processes also create data that can be mined and use to create models of processes that show how tasks and information flow through the process. Process mining can also map the social networks of the workers involved in the processes. In this chapter, the author explains how adaptive case management (ACM) can benefit from using process mining methods. Process mining is designed to discover, inspect, and enhance routine, repeatable business processes. Increasing the efficiency of routine processes increases the overall effectiveness of ACM processes. Further, process mining can be used to improve ACM processes by discovering hidden routine processes and helping knowledge workers reflect on and improve their case management methods.

2. What Is Process Mining

Process mining is an emerging management analysis field that uses workflow event information to discover and map processes. Like data mining, process mining is a data-driven approach to process improvement. Process mining can be used to discover a process model, check that an existing process conforms to a process model, or improve an existing process.

According to van der Aalst (2011), process mining arose from the explosion in data produced by information systems. Systems where able to capture more sophisticated data that led to being able to capture data on *events.* That is the key to process mining. Process mining can produce process models using event data captured in event logs that accurately reflect the actual process flow.

The following is an example of an event log:

Case ID	Event ID	Timestamp	Activity	Resource
1	3565	10/13/13 09:53	Register case	George
1	3566	10/13/13 10:01	Transmit case	George
1	3567	10/13/13 10:03	Case opened for investigation	Phil
2	3661	10/13/13 10:01	Register case	Stephanie
2	3662	10/13/13 10:05	Request demographic information for case	Stephanie
2	3663	10/13/13 10:07	Store case in pending information state	Stephanie
3	3331	10/13/13 10:07	Register case	Bill

Event logs will vary, but the essential components are when events occur, who handled the event, and which case was affected by the event. The event log is fed into an application that constructs a representation of the process by mining the events. Machine learning algorithms are used to create a Petri net model[1], Business Process Modeling Notation diagram[2], or similar process modeling method.

There are three ways to relate process models to event logs according to van der Aalst (2011). There is *Play-In* where the event log is used to create a process model. Play-In is how processes are discovered. In contrast, *Play-Out* is where the event log is compared to a pre-existing process model to determine how well processes conform to the process model. *Replay* uses both the event log and the process model to explain the model, diagnose processes, create predictions and suggest process enhancements.

There are eight uses for process models (adapted from van der Aalst 2011).
1. Insight into the processes,
2. Discussion with stakeholders,
3. Documenting processes,
4. Verification or error checking processes,
5. Performance analysis of processes and resources,
6. Animation of processes to allow for simulating various scenarios,
7. Specification for developing a process, or
8. Configuration of a set of processes.

Process mining is very useful, but the modeler must be wary of several challenges to developing process models. First, the modeler should be aware of the limitation of the machine learning algorithms used in creating a process model. Each algorithm makes certain assumptions about the data and how

---

[1] A good introduction to Petri Nets - http://www.techfak.uni-bielefeld.de/~mchen/BioPNML/Intro/pnfaq.html

[2] The Object Management Group's guide to BPMN - http://www.bpmn.org/

the data is represented which could distort the final process model. For example, if K-means clustering[3] is using cluster events from the event log, the initial choice of K can incorrectly classify some of the events.

Another issue is the quality of the event log. Are the events captured in the event log truly representative of the actual events in the process? Is the event log complete or is there missing data? Are there behaviors captured in the event log that are rare and infrequent which will distort the process model? The process model is only as good as the event log data so modelers should ensure they are working with quality event logs.

A final challenge of particular importance to adaptive case management practitioners is that process models are essentially two-dimensional slices of three-dimensional reality (van der Aalst 2011). As van der Aalst writes, "the discovered process modeling is *just a starting point* for analysis (italics in the original)" (p. 155). He further observes that "[o]ne should not seek to discover *the* process model. Process models are just a *view on reality* (italics in the original)" (p. 155). With this perspective in mind, the next section describes how ACM practitioners can use process mining to support ACM processes.

3. USING PROCESS MINING WITH ADAPTIVE CASE MANAGEMENT

At first, it would seem that process mining cannot be used for adaptive case management because process mining depends on repeatable processes while ACM is based on nondeterministic methods. ACM is based on how knowledge workers do their work which is often non-repeatable, unpredictable, emergent, and fits the variable conditions at that moment. (Swenson 2010). Modeling knowledge work would seem to be an impossible task because every event log would be very different from each other. The process model would continually change with each new case, and neither the event logs nor the process models would capture the complex reality of knowledge work.

Ukelson (2010) suggests that modeling routine processes still has a place in ACM. Most of the work in an organization is *expert work* that depends on the judgment and experience of the knowledge worker to apply the appropriate tools and methods to the current case. Even so, the knowledge worker often uses routine processes to accomplish some of his or her work. "Combining ACM systems with BPMSs [business process management systems] will finally enable true end-to-end visibility and control of the real-world business processes – structured, unstructured, and everything in between" (p. 39).

The most immediate effect of using process mining with ACM is to refine the routine processes that knowledge workers use during their ACM work. For example, a knowledge worker may choose from five different routine processes to handle the case. Process mining can refine three processes so that they are more efficient and suggests that routine process four could be eliminated because routine process five accomplishes the same procedures just as effectively. Streamlining routine processes and building routine processes that give more value for less effort can only enhance the overall effectiveness of the knowledge worker's ACM work.

Process mining could also be used to discover hidden routine processes in ACM work. As knowledge workers deal with more and more cases, they may

---

[3] Basic introduction to K-Means Clustering - http://home.deib.polimi.it/matteucc/Clustering/tutorial_html/kmeans.html

develop best practices in handling certain kinds of cases. Over time, these best practices are adopted by other knowledge workers. Best practices can be discovered, routinized, and refined through process mining techniques. Some best practices could be combined into a larger routine processes that can be optimized through process simulations.

Finally, process mining helps bridge the gap between business process management and adaptive case management. Manuel (2012) advocates pairing structured and unstructured processes in one enterprise architecture because of the need to align business processes with business strategy, objectives, and vision. Feedback is essential to increasing the efficiency of structured (routine) and unstructured (ACM) processes and value to the customer. ACM has feedback and alignment built into its method. With process mining, routine processes also benefit from feedback and alignment. In addition, process mining also prevents routine processes from drifting into irrelevance and barriers to the organizational effectiveness.

Even in highly-unpredictable knowledge work, there are some processes and practices that could benefit from process mining techniques. Modeling a unique event could start a dialogue on how to better handle a similar event in the future. Also, process mining can determine which resources may be overused and which may be underutilized. Think of process mining snapshots like these examples as *game films* for knowledge workers. How did he or she respond in the past and what could he or she do to improve their response to cases in the future?

4. SETTING UP ACM SYSTEMS FOR PROCESS MINING

Having discussed the value of pairing process mining with ACM, how does an organization prepare their ACM systems to provide the data necessary for process mining? Even though there are a number of ACM systems, all that is needed is to have the system produce an event log. Event logs have a simple structure as described in Section 2: case id, event id, timestamp, event and resource.

The hardest part is determining what to put in the event field. Choosing the correct event value will require the organization to determine an event taxonomy that is both comprehensive and flexible. A major issue is how granular the event is in terms of tasks. Shepherd (2010) gives an example of a task for a loan officer to calculate a risk score. The loan officer can use his judgment to calculate the score or use an automated calculator to create a score (p. 54). How would this example be reflected in the event log? Are the steps that the loan officer took to calculate the risk score individually recorded in the event log? Or is just the event "calculate risk score" recorded? If the score is created through the automated calculator is that the recorded event?

There has to be consistency to how the knowledge workers' events are described and recorded so that an accurate reflection of reality can be captured in the process model. Even so, the event taxonomy has to be flexible so that new events can be introduced into the event log. Consider the purpose for using process mining on the ACM processes. Is this to discover hidden routine processes? To refine an ACM process? Then, event descriptions must have a high degree of consistency. Otherwise, if the process mining is to start a dialogue or to provide feedback to knowledge workers, being less consistent and more flexible is desirable for the event descriptions.

Another rich source of information is mapping the flow of events between resources. As more organizations use social networking tools with ACM, it would be useful to diagram the social networks as events flow around a process. Social network mapping can help determine which resources are over-utilized and which are underutilized. A modeler can also tag resources with events to determine who is seen by other knowledge workers as the expert on certain types of events. A process miner may consider adding social networking data to the event log for a complete picture of event flow between resources.

A modeler can also add columns to the event log. For example, a column that tracks which templates were used for events. This way, one can develop a model that tracks templates over time. Which templates are the most used, which templates are being used less and less, and which templates seem to be on the rise? Are there templates that are being used for purposes other than what they were designed?

There are no limits to what can be added to the event log, but the ACM practitioner should start with the questions he or she wants to answer about the knowledge work. Each new column requires a data definition and a method for recording that data. Try to automate the process as much as possible so as to eliminate or reduce the recording burden on the knowledge worker.

5. INTRODUCTION TO PROM – PROCESS MINING WORKBENCH

Processmining.org[4] is maintained by van der Aalst (through the Processing Mining Group, Math&CS Department, Eindhoven University of Technology) and is a source for research and software devoted process mining. ProM[5] is an open source application developed to mine event logs and display process models. XESame[6] is a companion application to ProM, which extracts event data from non-event log sources.

Once ProM is installed, the process miner can import in an event log or use the XESame interface to map a non-event log data source into an event log format. After the event log data has been imported, ProM can model the processes and provide reports on the events and resources. For example, processes can be displayed as Petri nets and resources can be displayed as social networks. The ProM tutorial describes in detail the various questions that can be answered and visualized from the event log.[7]

ProM comes with a number of plug-ins that allows the user to try different machine learning algorithms. The ProM features exercise[8] for the user to learn how each algorithm works and displays information. ProM is easy to install, and it may benefit the ACM practitioner to experiment with building process models from the organization's ACM system.

6. CONCLUDING THOUGHTS

Data mining and process mining have greatly helped organizations in understanding their customers; refine their products and services; and improving their processes. Even ACM can benefit from process mining despite consisting

---

[4] http://www.processmining.org/

[5] http://www.processmining.org/prom/start

[6] http://www.processmining.org/xesame/start

[7] http://www.promtools.org/doku.php?id=tutorial:answers#verifying_properties_in_an_event_log

[8] http://www.promtools.org/doku.php?id=exercises:start

of unpredictable and non-repeatable knowledge work processes. First, process mining can make routine processes more effective and efficient thus increasing the overall effectiveness of knowledge workers. Second, process mining can discover hidden routine processes in ACM work. Third, process mining techniques can be used by knowledge workers as training reviews to help knowledge workers better their judgment and ability to innovate work methods. Finally, process mining can help visualize the relationships between resources in an ACM system and how templates and other ACM tools are being utilized.

7. REFERENCES

(Manuel 2012) Alberto Manuel. "Managing Structured and Unstructured Processes under the Same Umbrella." In How Knowledge Workers Get Things Done: Real-World Adaptive Case Management. Lighthouse Point, FL: Future Strategies, Inc., 2012.

(Shepherd 2010) Tom Shepherd. "Moving From Anticipation to Adaptation." In Mastering the Unpredictable: How Adaptive Case Management Will Revolutionize the Way that Knowledge Workers Get Things Done. Tampa, FL: Meghan-Kiffer Press, 2010.

(Swenson 2010) Keith D. Swenson. "The Nature of Knowledge Work". In Mastering the Unpredictable: How Adaptive Case Management Will Revolutionize the Way that Knowledge Workers Get Things Done. Tampa, FL: Meghan-Kiffer Press, 2010.

(Ukelson 2010) Jacob P. Nelson. "What To Do When Modeling Doesn't Work." In Mastering the Unpredictable: How Adaptive Case Management Will Revolutionize the Way that Knowledge Workers Get Things Done. Tampa, FL: Meghan-Kiffer Press, 2010.

(van der Aalst 2011) Wil M.P. van der Aalst. Process Mining: Discovery, Conformance and Enhancement of Business Processes. London: Springer, 2011.

Analyzing Communication Capabilities of CM/ACM Systems

With the help of Language/Action perspective

Ilia Bider, Stockholm University/ IbisSoft, Sweden

1. INTRODUCTION

Case Management (CM) and Adaptive CM (ACM) systems are aimed at supporting knowledge workers to run their knowledge intensive processes (Swenson, 2010). An essential part of such support is providing the process participants (i.e. knowledge workers) with the effective means of communication between them in the frame of each process instance/case. The implementation of means for communication/collaboration can differ from one CM/ACM system to another. Some systems may use the traditional message exchange means, others can exploit more modern means; the ones that are already widely employed in social software. To these means belong forums, bulletin boards, and other implementation of the concept of shared spaces. An example of using shared spaces in ACM systems can be found in the chapter "Means to Support Compliance and Flexibility" of this book.

To improve the communication means in the existing CM/ACM systems or design them for new systems, there is a need to have a framework that helps with conducting analysis of existing means and designing requirements on the new ones. Such framework should take the variety of possibilities that exist and could appear in the future for arranging communication between the instance/case participants. It should not, for example, assume that all communication is conducted through the messages in a natural language, written, or oral.

The paper presents a draft of a framework for analysis of communication capabilities in CM/ACM systems based on so-called Language/Action Perspective (LAP) introduced by Flores and Winograd and their associates in 1980s. This perspective, which is based on the speech act theory (Searle, 1969), has been originally suggested as guidelines for designing communication parts of business information systems (Winograd, 1987). Though this perspective had some success in designing commercial systems, it never became widespread as a basis for systems design beyond the organization that introduced it (i.e., Action Technologies).

This perspective has been also suggested for business modeling (see, for example, (Dietz, 1999)), and evaluation of information systems (see, for example, (Agerfalk, 2004)). After achieving some level of popularity in the academic world, LAP as a research field more or less died due to it being not able to find an area where it could be applied in practice (Lyytinen, 2004). The main reason for such an end, we believe, is trying to follow the patterns of communication found in natural languages for guiding development of software systems.

Though LAP did not show the way of how to design communication systems, we found it quite appropriate for analyzing communication means designed in the ad-hoc manner or based on some other principles, e.g. on shared space architecture. The framework, we have built based on LAP, was dubbed LAP-CA, which stands for LAP-based Communication Analysis. The framework, so far, consists of two steps check of communication capabilities provided by a computer system. The first step is a general one, and it can be used for testing communication capabilities of any system. The second one is specific to communication capabilities related to business processes. This step can be used for analysis of communication capabilities of any business process support (BPS) systems, including CM/ACM systems.

The two steps described in this chapter on their own are not sufficient for full analysis of communication capabilities built into a system, more steps are planned to add in the future. The current work does not describe a fully developed and tested framework; it rather present the evidence that such a framework could be built and be of use for practice.

The description of LAP-CA in this paper is done in parallel with the illustration of its usage on a CM system taken from our practice. The system called *ProBis* was built upon the state oriented view on business processes (Khomyakov & Bider, 2000), and it implements the idea of using shared spaces for communication.

The rest of this chapter follows the following plan. In Section 2, we describe the CM system used for illustrating the ideas behind LAP-CA. In Section 3, we describe the first step of LAP-CA. Section 4 is devoted to presenting and discussing the second step of LAP-CA. Section 5 contains concluding remarks and plans for farther development of LAP-CA.

2. DESCRIPTION OF THE EXAMPLE SYSTEM

The system we use in our initial test of LAP-CA is a CM system with shared spaces and collaborative planning (planning for each other) called *ProBis*. It was developed based on the state-oriented view on business processes (Khomyakov & Bider, 2000) for a Swedish interest organization in 2003-2006, as described in (Andersson et al., 2005; Bider & Striy, 2008). Though the system is under phasing out now, it was used in this organization up to 2013.

The reason we have chosen to investigate this particular system is purely practical. The author has participated in the development and introduction of *ProBis* into organizational practice, and has been using it himself for some period of time. Having intrinsic knowledge of the system, gave the knowledge needed for applying LAP-CA checks without the needs to investigate in details somebody's else system.

ProBis has no explicit data/information flow; all information exchange and communication is realized through shared spaces. A shared space in *ProBis* is presented to the end-user as a window separated in several areas by using the tab dialogues technique, see Fig. 1. Some areas of the window are standard, i.e. independent from the type of the business processes, others are specific for each process type supported by the system. Standard areas comprise such attributes and links as:

1. Name and informal description of a process instance
2. Links to the owner, and, possibly, the process team
   Links to the relevant documents, created inside the organization, and received from the outside.

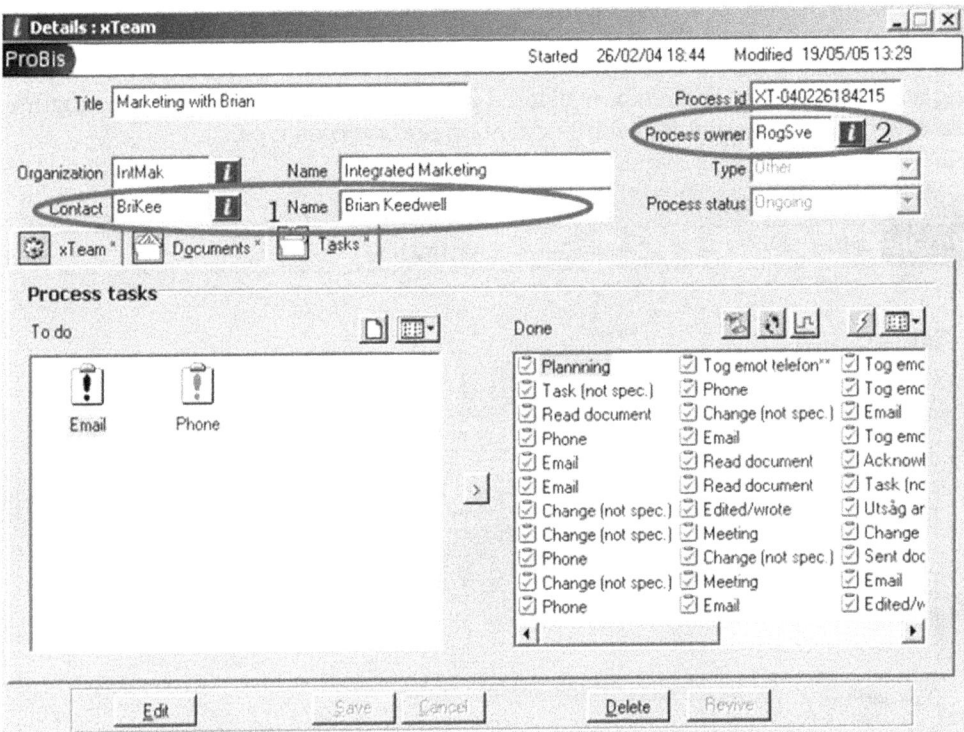

Figure 1. Task area in the ProBis shared space

The standard part of a ProBis shared space includes also the task area (tab) that contains two lists, as in Fig. 1. The *To do* list (to the left on Fig. 1) includes tasks planned for the given process instance; the *Done* list (to the right on Fig.1) includes tasks completed in the frame of it. A planned task defines what and when something should be done in the frame of the process instance, as well as who should do it. In *ProBis*, the process plan serves as a mechanism for issuing "invitations" to attend a particular shared space. All invitations from all process instances are shown in the end-user's personal calendar. From the calendar, the user can go to any shared space to which he was invited in order to inspect, change this space, or execute a task planned for him/her in it.

Process participants work with the shared spaces in *ProBis* in the following manner. A participant visits a shared space because a task has been planned for him/her in this space, or in the ad-hoc manner while browsing through the list of existing shared spaces (i.e., opened process instances/cases). When in the space, he/she can decide to make changes in it by changing the values of various fields, attaching new documents or persons to the shared space, etc. Any change in the shared space results in adding an event to the *Done* list of the tasks tab (see Fig. 1). If the change is due to the execution of some planned task, the event represents a report on its completion, otherwise the event represents some ad-hoc activity.

When changing a shared space, a participant can make changes in its plan (*To do* list) by adding new tasks, or augmenting or deleting the existing ones. When inserting a new task he/she can plan it for him-/herself or to any other person. The latter serves as an invitation for this person to visit this shared space.

As follows from the description above, the only way of communicating via *ProBis* is by assigning a task to the communication partner. This is done by filling a form as on Fig. 2. One chooses the task from the list, assigns it to another user of the system, and adds a textual description and some parameters, for example, by attaching a document that is already registered in the process. The task list is configurable and can be adjusted for each installation and process type.

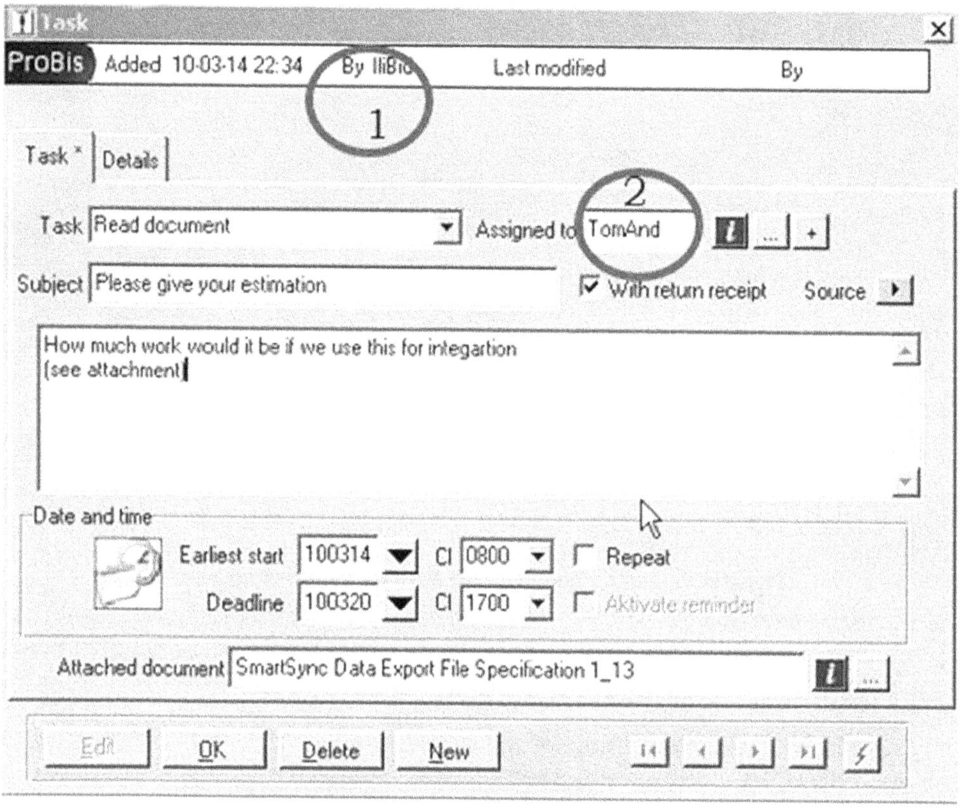

Figure 2. Assigning a task to another user in ProBis

To document the completion of a task assigned to a particular user, the latter moves this task from the *To do* list to the *Done* list via drag and drop, or via pressing the button placed between the lists (see Fig. 1). A report form, shown in Fig. 3, appears. This form is automatically filled with parameters and the task description from the original task assignment. The user just needs to add a textual report on completion of the task, and possibly make changes in other parts of the shared space.

The scheme as described above seems to be a one-way communication. This is not true, however. Consider a situation where the user who has just completed a task wants to notify the user who planned it. Information about who planned the task is shown in the original task form (see Fig. 2.). Notification can be manually issued by planning a special *Attention* task to the "planner" as the last act of completing the assignment. The planner gets this *Attention* task in his/her calendar and can view it in a window similar to Fig. 2.

To provide the user with information about the context of planning, there is a special button Source in the window in Fig. 2. Pressing the button leads to the item of the *Done* list that describes the event in which the planned task appeared in the *To do* list. This item is presented in a window similar to Fig. 3. The typical example of use for this button is when a user who has planned some task gets an *Attention* about its completion. Then, he/she can go directly to the completion report by pressing Source. There is no need to explain what *Attention* refers to when planning it, as the recipient of the *Attention* can go directly to the event that has caused this *Attention* to appear. In this way, many events in the *Done* list can be causally chained to represent various "conversations" in the frame of the process case/instance.

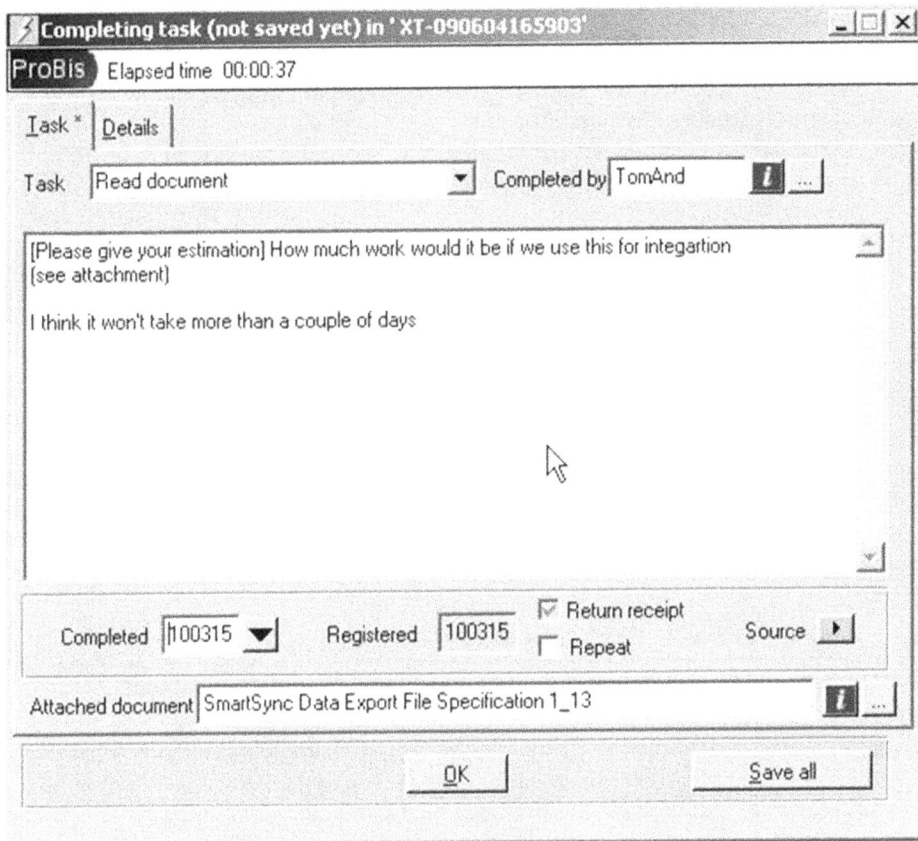

Figure 3. Completing a task in ProBis

The idea to introduce the *Source* button came from the following observation. From the time a person has got an *Attention* to the time he/she actually checks it, many new event items can appear in the *Done* list. The button gives a possibility to directly fetch the one that is relevant for the given Attention.

To simplify the attention scheme, a special check box is introduced in the task window (see Fig. 2) called *With return receipt*. When checked, a special attention-like task called *Receipt* is automatically planned as soon as the task is completed. This task is assigned to the user who originally planned the completed task.

To further facilitate communication, several more advanced features were added to *ProBis*. For example, there is a possibility to plan the same task to many users. Additional users can be added from the list with the "+" button (see Fig. 2), or can be fetched from a predefined group. Each user gets its own task in the calendar and will need to go and complete it independently from other users. Multi-user planning gives a possibility to easily raise attention of several people to some event that has happened in the frame of a particular process case/instance. Other advance features include automated planning (see (Bider & Striy, 2008)), and email notification when the new task has been added to a specific user, or has been changed (replanning).

3. LAP-AC: STEP ONE

The first step of LAP-AC is aimed at rough analysis of communication capabilities of a system. For this end, we use the notion of illocutionary points introduced by Searle (Searle, 1969). An illocutionary point represents an objective that can be achieved with a simple speech act. According to (Searle, 1969), there are five basic illocutionary points:

1. *Assertive*: Commit the speaker to something being the case - to the truth of the expressed proposition.
2. *Directive*: Attempt to get the hearer to do something. These include both questions (which can direct the hearer to make an assertive speech act in response) and commands.
3. *Commissive*: Commit the speaker to some future course of action.
4. *Declaration*: Bring about the correspondence between the propositional content of the speech act and reality (e.g., pronouncing a couple married).
5. *Expressive*: Express a psychological state about a state of affairs (e.g., apologizing and praising).

The first step of our framework is a check whether the system has means for expressing each type of the basic communication acts defined above. This is done by filling a table in which the first column lists basic illocutionary points, the second column describes in which way illocutionary points can be expressed in the given system, and the third column asses how well this ways are functioning or are supposed to function in the system. Table 1 illustrates application of the basic test to *ProBis*.

Table 1. First step of LAP-CA applied to ProBis

Illocutionary point	Way of expression in the system	Assessment
Assertive	Two ways: 1. By changing some attributes and links in the shared space. For, example, by changing the contact person in Fig. 1(see oval marked with number 1), we inform all participants of the process instance about changes that happened at our partner site. 2. By adding a new event to the *Done* list (see Fg. 1) where we can inform about the event through writing some text.	Functioned satisfactory.
Directive	By planning a new task to somebody else, i.e. when the link in the oval 1 in Fig.2 is not equal to the link in the oval 2.	Functioned OK if assignment was done by a manager. The users found it unnatural to plan for a manager and were reluctant to do so

Illocutionary point	Way of expression in the system	Assessment
Commissive	By planning a new task to him/herself, i.e. when the link in the oval 1 in Fig. 2 is equal to the link in the oval 2. As the planned task becomes visible for everybody, the act of planning for him-/herself functions as a promise.	Functioned satisfactory
Declaration	By changing some attributes and links in the shared space. For, example, by assigning the owner for the case in Fig. 1(see oval marked with number 2), we declare this person taking some responsibilities.	Functioned satisfactory
Expressive	Potentially can be done by adding specially designated "events" to the *Done* list, like *Opinion*, *Apology*, etc. The better way of handling expressive acts would be via using techniques implemented in social software, e.g. *Like*, *Dislike*, voting, etc.	Nobody used this type of communication acts.

As follows from Table 1, the communication system that is built-in in *ProBis* covers the five illocution points, but with different level of satisfaction.

4. LAP-AC: STEP TWO

Step 2 is elaboration of step 1 through creating a more detailed classification of the communication acts relevant for managing business process instances/cases. This classification has been built based on our own practical experience of process analysis, building business process support systems, and introducing them into organizational practice. Based on our experience, we identify the following areas of usage of communication in the frame of business process instances/cases:

- Reporting – knowledge transfer about the process instance state (assertive acts in the speech acts classification)
- Reflecting – exchanging opinions on the current state, and suggestions on how to proceed (expressive acts in the speech acts classification)
- Managing roles – assigning roles to participants of business process instances (declarative acts in the speech acts classification)
- Managing tasks – assigning tasks to participants of the business process instances, including self-assignment (a mixture of directive/commissive and declarative acts in the speech acts classification)
- Negotiating – requesting an authorization before assigning a role or a task for somebody or oneself, or asking for a change in already assigned roles and tasks. Negotiating also include agreeing to, or declining the requests. (A mixture of directive and commissive acts in the speech acts classification)

In each of these areas we identify a number of atomic communication acts that are described in more details in the subsections below. For each area we can create a table similar to Table 1 that can be used for analysis of communication capabilities of a particular BPS system.

Reporting

Report is a communication act that informs the recipient(s) about the development in the given business process instance. This act can be committed in various situations. For example, it can be committed as a reaction on the request for information from another process participant. It can also be committed after completing a task in the frame of the given process instance, or in connection to a task assignment act in order to provide a person who is to complete the task with the background information.

A report act, usually, has some dedicated recipients who need the information for their work, and the audience who might just be interested in this information (e.g., CC in case email is used as a media for communication). Reporting is always an assertive act in the speech acts classification.

We differentiate the following atomic reporting acts:
- *Status report* – report on what has being achieved in the process instance so far, how long are we from the goal set for the instance, what is planned for advancing the towards the goal, etc. Such reports could be prepared on the request from the management, or issued periodically to all process participants, or even to the external observers. A status report does not need to cover all details of the given process instance development, for example, it may just contain information about a particular planned task.
- *Task completion* – report on the planned task completed in the frame of the process instance, for example, goods sent to the customer (which ones and how much).
- *Event report* – report on the unplanned event, e.g. a customer calling and complaining on the quality of goods received.
- *History report* – report on the development in the process instance over some period of time, e.g. to update a participant on what has happened in the period of his/her absence.
- *Inquiry*. Besides the act of providing a report, this group includes inquiry – an act of requesting a report. Inquiry is a directive act in the speech acts classification. It presumes a response from the recipient(s) of the inquiry in the form of a report act.

As with illocution points, the reporting capabilities of a BPS system can be analyzed with the help of a table similar to Table 1. In Table 2, such analysis is done for *ProBis*.

Table 2. Analysis of reporting capability of ProBis

Type of report	Way of expression in the system	Assessment
Status report	The idea behind *ProBis* is that the shared space itself constitutes a status report, as it shows the current state of affairs in the given process instance/case. However, if the shared space is complex, there might be a need to highlight certain parts of it in the status report, e.g. to point out areas of risk. This can only be done by adding a special event in the *Done* list of Fig. 1 with textual explanations.	Functioned but not satisfactory. Would be better to have a possibility of highlighting certain areas with a set of colors, like red, yellow and green
Task completion	A report appears automatically when the task is moved from the *To do* list to the *Done* list in Fig. 1. At the moment of moving, the task per-	Functioned satisfactory.

Type of report	Way of expression in the system	Assessment
	former can add any text to comment the completion. Completion of a task that has not been planned in advanced is reported by adding an event directly to the *Done* list. If needed, attention of other processes participants to the report can be raised by planning an *Attention* task for them in the *To do* list. The report will be then automatically linked to this task completion.	
Event report	An event, e.g. a document received is reported by adding an event directly to the *Done* list. The document can be attached to the event, and/or to be inserted to the special tab of the shared space, see Fig. 1. If needed, attention of other processes participants to the event report might be raised by planning an *Attention* task for them in the *To do* list. The event report will be then automatically linked to this task.	Functioned satisfactory.
History report	*ProBis* automatically saves the history of changes made to the shared space. Any change generates an event, which the user can comment or leave without a comment. These events are merged with task completion reports and event reports (see above) to provide full history of the instance/case. The history can be searched by the event type, time, free text, and other parameters. In addition, *ProBis* can show how the shared space looked like before and after any event, producing the effect of a time machine. There is no way, however, to highlight certain events as being of importance for a particular history report. The only way of doing so is via writing a text.	Functioned satisfactory. However, a manual search is required to look for any specific event. It would be advantageous to add a feature that allows manual event grouping for a particular history report.
Inquiry	By planning a task, e.g. *Write a report*, or *Question* with return receipt, see Section 2.	Functioned satisfactory.

Reflecting

Reflecting means expressing personal opinion on the situation, possibly, including suggestions on how to proceed with the given process instance. From the speech act point of view, a reflection represents an expressive act.

ProBis does not have any special provision for reflections, except of adding opinions when producing reports More appropriate means for this type of communication acts would be forums, like/dislike and voting usual for social software.

Managing Roles

Role assignment is a communicative act that gives the recipient some permanent role in the given process instance, or relives him/her from an already assigned role. A role can be assigned to somebody else, or to oneself. To assign a role (or relieve somebody from a role), one have to have a right to do so. Such right can be derived from the person's position in the organization and/or the already acquired role in the given process instance. Alternatively, one needs to negotiate an agreement of such assignment/relieve. An agreement may be needed from the person to whom the role is being (or has been) assigned (if it is not self-assignment) or/and from other process participants who might object or agree to the changes in the distribution of roles.

Role assignment is a declarative act according to the speech acts classification as it directly changes the state of the business process instance. The managing roles capability of a BPS system can be analyzed with the help of a table similar to Table 2. In Table 3, such analysis is done for *ProBis*.

In its first version, *ProBis* did not have any provision for managing roles. Later, a special tab *Participants* was added to the shared space, where people engaged in the given instance could be listed along with their roles. In addition, the instance could be declared as *closed* for all others except its members.

Table 3. Analysis of managing roles capability in ProBis

Managing type	Way of expression in the system	Assessment
Assigning a role	Done by adding a person to the participants list with choosing his/her role from the predefined dropdown menu; the latter can be tuned for any *ProBis* installation. When a person gets a role first time in the given instance, an *Attention* task is planned for him/her with the text "You became a member of a team". This serves as an invitation to visit the instance and see what it is about. Multiple roles are allowed by adding several rows for the same person. Adding new participants generates an event in the *Done* list, where an explanation can be given about the motivation of the assignments.	Functioned satisfactory, except that any user that has access to the instance can add him-/herself or anybody else. There is no limitation on who has rights to manage which roles[1].
Removing the role	Done by removing a row related to a particular participant from the list. A comment can be added explaining why a person has been removed/removed him-/herself from the list of participants.	Functioned satisfactory, but with the same limitation as above.
Changing the role	Done by changing the role attribute for a particular participant. A comment can be added explaining why a person has received a new role.	Functioned satisfactory, but with the same limitation as above.
Negotiating	No special provision, except a person who gets a new role or changed role can reverse the action him/herself. Deleting the role can result the instance becoming inaccessible for this person; in this case the person cannot reverse the deletion. It would be advantageous to have a preliminary assignment which a person can confirm or reject. Asking for permission to become a participant (enrollment) is also a desirable feature.	

---

[1] Note that *ProBis* saves the history of all changes done to the shared space, which means that any manipulation with role assignments can be detected later.

Managing Tasks

Task assignment can be of two sorts, an assignment to somebody else, and self-assignment. Task assignment to somebody else is a communication act of asking the recipient(s) to complete a task in the frame of a business process instance. To assign a task, a communicator needs to have a right to make an assignment. Such rights can be of three origins:

- The communicator has some management position over the recipient, in general or in the frame of a particular process instance, that gives him/her a right to "order" certain tasks to be executed. The task planned should be of the sort that the recipient has rights and obligation to complete according to his contract with the organization
- The communicator holds no management position over the recipient, but the task being assigned falls into the sphere of responsibility of the recipient according to his/her position within the organization, or his/her role in the particular process instance.
- The communicator holds no management position over the recipient, but he/she has previously negotiated an agreement from the recipient, or/and from his/her manager.

Task assignment to somebody else is a mixture of directive and declarative communication acts in the speech acts classification. When it is an assignment of a relatively unimportant task to be completed more or less directly, the act is purely directive. No audience needs to be engaged in such communication act. However, if it is an assignment of an important task to be completed at some time in the future, the act besides being directive has also declarative nature. It changes the reality relevant to the given business process instance – a new element is introduced in the process plan. Such an act, normally have an audience (like a CC if email is used for communication), i.e. the audience is participants who need to know that the task has been planned, for example, for avoiding double assignments.

Task assignment to oneself also requires some rights from the communicator, which can be of three origins:

- The communicator has a right to assign him/herself this type of tasks according to his/her position in the organization or/and his/her role in the given process instance
- The communicator has an obligation to assign himself a task of this kind when a situation warrants it (again, according to his/her position in the organization or/and his/her role in the given process instance)
- The communicator has previously negotiated permission for self-assignment from some other process participant(s), e.g. management.
- Task assignment to oneself is a mixture of commissive and declarative communication acts in the speech acts classification. It is a commissive act as it constitutes a promise to do something, and it is a declarative act because it adds a new item to the process instance plan.

Beside assignments, this group includes task retraction, task change and reassignment. Negotiation may be required before such acts can be performed.

The managing tasks capability of a BPS system can be analyzed with the help of a table similar to Table 3. In Table 4, such analysis is done for *ProBis*.

Table 4. Analysis of managing task assignments capability in ProBis

Managing type	Way of expression in the system	Assessment
Assigning a task	Done by a user planning a task to him-/herself or somebody else. If the user has access to the *Tasks* tab in a particular instance, see Fig. 1, he/she can plan a task for him-/herself or for anybody else. There is no limitation to whom a task can be planned. However, some tasks types are reserved to the user with high access rights.	Functioned satisfactory, except that there is very limited control to what tasks can be planned and to whom[2].
Removing the task assignment	Any user who has access to the *Tasks* tab in a particular instance, see Fig. 1, can delete any task assignment, his/her own, or somebody else's.	Functioned satisfactory, but with the same limitation as above.
Changing the assignment	Any user who has access to the *Tasks* tab in a particular instance, see Fig. 1, can change any task assignment, his/her own, or somebody else's.	Functioned satisfactory, but with the same limitation as above.
Negotiating	No special provision for negotiation. It would be advantageous to have a preliminary assignment which a person can confirm or reject. Asking for permission to complete a certain task is also a desirable feature.	

Negotiating

This group includes a *request for engagement*, and *response* to it:

- *Request for engagement* is a question posed to the recipient inquiring whether he/she can think of committing him/herself to take a role or a task assignment (alternatively be relieved of a role or task assignment). A request can also be about permission to assign a role or a task to oneself (or relieve oneself from a role/task assignment). Request for engagement is a directive act in the speech acts classification. It presumes some action, e.g., a response from the recipient(s) of the request.
- *Response* is an act of accepting, conditionally accepting, or declining a proposal that comes in a request. This is a commissive act in the speech acts classification.

As has been already mentioned, *ProBis* has no specially designed provision for negotiation except of planning a *Question* task in the *To do* list, which is not a very convenient way to conduct negotiations. See also suggestions for improvement in tables 3 and 4.

5. CONCLUSIONS

The goal of this work was to draft a method of analysis of communication capabilities of a CM/ACM system, or even any other type of BPS systems. This method, called LAP-CA, is aimed for analysis of already existing systems and for guiding the design of new systems. To build LAP-CA, we used Language Action Perspective (LAP), but in a different way from those suggested by others. Instead of proposing of how communication should work technically, e.g. what kind of communication channels to use, we focused on identifying communication acts to be implemented in a BPS system, leaving the implementation details to the system designers.

---

[2] Note that *ProBis* saves the history of all changes done to the shared space, which means that any manipulation with task assignments can be detected later.

We tested LAP-CA in the analysis of an existing CM system of our own design to show that the method could be useful in practice. The system has been chosen because its non-messaging way of implementing communication that is becoming widely spread due to the advances of social software. The analysis showed that several types of communication acts where not implemented satisfactory in the system, e.g., reflections and negotiations. Such result would be useful for system redesign, had the system still been in operation.

To the best of our knowledge, there are no other methods especially aimed for analysis of the communication capabilities of BPS systems reported in the literature. Though LAP-CA requires farther development and testing, we believe that, even in its current form, it could be useful for practice.

6. ACKNOWLEDGMENTS

This work is based on our presentation at PoEM 2012 conference (Practical aspects of enterprise Modeling), and it constitutes a substantially extended and revised version of (Bider & Perjons, 2012).

7. REFERENCES

Agerfalk, P. (2004). Investigating actability dimensions: a language/action perspective on criteria for information systems evaluation. *Interacting with Computers, 16* (5), 957-988.

Andersson, T., Bider, I., & Svensson, R. (2005). Aligning people to business processes experience report. *SPIP, 10*(4), 403-413.

Bider, I., & Perjons, E. (2012). Reviving Language/Action Perspective in the Era of Social Software. *Short Paper Proceedings of the 5th Working Conference on the Practice of Enterprise Modeling.* Rostock, Germany: CEUR Workshop Proceedings, Vol 933.

Bider, I., & Striy, A. (2008). Controlling business process instance flexibility via rules of planning. *IJBPIM , 3*(1), 15-25.

Dietz, J. (1999). Understanding and Modelling Business Processes with DEMO. *18th International Conference on Conceptual Modelling (ER'99)* (pp. 188-202). Springer.

Khomyakov, M., & Bider, I. (2000). Achieving Workflow Flexibility through Taming the Chaos. *OOIS 2000 - 6th international conference on object oriented information systems* (pp. 85-92). Springer.

Lyytinen, K. (2004). The Struggle with the Language in the IT – Why is LAP not in the Mainstream? . *International Working Conference on the Language-Action Perspective on Communication Modelling (LAP).* New Brunswick, NJ.

Searle, J. R. (1969). *Speech acts.* London, UK: Cambridge University Press.

Swenson, K. D. (Ed.), (2010). *Mastering the Unpredictable: How Adaptive Case Management Will Revolutionize the Way That Knowledge Workers Get Things Done.* Tampa, Florida, USA: Meghan-Kiffer Press.

Winograd, T. (1987). A Language/Action Perspective on the Design of Cooperative Work. *Human-Computer Interaction, 3*(1), 3-30.

Enterprise as a System of Processes

Alexander SAMARIN, SAMARIN.BIZ

1.1 COMBINING CLASSIC BPM AND CLASSIC ACM

Both classic BPM and classic ACM are about coordination of business activities to achieve particular results. But both of them use different coordination techniques.

This chapter discusses coordination as a potential base for a common view on BPM and ACM. It is an updated version of my paper on how to understand how separate processes work together as one functional whole (i.e. a System Of Processes -- SOP) at the scale of an enterprise. Use of processes (and constructions related to them) will reduce the undesired complexity of an enterprise, improve understanding of its structure and behaviour, which thus facilitates the management and evolution of the enterprise[1].

1.2 BASIC BPM-RELATED DEFINITIONS

Enterprise functioning can be considered as business activity flows spanning the applications, employees, customers and partners within and beyond the boundaries of the enterprise. **Business activity** is a unit of work. Individual business activities are interrelated.

A **business process** is an explicitly-defined coordination for guiding the purposeful enactment of business activity flows.

Note: In its simplest form, a business process is an agreed plan to carry out (both parallelly and sequentially) some activities; the plan may include some variants and may be changed if necessary.

More about BPM-related definition can be found in [2].

1.3 FIND STABLE COORDINATION CONSTRUCTS

Explicitly-defined coordination is one way to bring some order into the structure and behaviour of interrelated business activity flows. The best-known coordination construct (or aggregation) is a business process. Other types of coordination construct can be revealed by analysing the degree of coordination between various activities, because coordination between activities can be strong (e.g. as in the army) or weak (e.g. as in an amateur football team). Usually, the degree of coordination between business activities which belong to a particular coordination construct is stronger than the degree of coordination between similar coordination constructs.

Let us consider four nested coordination constructs:

1. process pattern (a process fragment for the implementation of a good business practice);
2. process (coordination between process patterns and separate activities);
3. cluster of processes (coordination between closely-related processes, e.g. processes with the same business function);

4. system of processes (coordination between clusters of processes within an enterprise).

1.4 PROCESS PATTERNS

Although all business processes are unique, they are actually composed of similar process fragments or process patterns. For example, let us consider a typical claims process relating to a household repair: the process comprises claim making, evaluation of the repair needed, selection of a service provider, repair, control, invoicing and receiving the payment the repair activities from an insurance company. This process is actually composed of a few process patterns as shown in Figure 1; the patterns (red rectangles) are superposed on the process diagram.

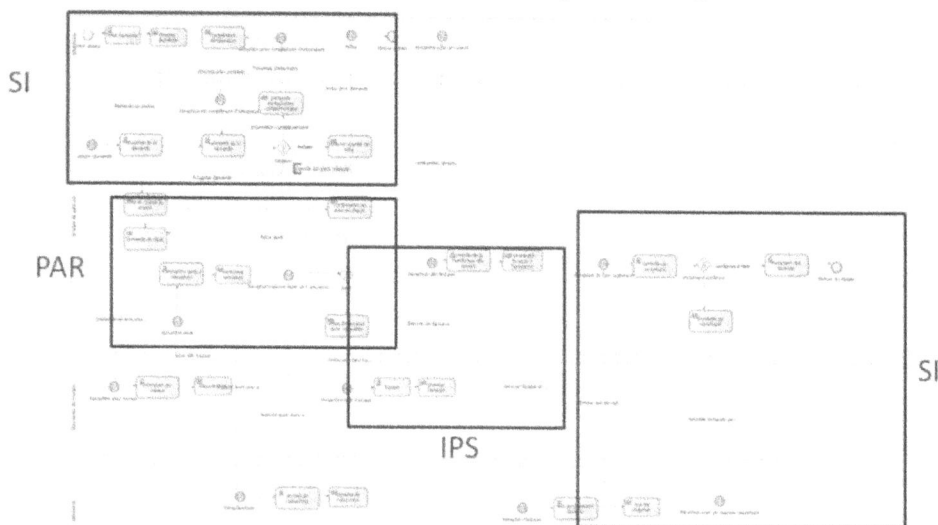

Figure 1 Example of a process diagram with the implicit use of process patterns

The patterns shown in Figure 1 are the following:
- the SI pattern– "Submission Interface", see [3];
- the PAR pattern– "Propose, Act and React", see 8.3.12 in [4];
- the IPS pattern– "Initial Process Skeleton", see 8.3.7 in [4].

Although a process pattern is a stable construct, they can be adapted for particular needs. For example, the Delegation of Authority Matrix (DAM) pattern (see [5]) is implemented differently in procurement and in project management.

Some process patterns are available at [6].

1.5 ANALYSING COORDINATION BETWEEN PROCESSES

Coordination between processes is usually event-based. In the simple variant, the finish of one process is the start of another (see Figure 2 in which the lightning symbol is used to represent events). Note that Figure 2 actually demonstrates the state-based coordination technique (see [7]).

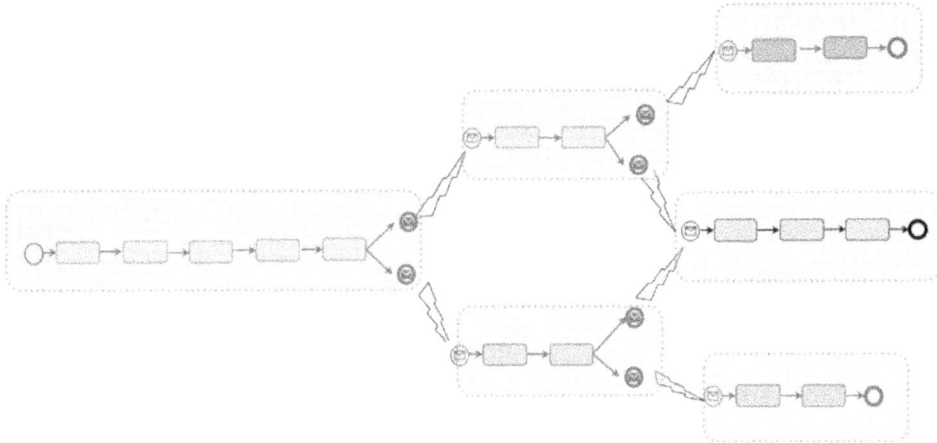

Figure 2   Simple coordination between processes

In reality, there are more complex interactions between processes as shown, for example, in Figure 3:

- the finish of one process is the start of another process – marked ①;
- start another process and wait for its completion (aka synchronous invocation) – marked ②;
- start another process and wait for its completion sometime later (aka asynchronous invocation) – marked ③;
- start another process and do not wait for its completion (aka "fire and forget") – marked ④;
- start another process from one process and wait for its completion in a third process – marked ⑤;

Another type of complex interactions between processes is "co-processes" (e.g. a pair of rock climbers tied together by a rope agree to climb one after the other, and not simultaneously – see [3]).

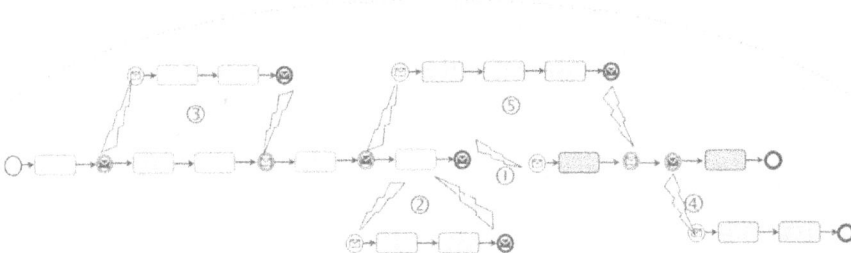

Figure 3   Examples of complex coordination between processes

Additional coordination techniques are also necessary because

- some events are generated outside of processes (a typical example is a database trigger), and
- events may be transformed between processes (see an example at [8]).

1.6 CLUSTERS OF PROCESSES

1.6.1 General

Processes which are strongly related to each other form a Cluster Of Processes (CLOP). Functional processes which are implemented in a particular business function, e.g. "Field Services", are usually a core part of a CLOP.

"Around" these functional processes there is a set of processes (called a halo of processes) which help to execute the functional processes. The processes comprising the halo are monitoring, operation, governance and management processes:

- monitoring processes are responsible for analysing the running functional processes – some sort of operational intelligence;
- operation processes are used for implementing operational changes (via available parameters);
- governance processes are used for controlling and directing the functional processes and other within an enterprise;
- management processes are used for the design and implementation of structural changes in accordance with the decisions from the governance processes.

Together, the halo of processes constitutes two control loops – an operational and a strategic loop (see Figure 4).

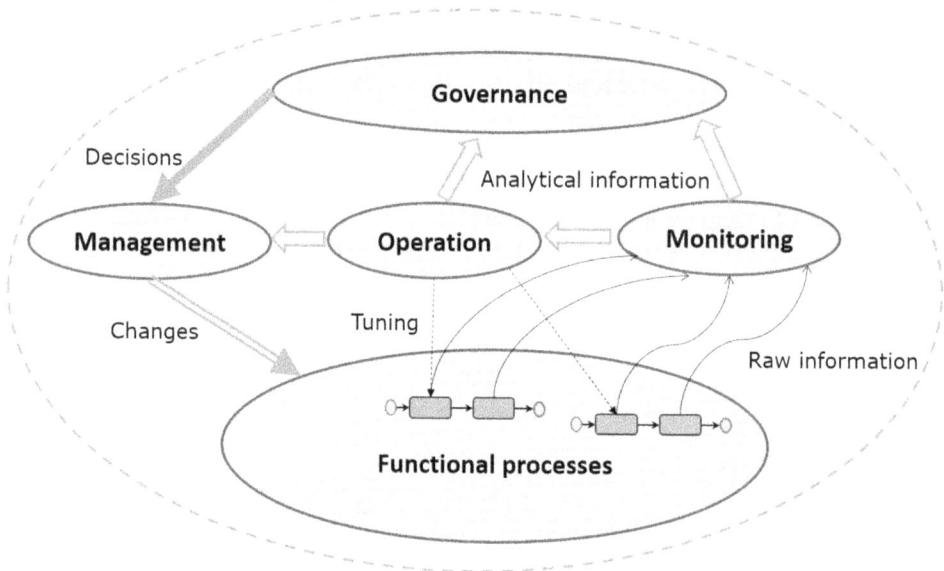

Figure 4   Internal structure of CLOPs

In the operational loop, the following coordination techniques (see [7]) can be used.

- Intelligence-based coordination technique – By using the data about the execution of functional processes, it is possible to predict the future behaviour of processes and to take proactively some mitigation measures to avoid trouble. For example, an insurance claim (functional) process may have an SLA related to the maximum execution time and some threshold to accept automatically small-value claims (i.e. claims which are not checked by an operator). If the monitoring process detects that there is a "wave" of claims and there is a risk that the SLA cannot be met because of staff resource limitations, then the operation process can temporarily increase the threshold to absorb the "wave".

- Goal-based coordination technique – Since a typical business goal is compound (imagine a "fish-bone" diagram) and different sub-goals are supported by different processes, then analysis of the actual situation with respect to the goal may reveal the need to adjust certain parameters in related processes or, even, to start certain processes. For example, if an organisation cannot fill some positions then a process for reviewing the job descriptions for those positions can be initiated. (The HR department is the owner of this process, but the content is provided by recruiting managers).

1.6.2 Generic relationships between CLOPs

Each CLOP may be related to an enabler group of CLOPS, a supporting group of CLOPs and a customer group of CLOPs (see Figure 5). The enabler group of CLOPS are typically specific for a particular CLOP while the supporting group of CLOPs are common to several CLOPs. Owing to natural recursion, a CLOP can be in the supporting group for other CLOPs. For example, a particular enterprise value system is a group of CLOPs which are supported by the finance CLOP, the IT CLOP, the HR CLOP and the procurement CLOP.

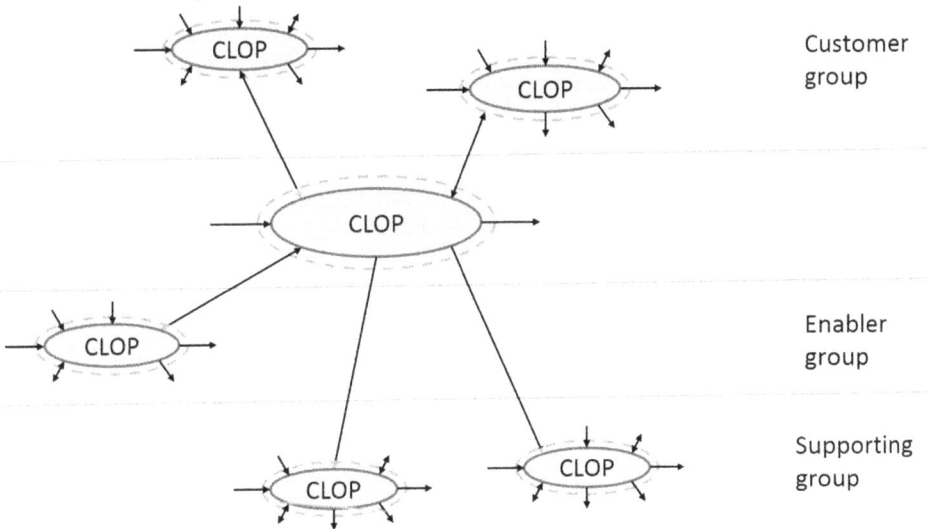

Figure 5   Generic relationships between CLOPs

1.6.3 Relationships between CLOPs

Let us look at the situation in which some activities from a CLOP initiate activities in other CLOPs. In a trivial case, explicit relationship via event-based technique is used in the form of "fire and forget". For example, a service technician finds that a particular piece of equipment needs to be replaced and he/she initiates a request to carry out this replacement.

Other examples of relationships between CLOPs include the following:

a) coordination for business objects such as products:

- a product life-cycle which requires some future work (e.g. the technical service of a car after every 20 000 km) – aka scheduling;
- the influence of the eco-system on the product, e.g. the end of support/production for some components of a particular product;
- technology progress, e.g. the availability of a cheaper material for/component of a particular product;

b) coordination for business objects such as resources:
- if a resource is not available then any processes that use that resource need to queue for it;
- a resource requires replenishment if its capacity is below a defined threshold;

c) coordination for business objects such as customers:
- offering new services and products as the result of field servicing;
- changing of legal conditions (to renegotiate a maintenance contract);
- marketing campaigns.

1.6.4 Implicit relationships between CLOPs

Implicit relationships between CLOPs may exist also and it is not easy to reveal such a coordination. There are many situations in which one process is changing a Business Object (BO) and some non-trivial actions are taken because of those changes. Also, a chain of changes may occur: a trivial change in a BO necessitates a change in another BO which necessitates a non-trivial action.

For example, a field service technician updates his/her work order (BO 1) with a report which contains some lessons learnt. Those lessons learnt, after validation, may be incorporated into the product maintenance guide (BO 2) or into the customer's profile (BO 3). An analysis of all customer profiles may reveal the need for some preventive maintenance (BO 4) or the opportunity for a custom project (BO 5). Figure 6 shows a possible implementation as a chain of changes.

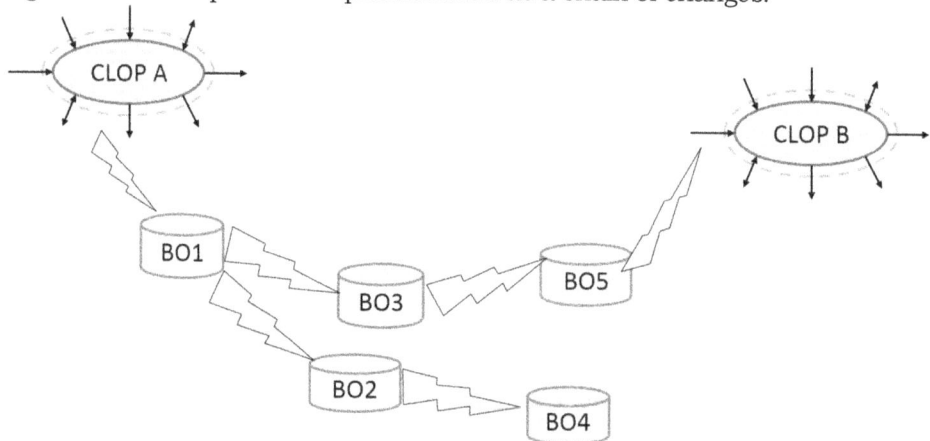

Figure 6   Implicit relationship between CLOPs a chain of changes

Figure 7 shows another possible implementation as a data integration to propagate changes among several business objects.

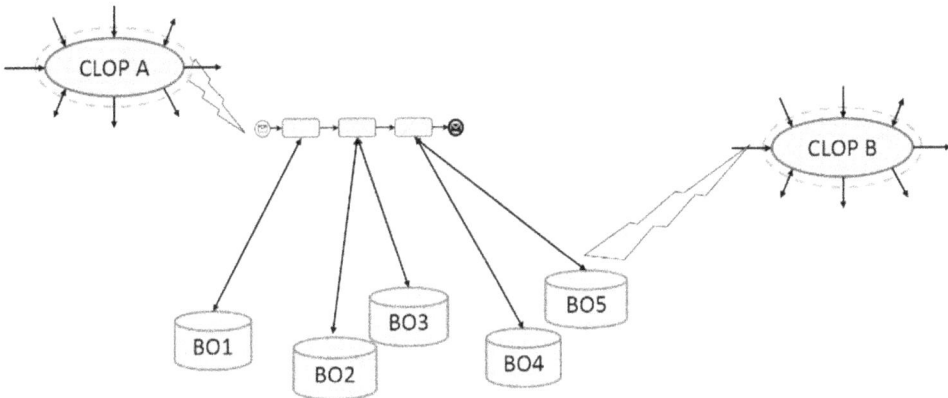

**Figure 7 Implicit relationship between CLOPs through a
data integration process**

Figure 8 shows yet another possible implementation as the "big data" or "business intelligence" approach when the data from various business objects is collected in one data warehouse and analysed.

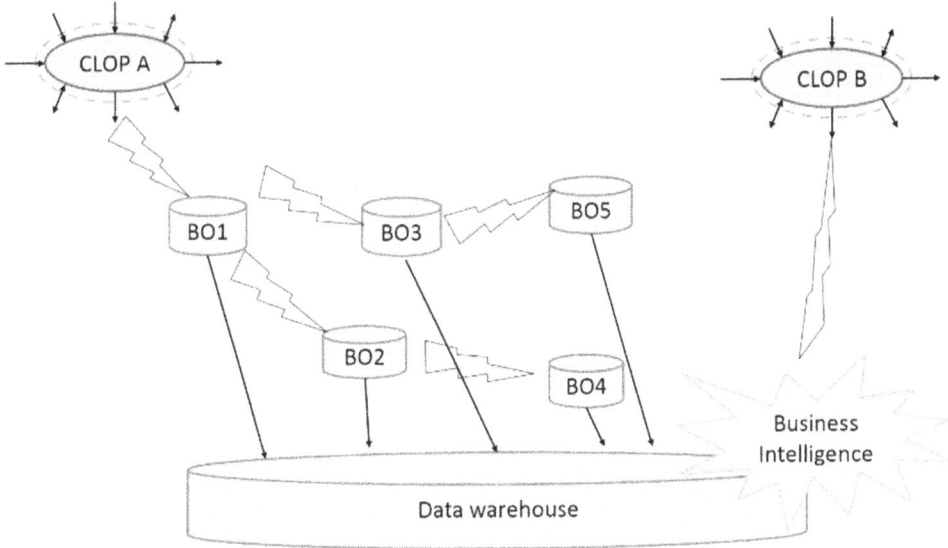

**Figure 8 Implicit relationship between CLOPs through
business intelligence**

The best implementation to be used depends on the particular situation.

1.6.5 Make relationships between CLOPs explicit

Implicit relationship between CLOPs may be converted into explicit one.

Firstly, the life-cycle of all business objects should be considered as a process (see [9]). This is shown schematically in Figure 9; the business object accepts some events and may generate other events.

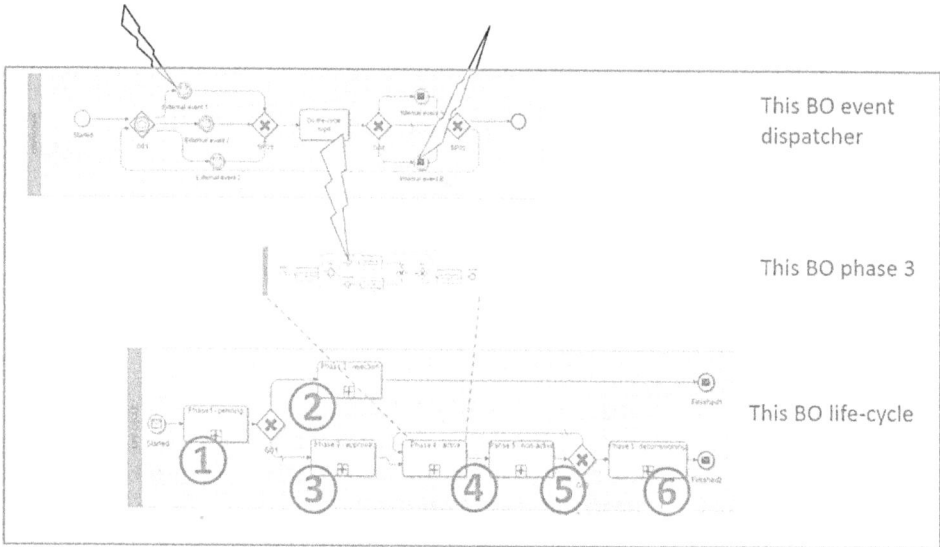

Figure 9   Business object life-cycle as a process

Secondly, an enterprise-wide event dispatcher should be available. As shown in Figure 10, the event dispatcher accepts all events, treats them and, possibly, generates some new events. This event dispatcher operates on the basis of rules, e.g. a change in the home address of an insured person should initiate the redefinition of his/her insurance contract (in the case that the premium is location-dependent).

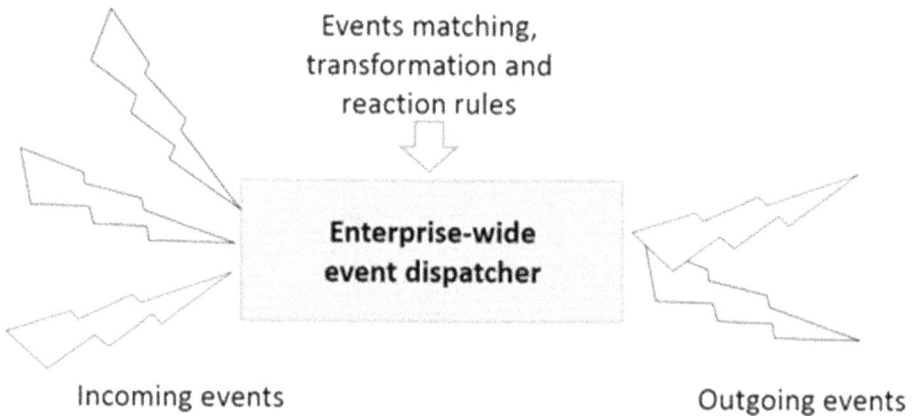

Figure 10   Enterprise-wide event dispatcher

Thus, the explicit link between two CLOPs may be established via the life-cycles of a few business objects and an enterprise-wide event dispatcher as shown in Figure 11.

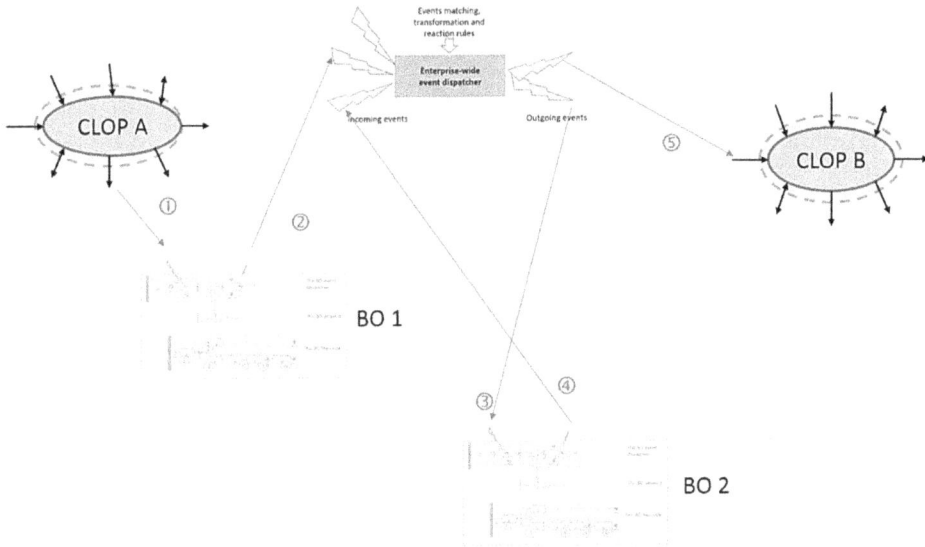

Figure 11   Explicit relationship between CLOPs

1.7   SYSTEM OF PROCESS

Classic value-streams and end-to-end enterprise processes are sequences of several CLOPs.

An enterprise may contains many end-to-end processes. As enterprise may comprise many value-streams.

1.8   FUNCTIONAL VIEW OF SYSTEM OF PROCESSES

A typical problem with cross-functional (or end-to-end) processes is that such processes are understood differently by different organisational functions that participate in the process. The root cause of this effect is that each organisational function sees the system of processes only from their functional silo (or "corridor").

For example, department ZZ understands their process as show in Figure 12.

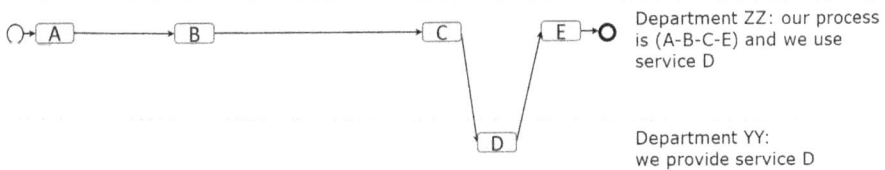

Figure 12   Department ZZ – Initial understanding of their process

Actually, the process of the department ZZ is part of the organisational value-stream as shown in Figure 13.

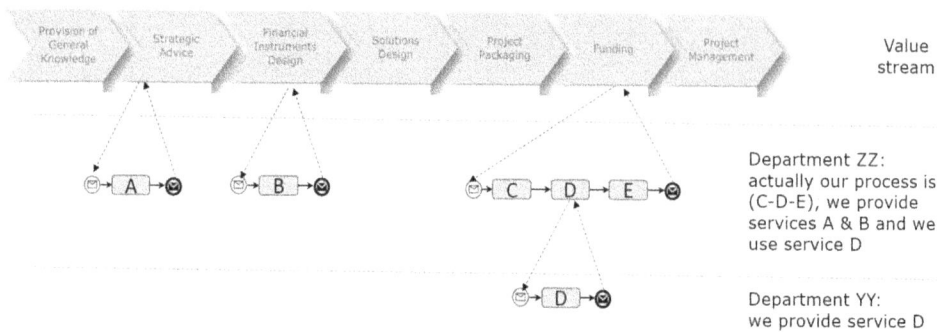

Figure 13   Department ZZ process as part of the organisational value-stream

Furthermore, activities A and B are from processes of other departments as show in Figure 14.

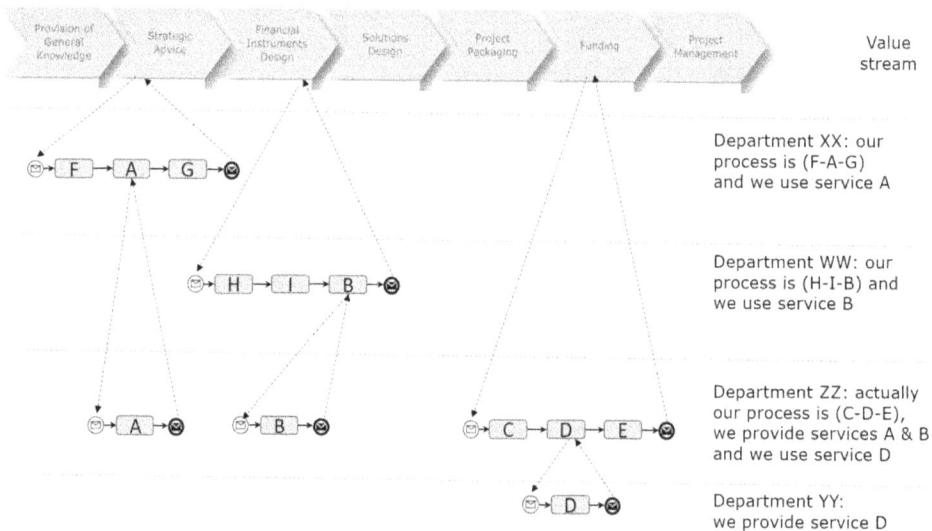

Figure 14   All departmental processes in the organisational value-stream

Again, the implementation separately of functional processes will create a lot of duplication and increase the undesired complexity.

1.9   IMPORTANCE OF THE CONSIDERING SYSTEM OF PROCESSES

1.9.1   Reducing complexity

In relation to 1.1 wherein we considered enterprise functioning as business activity flows spanning the applications, employees, customers and partners within and beyond the boundaries of the enterprise, the number of such potential relationships between those business activities is huge: $N \times (N-1)/2$ for N activities. This is the root cause of the effective complexity of modern enterprises. The determination of stable coordination constructs decreases the number of relationships between business activities and thus can be used to reduce the complexity of modern enterprises.

1.9.2 Objective estimation of potential performance

The use of executable processes enables the easy calculation of various performance indicators in an objective and timely manner. Their use also greatly helps the enforcement of SLAs (see [10]).

Most capabilities (where a capability is an assessment of the ability of a component to achieve a particular result – see [11]) are objectively calculated (possibly with the use of some simulation) from processes.

1.9.3 An insight for organisational structure

Knowledge of the processes may help to envision a draft organisational structure for these processes (see [12]) to be tuned.

1.9.4 Selecting the best coordination technique

Detecting several coordination constructs helps to find the best coordination technique for each particular group of activities. Some of them are best coordinated by classic templates (as in workflows), others are best coordinated by data, documents and knowledge based techniques (similar to ACM).

OTHER FACTORS TO CONSIDER

Note, so far, both implicit and explicit forms of processes were treated equally. Typically, implicit processes are implemented within custom-built applications and ERP systems. Extracting important events from existing applications/ERPs is mandatory to exploit the power of processes.

In the worst case scenario, some processes are defined only on paper by the business and ignored by the IT.

Ideally, the target is **explicit** and **executable** business processes.

1.10 REFERENCES

[1] http://improving-bpm-systems.blogspot.ch/2014/03/enterprise-as-system-of-processes.html

[2] http://improving-bpm-systems.blogspot.ch/2014/01/definition-of-bpm-and-related-terms.html

[3] http://www.slideshare.net/samarin/process-practical-patterns-si

[4] www.samarin.biz/book

[5] http://improving-bpm-systems.blogspot.ch/2012/07/practical-process-pattern-dam.html

[6] http://improving-bpm-systems.blogspot.fr/search/label/practical%20process%20patterno

[7] http://improving-bpm-systems.blogspot.ch/2014/03/coordination-techniques-in-bpm.html

[8] http://improving-bpm-systems.blogspot.fr/2011/01/explicit-event-processing-agents-in.html

[9] http://improving-bpm-systems.blogspot.fr/2013/11/practical-process-patterns-lifecycle-as.html

[10] http://improving-bpm-systems.blogspot.ch/2010/03/linkedin-how-do-we-measure-work-flow.html

[11] http://improving-bpm-systems.blogspot.ch/2014/08/concept-capability-for-bpm-entarch-and.html

[12] http://improving-bpm-systems.blogspot.ch/2011/10/enterprise-pattern-structuring-it.html

Real-World Award-Winning Case Studies

Cognocare, an ACM-based System for Oncology

Nominated by IActive US Corp, US

1. EXECUTIVE SUMMARY / ABSTRACT

Cognocare [0] is an ACM-based Clinical Decision Support System for Oncology that interprets clinical guidelines and expert knowledge, enabling a true dynamic and knowledge-based process generation based on Artificial Intelligence, where these processes are personalized treatments, adapted to each single patient condition. Physicians use it as an assistant to design, follow-up, modify and update fully detailed treatment processes in a very flexible environment.

2. INTRODUCTION TO COGNOCARE

Since receiving the 2012 WfMC Award for Excellence in Case Management in the Healthcare category, Cognocare has continued evolving by including new features and validating those features already introduced in the 2012 case of study. New features have been included under end-user demands and the main features have been validated with an independent observational study carried out over two hospitals in Spain and more than 200 pediatric oncology cases studied during the past six months. This might well be one of the first trials to provide independent, sound and scientific evidence of the advantages of using a case management software versus doing things manually.

Cognocare [0] is an ACM-based Clinical Decision Support System for Oncology that interprets clinical guidelines and expert knowledge, enabling a true dynamic and knowledge-based process generation based on Artificial Intelligence, where these processes are personalized treatments, adapted to each single patient condition. Physicians use it as an assistant to design, follow-up, modify and update fully detailed treatment processes under a very flexible environment.

Strictly speaking, after all the recent evolution of the ACM area [0] Cognocare is a Production Case Manager, since the "adaptive" flavor is missing in Cognocare. And we have to say that it has been an intensive subject of discussion among the members of Cognocare, IActive and also the clinical staff, because physicians do not have absolute freedom of choice when faced to the treatment of cancer, at least in the most well known types of cancer. They have to adhere to evidence-based treatment protocols, which, at the end, rely on long-term, costly clinical trials which produce these protocols. Therefore, the adequacy of the term "adaptive", as described in the references above, is still an open question for research from an operative, ethical and philosophical point of view.

The two most important sources of information for a CDSS like this are, on one hand, the access to clinical information about the patient (to personalize the treatment), achieved by implementing a virtual medical record that integrates with external EHR to obtain all the required information (Figure 1), and on the other hand access to clinical practice guidelines (as the main knowledge source on how to build a treatment).

Personalized treatments are timed processes with a flexible temporal representation scheme which encode start and end dates imposed by the guidelines, safety temporal constraints, milestones and deadlines to be met. They are stored in a local database, but since they are rich and structured information, they may be exchanged with the EHR at any moment or downloaded by patient through corresponding patients portals.

Practice guidelines need to be a structured knowledge representation, that is, an actionable representation that can be understood by the AI engine in order to compose appropriately the processes. In this case we use the freely available Knowledge Studio that fits into our AI engine (Figure 1) in a close collaboration of our physicians and our knowledge engineers.

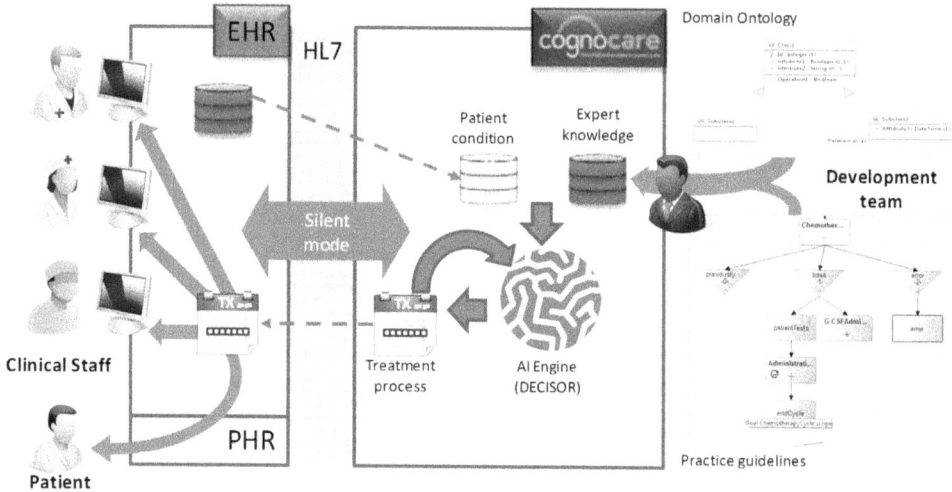

Figure 1. Architecture of Cognocare

A typical cycle (Figure 2) of use starts with an incoming patient with a confirmed diagnosis. Then, from the last laboratory tests and biometric and demographic data, Cognocare explores the practice guidelines and elaborates a personalized treatment or process in the form of a calendar (at different hierarchical levels showing the drugs, dosages and all the required information (even administrative tasks). When needed, physicians can modify many details of the treatment, mainly the details about the chemotherapy drugs, their dosage and timing, but respecting the critical backbone of the treatment in order to adhere as much as possible to the practice guideline. Since the outcome of the treatment may not be as predicted, Cognocare notifies (shadow) the part of the treatment that depends on an intermediate evaluation, or tests, of the condition of the patient, therefore it may be considered as a forecast.

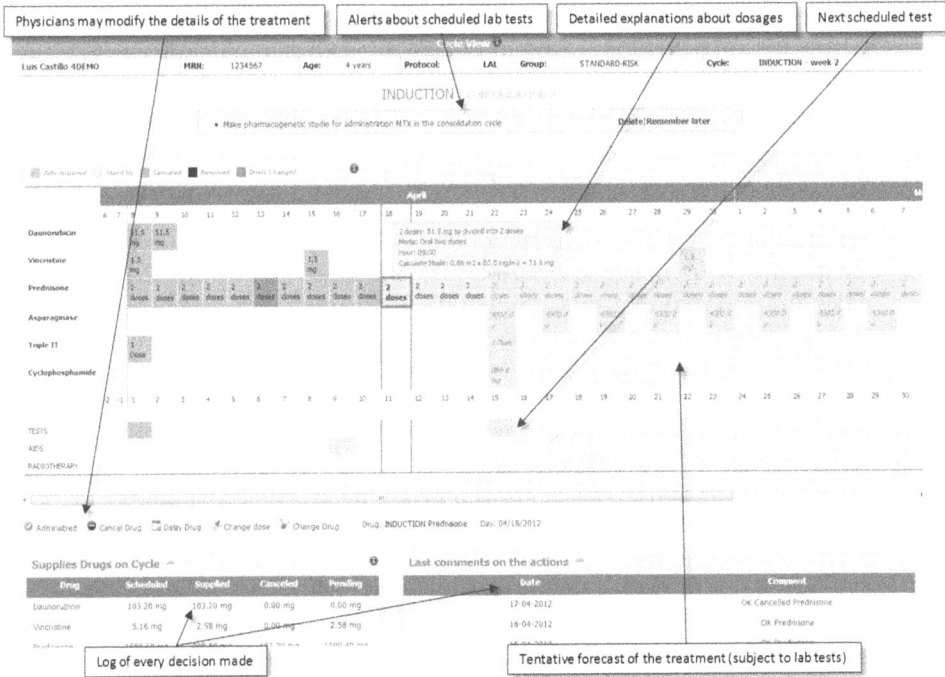

Figure 2. Cognocare screenshot

Since physicians or nurses can introduce daily values (body temperature) or even data coming from the latest laboratory tests, Cognocare always acts in "silent mode" monitoring these data in background and, in the case of a dangerous deviation from the expected values, it triggers a re-planning process to redesign on-the-fly a new treatment from that day on. This new treatment is always based on the same practice guidelines and on the process executed so far.

This cycle lasts until the patient completes the full protocol of the treatment and it is continued with follow-up sessions.

The main advantages provided by Cognocare are the following ones:

- Knowledge Sharing. All the physicians (knowledge workers) make similar decisions by sharing system's knowledge, in terms of both patient ontology extracted from clinical records and process templates to comply with standard practice guidelines. In addition to this, all the physicians involved in the treatment of the same patient (actors) share the same backbone of information: the treatment stored in the case of the patient.

- Dynamic. Unexpected events are managed on the fly by adapting the current treatment to the new conditions, generating new treatment steps by reusing the previous treatment process, if needed, and sending alerts for validation to physicians.

- Goal oriented. No matter what happens, it always tries to apply correctly practice guidelines, always with the same goal of healing the patient.

- Enables collaboration. Since every action in the process has an associated actor, the plan may be split into the profiles of actors and resources involved enabling a powerful collaborative care approach and increasing the coordination between different teams.

- Powerful reporting capabilities. Since all the information about the evolution of the treatment is logged in Cognocare, physicians may use its reporting capabilities to provided and enhanced situation awareness, like detecting meaningful deviations of the treatment and why, calculating the cost of the treatment beforehand, comparing the evolution of single patients respect to the average behaviour in the unit, etc.
- Patient engagement. The whole treatment is available in a structured representation since the beginning. This allows patients to download their treatment thru their patient's portals, integrate them into their personal calendar and make unprecedented decisions regarding the arrangement of their lives to met the scheduled treatment enough in advance (always subject to possible changes in the treatment).
- Productivity. Reduces physician's workload and allow them to focus on more treatments within the same time. An observational study is carried out in Spain in two different Hospitals within the Andalusian Healthcare System: Preliminary results show a dramatic reduction of dosage errors, a cut of time by ¼ and unprecedented higher awareness due to enhanced reporting capabilities.
- Comprehensive. Fully detailed treatments: dosages, clinical tasks, even parallel administrative tasks (automated reports, daily treatment flow-sheets, laboratory reports), are included in the process since the beginning, providing the basis for enhanced alerting and reminding capabilities.
- Errors management. Every decision made by the AI engine (like calculation of doses, changes of chemo cycles due to patient conditions, reminders of scheduled tests) may be shown to the physician, together with a brief explanation, beforehand reducing the likelihood of the errors due to shortage of time.
- Update to new treatments. Practice guidelines are not encoded within the source code, but as a separate file. Therefore, as soon as a new guideline is available for a disease, it is encoded in Knowledge Studio and made it available to physicians without having to reinstall or interrupt the software.

3. BUSINESS CONTEXT

Validating Cognocare has involved the design of a multi-center study, which was designed, under contract, by the Department of Statistics and Operational Research of the University of Granada in Spain and it was approved by the Committee of Ethics and Research of all of the hospitals. The goal was measuring both the impact in the design time of every chemo cycle and the impact in the early detection of errors.

In order to isolate interferences between the different players in the study which could affect the independence of measurements the study, the collection of data was designed as a random and blind process. Every chemo cycle had to be designed both by hand and by using Cognocare by two different physicians. Neither knew beforehand the name of the patient, or his/her pathology or his/her current condition. At the time of patient onboarding, an independent controller, which was hired exclusively for the purpose of the study, records the relevant information and randomly assigns a physician to the manual mode and the other physician to the Cognocare mode. The controller measures time and errors committed during the design of the chemo cycle. The results are explained in Section 4 .

The main stakeholders in the use of Cognocare are physicians, who are absolutely overwhelmed by information coming from clinical trials, different diseases, complex treatment protocols, dosage accuracy required and the continuous risks over patient lives. The impact on them has been measured and quantified by the independent observational study and we could go a little further and say that the final benefit is not only for physicians, but for patients who will receive better quality care. These results could also be expected in other hospitals or even augmented, depending on the degree of overload of physicians and, being more ambitious, it could also be projected over other applications of case management suites versus manual work.

As we said before, there are a number of features which have been added to Cognocare under physician's demand (both in US and Spain) which could provide higher value (not measured yet). We have included here these features because they have been demanded by real customers and which could also, in general, be extrapolated to other case management applications.

3.1 Taking advantage over resource scheduling thanks to predictive analytics

We could have all the long-term treatments beforehand, every disease implies a different number of days in the hospital and a different timeline of chemo cycles (see Figure 3), which, if put together could give the following added values. Hospital managers could have clues to hire more clinical staff or not in the face of a unexpectedly high number of patients, or even ask physicians about the possibility of delaying certain chemo cycles to keep the number of patients controlled depending on the number of available beds. Getting to know it these peaks of patients are going to happen during weekends is also important because the cost of hiring additional nurses is higher. In addition to this, knowing before hand and estimate of the amount of chemo drugs and side drugs which are going to be administered in the coming months could lead to buy these drugs in more economic batches.

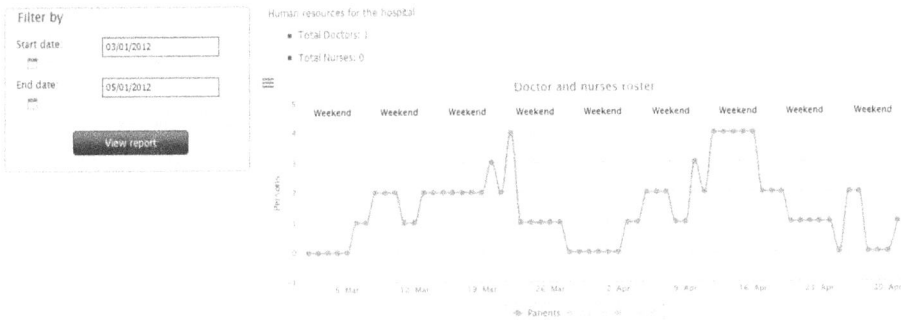

Figure 3. *Number of patients expected in the coming two months*

3.2 Introducing new dimensions in the management of costs

Since Cognocare keeps track of every decision made, it can produce reports about the real evolution of the treatment (driven by physicians, i.e. the knowledge worker) with respect to the expected evolution (suggested by the treatment protocol) as shown in Figure 4. These reports could be used to demonstrate adherence to evidence-based treatments and, therefore, to guarantee reimbursements like in the US healthcare landscape (not in other countries like in Spain).

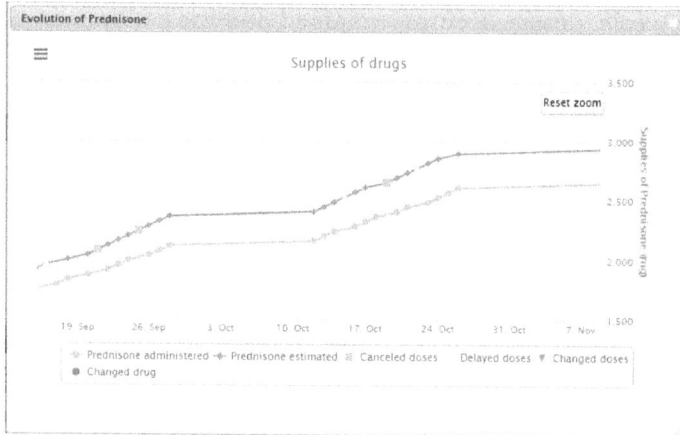

Figure 4. *Adherence to evidence-based treatments for a given drug "Prednisone". In blue the suggested dosage in the treatment protocol. In green the real (recorded) dosage. It can be seen that the administered drug does not exceed, at any moment, the recommended dosage and follows an equivalent curve along the time.*

In addition to this, since the dosage of every chemo drug is strictly quantified before hand, the whole cost of treatments might be discussed with physicians looking for alternative cheaper treatments when necessary.

3.3 Opening the doors for research or audit of every treatment

This exhaustive record of decisions made by the physicians along the treatment of a patient might be used to carry out comparative studies (see Figure 5) to detect hidden interferences of the treatment like the unexpected influence of an administered drug on the level of white blood cells.

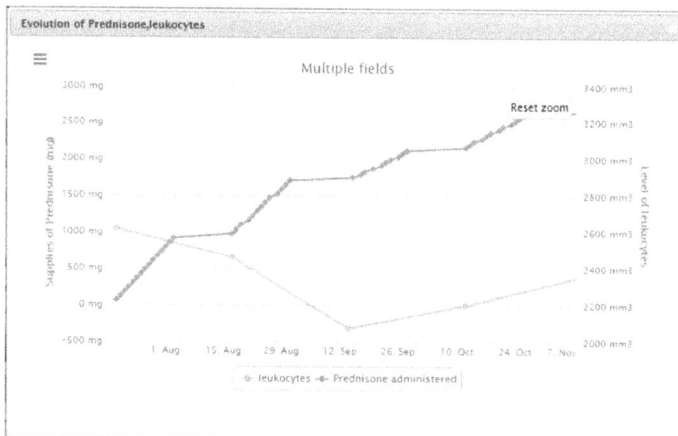

Figure 5. *Comparative study of administered drugs (Prednisone) and number of white blood cells to detect possible influences on each other.*

4. THE KEY RESULTS

All these results shown in this section have been proven and quantified by an independent observational study statistically well designed and approved by management staff of the hospitals included in the study [0]. We show here the most important qualitative results which could be summarized with the sentence with which authors close the statistical analysis:

"The Cognocare method is faster, less variable and is not different in reliability than the manual method for designing chemotherapy cycles in children with different types of cancer"

4.1 Impact on time

Cognocare takes much shorter time than the manual method, with a difference of between 524.1 seconds to 678.2 seconds with a confidence of 95% per every chemo cycle designed. These results imply a saving in time per cycle and patient of 8.75 minutes minimum and 11.30 minutes maximum. This effect is maintained with independence of the pathology and the physician who design the treatment.

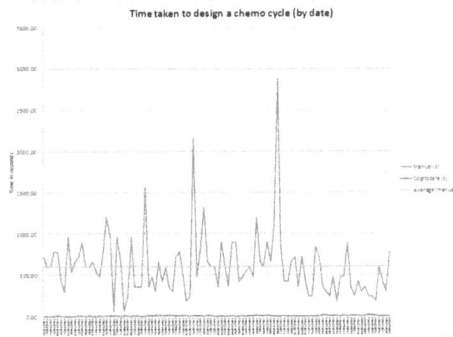

Figure 6. *Time taken (in seconds) with the manual method (in blue) and the Cognocare method (in red).*

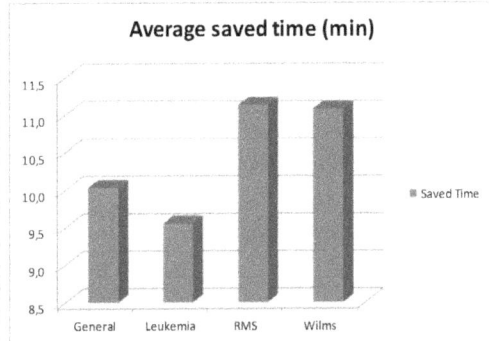

Figure 7. *Average time saved (in minutes) with the Cognocare method, split into the main pathologies during the study: Leukemia, Rhabdomyosarcoma, and Wilms Tumor.*

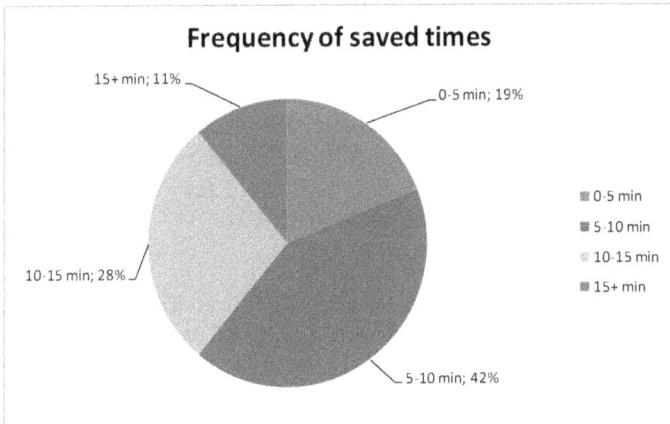

Figure 8. *Frequencies of saved times, by intervals, showing that in 39% of cases Cognocare achieves a saving of at least 10 minutes per patient.*

These results are, per se, really shocking. But if we consider an analysis of the worst cases it shows the following. There are singular critical cases due to high overload of physicians, or the critical condition of a patient, in which the saved time is meaningfully high reaching a peak of 48 minutes saved in a single patient. This delay in, just one single patient, could lead to a whole overload difficult to overcome in a regular day except for the professionalism and effort of physicians.

Maximum saved time (min)

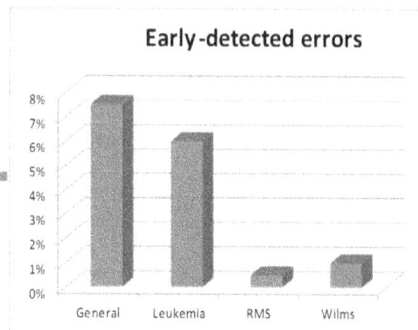

Early-detected errors

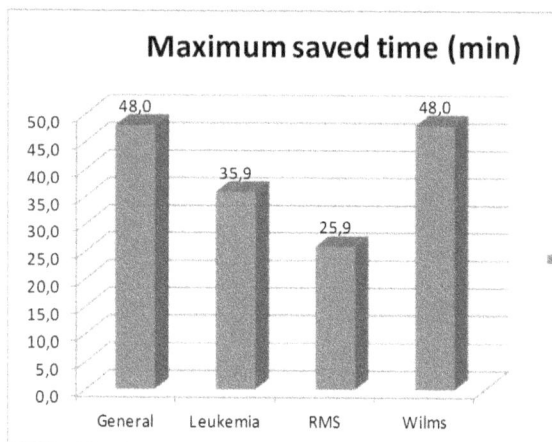

Figure 9. *Worst cases analyzed showing the highest savings in time thanks to Cognocare.*

Figure 10. *Percentage of early detected errors during the design of a chemo cycle, that is, errors committed with the manual method which were corrected with the Cognocare method.*

4.2 Impact on errors

The results here are even more important. In more than 7% of cases, Cognocare allowed for an early detection of an error in the plan of the chemotherapy cycle. If we take into account that a bad dosage can kill a patient, no more comments are necessary.

5. HURDLES OVERCOME

The adoption of Cognocare has not been an easy task and it required intensive training of the clinical staff, mainly physicians, during the study. The main obstacle to overcome has been the integration of Cognocare with heterogeneous sources of data in ancillary software settings. Although all of them use HL7[0] for information exchange, the truth is that each hospital use different encodings and different low level integration. Since this information is critical for Cognocare, we had to use external services [0] to unify the access to each EHR.

6. REFERENCES

Cognocare, an ACM-based System for Oncology. How Knowledge Workers get things done. Real-world adaptive case management. Future Strategies, 2012. www.FutStrat.com

Case Management: Contrasting Production vs. Adaptive. Keith Swenson. http://social-biz.org/2012/09/12/case-management-contrasting-production-vs-adaptive/, 2012.

M. del Mar Rueda, J. de Dios Luna, A. Arcos (Dpt. of Statistics and Operational Research, University of Granada). Report on the effectiveness of Cognocare during the smart design of chemotherapy cycles in children under different types of cancer, 2013. (In Spanish). Available under request to luis.castillo@iactiveit.com

HL7, http://en.wikipedia.org/wiki/Health_Level_7

CADUCEUS, Easy integration of clinical data. http://www.caduceus.es/

Assembled and written by Luis Castillo, Co-founder and Chief Technology Officer at IActive US Corp. luis.castillo@iactiveit.com

Crawford & Company, United States
Nominated by Appian Corporation, United States

1. Executive Summary / Abstract

With 700 offices in more than 70 countries, Crawford & Company provides claims management services used by the largest insurance providers in the world. A core part of Crawford's business is Global Disaster Response for incidents such as hurricanes in the U.S or tsunamis in Japan. Crawford must deploy small armies of claims adjusters to the world's most devastated regions so life – and business – can begin to return to normal in the quickest time possible. These adjusters are not Crawford employees, they are contractors who are un-schooled in Crawford business processes.

Using a modern work platform, Crawford built a series of Business Process Management (BPM)-based mobile and social business applications to streamline the management and execution of Case Management across all catastrophe-related resources and claims, from the assignment of insurance adjusters to the management of claims and final claim resolution. Applications include Claim Portal, Global Claim Intake, Claim Assignment & Scheduling (CAT Connection), Contractor Extranet (repairStream), Automated Claim Report Review/Approval, GTS Large Loss Management, Customer Billing, Employee On-Boarding, and more, all via a single platform.

Crawford calls this application set "Crawford Desktop + Mobile." The integrated solutions optimize automation of rote Case activities, while providing the enterprise data access and easy collaboration needed to improve and accelerate the non-structured aspects of Case Management.

Using this modern BPM approach to Case Management, Crawford has achieved tangible business growth. On the front-end, claim uptake and initial processing has accelerated by as much as 80%. On the back-end, invoicing to Crawford's major insurance carrier customers has accelerated by 70%. Crawford's legacy desktop system required 174 points of data entry per claim, while the new solution requires only 33 system touches per claim. This acceleration is crucial to Crawford's competitive advantage. Major carriers choose Crawford as their claims outsourcer because of the speed with which Crawford can conduct business in devastated areas. In addition, the dramatic acceleration of invoicing speeds revenue by decreasing DSO (Days Sales Outstanding).

2. Overview

Based in Atlanta, Georgia, Crawford & Company is the world's largest independent provider of claims management solutions to insurance companies and self-insured entities. Major service lines include property and casualty claims management, integrated claims and medical management for workers' compensation, legal settlement administration, including class action and warranty inspections, and risk management information services.

Appian was first introduced to Crawford during development efforts for repairNet, the company's managed repair service in the U.K. The BPM Software solution, called repairStream, enabled a series of operational and financial process improvements that dramatically accelerated claims fulfillment and quality of work across

Crawford's contractor network, ensuring that proper internal and customer reporting occurs at every stage.

Based on that success, Crawford acquired a global Appian license across an 18 project roadmap. The next major initiative was the creation of "Crawford Desktop + Mobile," a revolutionary set of applications combining BPM, enterprise data navigation, easy social collaboration and native mobility. The series of applications streamlines insurance claim Case Management across the spectrum of Crawford's core business, from the assignment of insurance adjusters to the management of claims and final claim resolution. Crawford Desktop + Mobile includes the Catastrophe Unit Personnel Tracker (CAT PT) mobile application. CAT PT uses Geo-Location capabilities of adjusters' mobile devices to allow Crawford to pinpoint the right adjuster to review a claim, based on location, capacity and a past performance scorecard. Adjusters then use the same mobile app to upload photos of a claim site, along with electronic claim forms directly from an iPad, iPhone, or Android device. The result is greater speed, participation and accuracy in Crawford's core company mission.

The next deployment, Customer Billing, removed friction and delay in the invoice process, while bringing Crawford's carrier customers more deeply into the process for greater engagement and satisfaction.

According to Brian Flynn, Crawford's Global Chief Information Officer, "The Appian BPM Suite, with its mobile and social capabilities, has changed the way we work with our business partners and ultimately how we service our clients."

3. BUSINESS CONTEXT

Prior to the adoption of the innovative BPM Suite, Crawford managed all its global catastrophe response efforts through spreadsheets, phone calls, and manual note taking documentation. Crawford needed a faster way to get a hold of adjusters in disperse locations, deploy them to the correct sites, and allow them to initiate and upload claim cases.

"The catastrophe team was using whiteboards to organize names and sticky notes to map who would go where to handle the claims. It was very chaotic," Flynn says. "As an IT team we said, 'Are you really doing this?' It was one of the deficiencies in IT. We don't get out as much as we should to see how things are working."

In order to further its mission for stellar service, and to reduce cost and friction from the Repair Claims process, Crawford identified the need to re-vamp management systems of all repairs cases, including repair contractor selection, claims processing and reporting, and accounting and invoicing. Existing Lotus Notes systems lacked the efficiency, effective social collaboration, and analysis reporting required to improve overall performance and profitability.

"An adjuster in the field doesn't always have 10 to 15 minutes to fire up a laptop. We wanted to be flexible by developing something that would work across any smartphone or tablet, regardless of the platform—Android, iOS, whatever," Flynn says.

Crawford realized that to continue to offer high quality customer service, improvements were needed to enhance the following:

- Claims management
- Claims Reporting internally and to the customer
- External Work Management controls

4. THE KEY INNOVATIONS

Mr. Flynn and his IT team decided a modern BPM platform could accelerate smarter decision-making and business action across all of its claim cases and sub-processes to improve business performance, increase customer satisfaction and enable continuous process improvement. Mr. Flynn believed BPM's ability to support rapid delivery of new solutions integrating mobility, collaboration, enterprise data, and process management would allow Crawford IT to help shape new, more modern work patterns across the organization.

After a rigorous vendor selection process, Mr. Flynn and his team selected Appian as Crawford's global BPM and Case Management platform. Crawford IT wanted to be as self-sufficient as possible, so Flynn organized a global BPM Center of Excellence driven by corporate IT and Business leadership. The COE follows an Agile methodology of rapid, iterative release cycles across global regions, typically starting in the US and moving out.

Leveraging the technology innovations integrated within the single platform has yielded dramatic business innovations for Crawford and Company. New modes of working have evolved that are fundamentally superior to the company's previous work styles and processes.

The initial claim uptake process is a prime example. Phone calls, spreadsheets and sticky notes have been eliminated. On-site adjusters no longer need to do duplicate work – initiating a claim on-site, then heading to an office to re-key claim forms, photos and other data.

The new CAT Connection application uses device geo-location and historical adjuster profile information to pinpoint the closest and best adjuster for a given claim site. Crawford then sends the assignment to the identified adjuster, who accepts it using the CAT Connection Mobile app. Adjusters use the app to upload photos of a claim site, along with electronic claim forms directly from an iPad or iPhone device. Forms then go into claim processing, various stages of review and reporting, through final settlement, customer communication and invoicing – all a single platform. The system provides the process guidelines, data access and collaboration required for all stages of claims Case Management, intelligently enforcing policies and procedures so that even adjusters with no prior knowledge of Crawford business processes can work quickly and effectively.

Snapshot of Crawford and Company Process Solutions:

Crawford Desktop + Mobile:
- mobile and social applications that streamlines all catastrophe-related resource management
- Catastrophe Personnel Tracker (CAT PT)
- Mobile claims assignment & scheduling w/Geo-Location
- Allows creation of ad-hoc teams of adjusters during major catastrophes
- Pinpoint the right adjuster based on location, capacity, past performance
- Adjusters upload photos with forms via mobile device to accelerate claims
- Tied to a virtual community for overall resource management

repairStream: end-to-end claims fulfillment service

Customer Billing: removes friction & moves customers into the process

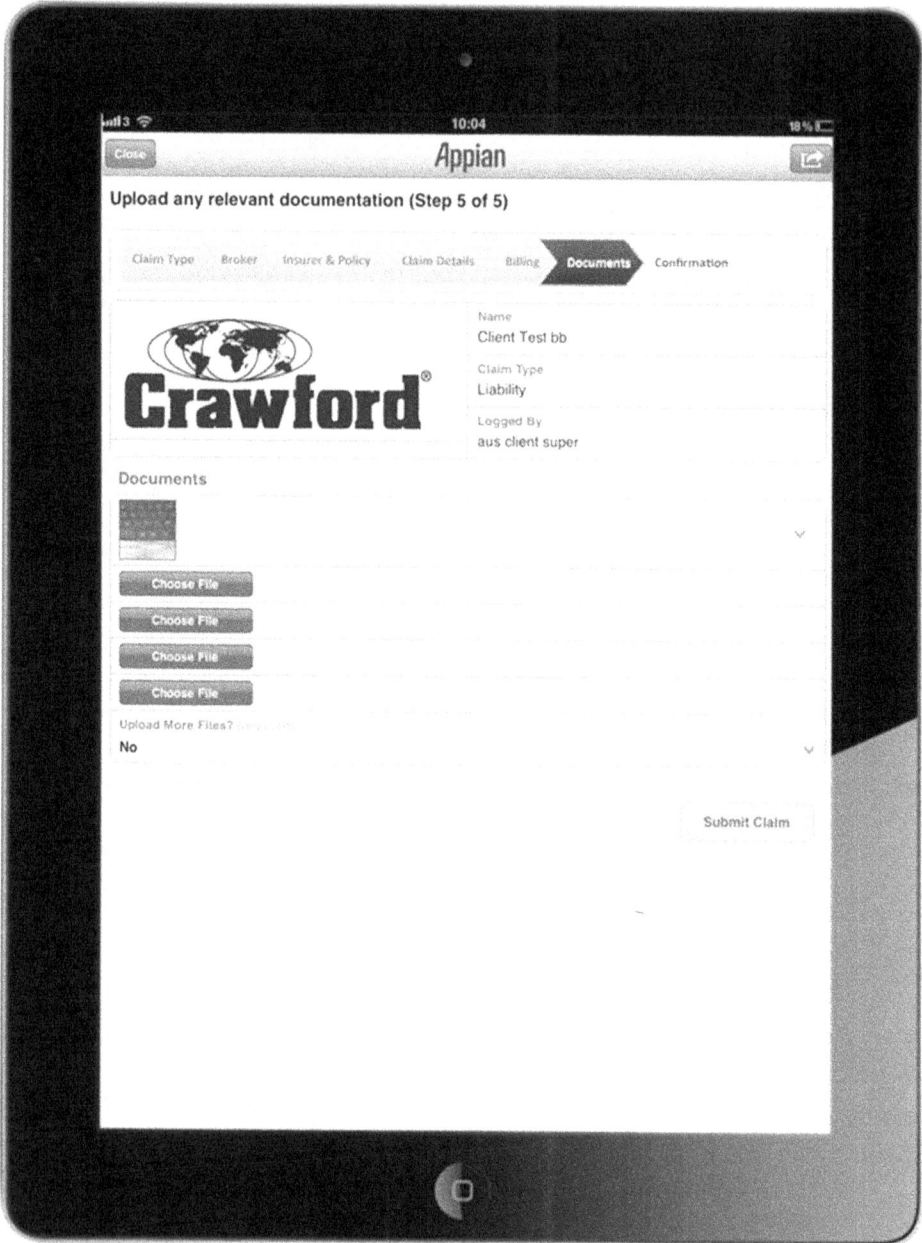

Crawford claims management request form as it appears on mobile devices

5. HURDLES OVERCOME

Crawford faced the common insurance industry pressures to modernize aging systems for great flexibility, mobility and social customer engagement, as well as the business process outsourcing pressures to reduce costs while delivering "personalized" processes to a global customer base.

With an unpredictable need for a larger and dispersed workforce, Crawford needed a social solution—something that would allow them to onboard new employees quickly and efficiently and also help them report on what they were seeing in the field during a disaster and stay in touch.

While choosing a solution was easy, convincing his team—and the business—that this was the right decision, wasn't, according to Flynn.

"This was very transformational for us—going from a waterfall to more agile development," said Flynn. "We had to convince our employees that this was the best thing."

The business, too, had a difficult time grasping the project.

"We thought this was something that they would have brought to us, and not us to them," says Flynn. Technologists think differently than businesspeople, and that was a challenge.

To get the business to believe in the project, Flynn says they reversed their approach and focused on helping them understand how their project matched their business and client needs.

6. BENEFITS

In the areas of claims management to which the modern process solution has been applied, Crawford Desktop + Mobile has accelerated operations by as much as 80 percent. Legacy systems required 174 points of data entry per claim. The replacement solution requires only 33 system touches per claim. Crawford has also seen an acceleration of 70 percent in invoicing speed over its previous paper-based bill review process.

For claims handled under Crawford's old systems, the average time from claim site visit to when the client received a claim report was greater than 2 hours. With a modern work platform, that time has shrunk to an average of 43 minutes. Crawford clients are ecstatic about these accelerated service level.

The business impact of smarter, faster decisions and actions was seen during the record-setting 2013 Canadian floods, during which Crawford was able to:

- Rapidly deploy 350 adjusters to specific sites in the affected region
- Handle 7,000 thousands claims from individuals
- Allow 60 carrier customers to begin processing those claims in only 6 weeks

For Hurricane Sandy in Jamaica, the Bahamas and the U.S., Crawford:

- Deployed more than 560 adjusters in the field
- Took over 44,000 calls
- Managed more than 48,000 claims

7. BEST PRACTICES, LEARNING POINTS AND PITFALLS

Best Practice/Lessons Learned:

✓ *Modernize architecture and software to minimize Catastrophe unit risk from extended downtime periods*
✓ *Utilize development tools that are well represented within the IT community in order to reduce delays in production support and enhancement*
✓ *Develop a mobile first strategy for business that requires workers to be able to work from anywhere at anytime*

Pitfalls to Avoid:

✗ *Don't fall into the trap of legacy IT systems; Embrace modern platforms that include mobile and social capabilities for workflow processing*

- ✗ *Avoid deploying one application at a time to improve process efficiency; Focus efforts that involve deploying a platform to address multiple process enhancements that is flexible to take on future challenges*
- ✗ *Modern business applications must include a mobile strategy; Without a mobile platform, an application is a legacy system from the moment it is rolled out to market*

8. COMPETITIVE ADVANTAGES

Appian continues to support and enable a series of operational and financial process changes at Crawford, as well as assisting in the interaction between all contractors, repairNet and Crawford UK.

The result is that Crawford is changing how the insurance industry reacts to major crisis – allowing the industry to more quickly and accurately process the individual and business claim cases that must be resolved for life to return to normal.

9. TECHNOLOGY

Crawford used the Appian BPM Suite to build the Crawford Desktop + Mobile, leveraging desktop, mobile and social business process applications with enterprise data access. This modern application platform helps drive better business decisions, actions and results. All the data, all the processes, all the documents and all the collaborations – in one environment, on any device, through a simple social interface.

In particular, Crawford relied heavily on mobile BPM capabilities to improve existing processes and design modern applications for claims adjusters to do real work in any location. Native mobile applications allow for work to be done on the go and collaboration to take place via any leading mobile device. The Crawford Desktop + Mobile can be utilized on all modern mobile device platforms with a web browser for 24/7 access.

The innovative work platform uniquely ties social business directly to the core enterprise systems on which Crawford's business is run. The platform offers real business value by integrating social collaboration and native mobile apps with the processes and data that drive the business. It delivers a new, highly transparent and collaborative style of work that results in productivity and better decision-making while creating a more informed and engaged workforce.

"The Appian BPM Suite, with its mobile and social capabilities, is truly an enabler that has changed the way we work with our partners, and how we service our clients."

-- Brian Flynn, Global CIO, Crawford & Company

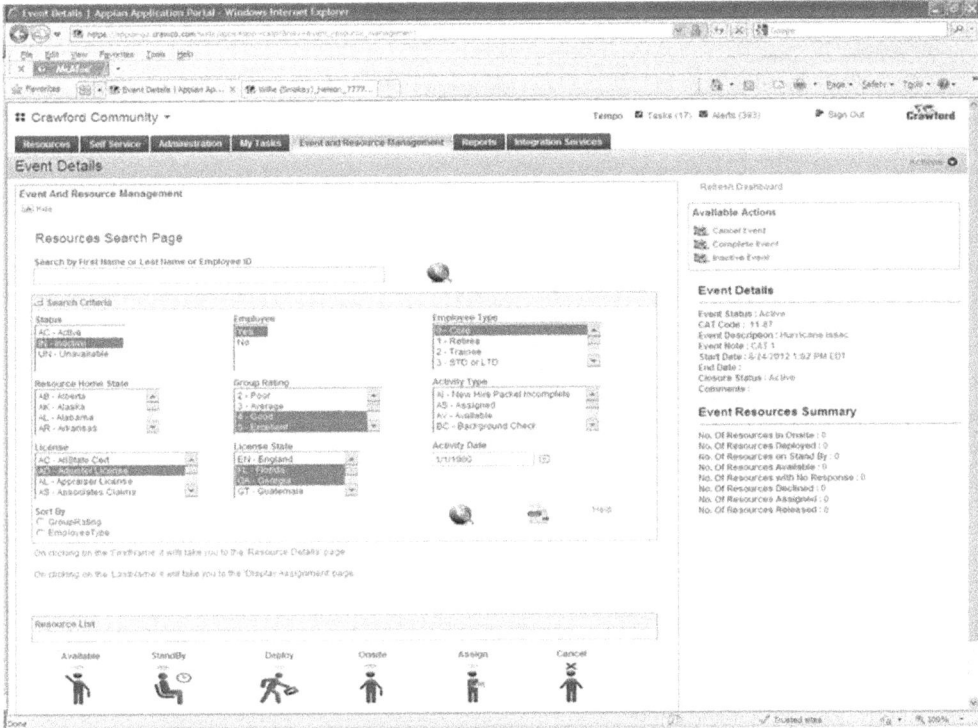

Crawford Desktop application in Appian portal view

10. THE TECHNOLOGY AND SERVICE PROVIDERS

As the market leader in modern BPM software, Appian delivers a Work Platform that unites users with all their data, processes, and collaborations – in one environment, on any mobile device, through a simple social interface. Appian's Business Process Management (BPM) Suite seamlessly integrates work automation with native mobile and social capabilities. Appian is available on-premise and in the cloud, with complete portability. More than 3.5 million users, from Fortune 100 companies to the mid-market and small businesses worldwide, trust Appian to power their critical business processes.

For more information, visit www.appian.com.

Infosys McCamish Systems, USA

Nominated by PegaSystems, USA

1. EXECUTIVE SUMMARY / ABSTRACT

The life insurance industry is complex – multitudes of products, different markets, each with their own unique set of processing rules, many policy owners holding multiple policies, spread across broad geographic regions – and each expecting the same customer care they experience when interacting with companies such as Apple, Amazon, etc. As a service provider, supporting call center and back office operations for 36 insurance carriers, this complexity increases exponentially. Call center and operational processes were carrier specific and the outdated/legacy system limitations acted as a bottle neck to consolidate and unify these processes. For every new client/carrier addition, we had to proportionately increase the team size to support the additional volume. Employee satisfaction and motivation levels were low since they had to refer to data from multiple systems to service a call. This was not a sustainable model.

We established a customer service optimization strategy (case management and workflow solution) with the main objective of providing the highest level of service possible for each individual customer, while still maintaining the carrier specific processes. Case management and workflow solution developed by leveraging the technical capabilities of BPM software and proprietary insurance industry specific framework of our vendor with our insurance industry expertise in call center and back office operations integrates with any backend systems, thereby providing a unified desktop to our customer service and operational teams.

This solution provided the customer service representatives and management with the right tool so they can deliver a customer experience on a highly efficient basis in a cost effective way.

- The application presents a single, 360-degree view of the customer in the integrated end-to-end solution - Scan and Intake, Content Management, Policy Administration, Commissions and Agent Licensing, IVR, Claims and Print Management, among others, and combines the information into a single configurable User Interface.
- The application keeps track of the execution of each automated process and maintains an audit trail of assigned tasks, the performance of the operators, and the performance of individual processes. Businesses can take any of their key performance indicators, drill down, apply and achieve immediate results.

2. OVERVIEW

Growing from a handful of clients (insurance carriers) to 36 different insurance carriers with operations supported by different technology, we realized the need to enhance our service offering and technology and embarked on a customer service optimization strategy. It was directly linked to our overall business strategy of delivering enhanced customer experience and reducing the cost of operations by implementing a best in class customer service platform.

Scope:

Business: Customer servicing & Claims administration of Life, Annuity & Worksite Insurance business

Objectives:
- Improve BPO operational efficiency
- Facilitate business process optimization within BPO
- Increase capabilities for reporting and management of client SLAs
- Establish foundation for functionalized approach to BPO work items (vs client)
- Improve scalability of BPO work activities for larger clients
- Streamline the process of on boarding new clients
- Modernize and Unify the customer service platform to deliver exceptional service, irrespective of Systems of Record
- Improve SaaS revenue

Team Organization:

The key stakeholders of the project were internal to the organization – i.e. platform development, solutions design, marketing and the Business Process Outsourcing (BPO) unit. The BPO unit is responsible for customer service functions.

Development Methodology:

Early on we partnered with a best in class provider and initiated a Proof-of-Concept (POC) phase to evaluate BPM providers and identify the Return on Investment to be expected.

During development of the core systems, agile development methodology was followed to ensure the stakeholders, especially those from BPO Unit, were onboard with the changes upfront in terms of system usage and processes.

Changes were managed primarily in three phases:
- Playback sessions during the product development phase
- Initial soft launch, focusing mainly the "Super Users"
- Product rollout in multiple waves.

This raised the adoption rate significantly by providing adequate time for internal change and acceptance. Assistance was on the floor during the soft launch for immediate response to issues. There was no need for "big-bang" change communications across the organization due to this approach.

Benefits Realized

After the implementation, customer representatives were re-organized into functional so that:

a) Each end customer experienced the same level of quality customer service across the entire organization and all of our clients;

b) They created more opportunity to develop functional expertise to raise the service to the level of 'trusted advisor' to the customer.

3. BUSINESS CONTEXT

Fig 1: Siloed Model – Split By Carrier

Prior to the customer service optimization strategy – the organization was structured into client teams based on carrier. Each team had separate processing units due to the specific carrier, channel and product features.

BPO Service Team

- The team used dual screens for servicing business due to the lack of BPM automation.
- Separate process guides were created for each clients.
- The team was required to pull up processing guides for each client on the exact processing rules on how to handle the transaction.
- Processing rules associated with documents, were integrated into the work flow.
- The team could not easily see the entire work flow without accessing the processing guides.
- The team could not easily see all the policies the client was associated with.
- Workflow processing was segregated from the policy administration system and required the team to access multiple systems to process each transaction and to move the process forward.
- Content Management was not integrated into the workflow.
- Any process improvements were not automated and when identified, required updates to the workflow and the processing guide.

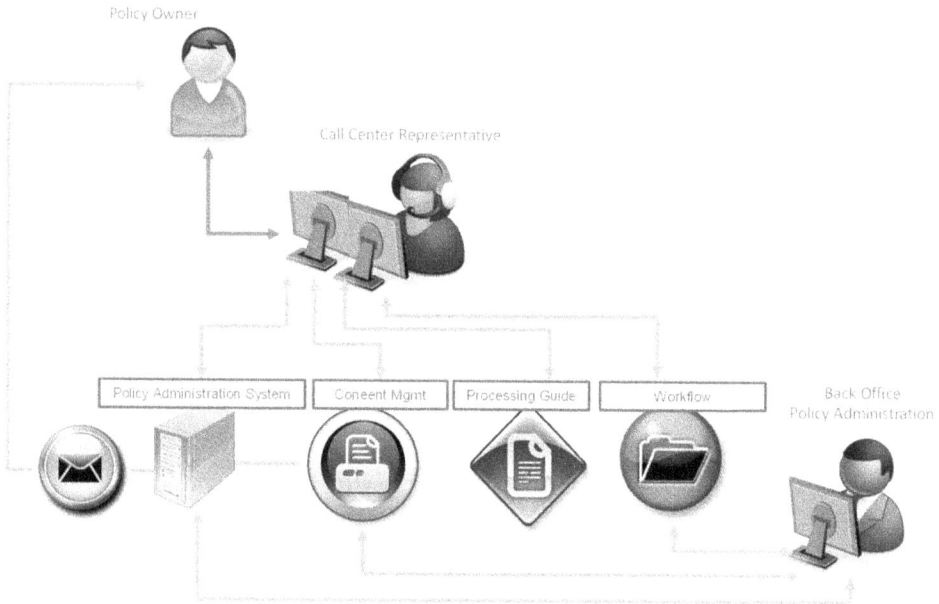

Fig 2 – Multiple Touch Points

The impact this processing model created:
- Inefficient and Inconsistent manual processes
- Call handling
    - High call waiting time, call abandonment
    - Low First call resolution, call backs and transfers
    - Inefficient complaint handling and incident reporting
- Inconsistent multi-channel experience
- Lack of 360 degree customer view
- Limited one and done processes
- Out-of-date self-service options
- Absence of real-time performance measurement and SLA
- Hard to compile metrics across channels
- Limited Process Improvements
- Pull method of handling work, which is less efficient
- Processes spanning across disconnected systems
- Decision by carrier, product lines, systems in "sticky notes"
- Lost opportunity in Business Intelligence to carriers

4. THE KEY INNOVATIONS

The objective of the project was to empower customer service representatives with the right tools so they can deliver best-in-class customer experience on a highly efficient basis.

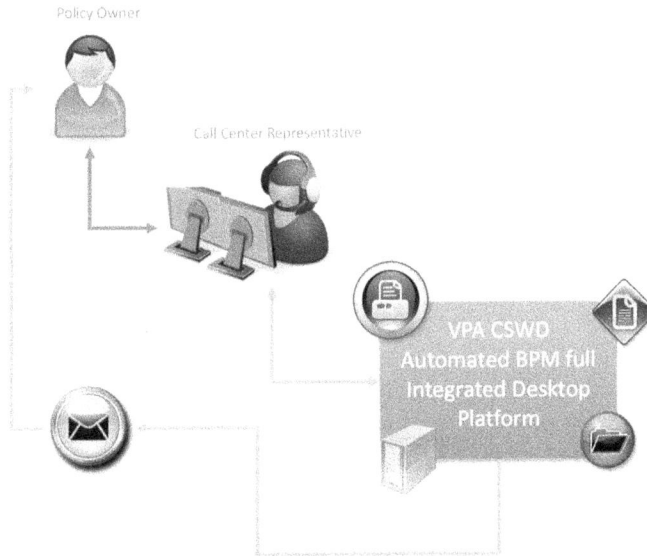

Fig 3—Customer Centric Service Model

Benefits Gained:
- Platform Consolidation - Creating an optimized front end which can be layered on top of both legacy and new platforms allowed us to provide our client in-surers high level service across all end consumers through one single desktop.
- Providing a customer-centric service model, allowing end consumer contact across all channels, with key focus on providing next best actions to our service reps in addition to optimized consumer interaction front end.
- Improvement in Operational Efficiency.

4.1 Business

Outcome:
- 20-30 percent Productivity Improvement in our operations
- 25 percent reduction in average call handle time
- 30 percent reduction in time to complete after call closure activities
- Training / onboarding of new associates reduced from six weeks down to four days
- 20 percent reduction in re-work
- Experience Indicates an ROI of 25 to 30 percent, based on the transactions processed during this period
- Traditional, Predictive or Adaptive Models- Extensive and comprehensive support for adapting by continuously monitoring measurable business objectives.
- Multi Tenant Architecture allows for shared process, or client rules while maintaining the ability for product specific rules within the Policy Admin System.

4.2 Case Handling

From a case handling perspective, the outcome allowed:
- Guiding call center service representatives through transactions without having to reference multiple procedure sources during processing,
- Facilitating service across all communication protocols (web, mobile, etc.), irrespective of distribution channel, insurance product or underlying Policy Administration Systems.

- Individualizing screens to display information as needed, based on information pertinent to the caller (i.e., agent, advisor, owner, etc.), the product or the service request.
- Improvement in Average Call Handle Time
- Reduction in re-work
- Improve the percentage of first call resolutions
- Reduction in call abandon rate
- Reduce specialized training / onboarding time
- Improvement in employee job satisfaction
- Reduce effort to validate after-call closing /validation activities
- Interactive and efficient processing to the call center representative

Interaction Driver
- Delivers personalized customer interactions
- Improves FCR and reduces escalations
- Eliminates manual activities

Dialogue Management
- Personalized experience for each customer
- Consistent experience across all CSR's
- Adapt level of scripting to role and specialty

Knowledge Management
- Re-use knowledge sources from around the enterprise without replication or consolidation
- Improve customer experience with personalized treatments

Interaction Coaching
- Improves CSR performance
- Makes every CSR more like your Best CSR
- Reduces training time
- Improves service quality and consistency

360° View of the Customer
- Leverages enterprise data sources without replication or consolidation
- Improves CSR productivity and reduces training time

Role Based Portals
- A common system specialized by role, tasks and experience to manage a customer across the lifecycle
- Increased productivity through guided interactions

Additional benefits
- Many more one and done transactions processed reducing significantly back office processing costs.
- Customer satisfaction (More efficient processes, Better service levels, Client specific scripting, Adaptive analytics),
- Easier adoption of delivery channels ((Web self service, Mobile, Social media),service orientation (Customer Centric – Easy assembly of data from multiple LOBs, Potential use of Cross-carrier analytics),

4.3 Organization & Social

In developing the application we leveraged our service team's extensive experience in BPO operations and Call Center allowing us to optimize each process for customer interaction. We formed a Center of Excellence:

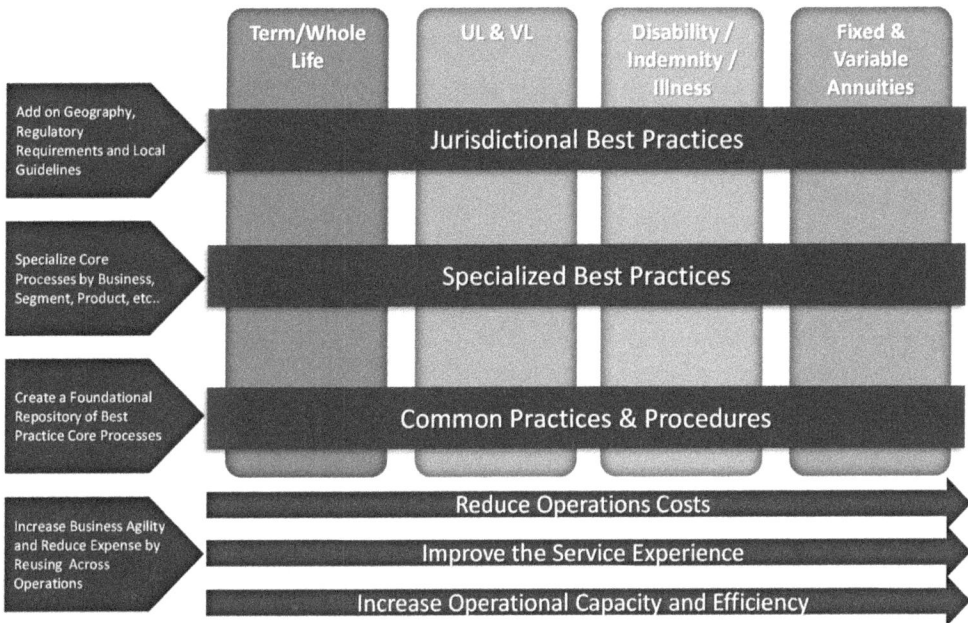

After the implementation, customer representatives were re-organized into functional groups so that:

a) End customer experienced the same level of quality customer service across the organization for all of our clients.

b) Created more opportunity to develop functional expertise to raise the service to the level of 'trusted advisor' to the customer

"The CSRs feel their productivity has improved significantly with a reduction in after call work time. The updates to policy records and workflow creation are much easier and quicker to perform. For call handling, they like the streamlined access the 360 degree view provides to the most commonly accessed policy information and to validate callers."
-- Lisa Johnson, Head of Insurance & Annuity Operations

VPA CSWD				
Web Services				
New Business Platform	Policy Administration System	BPM / Work Flow	Content Mgmt	Producer Management
View Pending Applications	Client Summary	Chronological View of Every Event Transactions,	Logical Views of all In-bound	Provide Hierarchical
	Policy Summary		and Out-bound	View to
By Client	Policy Maintenance	Letters/Notices	Policy	Locate Policies
By Agent	Transaction History	Service Notes	Documents	by Agent and
By Agency	Transaction Submit	Integration with BPM and Workflow		Agent Hierarchy

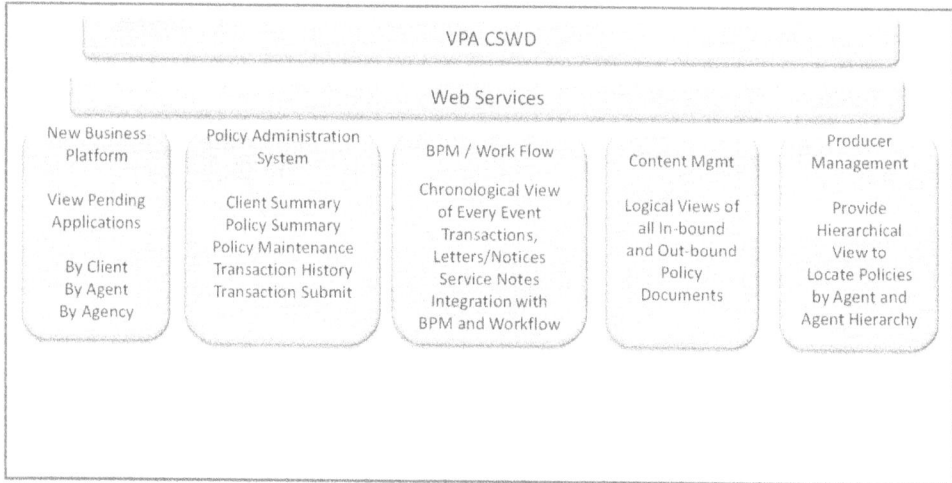

5. HURDLES OVERCOME

The project team adopted an agile approach to implement this solution, initially offering integrated workflow, system integration and responses to the questions asked most frequently by our call center clients.

The second and subsequent phases consisted of enabling increasingly complex transaction processing and integration points such as the transition to a new document management system. This gradual implementation helped us to circumvent a number of common hurdles simultaneously.

Being in a risk adverse industry, our clients are most concerned about data integrity and privacy, followed by customer experience. By implementing the solution using agile methodology, we were able to assure our clients that the strategic direction that our company was taking was not only a safe one, but the right one.

This also worked to the benefit of our customer agents who were not required to re-learn and execute on a new system from day one. Instead, they were able to easily settle in with the look and feel of the new interface from a very basic perspective, and were comfortable with the application, as more of the functionality and transaction processing was transitioned from our Base Administration System to our case management solution.

Management

Our Variable Product Administration System has been the backbone of the McCamish Systems, and Infosys McCamish's service offering for over 20 years. That, coupled with the obvious investment required to implement a new fully integrated front end, workflow and policy servicing system comes with inherent risks and skepticism; however through the extensive due diligence conducted with our business partners, and the vision of our senior executives and system architects we were convinced from the onset that our case management solution, was our future and what would set us apart from our competition.

Questions from management perspective are listed below. The project team was able to demonstrate the solution capabilities addressing these questions during pilot phase. :

- **Return on Investment** : This program required a commitment of $5 - $6 Million USD. Management was concerned about the ROI from this investment and also whether this is the right investment. The pilot phase of this solution demonstrated a potential of 25% to 30% ROI and also offering new service models.

- **Market Differentiator** : This solution is designed using insights gained from our vast experience in servicing customers in the insurance industry, combined with BPM capabilities of the vendor framework. Hence, the solution can be quickly implemented / adopted by other customer insurance organizations, differentiating us from competition

- **Risk of Execution**: Developing this solution required resources with BPM skillset, a skillset that did not exist in the organization. The project team partnered with the vendor organization's training division and put together a training program to train in-house resources and deploy them on this project.

- **Change Management** : Resources in the organization (both operations and application development teams) have been using these legacy applications for more than 15 years. To drive this change, the project team worked closely with business users to implement this in agile methodology and scoping smaller releases instead of taking a BIG-BANG approach.

Business

As previously mentioned, the Insurance, Annuity, and Retirement marketplace is extremely risk adverse, and while not all consider the industry a commodity, customer experience is key to persistency. Most of our clients have been doing business for years on antiquated, legacy systems which provide stability but lack flexibility.

Our policy administration system offered both stability and flexibility, offering short time to market for new products, resulting in a steady increase of policy volume and revenue.

When presented with the alternative that our new case management system provided to a linear increase in customer service and administrative resources, the reduction in training and onboarding times, consistent delivery and metrics, coupled with our roadmap of end-to-end processing capabilities, our clients recognized that our case management solution was a better business solution.

- **Scope Management** : Initiated a Six Sigma exercise to identify process improvements and eliminate unwanted operational processes from being replicated on the new solution.

- **Change Management** : Business/Operational users have been using the legacy applications for more than 15 years. In its end state, the Case Management solution was significantly going to change the Operating Model. To minimize/eliminate disruption.

- Implemented this solution using agile development methodology, with functionality deployed in small phases.

- Bi-weekly play back sessions, so the users are well aware of the proposed solution and actively participate in the solution design

Organization Adoption

Expectation Setting :

- Managing the enthusiasm and excitement of sales and operational teams, regarding the implementation plan of this solution to our current and prospective clients.

- For architecture and development teams to understand that the case management solution was not being developed to replace our existing

System of Records/Policy Administration System, but rather to enhance it through seamless integration.

6. BENEFITS

6.1 Cost Savings / Time Reductions

We are applying a Six-Sigma methodology to determine what our actual realized savings and cost reductions are, although the results from our POC and pilot program were encouraging.

For our POC we reviewed the current steady state processes that would be included with our initial and subsequent releases and the steps involved for each. We then compared the to-be process against that base line to predict the cost savings and time reductions.

During our Pilot program, we used actual Call Volumes, Average Wait Times and Average Handle times from the current steady state and compared those to the time we were seeing post implementation of the case management system.

The POC indicated a cost savings of 25 -30 percent. Based on our current experience with 50 percent of the overall project complete, we are realizing a cost savings of approximately 19 percent. Upon completion of the project we expect to see a cost savings of 30 percent. (Additional details can be provided upon request). Important factors contributing to cost savings are listed below:

- Effort Reduction -- Information required to service a call is presented by a single application, instead of accessing multiple applications.
- Reduction in Training Time -- Training time to enable new joinees reduced from six weeks down to four days.
- Individual Productivity Improvement –
    - Case management solution guides through the next appropriate action, instead of Customer Service Representatives manually processing these activities by referring to process manuals
    - Reduction in re-work and increase in motivation levels

On the development side, we have been able to cut down the development and testing effort significantly (by approx. 50 percent) using the "Wrap and Renew" approach and still deliver comparable benefits to our business partners.

6.2 Increased Revenues

Since our case management solution is a stand-alone component capable of cross platform integration, we can now offer our clients SaaS, and Lift and Shift implementation and service models to open up new channels of revenue streams.

Once again, the 'Wrap and Renew' architecture provides a cost savings as well, by reducing implementation costs and increasing margins.

Our case management and workflow solution presents additional revenue options, both for organization as well as our clients (Insurance Carriers).

This solution increases the revenue potential for our organization due to the following reasons:

- New Service Model -- Using our case management and workflow solution, we are able to offer our services in a SaaS delivery model. In the past nine months, two new client wins has been attributed to this solution.
- Stand-Alone Option – Our case management and workflow solution can be implemented as a "Stand Alone" application and can be readily integrated with the insurance carrier's back end systems.

- Alternative Option to Policy Data Conversion -- Traditionally, the majority of our new client acquisitions involves policy data conversion from clients' platforms to our platform. This is time consuming and also involves risk. With the case management solution, we are able to offer our services in "Wrap and Renew" model, using which our clients will start realizing the benefits very quickly (three-to-six month period).

For our clients, our case management solution presents

- A 360-degree view of the customer, there by efficiently service the customer, resulting in improvement in customer satisfaction levels.
- Additional upselling and cross selling opportunity by offering products that better suit customer needs.

6.3 Quality Improvements

Complexity and touch-points have an inverse relationship to quality. Where our customer agents and analysts previously had to access multiple UIs to answer many of the client inquiries, our case management implementation has streamlined that process so that all policy information is easily accessible and available, regardless of which system the data is currently residing.

This is more evident in a multi-client environment where each client has its own rules and processes. Our solution and workflow walks the processor through each process step by step by using our rules engine in the BMP framework to drive the flow, rather than leaving it up to a subjective decision process and duplication of processes.

7. BEST PRACTICES, LEARNING POINTS AND PITFALLS

7.1 Best Practices and Learning Points

- ✓ Six Sigma exercise conducted before the start of the case management solution development phase helped us in identifying process improvements and refine the operational processes. This helped us in filtering out inefficient operational processes and avoiding them from being replicated on the new system.
- ✓ Agile implementation allowed us to use the 80/20 rule to identify the processes that have the most impact on our customer agents and implement those in a timely manner.
- ✓ Regular play-back sessions with business/end users of the application, so they understand and are aware of the changes. This helped in the users embracing the change in operational processes as a result of implementing the new system.
- ✓ A multi-tenant environment provides a call center agent with the ability to handle multiple clients without having to learn multiple systems, or user interfaces.
- ✓ A unified platform allows us to Engage, Simply, and Change rapidly to meet a clients' market demands.
- ✓ Once built, rules, workflows and scripts can be easily changed to accommodate individual clients without development overhead, allowing us to design once and deploy in many places.
- ✓ Allows Infosys McCamish to provide new servicing options such as SaaS, Lift and Shift, Rebadging and Hybrid models, outside of the standard License, Conversion or BPO models by providing a Wrap and Renew approach.
- ✓ Integrated Workflow and Metrics allows a team manager to make on the fly decisions based on real time analytics to improve operational efficiencies.

7.2 Pitfalls

✗ *The capabilities and visions for our solution offers unprecedented options so it is important to carefully plan the roadmap and development process to develop a solution with fully functional features rather than just features that do not deliver to 100 percent of our expectations.*

✗ *It is important to manage the clients to the projected roadmap.*

✗ *A knowledgeable development and architecture team with skillset and understanding of BPM methodology must be established before we commit to roadmap timelines.*

✗ *Not knowing to the full extent all of the underlying framework's features, initially resulted in unnecessary custom code development while the functionality was already available as out-of-the-box functionality.*

8. COMPETITIVE ADVANTAGES

Our case management and workflow component is a game changer for Infosys McCamish both as a BPO and as a solution provider.

End Customer Experience --

- Provide consistent, streamlined call center and back office administration services to our new and existing clients.
- Complete metrics, real-time drill-down data and graphical reporting and predictive and adaptive analytic capabilities provides our manager and clients with a snap shot of the business at any point in time.

Operational Efficiency

- Improvement in operational efficiency of our customer service and back office operations group, since the case management solution supports these transactions end-to-end, instead of referring to multiple applications to do the same

Alternate Service Models : Using this case management and workflow solution our services can be offered using any of the service models, that best fits the client needs:

- Full or Partial BPO
  - Legacy Conversion
  - Lift & Shift
  - Wrap & Renew
- Licensing
- SaaS

Unified Customer Service Layer

- Can integrate with multiple administration systems to provide a true 360° customer view and multi-channel service
- Leverage the client's in-house expertise, a model in which client's customer service representatives use this case management and workflow solution in a Wrap & Renew model

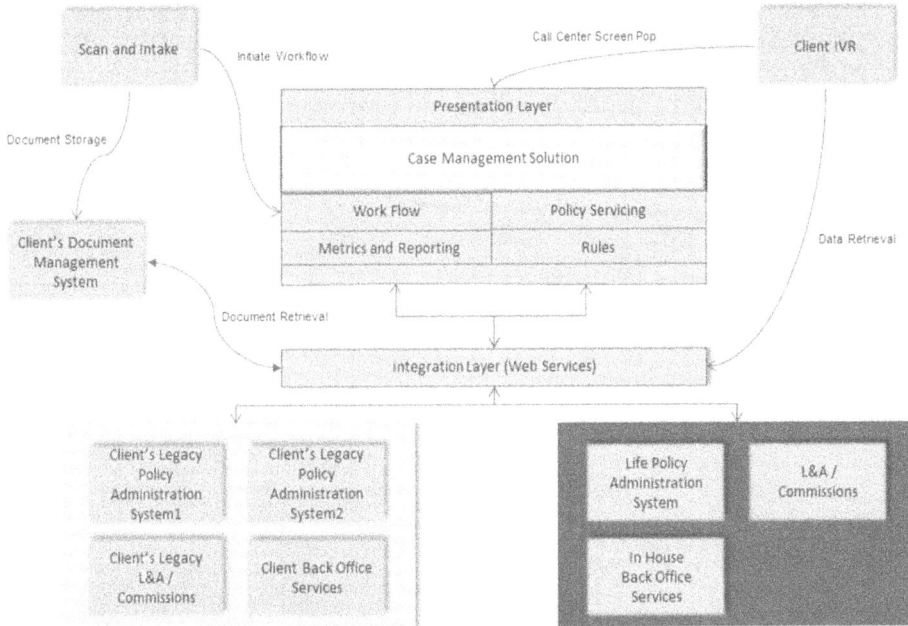

Fig 4 – Solution Implementation View

9. TECHNOLOGY

Layered software architecture

- We architected our solution in a layered way, giving us the ability to encapsulate the most common industry practices and processes in the lowest layer. We built additional layers on top of these framework layers for relatively higher variability requirements such as unique carrier nuances. This layered concept helps us adopt a more agile and iterative cycle of development too.

- The benefits are increased reusability and reduced cost, higher standardization of processes, quicker time to market, higher maintainability

Configuration as opposed to customization

- Unlike other web applications, the degree of configurability is much higher in our architecture, giving rise to less deviation from the standards, lower defects, higher maintainability of the overall solution

Integration services

- The details of dealing with different policy admin systems behind the scenes are encapsulated in a separate service layer. This helps our solution to focus on process automation and not the details of communicating with those systems in their language and protocols.

Self-service capable

- Taking advantage of the HTML 5 compliant user interface as well as security architecture gives us ability to enable self-service of select use cases using the same underlying infrastructure. The technology is also adaptable to delivery of the same services through mobile channel for end customer or customer representatives.

Multi-geo capable

- The technology and architecture used in our case management solution is capable of supporting multiple geographies with minimum configuration change.

10. THE TECHNOLOGY AND SERVICE PROVIDERS

Our case management solution was built on Pegasystems BPM platform - www.pega.com. Training on the platform was provided by Pegasystems and our staff was initially augmented by Pegasystems consultants, who were phased out as our development team developed the skill set's necessary to become self-sufficient.

JuriShare - Contract Generation System

Nominated by Camargo Correa Engineering and Construction, Brazil

1. EXECUTIVE SUMMARY / ABSTRACT

The Contract Generation System, named JuriShare, designed for contracts, was developed on a Sharepoint platform and consists in creating documents based on templates that are part of a workflow solution. This solution automates the analysis processes and establishes a workflow for internal approvals, enabling lawyers to focus on the document's legal aspect.

The system is designed for contracts with suppliers and with the Company's public or private Clients. The Company refers to the first type of documents as "non-strategic" and the second type as "strategic". For both types of documents, a distinguished workflow was established by the legal department of the Company through which the users may either generate a contract using the system or it may use the system to store the document and to control its status.

The system had a significant impact which resulted in cost and time savings, work transparency and quality, as well as monitoring management of documents. Additionally, it enabled control of potential risks, centralized access to documents and decentralized its usability, since some users are remotely established. Overall, the tool stimulates a collaborative and integrated environment among all areas, including the many construction sites which are located throughout Brazil, Headquarters and back office. It also allows all the lawyers spread throughout Brazil and in other Latin American countries to have access to all of the documents included in the system, being an integrative tool which allows the Company to have a better management of all of its contracts.

Operating for five months now, the system has generated almost 706 non-strategic documents, 450 of which were created automatically. Also, the system has 268 strategic documents stored. Prior to JuriShare, the analysis of documents would take seven work days.

Lawyers operate the system when they are notified, as established in the workflow rules, and also by other collaborators who insert new assignments which start the workflow. These collaborators can be located in the administrative, commercial or supply areas in the over 30 construction sites of the Company or in the Headquarter. Directors and Vice-Presidents are also involved in the process, as they are responsible for approving documents when greater risks are identified by lawyers. In sum, this system has a significant impact in all areas of the Company, at the same time that each area is a contributor in operating the tool.

2. OVERVIEW

JuriShare is a system developed on SharePoint platform with the purpose to generate, track and organize strategic and non-strategic contracts issued by the Company, in the over 30 construction sites spread throughout Brazil and in other countries where the Company has construction and engineering projects, such as Venezuela, Peru, and Angola.

The system is composed of fourteen (14) pre-approved non-strategic contract templates which shall be filled in by the Company's internal client (hereinafter referred to as "user") and JuriShare will generate the contract accordingly to the workflow established by the Company's legal department. The analysis behind the establishment of such workflow will be explained in item 3 – Business Context, below.

Each pre-approved contract is composed of two complementary, but distinct documents named "General Conditions" and "Specific Conditions". The first document is composed of generic, conceptual and legal conditions, such as, obligations and responsibilities of the parties and the second document is composed of the singular, technical and commercial conditions, e.g., qualification of the parties, work scope and term of the contract.

The legal department established that the General Conditions of the contract are immutable and that any alteration to the legal terms shall be made in the Specific Conditions.

In order to generate a non-strategic contract, the user shall access JuriShare and choose one (1) of the fourteen (14) contract templates available in the system. It will have access to the Specific Conditions of the contract and shall fill in the template including all the commercial terms. At the meantime, the user shall send the supplier the General Conditions of the contract and if the supplier does not accept any of the legal terms, the user shall include such observation in the system. Such observation will alter the workflow of the contract and the contract will not be automatically generated by the system, being necessary the analysis of a lawyer. However, if the supplier accepts the General Conditions of the Company, the system will generate the contract in Portable Document Format (pdf) and the document will be in its execution version.

As for the strategic contracts, the workflow may be initiated by a user or by the lawyer. Either party shall include the strategic document in JuriShare. The lawyer responsible for that project will be notified that a contract is available for its analysis. The analysis shall be made in the system, which will store and track all the alterations made to the document, permitting any user or lawyer of the Company to have access to the document and also its status.

This system ensures the preservation of information, allows the user and lawyers to accompany the status of the contract (either if it is in analysis with a lawyer, in analysis with the supplier, approved by the parties or in process of signature), and permits the Company to have a tool integrating all the contracts entered by the Company with suppliers.

The final execution version of the contract is also available for consultation and the signed version must be filed in the system's library.

What may seem as a simple automation system is actually a well-structured intelligence which allows the lawyers to focus on strategic legal items of the contract and not on standard clauses that are well-known and accepted in the market. Additionally, the lawyers may concentrate their knowledge on contracts which the Company classifies as of greater risk, accordingly to the workflow described in item 3 – Business Context, below.

In the event of identification of a risk, the lawyer will evaluate if it is the case of altering the General Conditions included in the system in order to mitigate any losses and damages which may be incurred or suffered by the Company. If it is the case of altering the General Conditions, the lawyer will draft the alteration necessary and circulate to all the areas involved in the negotiations and responsible for that contract and verify if such areas have any suggestions or inputs for such document. If the General Conditions are approved by all areas, the document is uploaded to the system and any contract that is generated from that day on will be updated and will contain the provision necessary to mitigate the verified risk.

A clear example of this is that on August 1st, 2013, the President of the Federative Republic of Brazil approved an Anti-corruption Law (Law no. 12.846/2013) which addresses the liability of legal entities in administrative and civil spheres for the practice of tortious acts, especially those practiced in relation with a public official at the international, national or local level.

The Company verified the necessity to include a clause in all of its contracts considering such matter. The legal department drafted a clause, sent to the approval of the areas involved in this matter and included in the General Conditions of all of the fourteen (14) pre-approved templates. Such clause is present in all the contracts generated from the date of its insertion and then, immediately available for all the Company, including the construction sites.

3. Business Context

The project was created after observing that the Company's legal department was emitting a large quantity of non-strategic contracts of the same type and that these contracts, in general, followed the same legal premises. The Company also noticed that most of its suppliers accepted its legal terms and that the negotiation was based on commercial terms, such as price and term of the contract.

Also, the legal department observed that the Company did not have a program or tool which centralized all the strategic and non-strategic contracts issued by the Company, being that in many cases the Company's internal clients, located at worksites throughout Brazil, issued a large amount of contracts in which the legal department was not involved and/or did not have any knowledge of its issuance. The legal department would only be aware of such contract when a lawsuit was filed against the Company.

With this observation, the legal department of the Company decided to elaborate drafts of pre-approved non-strategic contracts which were endorsed by all the areas involved in the negotiation and contracting process. This would allow the corporate area to issue the contract without the necessity of any evaluation by the legal department if all of the legal premises (General Conditions) were not altered.

At the same time, the legal department also evaluated the amount of judicial lawsuits filed by suppliers against the Company and verified that most of the lawsuits were filed due to contracts that were not analyzed by the legal department and that did not contain all the premises of the Company and legal certainty. The legal department also verified that more than 60% of the contracts issued with suppliers did not surpass the amount of R$ 2,500,000.00 (two million, five hundred Brazilian *reais*; equivalent to USD 1,000,000.00).

The idea of creating pre-approved non strategic contracts emerged from the facts above mentioned. With this, the legal department created a workflow in which the system's users would be able to fill out a form with the commercial terms of the contract and the system would generate the contract. This would allow the contract to have appropriate wording, encompass all the Company's premises (and when such premise is not accepted by the supplier, the risk is analyzed by lawyers, who try to mitigate them and, if such risk persists, the General Counsel submits the risk to the Director or Vice-President of the Company's approval) and provide greater legal certainty to the Company.

In order to implement this idea, the legal department verified the types of contracts that were most frequently celebrated with the suppliers and determined which documents could or could not be issued automatically by the system, along with the workflow involved, all verified accordingly with the risks involved.

Thus, the legal department created two complementary but distinct documents that meet the legal and commercial needs of the Company, named, (i) "General Conditions" comprising the generic, conceptual and legal conditions, e.g., obligations and responsibilities of the parties; and (ii) "Specific Conditions" that are composed of the singular, technical and commercial conditions, e.g., qualification of the parties, work scope, price and term of contract.

4. THE KEY INNOVATIONS

4.1 Business

With the implementation of JuriShare, the Company verified a positive impact in the management of its strategic and non-strategic contracts, integrating all the documents executed by the Company in a single tool. Also, the legal department observed that some of the non-strategic contracts were issued in one business day, reducing the analysis period in six business days, therefore, granting efficiency in the execution of contracts.

With the standardization of the non-strategic pre-approved contracts, the Company is certain that all of its premises are attended, mitigates the risks involved in the contracting process, has greater legal certainty and assures the quality of the legal department's work.

In addition to the above mentioned, the legal department noted cost and time savings with the implementation of the system, for the lawyers would be able to analyze the contracts in a short period of time and any and all users of JuriShare has access to all of the documents issued by the Company, not being necessary for a worker to obtain and send a copy of the document to the other.

In the past five months, since the system has been fully operating, a considerable amount of documents has been emitted by JuriShare, which demonstrates that the Company has widely accepted the system and that it is a strong tool when contracting suppliers. Altogether four hundred and fifty (450) documents were automatically approved and emitted by the system and two hundred and fifty six (256) documents were approved and emitted after the analysis of the legal department.

Moreover, the amount of strategic contracts issued by the Company from the period of December 2013 to April 2014 are: fifty two (52) consortium contracts, twenty nine (29) contracts with private clients, forty six (46) contracts with public clients, sixty nine (69) Memorandums of Understandings (MOU), and seventy two (72) Non-Disclosure Agreement (NDA).

4.2 Case Handling

Before JuriShare was created, the Company's internal client would send an e-mail to a lawyer requesting the preparation of a contract. The lawyer would have seven (7) business days to analyze the documents supplied by the Company's internal client and would emit a contract on the seventh day.

The commercial and legal terms of the contract were concentrated on a single document, which made it harder to identify the specific conditions of the contract and the standard terms and conditions were placed in different clauses of the contract, therefore, this demanded more time in the lawyer's analysis after its execution.

As mentioned above, the project was created after observing that the Company's legal department was emitting a large quantity of non-strategic contracts of the same type and that these contracts, in general, followed the same legal premises. In addition, the legal department observed that the Company did not have a program or tool which centralized all the strategic and non-strategic contracts issued by the Company.

In views of solving these issues, the legal department conceived the idea of implementing a system which is similar to a form any person needs to fill out when registering in any shopping website. With this idea, the legal department verified the amount of lawsuits filed against the Company, which contracts were the most executed by the Company and decided to elaborate drafts of pre-approved non-strategic contracts. In addition, it expanded its initial idea to become a tool in which all the users would be able to access the documents stored therein.

With the implementation of the system and creation of the General Conditions and Specific Conditions, being that the General Conditions of the contract are immutable and that any alteration to the legal terms shall be made in the Specific Conditions, the Company had a better management of all of its contracts and this simplified the analysis of the contracts for the commercial terms of the contracts were consolidated in a sole document.

Just as described above, the template may be altered at any time according to the evaluation of the legal department and the Company's necessity. If it is the case of altering the General Conditions, the lawyer will draft the alteration necessary and circulate to all the areas involved in the negotiations and responsible for that contract and verify if such areas have any suggestions or inputs for such document. If the General Conditions are approved by all areas, the document is uploaded to the system and any contract that is generated from that day on will be updated and will contain the provision necessary to mitigate the verified risk.

Reproducing the example previously described, on August 1st, 2013, the President of the Federative Republic of Brazil approved an Anti-corruption Law (Law no. 12.846/2013) which addresses the liability of legal entities in administrative and civil spheres for the practice of tortious acts, especially those practiced in relation with a public official at the international, national or local level.

The Company verified the necessity to include a clause in all of its contracts considering such matter. The legal department drafted a clause, sent to the approval of the areas involved in this matter and included in the General Conditions of all of the fourteen (14) pre-approved templates. Such clause is present in all the contracts generated from the date of its insertion and then, immediately available for all the Company, including the construction sites.

4.3 Organization & Social

The system had a significant impact which resulted in cost and time savings, work transparency and quality, as well as monitoring management of documents. Additionally, it enabled control of potential risks, centralized access to documents and decentralized its usability, since some users are remotely established. Overall, the tool stimulates a collaborative and integrated environment among all areas.

With the standardization of the non-strategic pre-approved contracts, the Company is certain that all of its premises are attended, mitigates the risks involved in the contracting process, has greater legal certainty and assures the quality of the legal department's work.

With the standardization of the pre-approved contracts, the Company is certain that all of its premises are attended, has greater legal certainty and assures the quality of the legal department's work. It is also certain that the contract will be celebrated before the execution of the scope of the contract.

5. HURDLES OVERCOME

The system was implemented after the legal department also evaluated the amount of judicial lawsuits filed by suppliers against the Company and verified that most of the lawsuits were filed due to contracts that were not analyzed by the legal department and that did not contain all the premises of the Company and legal certainty.

The legal department also verified that more than 60% of the contracts issued with suppliers did not surpass the amount of R$ 2,500,000.00 (two million, five hundred Brazilian *reais*; equivalent to USD 1,000,000.00) and that 70% of the contracts issued at the worksites were not analyzed by the legal department and did not contain all the legal premises.

With this observation, the legal department of the Company decided to elaborate drafts of pre-approved non-strategic contracts which were endorsed by all the areas involved in the negotiation and contracting process.

The main challenges observed by the Company was the interaction with all of the areas involved in the process of contracting a supplier, fulfilling all the needs of these areas and develop a single tool which would allow the Company to emit contracts with legal certainty and facilitating such process for the Company.

Since the establishment of JuriShare, all the contracts are issued in accordance with the corporate rules and following the legal premises of the Company, being that 70% of these documents are issued automatically.

6. BENEFITS

6.1 Cost Savings / Time Reductions

The Company also verified cost and time savings with the implementation of the system, considering that the lawyers were able to quickly identify the alterations made in the General Conditions by analyzing the Specific Conditions (as previously mentioned, the General Conditions are immutable and any alteration to the legal terms shall be made in the Specific Conditions). Also, the Company verified that since the creation of the system, the amount of lawsuits filed against the Company has decreased, therefore reducing costs with lawsuits and external contracting.

Notwithstanding the abovementioned, the Company also reduced costs with lawyers who analyzed the non-strategic contracts, considering that the quantity of contracts that should be analyzed by the lawyers reduced considerably.

6.2 Increased Revenues

In 2013, the Company observed that it saved R$ 80,000.00 (eighty thousand *reais*; equivalent to USD 32,000.00 – thirty two thousand dollars) per year since the implementation of JuriShare. This was due to the fact that the amount of contracts sent to analysis of the lawyers were reduced, considering that if the General Conditions of the contract were not altered, the contract can be generated without the analysis of the lawyer. Also, the system saved time of all of the other employees involved in the process.

Furthermore, considering that the system was develop in-house and that it can be access directly from the Company's intranet, there is no additional cost or charge for its use.

Finally, it is important to be considered that 70% of the contracts issued at the worksites were not analyzed by the legal department. So, the Company should hire many lawyers if all of those documents would be analyzed by the legal department. Since JuriShare was implemented it was possible to reach all of the legal documents issued by the Company without any other lawyer hired.

6.3 Quality Improvements

With the creation of the pre-approved contracts and JuriShare, the legal department met the legal and commercial needs, for some of the contracts could be generated without the necessity of analysis of the lawyer, if the General Conditions of the contract were not altered, since all the premises of the Company were met.

With the standardization of the pre-approved contracts, the Company is certain that all of its premises are attended, has greater legal certainty and assures the quality of the legal department's work.

- Lastly, the system allows the Company to standardize the contracts issued and that any improvement made to the document will be easily and rapidly incorporated to all of the contracts generated by the system.

7. BEST PRACTICES, LEARNING POINTS AND PITFALLS

7.1 Best Practices and Learning Points

✓ Approval: the schedule shall include a period of dedication of the team that will use the system in order that the workflow is reviewed in a detailed manner in order to avoid bugs on go live and operation.

✓ Establish a test schedule in order to guarantee that all of the functions of the system are operating according to its objective, which shall be attended by all the areas involved in the contract elaboration process, ensuring the stability of the system before go live.

7.2 Pitfalls

✗ Detailed Specification of the System: the people involved in the creation of the system shall dedicate time to analyze the document specifying the Project in order to avoid different interpretations of the system vs. developer of the system.

✗ Interview stakeholders: when detailing the system, all of the areas involved in the workflow process shall send their inputs. This will allow the system to meet the expectations and needs of all the areas of the Company.

✗ Hotline: it is crucial to create a hotline, before go live, that allows employees of the Company to inform the problems that they are having with the system and also allow them to submit their questions regarding the system.

✗ Support: include in the budget costs with developer's support during the stabilization period of the system in order to ensure immediate correction of any bugs or implement small adjustments identified in the go live.

✗ Communication Program: include in the project a budget to contract a company that will give publicity to the system in the Company.

8. COMPETITIVE ADVANTAGES

The system ensures that the contracting process will be more efficient and secure for the Company and the supplier since its elaboration to the effective execution of the subject matter of the contract, thus benefitting the competitive advantage of the Company in the market.

9. Technology

The technology chosen for the development of JuriShare was the Microsoft program "SharePoint Server 2010". The workflow customization was developed using the following technologies:

- Operating System: Windows
- Platform: Net.
- Devices: Web
- Technology: SharePoint 2013 Standard
- Services: No WCF
- Language: ASP.NET and C #
- Framework: 4.0
- Database: MS SQL SERVER 2008 R2

10. The Technology and Service Providers

The consultants and suppliers involved in the elaboration of JuriShare are:

- Mind Services - http://www.mindservices.com.br/
- Microsoft - http://www.microsoft.com/pt-br/default.aspx

The National Police Immigration Service, Norway

Nominated by Computas AS, Norway

1. Executive Summary / Abstract

An asylum seeker's first encounter with Norwegian authorities is through the National Police Immigration Service (NPIS). The NPIS collects information about each immigration case, prior to application handling by the Norwegian immigration authorities. A large percentage of asylum seekers have no passport or valid ID, and many provide inaccurate information, adding to the complexity of identity determination and case investigation tasks.

UTSYS is the NPIS' ACM solution. Used by all operational personnel, UTSYS supports registration, identity analysis, interviews and forcible return, as well as managing Norway's asylum seeker detention center. UTSYS helps NPIS monitor every pending asylum case, continually updating and completing case information. Case managers are responsible for a portfolio of cases that they own throughout the case lifecycle. Using case context, UTSYS offers the case manager suitable functionality for resolving the case effectively.

Case managers collaborate extensively with regional police authorities, identity analysts, legal experts, as well as experts on the state of affairs in receiving countries. A rejected asylum application triggers a process that may take any number of directions, all with the ultimate aim of returning the unsuccessful applicant to the country that will rightly accept the return. Return cases are highly unpredictable, with constantly changing circumstances both locally and in receiving countries, depending on a wealth of information from national and international authorities and agencies.

In 2013, UTSYS helped the NPIS achieve a 64% increase in the proper and efficient return of persons without legal residence in Norway.

2. Overview

In Norway, asylum applicants are handled by two authorities, the NPIS and the Norwegian Directorate of Immigration (UDI). The UDI has the overall responsibility for coordinating the immigration service whereas the NPIS has the executive power of the police.

The UDI processes applications for asylum, visas, family immigration, work and study permits, citizenship, permanent residence permits and travel documents, and make the decisions in asylum cases. In addition, the UDI is responsible for ensuring that all asylum seekers are offered accommodation while they await a decision, and for finding good solutions for those who voluntarily return to their home countries.

The NPIS is responsible for the initial registration of asylum seekers, identity verification work, and eventual enforcement of rejected asylum cases. This includes coordination, execution and quality assurance of the transportation out of the country. The process may take anything from weeks to several years to carry through. Furthermore, the NPIS is responsible for operating the national immigration detention center.

The two authorities cooperate closely in providing input information for the applications and executing arrests, detention and deportation when required. The decisions are made by the UDI, and the NPIS implements. This includes handling of illegal immigrants and cases where the rejected asylum seeker chooses not to act in accordance with the decision.

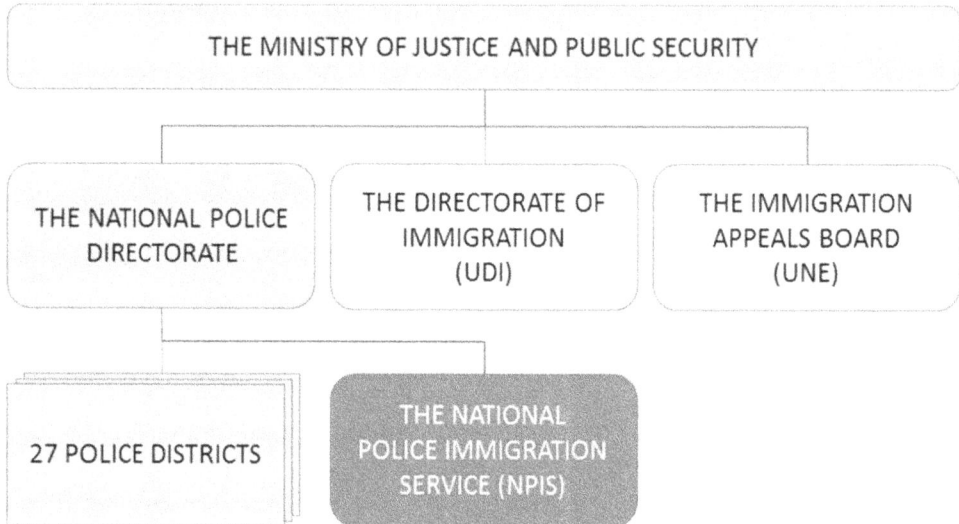

Figure 1: The national police immigration service in the immigration administration

3. BUSINESS CONTEXT

The NPIS is in charge of forcible returns from Norway, cooperating with local Norwegian police forces to return persons without legal residence. Subjects are returned to their home countries or other European countries where they have previously applied for protection – so-called Dublin return cases – or get a permanent residency. Norway's capacity for asylum is limited, so the purpose of rejection is ensuring that asylum is granted only to those in genuine need of protection. Prompt deportation of failed applicants with criminal records has first priority, this group constituting 38% of the approximately 6000 subjects returned in 2013.

Although an end-to-end process with deviations can be described for the overall application process, the situation looks more chaotic from the proceedings of the particular case. An identification status of a subject, that was considered sufficient at one point in time, may later be regarded as incomplete or wrong due to events producing new information. Many subjects actively try to disguise their real identity by supplying false information through forged documents, or hiding information by sandpapering fingers and removing labels from clothes. A disappeared person may turn up again in unexpected situations. Changed circumstances in the subject's native country may completely alter the course of events. The knowledge and expertise of NPIS staff is a vital resource in performing the necessary investigations.

A case in UTSYS represents an asylum application. The NPIS initially registers and prepares the asylum case for UDI. The legal processing, preparation and decisions regarding the asylum application is handled outside UTSYS. If the application is rejected and the subject does not voluntarily return, the NPIS carries out deportation. This work consists in verifying that the subject is returnable to the country in question, providing sufficient documentation to satisfy domestic authorities regarding the subject's identity, and ensuring the receiving country's willingness to assume responsibility for the subject. It also involves planning the transportation, possibly with police escort, locate and detain the subject, see him off on a plane, and, if necessary, escort him to his destination.

Each case is assigned to a case manager, as part of his case portfolio. At all times, a case has one of the following states:

- Pending: Awaiting a final decision from UDI or UNE (the immigration appeals board) whether asylum is granted or not.

- ID verification: The subject's asylum application is finally rejected, and necessary work to document his ID has started.

- Effectuation: Planning and implementing the deportation.

- Finalization: Preparing closing of the case after the subject's deportation, residence permit or death.

- Closed: The case is closed in UTSYS and can no longer be changed. Future events regarding the same subject may lead to the creation of a new case.

The case manager manually changes the case state to support coordination across cases.

4. THE KEY INNOVATIONS

UTSYS was conceived to serve the dual purposes of visualizing overall progress and simultaneously orchestrating and supporting the tasks to be performed by the different roles involved. Eventually, UTSYS has also proved to be an enabler of organizational adaptions.

4.1 Business

Event-driven and goal-seeking case handling using UTSYS blackboards

In movies, we often see criminal investigators organizing their work around a physical blackboard with notes, photos, maps etc. Its purpose is to create a shared view of a complex and changing state of affairs.

UTSYS supports police work, and the system can be seen as using blackboards for supporting parallel lines of work. Instead of letting these different lines of work exchange information bilaterally or on request, case workers post all information, results and plans to the shared blackboard, ensuring real-time multilateral coordination. An UTSYS blackboard exists from the arrival to the deportation of a subject.

The process required to return an illegal alien successfully is goal-seeking. The overall goal is to get the subject transported out of the country. To achieve this goal, there are several subgoals:

- Establish the identity of the subject

- Produce the necessary travel documents (passport, laissez-passer) required by transit state authorities and the receiving country

- Make sure the receiving country will accept the subject

- Make sure that the whereabouts of the deportee can be controlled prior to departure

- Produce a traveling plan

- Effectuate the physical travel

As the work proceeds, these subgoals are influenced by multiple events that may result in goals becoming satisfied or no longer met. Failing a subgoal may cause change of case state and necessitate more work to re-establish the subgoal. Receiving countries may change their policies and need for travel documents, it may be impossible to effectuate a planned travel, causing the creation of a new traveling plan.

UTSYS is non-monotonic in the sense that an achieved subgoal may get undone by new events. To satisfy the ultimate deportation goal, all subgoals must be satisfied simultaneously. UTSYS work is event- and time critical. By failing to act when a time window opens, progress may turn into relapse. Prompt action after a subgoal is reached or before a deadline expires is therefore of utmost importance, and a key feature of UTSYS is to support the knowledge worker's overview and basis for swift action.

Figure 2 shows a simplified case scenario, and how the blackboard concept provides shared overview.

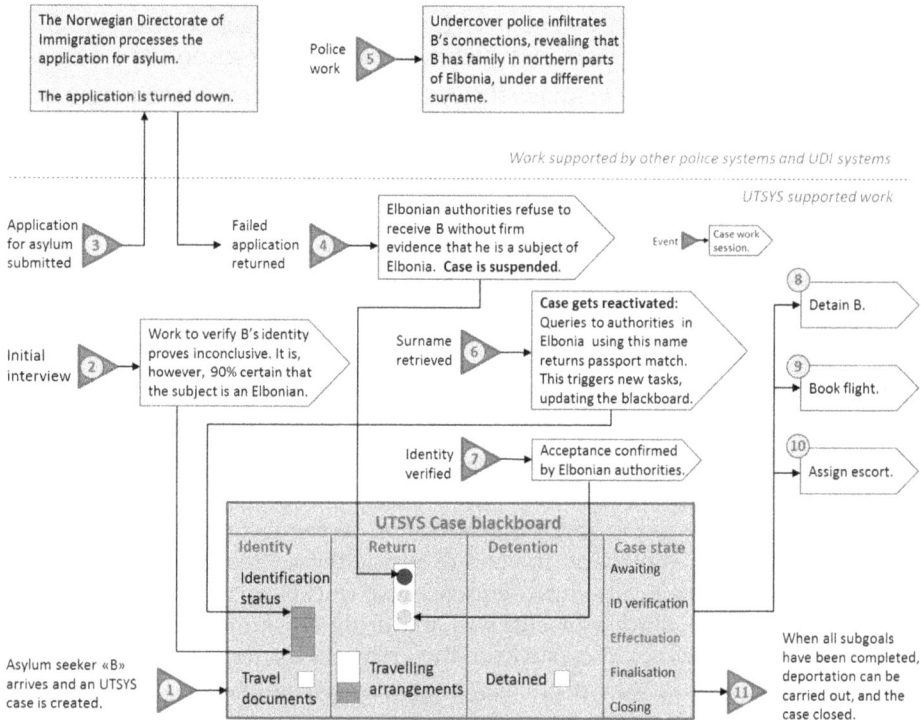

Figure 2: Event- and goal-driven case handling using UTSYS blackboards

Each line of work – identity, return and detention – has its own blackboard area. Identity work may take place from the registration and preparation of the case until the deportation is completed. The need for detention may arise independently. The transport planning may be interrupted due to new results from the identification work, to a change in the receiving country, or to the disappearance of the subject.

Case portfolio and deadline management

Case portfolios are collections of cases under a particular responsibility. Each case manager has his personal portfolio to keep track of the work of all the cases he is responsible for. Personal case portfolios can be aggregated at a department level or across all NPIS cases.

Figure 3 shows the top NPIS portfolio with its overview of important deadlines, case state versus criminal record overview, and drill-down area. The portfolio is zoomed to *Effectuation* of subjects with *Criminal records* with its corresponding list of cases, of which one is further inspected in a popup window with a summary presentation of the case.

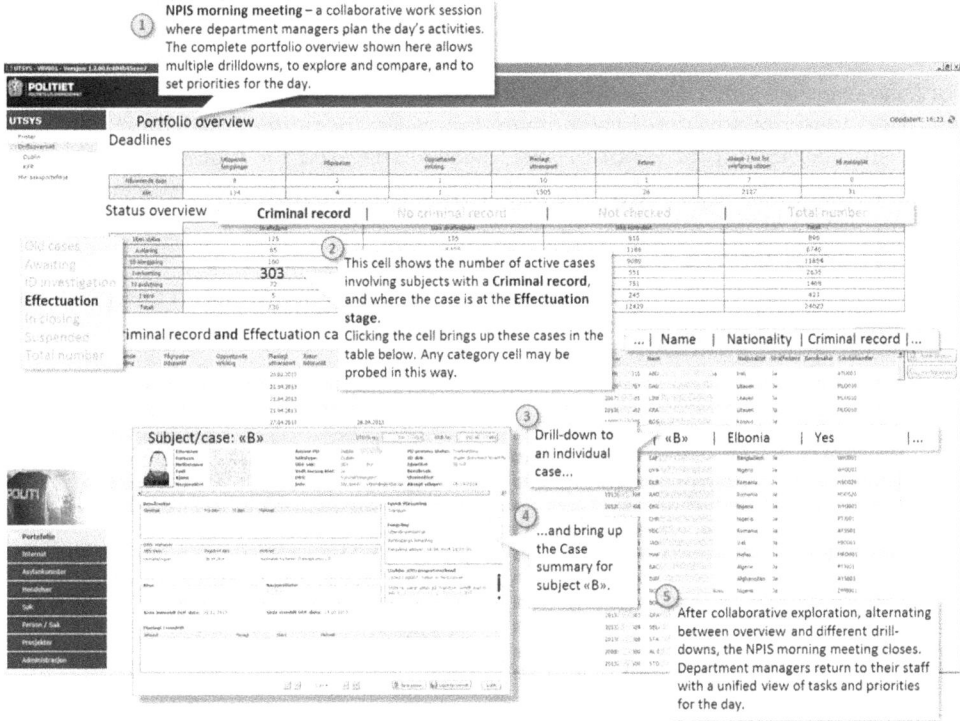

Figure 3: Scenario showing how the aggregated portfolio is used to support collaborative work at management level.

Case portfolio overviews are frequently used in regular morning meetings for prioritization of cases and planning the day's work. Typically, in a morning meeting, managers will inspect the important deadlines, such as detentions that expire or expiry date for returns to a country of first entry, and decide on the necessary means to handle these.

The meeting will also go through the most important cells in the case state overview, inspecting the list and zooming in on particular cases when in need of more information.

A case is suspended when actual deportation turns out to be impossible for some reason. A case remains in suspension until all reasons for suspension have been eliminated. Work regarding the forced return is put on hold, while identity and detention work proceeds reflecting external events. A suspended case keeps its original case state, but is on a side-track for one of various possible standard reasons:

- It is temporarily not possible to deport the subject to his homeland or a country where he has a residence permit.
- Due to health conditions, the subject cannot be transported, even with the assistance of a healthcare professional.
- The case is given postponement by the Immigration Appeals Board.
- An application regarding voluntary return is being processed.

- There is a dependency to a non-asylum UDI case, for instance a family re-union case.

- The subject is involved in an unsettled criminal case and the prosecution lawyer has decided that deportation shall be suspended.

- In addition, the case worker may also specify other reasons why the subject currently cannot be deported. These are documented by logging an event in UTSYS.

Portfolio overviews provide access to the suspended cases. Drilling down to these may lead to actions to get these suspended cases "back on track". Portfolio over-views are also useful for event-driven reviews, triggered for instance by changed homeland conditions, making it feasible to return larger groups of subjects to that homeland with less effort.

4.2 Case Handling

Planning and execution of UTSYS work relies on four main tools: case portfolios, designated overviews, individual case blackboards with worklists, and campaigns.

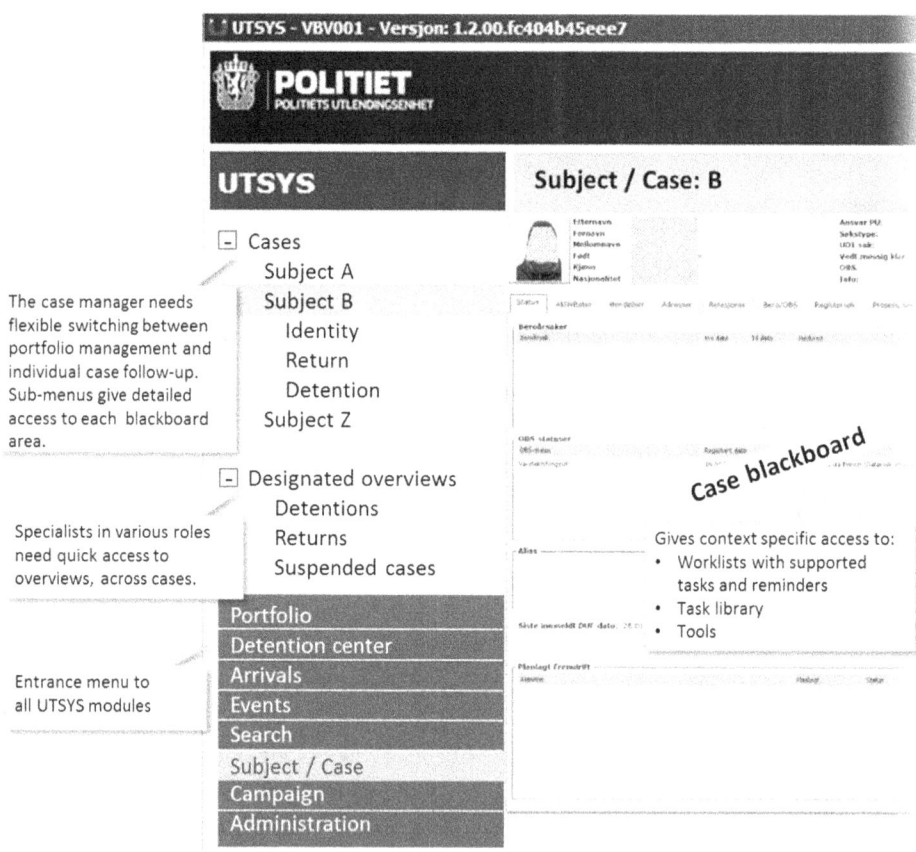

Figure 4: UTSYS access structure, showing case-specific and designated overviews.

Designated overviews

The designated overviews present all cases across portfolios, albeit restricted to the needs of a particular line of work. These are customized for discipline specialists wanting to supervise all cases relevant for their discipline, and possibly take action regarding their area of expertise. Detentions and Dublin returns are examples of lines of work in which experts such as prosecution lawyers or experts on the Dublin agreement need overview and deadline monitoring.

Blackboards to organize and support case overview and lines of work

In contrast to many case management systems, there are no personal worklists in UTSYS. UTSYS worklists are either shared for a particular function (registration, detention center management) or they belong to a case blackboard. Collaboration is essential in all UTSYS work, therefore the blackboard approach is favored over personal worklists.

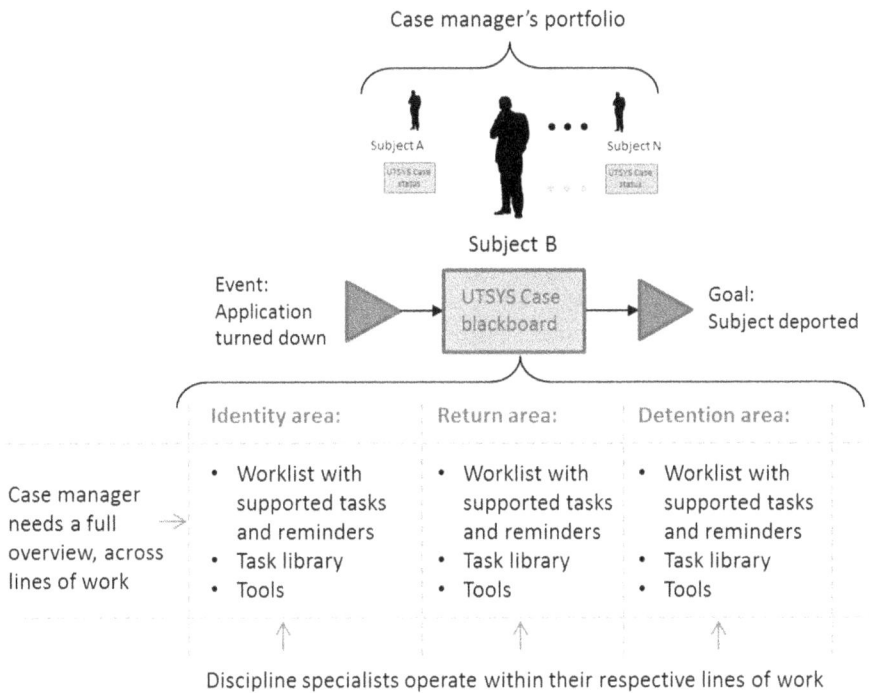

Figure 5: One blackboard per case, with dedicated areas for the different lines of work

Every case is organized into lines of work, each represented as an area of the blackboard. This contains shared information and a dedicated worklist providing overview of tasks that are in progress or planned. Each blackboard area addresses one or more of the subgoals.

The information in the Identity area is maintained and will serve as part of possible future cases regarding the same subject. The information in the Return and Detention areas may be wiped out when that line of work is restarted, e.g. a person may manage to travel straight back to Norway after a deportation, thus needing another transport in the same asylum case. The blackboard area for transport planning or detention represents only the current transport or detention.

Worklists and work support in UTSYS beyond the case level

UTSYS provides active task support similar to other documented case management solutions based on the same ACM framework. Task libraries enable the user to instantiate tasks with active task support. In UTSYS, such task libraries have been defined for each of the case blackboard areas. There are also functional task libraries for registration handling and for operating and managing the detention center. Similarly, there are worklists for registering asylum applicants and for managing and operating the detention center. These worklists provide a shared overview of ongoing tasks.

Planned work / Reminders / Coordination

All UTSYS tasks have a title, a responsible and a deadline, and come in two varieties. Structured tasks are predefined, with a formal task definition with a corresponding runtime task instance providing the user active task support. Unstructured tasks are used as reminders and for note keeping; they are flexible and open-ended with no active task support.

For structured tasks, the lines of work are associated with task libraries collecting useful recurring tasks. In addition to the active task support, these task definitions are used to ensure the correct performance of tasks, in accordance with immigration legislation and NPIS policies. Both unstructured and structured tasks are part of worklists, case blackboard or other.

In UTSYS, the individual case manager may build his own library of unstructured tasks, making it is easy for him to use the same type of reminder for recurring purposes. This also enables use of such unstructured reminder tasks for reporting purposes. Growing reminder libraries provide user-driven inspiration for future development of UTSYS. Some of these reminders may easily be enhanced with active task support in the future, making them to be fully fledged structured tasks with execution support.

For individual cases, the case blackboard with shared information and tasks are adaptivity-enhancing features. Not only is the information result of the work that has been performed available, but the reminders can be used for articulating further work and communicating fragments of plans among co-workers.

4.3 Organization & Social

Enabling a more adaptive NPIS organization

Since 2012, the NPIS has grown from 400 to 600 employees. UTSYS was launched in October 2012, and the system has been developed incrementally in parallel with the organizational development of NPIS. With its previous organization into country-specific departments, it became increasingly hard to utilize these resources effectively, as the growing influx of asylum seekers has tended to come in waves from specific countries or regions. UTSYS has provided the means for opening up the organization, letting specialists contribute across department borders, and enabling flexible mating of cases, tasks and available resources. Due to this, UTSYS has become a cornerstone in the continual adaptation of the NPIS organization to changing demands.

UTSYS portfolio management has made the NPIS less dependent on a fixed department structure. Lines of work across departments increase organizational flexibility, enabling co-operative work and contributing to more uniform practices. Working together across departments provides a wider frame of reference and provides staff with new opportunities for learning.

Campaigns

A *campaign* is a collection of cases, grouped by a team manager or case manager. Campaigns enable coordinated work on collections of cases in a brief time window, followed up as a whole. A campaign has its own blackboard with overviews, tools and a worklist of reminders.

The campaign concept is an example of how UTSYS boosts the effectiveness and productivity of the NPIS as a whole. Sometimes, an event can change the circumstances for a larger set of cases. In such situations, there is much to be gained by handling several cases collectively, as one group. The salient event may be a political decision by Norwegian authorities or a change of circumstances in a receiving country.

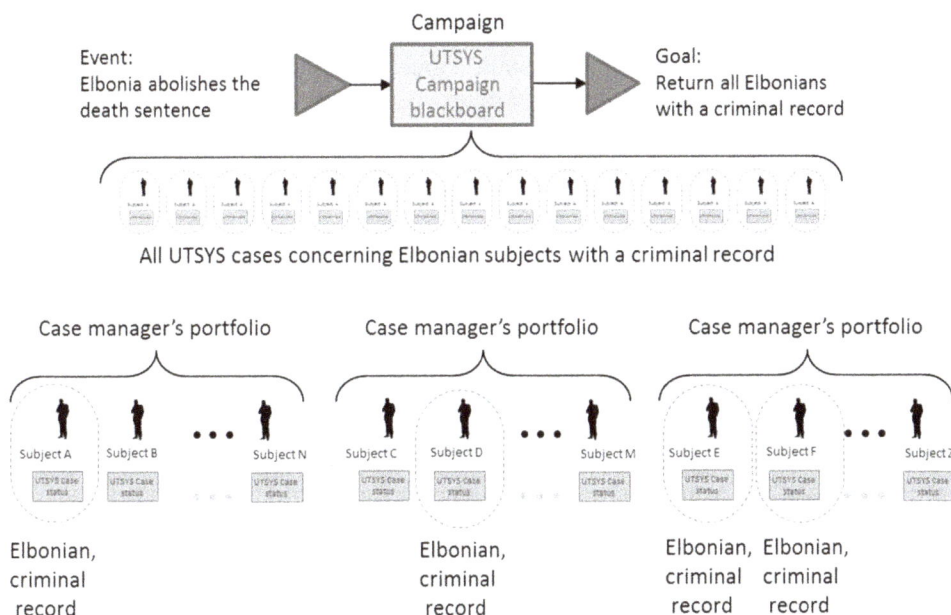

Figure 6: Organizing a campaign for mass return of criminal Elbonians

The campaign mechanism is used for working with sets of cases independently of pre-defined case characteristics. Figure 6 shows a campaign handling several cases involving the same home country, established due to changed domestic conditions. Other examples include handling of cases that may utilize shared transport planning, with chartered airplanes going to a transit stop or final destination, or even ad hoc campaigns for the individual case manager.

The possibility to create campaigns and build task libraries with reminder names provides a flexible mechanism for coordinating, planning and executing work.

UTSYS administration module supports organizational flexibility

Mass transfer of cases between case managers and responsible departments helps accommodate organizational changes. Referring to the example in Figure 6, a new department may assume responsibility for deportations to Elbonia. Or a case manager may quit. In both situations, relevant blackboards and responsibilities are transferred in one operation.

Reference data are maintained in the administration module as codes and code relations. Organizational structure, case event types, detention warrants, ID status, case state and suspension reasons are editable reference data, making the system resilient to business- and organizational changes.

5. HURDLES OVERCOME

Management

Manage the case volume fluctuations

Changes in country situations may lead to a sudden increase or decrease in the number of asylum applicants. A new political or legislative situation may open the possibility of safely returning subjects to a given country. The NPIS must then be able to change priorities and reallocate resources swiftly. The need for a more flexible and adaptive organization was identified and taken into account early in the UTSYS project, and the resulting system concept helps NPIS meet these fluctuations. When the need arises for more effort in one area, the case managers and discipline experts may easily change which cases they address. The NPIS experts on national and regional matters continue to work in a specialist role, but the case manager can now confidently operate across national lines, working within a unified system in a uniform way.

Participatory design

In order to meet the fundamental needs of NPIS, the project depended on close participation and contributions by NPIS top management and seniors. Some functional decisions were made before the development project started, and for the first release the project profited from the use of a core team with very experienced case managers authorized to make rapid decisions. For the more recent development, NPIS have allocated experienced and authorized case managers to provide expertise for new parts of the system, contributing to new functionality.

Business

Effective resource utilization in a rapidly changing business environment

Previously, NPIS department structure was considered to restrict the effective use of its resources. UTSYS has helped move the case as such to the center of the stage, across departments. Cases are now handled similarly and the information is maintained in the same way throughout the organization. UTSYS provides the basis for the generalist case worker to handle a wider range of case types, in a uniform manner, assigning specialist work to available experts.

Re-prioritization due to changing political signals

Changing political signals often entail that the NPIS must change its priorities. The administration module for defining codes enables the NPIS to create new tags with which to flag cases to provide overviews along new lines. This makes it possible to adjust the portfolio overviews in accordance with the new political picture. The campaign mechanism makes it easy to launch directed efforts on a short term basis.

Organization Adoption

Establish uniform work practices

More collaboration and extensive use of common overviews leads to more uniform practice, as well as more confident staff. The blackboards provide a common way of viewing the cases, and working through common overviews ensures uniform registration of data. Each case manager can work on cases and prioritize through his own portfolio overview.

Empowered users continually challenge established practices

Having one common system stimulates the attention to common routines and procedures. A flexible system must strike the right balance between structure and freedom. Empowered UTSYS users are encouraged to look for possible improvement to existing routines and to suggest new procedures. Working bottom-up with the case workers to describe procedures and work support is paramount to keeping the system customized for the actual needs, and creates user enthusiasm.

Focus on cases and professional work, not on the UTSYS system as such

With UTSYS, the user experience is that the system is sufficiently intuitive to be transparent. The users relate to cases, portfolios, blackboards and designated overviews, directly articulating their work. NPIS training concerns domain issues and the different lines of work, not how to operate the UTSYS system as such.

6. BENEFITS

6.1 Cost Savings / Time Reductions

Providing overview – meeting deadlines and avoiding extra work

Prior to UTSYS, the investigation work relied on standalone databases and spreadsheets to handle day-to-day overview and follow-up. Case details were scattered through several systems and police logs, making it hard to grasp the overall situation for a case at any given point of time. The case manager had to manually construct his understanding of the situation. This was cumbersome, with an added risk of missing overview and deadlines and hence leading to extra work and costs.

Today, the UTSYS blackboard concept creates a shared status overview of each case and makes it easier to follow up deadlines and priorities for the workday, with a transparent planned progress and reminders and due dates linked to case tasks in worklists. The blackboard provides a single access point for all personal information about a subject. Some of this information is fetched from UDI systems, but all information is available through UTSYS.

In addition to the single case overview, the use of portfolios provides aggregated overviews across cases. Portfolios combined with tagging of cases makes it easier to see the overall picture and set the priorities accordingly. Working with similar cases in a portfolio saves time and increases quality.

UTSYS has vastly improved data registration processes both regarding arrival and detention registration. Arrival registration allows for mass registration of groups with off-beamed individual registration following the same process. Detention registration used to take 20 minutes, with UTSYS it is down to 4 minutes.

Improved collaboration across department borders

With shared case blackboards, communication between officers at the detention center and the UTSYS case workers is improved and less dependent on phone, fax and email. NPIS employees all work on the same cases, supported by the same system, getting an overview of case state and ongoing work. A shared worklist highlights planned, ongoing and finished tasks at the detention center, with due dates and reminders. Detention center staff no longer need to check out several sources to establish their daily working plan.

For sharing experiences related to deportations, UTSYS integrates a country database collecting updated information about receiving countries, with references to domestic conditions and acceptance criteria. The country database also includes operational information for escorting officers, such as vaccines, visa and safety conditions.

Shorter stay in asylum centers

Primarily due to faster and better identification work, the NPIS has made a big contribution towards achieving the goal of reducing asylum seekers' length of stay in asylum centers. Accumulated over thousands of cases, this amounts to significant savings in the Norwegian immigration sector.

Increase in handled deportations

Assisted by UTSYS, the NPIS has significantly overachieved the goal of a 5 percent increase in deportations. 2013 saw a total of 5934 forced returns, an increase of 64 percent. 2224 of these deportees had criminal records. This increase continues to rise, so far by another 37 percent in the first quarter of 2014.

NPIS performance is being monitored by politicians and the press, and monthly statistics are published at their website www.politiet.no/pu.

6.2 Increased Revenues

The NPIS does not have revenue generation as a goal, but the organization has grown considerably over the last few years, due to the steadily increasing numbers of asylum seekers. UTSYS provides the NPIS with the means to handle this increasing workload in a developing organization. Employees challenge existing ways or working as part of the ongoing organizational development, and their contributions are inspirations for future functionality in UTSYS.

6.3 Quality Improvements

Improved data quality

With UTSYS the data quality in deportation cases has increased significantly. Instead of registering the same fact several times, in several systems, case information is handled by one system where it is easier to retrieve, and where different users collaborate on the same data. Increasingly uniform practices in describing the cases has also made a positive contribution, and data quality is expected to continue to improve.

Preventing misuse

Asylum is intended for those in genuine need. The NPIS shall ensure that asylum is not misused by subjects who have no right to stay, or who are trying to obtain residence based on false identity information. UTSYS contributes to crime prevention and to identify crime related to immigration, such as human trafficking, smuggling, war crimes and terrorism.

It is an important political signal that criminals without legal residence in Norway are prioritized and deported quickly. An annual allotment letter sets a target number of deportations. The results achieved in this area greatly influence the attitudes of the general public in Norway.

Goal-driven resource prioritization

Based on UTSYS portfolio overviews, codes for tagging of cases and the campaign-mechanism, the use of NPIS resources in the different lines of work can be prioritized in accordance with set goals. This ensures that resources are put where they make the greatest contribution towards goal achievement.

7. BEST PRACTICES, LEARNING POINTS AND PITFALLS

7.1 Best Practices and Learning Points
  ✓ *The use of the blackboard system architecture as a metaphor is useful for organizing case management solutions where several disciplines collaborate*

on the same case. The blackboard metaphor may point forward to incorporation of intelligent agents to assist in the collaboration.

✓ Strive to provide functionality both for working at the case overview level and at the individual case level. For UTSYS, case portfolio management is vital in prioritization of work within single cases and across cases.

✓ In prioritizing across cases, support for mass handling in campaigns was a useful addition to the system.

✓ The current UTSYS is a good host for augmenting with more active task support as documented for other operational ACM solutions based on the same ACM framework. UTSYS users had experience with using UDI's case handling systems, but were initially afraid that active task support would result in a straitjacket not suitable for supporting complex police work. With the necessary flexibility in place, active task support looks promising for future extensions.

7.2 Pitfalls

✗ Avoid too detailed assumptions regarding complex processes, especially when they involve collaboration across multiple roles and disciplines.

✗ Avoid exploring peripheral functional areas too deeply; maintain a good balance across the functional areas.

8. COMPETITIVE ADVANTAGES

As a government agency, the NPIS is not assessed in terms of competitiveness. There is, however, considerable public attention concerning how well they solve their mission. Now in daily use by all operational personnel, UTSYS has become the key case management platform of the NPIS. The system is instrumental in achieving the goals and KPIs set by Norwegian authorities, and continues to serve as a basis for developing more uniform and coherent work practices. Providing overview, space for collaboration and resource management, UTSYS is a flexible basis for the further development of the NPIS organization and its future ways of working to solve its mission in Norwegian society.

9. TECHNOLOGY

UTSYS is developed with Microsoft .Net 4.0 using Windows Presentation Foundation (WPF) for visualization, and Windows Communication Framework (WCF) for handling the communication between clients and server, and between server and external systems. The chosen database is Oracle relational database. The use of stateless application server with continuous data-persistence supports scaling, both horizontally and vertically, and ensures rapid availability of information across clients – suitable for supporting blackboard updates in real time.

There is integration with UDI's services as the joint hub for immigration management cases, and with ELYS, the national police register for inquiries giving access to the registers of Interpol and Schengen.

Worklists and the active task support were implemented using an ACM framework that has hosted several operational ACM solutions developed for and used within the Norwegian public and private sector during the past 15 years. In UTSYS, this ACM framework was used in its Microsoft .Net version.

10. THE TECHNOLOGY AND SERVICE PROVIDERS

Computas AS is an employee owned Norwegian IT consulting company with around 250 consultants, which provides services and solutions for business processes and co-work. Computas AS has delivered numerous work process support applications to the Norwegian public sector and private enterprises, based on the ACM framework FrameSolutions™.

FrameSolutions™ currently has more than 100 000 users, and handles an annual cash flow of around 50 billion NOK. IT solutions based on FrameSolutions provide work process support and task support resulting in higher efficiency and quality in organizational processes. FrameSolutions is a framework for realizing bespoke process-centered case management solutions.

Assembled and authored by Helle Frisak Sem, Steinar Carlsen, Gunnar John Coll, Geir Borgi, Steinar A. Kindingstad, Computas AS. Bios are available in the Author Appendix.

The Office of Secretary to the Government of Federation of Nigeria

Nominated by Newgen Software Technologies Limited, India

1. EXECUTIVE SUMMARY / ABSTRACT

The Office of Secretary to the Government of the Federation (OSGF) of Nigeria is responsible for effective coordination and monitoring of the implementation of Government policies. The Cabinet Secretariat office of OSGF collates, vets and disseminates memoranda and associated documents from various Council Members, Ministries, Departments and Agencies (MDAs) of the Government. These memoranda and documents form the basis of agenda setting and discussions at the Federal Executive Council (FEC) of the Nigerian government. The FEC comprises of ministers handpicked by the President of Nigeria to spearhead different ministries and businesses of the Nigerian government.

The memoranda and documents have dynamic lifecycles undergoing several levels of checks, iterations and annotations. This was largely handled manually, causing problems such as slower processes, manual errors and high operational costs. Maintaining security of information was a challenge too. To overcome these impediments, the Government delegated Galaxy Backbone Limited, its wholly owned ICT subsidiary to create the right solution to this challenge. Galaxy Backbone launched its *1-Gov.net program,* which would create a common Information and Communication Technology (ICT) platform for all Ministries, Departments and Agencies of the Federal Government.

Galaxy Backbone decided to leverage a BPM and ECM (with in-built EDMS) platform to respond to these challenges. It chose Newgen's e-Gov solution to bring about the following process transformations:

- Automation of the Memoranda Submission and FEC meeting Agenda listing process.
- Automated capturing of conclusions reached at FEC meetings, preparing extracts (decisions of FEC) and sending them to specific MDA for implementation on request.
- The system provided **two-tier security** to documents by integrating RSA security solutions like Authentication Manager, Secure ID and DLP
- **Storage and retrieval** of documents in digital format.

2. OVERVIEW

The Office of Secretary to the Government of the Federation (OSGF) of Nigeria plays a pivotal role in ensuring the effective implementation, coordination and monitoring of Government policies. The Cabinet Secretariat office of OSGF collates, vets and disseminates memoranda and associated documents from various Council Members, Ministries, Departments and Agencies (MDAs) of the Government. These memoranda and documents form the basis of agenda setting and discussions at the Federal Executive Council (FEC) of the Nigerian government. The FEC comprises ministers handpicked by the President of Nigeria to spearhead different ministries and businesses of the Nigerian government.

The memoranda and documents had dynamic lifecycles undergoing several levels of checks, iterations and annotations. This was largely handled manually, causing problems such as slower processes, manual errors and high operational costs. Maintaining security of information was a challenge too. To overcome these impediments, the Government delegated Galaxy Backbone Limited, its wholly owned ICT subsidiary to create the right solution to this challenge. Galaxy Backbone launched its *1-Gov.net program,* which would create a common Information and Communication Technology (ICT) platform for all Ministries, Departments and Agencies of the Federal Government.

Galaxy Backbone decided to leverage a BPM and EDMs platform to respond to these challenges. It chose Newgen's e-Gov solution built on a Case Management platform to revolutionize the following processes:

- Automation of the Memoranda Submission and FEC meeting Agenda listing process.
- Automated capturing of conclusions reached at FEC meetings, preparing extracts (decisions of FEC) and sending them to specific MDA for implementation on request.
- The system provided two-tier security to documents by integrating RSA security solutions like Authentication Manager, Secure ID and DLP
- Storage and retrieval of documents in digital format.

In terms of functionality, the solution treated each memo as a case file, as they required high level of collaboration for decision making and the future of each memo evolved with multiple iterations and annotations. Eventually some of the memos would be featured in the Agenda of the FEC and tabled for discussion. Once the memos were tabled and discussed the Cabinet Secretariat disseminates the conclusions of each meeting to the FEC.

These conclusions are then tabled at the next council meeting for consideration, and approval. Once approved, the Cabinet Secretariat prepares extracts (extracts are decisions taken by the FEC) which are then sent to specific MDAs for implementation.

This entire process was being handled manually and relied heavily on physical documents. The OSGF realized that the process was prone to manual errors, as is common with manual handling of information and was also highly time consuming. The existing system was prone to security lapses, with the possibility of confidential, State level information being leaked into the public domain, especially media.

The E-Gov solution combined its BPM, ECM and Case Management domain expertise to automate and streamline the entire process through which the collaboration of Memos is performed. Each memo is archived into a case file which goes through multiple approval/reviews and iteration stages. While the movement of these memo files is more or less structured but sometimes ad-hoc routing was required for special approvals and iterations. The implemented solution supports ad-hoc workflows and tasks, making such unprecedented activities possible without loss of time or additional overhead costs.

The solution had a Case Management functionality baked into it and hence each participant within the process flow was empowered as a Knowledge Worker. Participants could easily take on ad-hoc developments on each Memoranda and Agenda Listing.

The solution also provides a two tier security, which was developed bearing in mind the sensitive nature of the information which OSGF was handling and needed to manage.

Benefits

- Improved life-cycle management of Memoranda from the creation to the implementation as a policy phase.
- Memoranda and other confidential FEC documents were stored and archived electronically, making retrieval easier and hassle free. Since documents do not have to be moved physically, the incidence of loss or pilferage was greatly reduced
- Automated Memoranda Submission and Agenda listing processes along with vetting, production & Circulation of Draft conclusions and extracts of council meetings ensured effective cycle times with FEC stakeholders being able to access information at a click of a button.
- The RSA security system to certify that only authorized persons are allowed to access documents in the Electronic Document Management System (EDMS) and prevented leakage of highly confidential data.

Challenges

- Change management & Capacity building as business users were resistive to change.
- Integration with ISMS (RSA) and VANSO SMS gateway.
- Setting up the network infrastructure to connect various ministries with production data centre at OSGF.
- Setting up the scanning shop for the digitization of legacy data present as physical archive of OSGF.

3. BUSINESS CONTEXT

It is critical to understand the structure of the organization prior to elaborating the sequence of the following activities which were transformed with the help of the solution:

1. Memoranda Submission and Agenda Listing
2. Vetting, production and circulation of draft conclusions & extracts of the FEC Meeting.

The Cabinet Secretariat OSGF is structured into three departments Economic Matters, Social Matters and Monitoring and Evaluation of Policies.

The Permanent Secretary is the Administrative Head of the Office. He is assisted by the following

- 2 Directors,
- 3 Deputy Directors,
- 7 Assistant Directors,
- 1 Chief Administrative Officer,
- 2 Assistant Chief Administrative Officers,
- 3 Principal Administrative Officers,
- 8 Senior Administrative Officers,
- 2 Administrative Officers I
- 3 Administrative Officers II.

There are also Confidential Secretaries and clerks who see to the production, collation and dispatch of the Council documents. The organization structure has been elaborated as below:

Organization Structure Cabinet Secretariat, OSGF

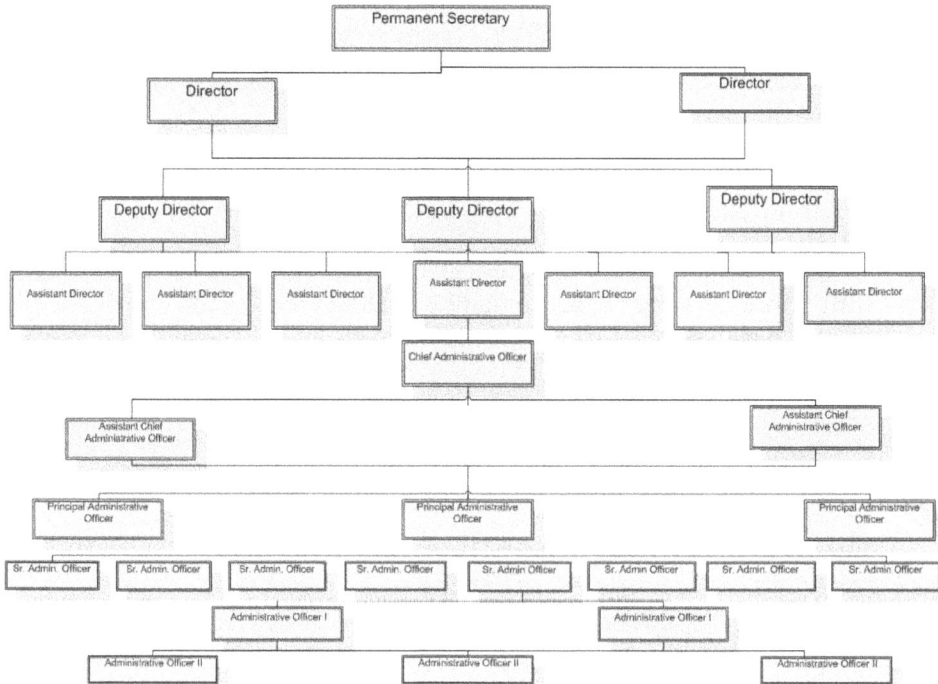

Permanent Secretary

Director — Director

Deputy Director — Deputy Director — Deputy Director

Assistant Director — Assistant Director — Assistant Director — Assistant Director — Assistant Director — Assistant Director — Assistant Director

Chief Administrative Officer

Assistant Chief Administrative Officer — Assistant Chief Administrative Officer

Principal Administrative Officer — Principal Administrative Officer — Principal Administrative Officer

Sr. Admin. Officer — Sr. Admin. Officer — Sr. Admin. Officer — Sr. Admin. Officer — Sr. Admin Officer — Sr. Admin Officer — Sr. Admin. Officer — Sr. Admin Officer

Administrative Officer I — Administrative Officer I

Administrative Officer II — Administrative Officer II — Administrative Officer II

The Office has some sub-units, headed by relatively senior officers. These are:

Internal Administration- The Internal administration unit sees to all the administrative processes of the Office.

Archives- The central repository of all Council Memoranda and Conclusions which are systematically preserved for posterity.

End room- Staffed with specially selected Confidential Secretaries the end room is where the Memoranda, Notes and Conclusions assume their final form and shape before they are circulated to Council Members. The success of the Secretariat depends largely on the quality of work finally produced by the End Room.

Distribution Unit- is where completely processed Council documents are received and parceled for distribution to the Council members. It is also staffed with specially selected Confidential Secretaries and Clerks.

Prior to the Implementation both the processes were being operated manually, where the movement of documents and information happened physically. The process flow for the same has been enlisted below:

The Memoranda Submission & Agenda Listing Process Prior to Implementation

- *The "Memoranda Submission and Agenda Listing Process" started with the manual submission of Memoranda/Notes by office of the Permanent Secretary of a Ministry between Monday morning and Thursday evening for the FEC meeting scheduled on the Wednesday.*

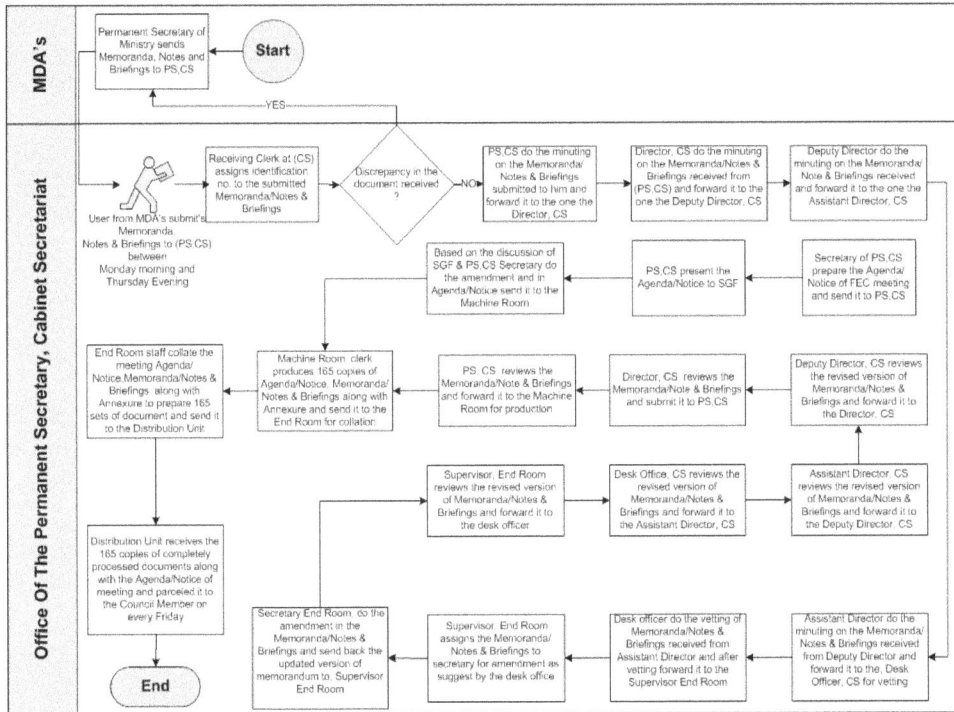

MDA's / **Office Of The Permanent Secretary, Cabinet Secretariat**

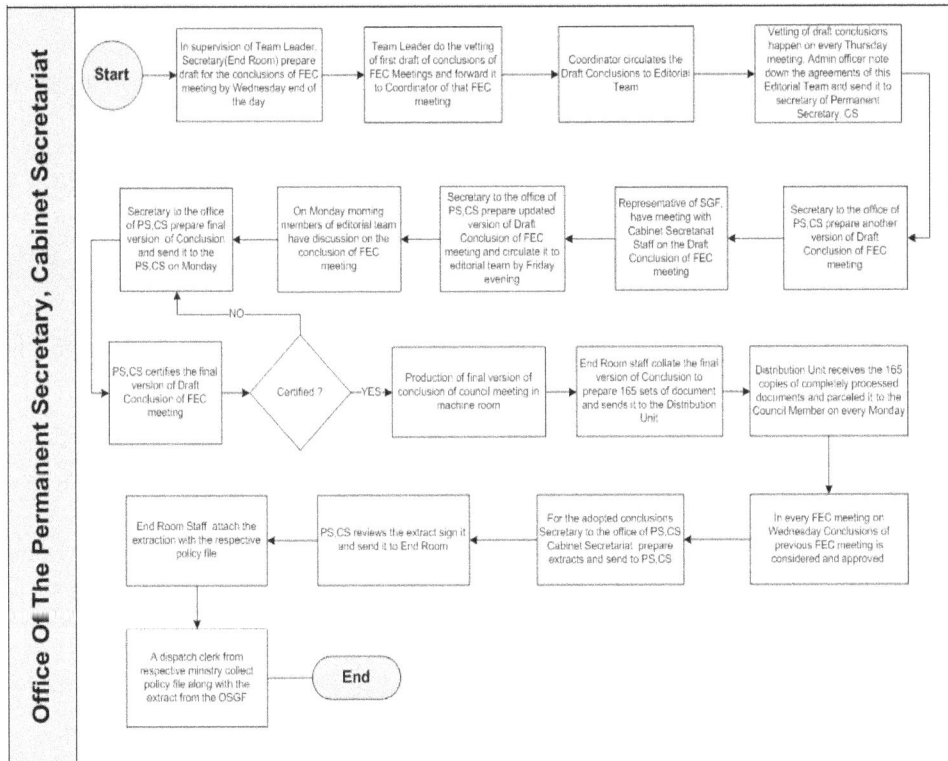

The Vetting, Production & Circulation of Draft Conclusions and Extract Council Meeting Process Prior to Implementation

- *At each level of the Memoranda Submission and Agenda listing process, minutes were created (after necessary action was initiated) and in case of discrepancies the progressing level would revert to the preceding level for rectifications.*

At any point in time, changes would mean alteration in the sequencing of close to 165 copies of the same document. Moreover since these discrepancies and exceptions were handled manually, it would mean valuable time lost caused by manual hand-offs, routing and re-routing of documents physically.

- *Each Memorandum had a different purpose and each exception handling could bring about new challenges.*

4. The Key Innovations

The OSGF needed a solution that would help it simplify the processes (Memoranda Submission, agenda listing and vetting, production, circulation of draft conclusions of the FEC meetings). The implementation gave OSGF the freedom to automate a complex and tedious document and intensive procedures.

The solutions Case Management capability allowed OSGF users to operate as knowledge workers. Each user could engage in dynamic changes across multiple levels in the process chain.

Some other key functional innovations are listed as below:

- A unique user interface was developed that would enable ministers to view the Agenda Listing and the Memoranda notes and details through the iPads.
- Integration of EDMS application with Audio Visual conferencing system to access the document images stored in EDMS application for presentation during FEC meeting at Council Chamber.
- Integration of application with SMS gateway/server to send SMS notification to business users of Memoranda Submission & Agenda Listing process.
- Integration of application with E-mail server to send E- notification to business users of Memoranda Submission & Agenda listing process.
- Integration of application with RSA security system to certify that only the authorized person is allowed to access the documents in EDMS repository. To monitor the events and to avoid data leakage.

4.1 Business

Following the implementation, while the Memoranda notes, agenda listing and vetting process happened between the same stakeholders, the entire process was automated. The key process points are mentioned as below

- *To be "Memoranda Submission & Agenda Listing Process" will commence with the submission of Memoranda/ Notes or Briefings by office of the Permanent Secretary of a Ministry between Monday morning 9 A.M. and Thursday evening 6 P.M. for the FEC meeting scheduled on next Wednesday.*

A user from the office of the Permanent Secretary of a Ministry is able to commence the process by two ways:

- By uploading the scanned copy of all the documents along with the softcopy of the Memorandum. The process can also be initiated without scanned annexure to the Memorandum/Note. If a user at MDA does not scan the annexure along with the Memorandum and other documents like covering letter then after initiating the process they need to note down the system generated unique Memorandum file on a sticky note and paste it on the top page of the annexure and give it to the dispatch clerk along with policy file for the manual submission at the Cabinet Secretariat. The annexure will be scanned and uploaded at the Cabinet Secretariat.

- Manual Submission of all the documents Memorandum/Note, Covering Letter, Annexure & Policy File etc. to the office of Permanent Secretary, Cabinet Secretariat.

In case the Permanent Secretary's office is receiving the hard copy of the docket, then the documents will be scanned and exported to the E-gov application. At this stage each Memorandum and its associated documents receives a user identification number which becomes its identity through-out its lifecycle. Users from Ministries are allowed to initiate the electronic file of Memoranda/Note for processing between Mondays 9 A.M. to Thursday 6 P.M. for the FEC meeting scheduled on Wednesday of next week.

Once documents are exported into the system, it flows between members of the Internal Administration team, the Distribution Unit, the End Room and finally to the Archival team. Each Memorandum witnesses some dynamic movement between the Internal Administration team and End Room team, where maximum value additions are made in terms of minutes, recommendations and rectifications.

At each level participating users can route the documents back to their predecessor in case of discrepancies or missing links. At certain levels, participants can connect with officials from other ministries where vital pieces of information are to be attached as part of the Memorandum. On every movement of a document, succeeding recipients receive automatic system generated E-mail and SMS alerts.

Once the documents have been vetted, they are handed over the Secretary End Room, where final amendments to the soft copy of the Memorandum are made. On completing amendments, the document are routed back all the way up to the Directors and sometimes even Permanent Secretary for finalization of the Agenda Notice.

On finalization and review from the Permanent Secretary, the Agenda Notice is finally submitted to the Secretary to the Government of Federation of Nigeria for review. The Memorandum then travels back to the Permanent Secretary Cabinet Secretariat with final comments and amendments. Once these are inculcated, the Permanent Secretary's office circulates 165 copies to the respective FEC members.

Each Wednesday once the FEC meeting concludes, the Secretary end room drafts the conclusion in supervision of the Team leader of the respective FEC meeting. The Conclusion will be generated as an electronic file, carrying a unique identification number and will be uploaded as a Draft Conclusion of that particular FEC meeting.

Each Thursday the Permanent Secretary and his team meets to discuss the draft conclusion, prior to which they have already received electronic copies of the draft. The document then passes through several levels of vetting, where versions of the conclusion are created. The FEC conclusion has an editorial team which at all times along with the Permanent Secretary can view the document simultaneously in read-only format and can chip-in with suggestions for changes. Each Monday the Permanent Secretary, Cabinet Secretariat, meets the editorial team and based on their discussion, the final version of the Conclusion is created. After a review and buy-in from the Secretary, Government federation, the conclusion is sent to 165 council members electronically.

The conclusions are finally discussed in the FEC meetings and then made into policies. Extracts of each meetings are created and sent to the Permanent Secretary who then signs the Memorandum and sends it to the respective MDA

4.2 Case Handling

The entire process involved the following steps:

Memoranda Submission and Agenda listing process- To initiate the process within the solution all Memoranda and associated documents are scanned, indexed and uploaded into the EDMS. Within the EDMS application users can create a file for the document in application and tag the file with unique identification number. The document will travel through an extensive process before it moves on the next step.

The process for this stage is elaborated below:

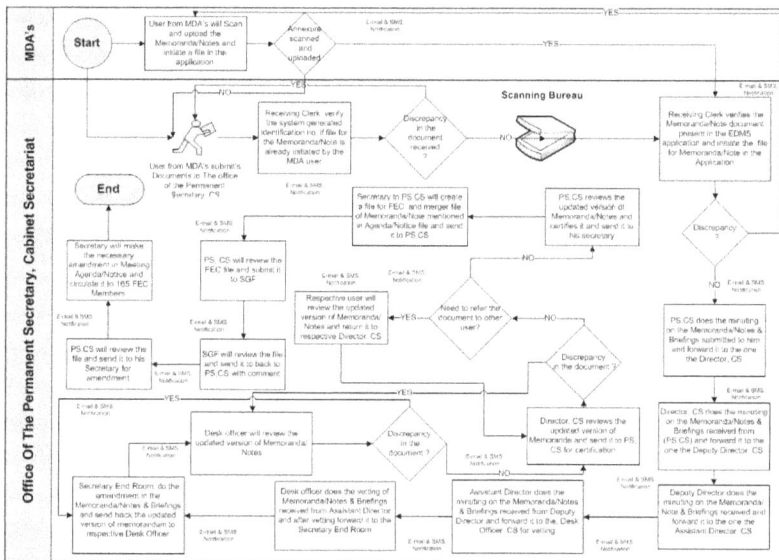

Memoranda Submission and Agenda Listing Process post implementation

At each level, the documents can be routed back to preceding officers in case of exceptions and discrepancies. Sometimes documents may be incomplete and need to be moved across departments and ministries. These activities are rules defined and exception handling becomes effective and astute. Every movement of a Memorandum or associated file is accompanied by an Email and SMS notification.

Once the documents are scanned, indexed and titled in the EDMS users can introduce them into the vetting, production and circulation process. The solution combines its workflow technology along with a case management platform to drive the below mentioned process

At the time of implementation defined a structured framework for initiation of each new case or Memoranda submission was created. Once the documents are scanned and exported to the main application, each new case would begin reflecting within the participant's domain. Thereafter the following tasks could be accomplished:

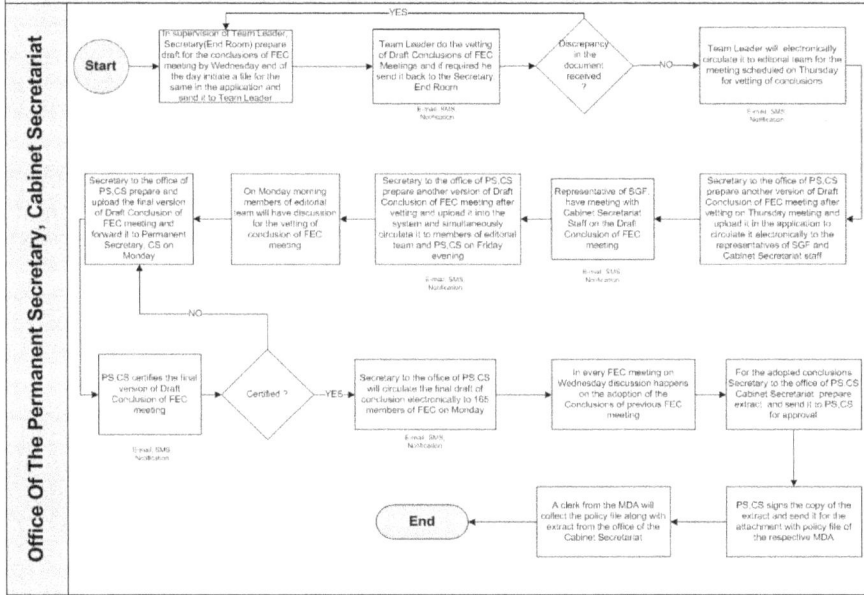

Vetting, Production & Circulation of Conclusions, Extracts of FEC Meetings

Checklist- Each submission has to be backed with some mandatory documents along with each Memorandum copy. The checklist was to ensure that all relevant documents were attached with the electronic copy of the Memorandum. The checklist window has been showcase below

Agenda/ Memo- This is to define the Name of the Case (Agenda Listing or Memorandum) which would become its key recognition characteristic across the case lifecycle.

Task Handling- This would enable the setting of a To-Do list which would then govern the activities which need to be accomplished across a Case (Agenda/ Memo) lifecycle.

User Selection- A rules based defining of the flow through which a particular document or case will be handled. The solution drove structural movement of documents and actions performed on each document. With a baked in Case Management capability the system provided flexibility to move workflow on an ad-hoc basis as well.

During the user selection, work on different cases (Agenda Listing / Memoranda) could be prioritised, governing the dispatch and movement of documents within the system. The system also provided the ability to set a definitive time period by which a particular user had to check-out the document from their end.

Key roles

The participating members and agencies in each processes are listed as below

Permanent Secretaries- Were assigned from each Ministry, Department and agency who would work on respective Memoranda and briefings and send the same to Permanent Secretary Cabinet Secretariat for creation of minutes.

Permanent Secretary Cabinet Secretariat- All Memoranda from across Ministries and departments will be submitted to the Permanent Secretary, Cabinet Secretariat who is responsible for creating the minutes of each Memoranda.

Director / Assistant Director / Deputy Director Cabinet Secretariat- Each of these participants enriched the Memoranda and created a level of minutes

Desk Officers- The Desk officers are responsible for the first round of vetting of the Memorandum notes. The Memorandum note is handed over to the Desk officers by the Deputy Director.

Team Leader End room- Each Memorandum has an associated team leader who oversees the amendments being made to the Memorandum and associated documents by Secretary End Room.

Editorial Team- Works closely with the Team leader to provide suggestions on the content of the Memorandum. They can make recommendations which are collected at the end

Secretary End room- All Memoranda following amendments and minute creations reach the end room. The secretary end room is responsible for given all Memoranda Notes and Conclusions their final shape for circulation to the council.

Memoranda and Associated documents- Are essential information forming the backbone and basis of each Policy the Nigerian government introduces. These documents are mobilized among stake holders such as Ministers, Ministry departments and the FEC through a synchronized process leveraging the solution.

- Physical copies of the Memoranda and other associated documents are converted into digitized documents through scanning and are then uploaded in to the EDMS. Once the upload is completed these documents receive unique identification numbers and continue through a process flow before they are featured into the FEC Agenda.
- FEC Meeting Details- Once a Memorandum is featured in the Agenda, the FEC undertakes discussions and passes conclusions on specific actions and policies. These are relevant information which undergo a vetting process and require several levels of check, iterations and annotations. The documents are routed through a process flow, before they can be presented as policies. Once the FEC comes to a conclusion a summarised the Memorandum is signed and made available as part of the policy file under the respective MDA.

4.3 Organization & Social

The implementation completely transformed the performance of the OSGF. The process being followed prior was sluggish and ineffective. The implementation brought about some refreshing changes in terms of the organization's ability to handle processes. Ministers and their support staff no longer need to lug large volumes of physical documents to FEC meetings. The use of paper was drastically brought down.

Prior to the implementation, 165 copies of each Memoranda Note and associate documents were circulated across ministries. Each copy could carry up to 800 pages. There used to be a separate mail and delivery facility which was pressed into service for making each batch available across ministries. The implementation enabled OSGF to do away with this entire practice, thus reducing impact on the environment and also enhancing its cost efficiency.

With the elimination of physical documents and several manual procedures, officials within the OSGF organizational structure were now diverted into high value tasks. Improving the overall quality and efficiency of work put forth by the OSGF.

The Memoranda process encompasses some highly strategic decisions, which are often of national importance such as infrastructural projects or fiscal commissions. The process being followed prior to the implementation was time consuming as approval processes were manual and could be stalled the moment one member of the chain was missing. With the implementation most of this process was automated and approval processes, exception handling and even routing and re-routing of documents was done online. As a result the through put time of each team was brought down substantially. This enabled OSGF to churn out FEC documents faster and invariably create faster decision making within the government.

The implementation implied a huge change over from the existing mechanisms used by the Ministries and the OSGF for accomplishing the Memoranda Notes, Agenda Listing and the entire vetting process. The transition from a legacy manually driven process to a completely automated procedure, was causing some restive moments across the framework. To smoothly drive this change, Newgen with the help of Centrifuge consulting set up a Centre of Excellence, that would help members involved in the process effortlessly slide into this transition. An extensive hand-holding of the participants who were to operate the systems on a regular basis was done. Change Management was critical to the success of this project. Product experts were stationed onsite to help with the same. Some experts were stationed for over 6 months.

5. HURDLES OVERCOME

Management

A major concern for the management (in this case Ministers and Head of Departments) was the security of the information which was being exchanged across the board for the Memoranda Note, Agenda Listing and Vetting process. The information was mostly of a sensitive nature and needed to be guarded effectively. This concern was addressed by integrating a RSA secure token ID with this application. This was user driven and needed two levels of password clearances prior to a user could login and use the system.

Business: Organization Adoption

At the organizational level, the critical challenges were several. To begin with, the penetration of computer literacy was low within the structural framework. So for most users on the face of it the system appeared to be complex. The common mind-set was that to be able to use this technology most would have to go through some grueling training. The changeover was a huge concern for most employees.

Several initiatives were taken to make this transition possible:

- Formation of a CoE to handle the Change Management
- Basic to advance training on how to effectively leverage the system to end users. This also led to the formation of training centers.
- Regular awareness programs to enable users understand the benefits of the implementation.

6. BENEFITS
6.1 Cost Savings / Time Reductions

Cost Savings- While it will not be possible to disclose the monetary figures, the implementation has enabled 60% cost reduction in the entire procedure

Time reductions- The through-put time for each approval process was brought down by 70-80% depending on the volume of the project.

6.2 Quality Improvements

The most apparent quality improvement effectuated by the implementation was the bringing down time taken to arrive at right decisions by stakeholders such as ministers and head of departments. Thereby enhancing the speed at which strategic government decisions were cleared.

7. BEST PRACTICES, LEARNING POINTS AND PITFALLS
Pitfalls

After mapping the entire process followed for the Memoranda and Agenda Listing process *the team* recommended that the following actions could be avoided

- ✗ *Duplication of activities- At the time of implementation it was found that some of the re-routing of documents once the Memoranda, associated documents or agenda listing had been updated were unnecessary and added to process time.*
  For example once the Secretary End room has updated a document, he no longer needs share the same with a supervisor so that it can reach the relevant Desk Officer. The Secretary End room now shares the updated document directly. In another case updated documents now no longer need to pass through Deputy Directors and Assistant Directors prior to reaching the Director. Thus the channel between a Desk Officer and Director was open and direct.

8. COMPETITIVE ADVANTAGES

The implementation done for OSGF Nigeria is one of the largest Digital transformation projects across the globe. The project came with its share of typical as well as unusual challenges.

Driving the change management for a completely manual driven process was a key achievement. Then for those who understand how governments operate, the entire deployment was attempted in a domain where a lot of protocol had to be observed while ensuring that the best was drawn out of the implementation. Last but not the least, the elimination of paper from the entire process was a remarkable milestone. Each FEC Agenda discussion needed close to 13,200 sheets of paper.

Newgen over the last few years has gained considerable expertise in developing and delivering large critical projects for government departments across the globe. In one of its largest implementation ever, over 8 billion document for a India's largest government affiliated Insurance organization were digitized.

The key competitive advantages which were created with through this implementation are enlisted below:

Faster Decision Making- The implementation at OSGF has vastly improved the process times for circulation of relevant documents aiding faster approvals and thereby faster time to arriving at critical decisions

Compliance- There is always a high premium attached to all forms of Compliance to projects such as the OSGF. The implementation provided extensive compliance coverage for OSGF. Right from document storage to secured authentication and access to information.

Cost Benefits- Cost impact is a key driving force for any technology investment made by an organization (does not have to be Government agency). The implementation at OSGF delivers cost benefits across several levels. Firstly the implementation delivered is quite cost effective, built on innovative technology which is frugal yet smart. Secondly, as has been mentioned previously the OSGF was able to cut down drastically on handling physical paper there by reducing costs associated with transportation, storage, retrieval and complete information management.

9. TECHNOLOGY

The implementation at the OSGF Nigeria has an underlying Business Process Management and an Enterprise Content Management platform. The solution has also been configured to bring about important Case Management capabilities where-in ad-hoc incidents can be managed effortlessly.

The ECM and BPM platforms combine together to provide effective capture, indexing and creating storing conventions for the Memoranda and other critical government documents. They enable the OSGF to orchestrate the entire lifecycle of Memoranda till they time they become policies or otherwise.

Newgen combined its following products to streamline the processes:

OmniScan- An enterprise scanning solution which is used for effective digitization of all Memoranda and Agenda listing documents. Once documents are scanned using OmniScan, the application allows systematic tagging and indexing of the documents. This simplifies search and retrieval of documents in the Enterprise Content and Document Management application to which the Memoranda and Agenda Listings are exported to. The application also creates folder structures which can be reflected in the ECM system.

OmniDocs- The Enterprise Content Management platform and Document Management solution tightly integrates with OmniScan and the BPM tool OmniFlow. The OmniDocs application provides the underlying base for document intensive collaboration. The ECM application enables tight version controls at the same time providing effective collective collaboration on Memoranda and Agenda listings spanning across ministries.

OmniFlow- A robust BPM application, which is scalable and platform independent. The application has an in-built Case management tool, creating remarkable exceptional handling. The BPM tool also helped design the appropriate flow and rule based delivery and exchange of documents, saving effort and time spent otherwise on manual movement and handoffs of document.

Business Activity Monitor (BAM) - The BAM tool is integrated with the BPM tool and provides valuable insight in process performance. Real time summaries of each function within the solution value chain can be accessed and understood through BAM. The BAM tool effectively eradicates bottlenecks as they arise and provide valuable process insight.

Unique benefits

- Automation of Memoranda Submission and Agenda Listing Process has improved the turnaround time for the OSGF. Information which was previously stored as paper, can now be distributed to targeted users electronically. This has resulted in bringing down the time and cost impact of creating 165 copies of the same document and circulating it physically to FEC members has been eliminated.
- Documents were stored electronically for effective retrieval and better compliance bringing down costs associated with physical storage and manual handling of paper. The EDMS which is a part of OmniDocs drives impeccable document management with smart indexing and folder structures. Applying single or multiple taxonomy or categorizations to a document folder was now possible.
- The flow of documents between officers and departments is rules driven. Therefore minimal time was lost with respect to routing of documents, raising queries and handling of exceptions.
- Response times have dramatically improved as participants' obtain prior notification of an impending task through emails and SMS.
- The solutions case management capability allows smart responses to dynamic scenarios and unscheduled requirements.
- A unique user interface enables ministers to view the Agenda Listing and the Memoranda notes and details through the iPads improving approval cycles.
- Integration of EDMS application with Audio Visual conferencing system to access the document images stored in EDMS application for presentation during FEC meeting at Council Chamber makes way for cohesive and collaborative decision making within the structural framework.

10. THE TECHNOLOGY AND SERVICE PROVIDERS

Galaxy Backbone Nigeria-
http://www.galaxybackbone.com.ng/Pages/default.aspx

Galaxy Backbone Limited is an Information and Communications Technology Services provider, wholly owned by the Federal Government of Nigeria. Galaxy Backbone Limited was established in 2006 by the Federal Government based on the need for Government to pursue a coordinated and harmonized approach to information and communications technology acquisition, operation and use in the public sector. The intent for the establishment of Galaxy Backbone was, therefore, to enable the Federal Government derive more value from its investments in information and communication technology by eliminating duplication, establishing economies of scale, enhancing interoperability of systems and improving Government's capacity to deliver electronic services.

Galaxy Backbone worked with Newgen as a partner. Galaxy was pivotal for in helping develop an understanding of the exact nature of the technology demanded by OSGF.

Pershing LLC,
a BNY Mellon Company, USA

Nominated by Pershing LLC, a BNY Mellon company, USA

1. EXECUTIVE SUMMARY / ABSTRACT

Prior to implementing its Task Management solution for onboarding new clients to Pershing LLC, a BNY Mellon company, the Client Transition (conversion) team relied on a highly manual, paper-intensive project planning system to track the conversion process and manage multiple tasks.

This required frequent in-person meetings, e-mails and phone calls among departments. Administration was difficult and time consuming as project plans had to be printed and shared prior to each meeting and updates were restricted to a single team member from each department.

The new automated task management solution allows the conversion team to access and adapt up to 1,100 steps within the master conversion plan for the new client and distribute the plan to more than 150 impacted team members. It also allows all team members in real time to:

- Access the project plan, carry out tasks and update status.
- View an overview of status, including open items and the percentage of project completed.
- Capture and archive documents with a built-in imaging system for audit and recordkeeping.
- Receive alerts when tasks are added, coming due or past due.
- Add comments to tasks or steps, improving both communication among team members and information retrieval.

Since its implementation in 2013, the project has met its objectives with:

- Improved access to information and documentation across the firm.
- Easy project updates and administration across 43 groups in Pershing.
- Enhanced project oversight and communication among diverse teams.
- Time and resource savings on project planning.
- Improved quality by using standard checklists for processes in adherence firm guidelines and regulatory requirements.
- Reduction in project administration from days to minutes.

2. OVERVIEW

The task management solution was designed to provide full transparency, accountability and insight into the new client onboarding process at Pershing, which engages up 43 internal departments, such as technology, trading, tax reporting, statements, new accounts and mutual funds, all while storing the documentation and history in one centralized location.

Since every client that is onboarded at Pershing has a different set of requirements, the team required a task management system that could be tailored by the type of client and for individual client engagements, improving both project delivery and team communications across Pershing.

The basic components of the task management solution include:

- **Tasks**—Tasks consist of one simple step or may be more complex, involving multiple steps.

- **Steps**—Steps are a sub-step attached to the task.
- **Checklists**—Checklists are a group of related steps attached to a task that help create repeatable business processes. Timelines are then created for completion of the checklists.
- **Alerts**—Users can receive alerts when tasks are *added, coming due* or *past due*, via e-mail, text, pop-up alert, blink in task bar, or view all alerts upon logging into the system.

Each of the 43 departments creates the tasks, checklists and steps for the each of the five conversion types at Pershing: incoming (new clients), in-house (internal transfers), start-up (new broker-dealer businesses), deconversions (exiting clients) and managed investments.

Each step in the checklist (see Figure 1) can be assigned to either a user group or individual. All task checklists for the particular conversion type (up to 1,100 steps) are embedded into a master conversion template, used to create the new project plan when a new client is onboarded.

Since financial services is a heavily regulated industry, departments must create the checklists according to regulatory requirements and the guidelines listed in Pershing's policies and procedures manual to ensure tasks are completed correctly. Certain departments, such as the Anti-Money Laundering team, may have concerns about confidentially, so have the option of designating checklists as *public, private* or *shared.* If private, only the team members assigned to that task can access and update the item.

Checklists ensure that the tasks and, ultimately, the entire conversion, are performed consistently and correctly across a high volume of conversions, regardless of the project size or complexity. For each of the 500 checklists involved in a conversion, the individual responsible for the task is required to complete all of the checklist steps to close out the task.

Figure 1

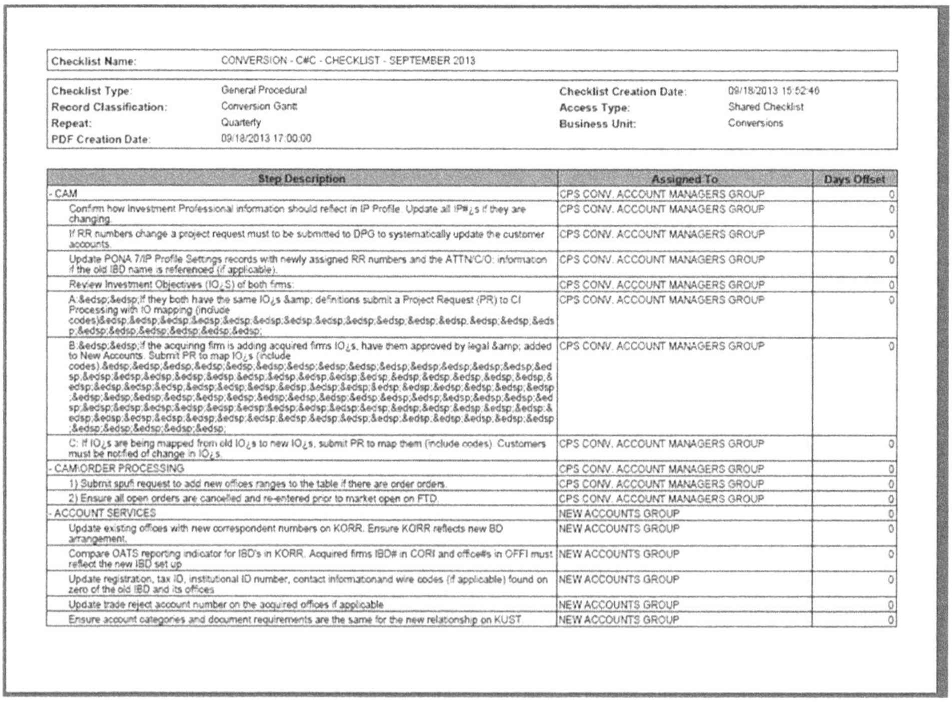

Checklist Name:	CONVERSION - C#C - CHECKLIST - SEPTEMBER 2013		
Checklist Type:	General Procedural	**Checklist Creation Date:**	09/18/2013 15:52:46
Record Classification:	Conversion Gantt	**Access Type:**	Shared Checklist
Repeat:	Quarterly	**Business Unit:**	Conversions
PDF Creation Date:	09/18/2013 17:00:00		

Step Description	Assigned To	Days Offset
- CAM	CPS CONV. ACCOUNT MANAGERS GROUP	0
Confirm how Investment Professional information should reflect in IP Profile. Update all IP#¿s if they are changing.	CPS CONV. ACCOUNT MANAGERS GROUP	0
If RR numbers change a project request must to be submitted to DPG to systematically update the customer accounts.	CPS CONV. ACCOUNT MANAGERS GROUP	0
Update PONA 7/IP Profile Settings records with newly assigned RR numbers and the ATTN/C/O: information if the old IBD name is referenced (if applicable).	CPS CONV. ACCOUNT MANAGERS GROUP	0
Review Investment Objectives (IO¿S) of both firms:	CPS CONV. ACCOUNT MANAGERS GROUP	0
A:&edsp;&edsp;If they both have the same IO¿s & definitions submit a Project Request (PR) to CI Processing with IO mapping (include codes)&edsp;&edsp;&edsp;&edsp;&edsp;&edsp;&edsp;&edsp;&edsp;&edsp;&edsp;&edsp;&edsp;&edsp;&edsp;&edsp;&edsp;&edsp;&edsp;	CPS CONV. ACCOUNT MANAGERS GROUP	0
B:&edsp;&edsp;If the acquiring firm is adding acquired firms IO¿s, have them approved by legal & added to New Accounts. Submit PR to map IO¿s (include codes).&edsp;	CPS CONV. ACCOUNT MANAGERS GROUP	0
C: If IO¿s are being mapped from old IO¿s to new IO¿s, submit PR to map them (include codes). Customers must be notfied of change in IO¿s.	CPS CONV. ACCOUNT MANAGERS GROUP	0
- CAM\ORDER PROCESSING	CPS CONV. ACCOUNT MANAGERS GROUP	0
1) Submit spufi request to add new offices ranges to the table if there are order orders.	CPS CONV. ACCOUNT MANAGERS GROUP	0
2) Ensure all open orders are cancelled and re-entered prior to market open on FTD.	CPS CONV. ACCOUNT MANAGERS GROUP	0
- ACCOUNT SERVICES	NEW ACCOUNTS GROUP	0
Update existing offices with new correspondent numbers on KORR. Ensure KORR reflects new BD arrangement.	NEW ACCOUNTS GROUP	0
Compare OATS reporting indicator for IBD's in KORR. Acquired firms IBD# in CORI and office#s in OFFI must reflect the new IBD set up	NEW ACCOUNTS GROUP	0
Update registration, tax ID, institutional ID number, contact informationand wire codes (if applicable) found on zero of the old IBD and its offices	NEW ACCOUNTS GROUP	0
Update trade reject account number on the acquired offices if applicable	NEW ACCOUNTS GROUP	0
Ensure account categories and document requirements are the same for the new relationship on KUST	NEW ACCOUNTS GROUP	0

Once the conversion template has been created, an e-mail notification sent to all business areas kicks off the new client onboarding process. As soon as the team receives the e-mail, the team member assigned to a particular task "locks" it so only he or she can work on it. This ensures that multiple people from one team do not work on the same task.

Once a task is locked, the team member begins working on it or can reach out to the conversion manager with any questions. If a task is not required for that particular conversion, it can be closed out immediately.

To keep the project on track, the system accommodates for changes in staffing and assignments. If a team member is away, he or she (or an administrator) can unlock a particular task and send it back to the group for another team member to lock and complete. If an item becomes past due, reminders are sent to the individual concerned to complete the task.

Team members receive alerts or notifications when a task they are assigned to, or have created and assigned to someone else, is added, coming due or past due, so that all members are aware of their project action items.

To determine the status of a conversion, the conversion manager, or business area conversion liaison, can log onto the system at any stage to view open items and the percentage of the project complete (see Figure 2). This provides clear insight into who needs to be contacted for open tasks and enables the conversion manager to determine if any issues need to be resolved to keep the project on track.

The solution allows users to add comments at the task or step level (see Figure 2). These notes become a permanent part of the project record, and can be helpful if an item needs to be researched at a later date. For instance, if a particular task is not required for a conversion, it can be marked "N/A" in the system so the item and the reason it is missing is recorded.

If a document is missing, this can also be noted. Capturing documents and notes aids in both communication among the team members and provides overall transparency, including for audit purposes.

Figure 2

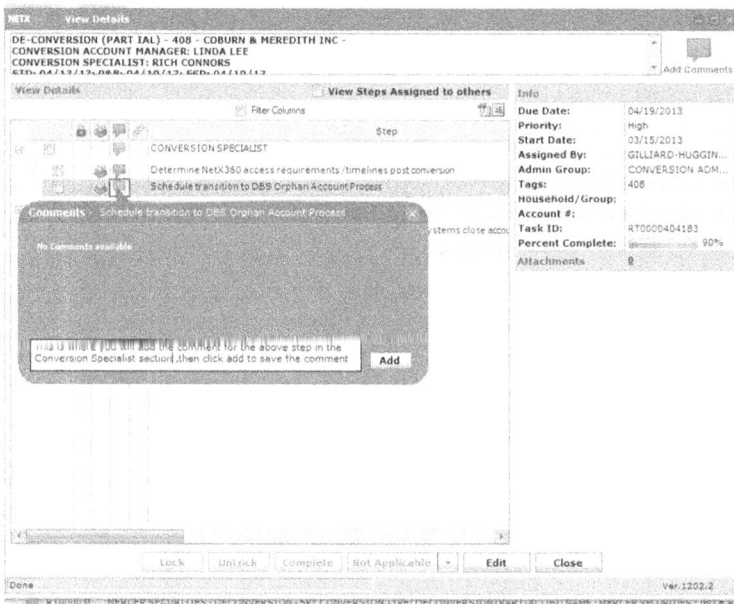

Once the project is completed at 100 percent, it is automatically moved into an imaging warehouse (see Figure 3). All documentation, project history, team members, dates of completion, and other project details, are stored in compliance with books and records and external regulations, for three to five years, in one centralized location.

Figure 3

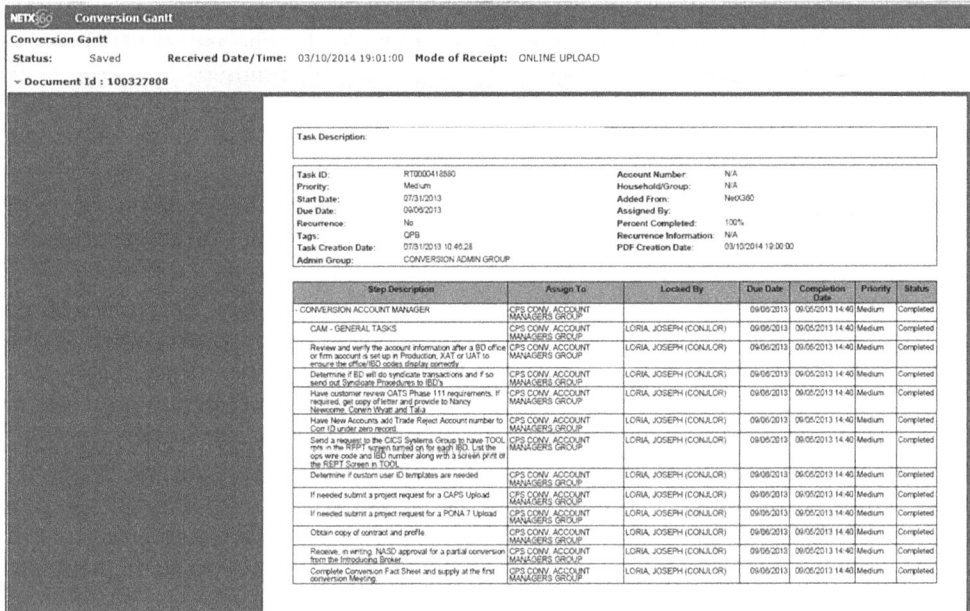

3. BUSINESS CONTEXT

Prior to implementing task management for client onboarding, the Client Transition team and up to 43 departments relied on a paper-intensive project plan to track the onboarding process and manage the approximately 500 tasks involved in each of the five conversions that typically take place in a week.

This included frequent in-person meetings, e-mails and phone calls among team members and departments. Administration was time-consuming and difficult, as project plans were printed and could only be updated by a single team member from each department. If a team member assigned to a task was away or sick, the task could not be accessed or reassigned, causing delays in the onboarding process. The system relied on team members individually tracking progress on tasks and following up with each other for status.

If a client requested a status of the conversion, it was a time-consuming, manual process involving phone calls and e-mails to the business areas. Since information was not centrally located, documentation and project information needed to be looked up on various systems and hard drives throughout the firm.

This paper-based system was eventually migrated to a semi-automated system, Project and Portfolio Management (PPM), modeled on Microsoft Project. However, this was also heavily manual and time consuming to administer. Only one team member could be assigned to tasks in PPM, making it difficult to update items. It also did not provide an oversight function or the ability to attach documents, add comments or sign up for alerts.

4. THE KEY INNOVATIONS

A previous paper-based system that housed documents and related project information on various shared drives and hard drives throughout the firm was replaced with a centralized, transparent process that stores all documents, comments and project information in one place for up to five years. The new solution improves project delivery across the firm, as well as accountability, manager oversight, team communications and project timeliness.

4.1 Business

Since this is an in-house solution, it primarily impacts the ways internal business teams interact with one another, including the Client Transition team responsible for leading conversions and 43 different business areas impacted by the conversion process.

Instead of requiring representatives of the departments involved with a conversion to attend in-person meetings and manually update paper-based project plans, team members now access and update tasks in real time in a centralized location. This has delivered significant time savings for the Client Transition team that manages conversions and for the conversion liaison in each department. These time savings have resulted in ease of tracking projects, reduction of printed reports, and decrease in manually inputting of project data.

Bottlenecks in task management have been improved. Instead of only one individual being assigned to a task per department (preventing progress if away), teams can now be assigned to tasks. Instead of individuals being responsible for remembering specific tasks and due dates for completion, features embedded into the system, such as checklists and alerts, provide this function.

Transparency has also been improved as business users, client management and the conversions team can all view progress of each conversion, as well as tasks completed and in the queue for completion. Users can also view interdependencies so that they can work effectively with others responsible for tasks during the conversion.

Reporting to clients has improved as clients can now receive real-time updates on the status of open items. Data can also be easily extracted into a Microsoft Excel or Adobe Acrobat file (this was previously a manual process) to provide clients with a status report or open items list. Otherwise, the transition to the new solution has been seamless for Pershing's clients.

The Product Management Group that developed the solution regularly interacts with both the Client Transition team and departments to obtain "voice of the customer" feedback for possible future enhancements.

4.2 Case Handling

Prior to implementation of the task management solution, the previous paper-based system meant that there were more in-person meetings, e-mails and phone calls among the Client Transition team members and internal departments. Only a single person per department could access and update the project plan. If that person was away, progress would stall. Documents and information were stored on various shared drives and hard drives throughout the firm.

With the new, automated system, e-mail notifications are sent to all groups as soon as the conversion template has been created. Progress begins immediately and managers benefit from full transparency, as they can easily log into the system to find out the overall percentage of project complete, open items and who has been assigned to tasks. When the project is complete, all documents, comments, task assignments and completion dates are stored in the system for up to five years.

Processes for onboarding had already been defined over a period of time to comply with business needs and regulatory requirements prior to implementation of the solution. Processes were moved into checklists and validated with all business areas and the conversion team to ensure they met business requirements.

The overall system architecture.

The task management solution was based on the "Getting Things Done" [1](GTD) methodology, which is based on two key objectives:

1. Capturing all the things that need to get done—now, later, someday, big, little, or in between—into a logical and trusted system outside of your head and off your mind; and

2. Disciplining yourself to make front-end decisions about all of the "inputs" you let into your life so that you will always have a plan for "next actions."[1]

The task management solution is an automated, simplified system that requires each of the business areas to create step checklists for tasks. The system then sends notifications related to these checklists to all team members to ensure they are completed on time. It provides oversight by allowing anyone with access to hover over a task icon to see who is working on it and provides an overall status with the percentage of tasks complete. When the project is complete at 100 percent, any documents attached and the complete project history are stored for up to five years.

The case templates for the five different conversion types performed at Pershing were defined based on the approximately 500 existing tasks and 1,100 related steps across 43 business areas required to complete a conversion. Since financial services is a heavily regulated industry, the tasks and steps were already in place and being tracked on a Microsoft Project Gantt chart.

The key roles

The key roles in the task management solution are conversion manager, conversion specialist, business area manager and individual user. These roles are assigned and managed as follows:

- Conversion Manager—Manages the entire conversion process, serving as the liaison between the client and Pershing's internal business areas.
- Conversion Specialist—Coordinates data files for the conversion in collaboration with the client and Pershing's technology team.
- Business Area Manager— Serves as a liaison to the Client Transition team, as a representative from one of the 43 internal departments impacted by conversions. Manages the user group assigned to tasks.
- Individual User—Performs tasks, updates tasks and closes out tasks.

Access to the task management solution and permission to perform the functionalities available within it are managed by 30 different entitlements, such as creating and assigning tasks, adding or modifying checklists, establishing user groups, attaching documents and accessing the imaging system.

The main business entities

The main business users include 43 internal departments impacted by new client conversions, including technology, trading, tax reporting, statements, new accounts and mutual funds. These areas create task checklists, assign groups, update tasks, add documents and comments, and manage the overall completion of

---

[1] [1]Getting Things Done, Penguin Books, David Allen (2003)

tasks. Each business has a conversion liaison responsible for managing tasks and assignments for their team.

The group most significantly impacted by the new task management solution is the 30-person Client Transition team, responsible for leading the onboarding of all new clients to the firm.

The case template

Based on the type of onboarding (new client, in-house transfer, start-up client, de-conversion or managed investments) a different conversion template is used. The checklists and steps contained within these templates do not change per conversion, but are updated and subject to supervisory review periodically. This ensures consistency of results regardless of conversion size or complexity, or volume of conversions taking place.

4.3 Organization & Social

Although all employees on the Client Transition team and departments reported significant time savings and greater ease in accessing the system and making updating, most impacted was the individual responsible for maintaining the system, loading tasks and communicating the kickoff to the business areas.

Previously, more than 75 percent of this individual's time was dedicated to managing the conversion process. With the new system, this percentage has decreased to below 50 percent. Instead of manually loading hundreds of tasks, the conversion template now stores these items. Instead of holding regular in-person meetings, the system now alerts users when items are added, coming due or past due. Finally, instead of distributing hard copies of project plans, team members now electronically access and update the plans.

According to users, the solution is "more user friendly and easier to work with" than PPM, the previous Microsoft Project-based system. While PPM proved useful for IT project management, it was not particularly suited to different client conversion types, along with multiple tasks, checklists and steps. It did not have the capability to add documents and comments or house all of the components in a centralized location. While PPM automated some tasks, it still required hours of manual updates and was therefore an interim step between the one hundred percent manual, paper-based system and the fully automated and centralized task management system currently in use.

"It previously took more time, sometimes 30-40 minutes or more to look up something related to a project. Now, with the new system, it's 1, 2, 3. I just put my cursor on the icon and the information pops up," said one user (see Figure 4). "It has drastically reduced the number of steps it takes to complete a task."

Figure 4

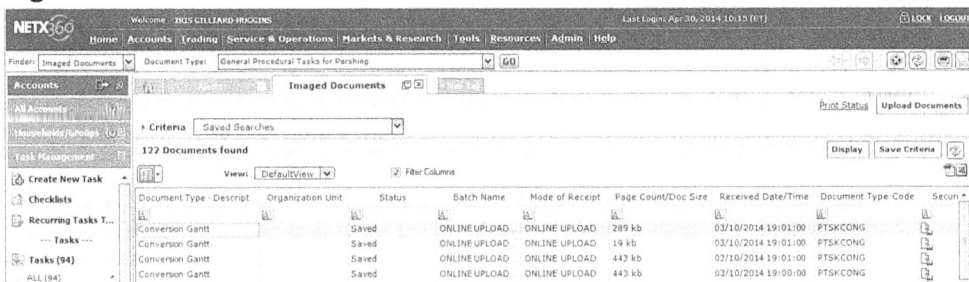

With task management, tasks can be added in one or two minutes and people can be added to groups as needed. Said another user, "It is a great enhancement, especially for tracking purposes."

A completely in-house solution, over 46 members of the Product Analyst Group at Pershing worked on implementation of the task management solution over a two-and-a-half year period, spending over 20,000 hours. With an open flow of communication, feedback was readily received from the business areas and the implementation team could add new functionalities to help evolve the solution to meet the complex business needs of the conversion team. At all stages, processes were checked and validated with senior management and users to ensure that they would meet business and operational needs.

The implementation team also leveraged the Center of Excellence (CoE). The Center of Excellence supports BPM development projects across Pershing. The CoE monitors the results of program execution by capturing and reporting on Business Process Analytics. The BPM is transparent to business process owners and BPM initiatives are supported by the Executive Committee. Available metrics provide the CoE, process owners and the Executive Committee insight into the following KPIs:

- Process adoption
- Increased productivity

The BPM CoE has a governance model and relies on partner groups, including Project Management, Business Analysis and Technical Architecture. All participants are aware of and support the Software Development Life Cycle (to allow for a defined, repeatable, approach in creating new process flows and enhancing existing ones). Each technical service in the BPM Solution space feeds information to the BPM CoE and has its own strong governance, including defined business and product ownership. With the practices in place, and the results of the BPM program as reported, the CoE has a profound impact on the entire organization. All team members, from project sponsor to developers, are encouraged to ensure that BPM practices are well represented.

5. HURDLES OVERCOME

Management

Specific requirements for the solution were not provided, so the development team conducted significant research to determine how other systems that required repeatable tasks, such as Microsoft Outlook behaved. They also experimented with different process flows and communicated regularly with future users and senior management to validate whether the solution, at each stage of development, would ultimately meet their needs. Senior management appreciated the accountability and traceability the solution provided as well as the ability to scale it for both external clients and for internal business needs.

Business

Based on early demos to the business areas, feedback was shared on functionality that could help improve business processes. This resulted in several features and functions being added to each new release. These included assigning tasks to user groups, not just individuals; attaching and storing documents at the task and step level; making checklists confidential and capturing comments as part of the project.

Organization Adoption

The Client Transition team worked hard to train users on the new solution and ease the transition. This included overview training to groups and time spent at the desks of individual users. The intuitive nature of the automated system and its user-friendliness has resulted in training time being drastically reduced with the new solution. Associates easily grasp how it works, reducing training time to a half-hour in most cases. The previous system required hours of training, with users relying on "cheat sheets" to perform certain functions.

Ultimately, the task management solution has been very well received by both employees on the Client Transition team and the business areas. As one user put it, "The simplicity makes performing work much easier. With the new solution, tasks now appear automatically. It's very self-explanatory."

6. BENEFITS

6.1 Cost Savings / Time Reductions

Task management has helped the team at Pershing standardize its onboarding process and improve productivity. The new tool and associated processes has meant that the team can handle new client transitions more efficiently and achieve better transparency into the numerous tasks involved in a conversion.

- Project initiation happens in real time across 43 departments at Pershing, instead of taking days to set up and load tasks.
- Training has been reduced from hours to 30 minutes as trainees easily grasp the new solution, whereas the old system took several hours to train and users relied on "cheat sheets" for certain tasks.
- Users can now respond to client inquiries in real time by pulling up documents housed in the imaging system, whereas it previously took 30-40 minutes, or longer, to research items.
- Loading a task or adding a new user only takes one or two minutes, as opposed the 15 minutes previously.
- Time management for teams and individuals improved dramatically, enhancing the overall project efficiency and individual productivity.
- Automation of projects helps groups and individuals manage time and business efficiency.

6.2 Increased Revenues

Since implementation of the task management solution is an internal project, it does not have a direct impact on firm revenue. Task management has however, reduced business costs, including for personnel, training and paper use. Since it is an in-house system, the need to pay any licensing fees to external vendors has been eliminated.

6.3 Quality Improvements

The move to the new task management solution has enabled the Client Transition team and business areas impacted by the conversion to realize quality improvements in various areas, including:

- **Consistency**—By adding checklists that follow both regulatory requirements and Pershing's policies and procedures, a consistent outcome is ensured with each project.
- **Centralization**—Using a built-in imaging system, all documents, comments and history are recorded and archived for the time period required by books and records or external regulators.
- **Automation**—The need for individuals to track specific tasks, remember what steps need to be performed in what sequence, and the length of time documents need to be stored for books and records is eliminated. These features are embedded into the system.

- **Transparency**— Information, documentation and comments are easily accessed by all team members, providing accountability for up to 1,100 steps per conversion.
- **Easy Updates**—Individuals can easily update the status of tasks and close them.
- **Confidentiality**—Since checklists can be created as public, private or shared, this eliminates the risk of sharing sensitive or confidential information with the wrong individuals.
- **Green**—Paper use is essentially eliminated as tasks, steps and checklists are available electronically, removing the need to circulate copies. Audit and client inquiries are also responded to electronically. An estimated 5,200 sheets of paper have been saved each year.

7. BEST PRACTICES, LEARNING POINTS AND PITFALLS

7.1 Best Practices and Learning Points

Based on the experience of the Product Analyst Group, Client Transition team, and 43 internal departments involved, several best practices and learning points were noted, such as:

- ✓ *Hold frequent demos with the impacted business areas during development to receive feedback and add functionalities to help meet business needs.*
- ✓ *Track metrics such as efficiency, productivity and paper use at the beginning of the implementation and again at the end to show improvements.*
- ✓ *Follow the rules of any external regulators and internal policy and procedure guidelines when creating the steps for task checklists.*
- ✓ *Assign user groups, not just individuals, to tasks to ensure there is a Backup for completing tasks.*
- ✓ *Add a comments field for tasks and checklists, which then becomes a permanent part of the project's history.*
- ✓ *Review checklists on a half yearly basis to ensure they still meet regulatory requirements and business needs.*
- ✓ *Integrate with existing platforms to make it easier to view and track tasks and project deliverables.*
- ✓ *Add "hover over" icons to view user groups, individuals assigned to complete tasks, comments, etc.*
- ✓ *Integrate an imaging system to attach documents and store at the task or step level for the period required by books and records.*

7.2 Pitfalls

The project encountered few pitfalls as the new process represented a major improvement over the previous paper-based, semi-automated process, however, the following pitfalls were encountered:

- ✗ *Not creating checklists to follow firm guidelines and procedures could result in tasks not being completed successfully.*
- ✗ *Making changes to checklists or tasks could result in inconsistent outcomes across projects.*
- ✗ *Not providing an option to make checklists confidential could present a conflict for some business areas.*
- ✗ *Allocation of additional storage space in the back-end system is needed if a large number of tasks are planned.*

8. COMPETITIVE ADVANTAGES

Since the task management solution was developed in-house and on a flexible platform, it can be easily adapted as the business needs of the Client Transition team and internal departments evolve.

The adaptability of the master conversion checklist and ability to modify and add steps in the conversion process, plus attach notes and documents to tasks and steps means that the processes can be adapted as business requirements and regulations change. This enables Pershing to be more nimble when onboarding new clients and helping clients onboard additional firms due to mergers and acquisitions.

Going forward, the Product Management Group will interact regularly with the Client Transition team as well as the BPM Center of Excellence to ensure the solution continues to meet Pershing's business needs.

9. TECHNOLOGY

The development of the task management solution was based on the "Getting Things Done" (GTD) time management methodology, which is based on two key objectives:

1. *Capturing all the things that need to get done—now, later, someday, big, little, or in between—into a logical and trusted system outside of your head and off your mind; and*

2. *Disciplining yourself to make front-end decisions about all of the "inputs" you let into your life so that you will always have a plan for "next actions."*[1]

Since there are many tasks, either simple or more complex, performed by the Client Transition team and departments involved in a conversion, the objective was to create a system to track these tasks and provide transparency, accountability and traceability, all while storing the documents and history in a centralized location.

The front-end of the solution was implemented based on .Net 2.0, a Windows platform, which offers improved graphics and a richer user interface than web-based solutions.

The back-end of the solution was created based on Pershing's existing Oracle back-end system, which the team felt offered enhanced system performance. Extra storage space was allocated due to the large number of tasks involved in client conversions.

Based on feedback received from business areas during implementation, the following additional functionalities were incorporated:

- **Alerts**—Alerts notify user groups or individuals about tasks that are added, coming due or past due, serving as useful reminders to complete tasks and keeping the overall conversions on track.
- **Comments**—Adding comments at the step or task level means that team members no longer have to remember the details or dates associated with each task. If you need to look up an item several months later, it is easy to call up the project history. Everything is in one place.
- **Imaging**—Attaching documents ensures that documents associated with a task or step stays with the task or step, and are stored in the imaging system for the time allocated by books and records.

10. THE TECHNOLOGY AND SERVICE PROVIDERS

NetX360® Task Management helps users manage their time and business processes more efficiently by enabling them to create, organize, process and monitor tasks. With NetX360 Task Management, users can collect, organize, process and monitor on a wide range of tasks, streamline daily processes by automating simple, one-step, or multi-step, complex tasks on a one off or recurring basis, assign tasks to a single user or a user group to minimize effort, and subscribe to task alerts so they are notified of tasks requiring attention. Users can also create and deploy standard checklists such as create a financial or project plan to ensure staff complies with policies, and procedures and customize them to business needs. Task Management is integrated with Pershing's NetX360 solution so users can access all task management functions from a single platform and see all tasks in a single inbox. The tool is offered as a complementary addition to NetX360 for Pershing clients.

Albridge Document Management was used to implement the imaging system. Albridge Document Management stores vast quantities of web-accessible e-documents in easily searchable formats, a few keystrokes away. Incoming paper documents are scanned locally, quickly and easily.

Albridge is an affiliate of Pershing LLC, a BNY Mellon company.

We Are Pershing, a BNY Mellon company

Pershing, a BNY Mellon company, and its affiliates provide global financial business solutions to advisors, asset managers, broker dealers, family offices, fund managers and registered investment advisory firms. A financial services market leader located in 23 offices worldwide, we are uniquely positioned to provide advisors and firms global insights into industry trends, regulatory changes and best practices, as well as shifts in investor sentiment and expectations. Pershing provides solutions–including innovative programs and business consulting–that help create a competitive advantage for our clients.

Pershing LLC

As the New Model Clearing FirmTM, Pershing LLC provides a broad suite of financial business solutions so advisors and broker dealers can drive their business forward in a dynamic industry and regulatory environment. We are the #1 clearing firm in the U.S.* and our clients range from full service, institutional and independent firms to self-directed and bank-affiliated broker-dealers and span the globe. With a keen eye on delivering dependable operational support, robust trading services, flexible technology, an expansive array of investment solutions, practice management support and service excellence, our solutions help advisors and firms manage their businesses efficiently and serve their clients effectively.

* Based on number of broker-dealer clients, InvestmentNews August 2013

Important Legal Information—Please read the disclaimer before proceeding

• Information and content presented in this document are not intended or construed as an offer, solicitation or a recommendation to purchase any security. Pershing LLC and its affiliates do not provide legal or tax advice. The information and tools herein are not intended nor written to be used for the purpose of avoiding tax penalties that may be imposed on the taxpayer. You should consult your own legal advisors and/or tax advisors to understand the legal and tax related consequences of any information or actions described herein.

• The contents may not be comprehensive or up-to-date, and Pershing LLC will not be responsible for updating any information contained within this document. Pershing makes no representation as to the accuracy, completeness, timeliness, merchantability or fitness for a specific purpose of the information provided in this document.

Pershing assumes no liability whatsoever for any action taken in reliance on the information contained in this document, or for direct or indirect damages resulting from use of this document. Any unauthorized use of material contained in this document is at the user's own risk.

Copyrights and Trademarks

All information contained in this chapter may not be reproduced, transmitted, displayed, distributed, published or otherwise commercially exploited without the written consent of Pershing LLC.

State of Hawaii
Department of Human Services, U.S.
Nominated by Imagine Solutions, U.S.

1. EXECUTIVE SUMMARY / ABSTRACT

Who: Citizens of Hawaii seeking services and support for food, shelter, childcare assistance, employment support and work training, and dependency diversion and prevention.

What: State of Hawaii, Department of Human Services (DHS), Benefit, Employment and Support Services Division (BESSD). BESSD is the largest division in the Department of Human Services and provides services through nine programs that serve different populations. There are 14 processing centers statewide with a total of 34 physical locations.

Why: A common theme with Health and Human Service agencies is tackling an increasing need for citizen support by leveraging case management solutions (CMS). For Hawaii's BESSD, did so their objective was to improve data quality, eliminate errors, and manage more efficiently an increasing number of cases, without increasing staff, as well as to eliminate the restriction for citizen documentation to only be accessible at one location, on any island.

BESSD's new CMS application interfaces with the DHS system of record and supports integrated capture, routing, review and archival of case documents. The solution maintains an electronic format that supports automatic recognition and classification of citizen-provided forms, minimizing the need for manual intervention leading to improved accuracy for form validation. Documents are then routed to an electronic case folder; staff are empowered to view household information, case documents, and manage pending requests facilitating accelerated case processing times. Overall, the CMS supports more consistent process management, better mitigates fraud, and provides instant accessibility to the information captured with a 360^0 case view from any of the 34 distributed locations.

2. OVERVIEW

Business Context

Through nine programs that serve different populations, State of Hawaii's DHS/ BESSD staff provides a continuum of services that include food, shelter, and child care assistance, as well as employment support and work-training, and dependency diversion and prevention, all requiring substantial case documentation. The state provides these services at 34 branch locations across the islands.

The State of Hawaii's DHS/BESSD agency recognized their existing human services application was due for an overhaul when symptoms included misrouted and lost documents, manual indexing and reporting, and manual process management. Worst of all, the delays in pending requests for missing documentation often lead to delayed distribution of benefits to families in need. The overall citizen experience was poor, and, employee confidence in the system was low due to inconsistencies and holes in the system where accuracy could be bypassed.

The DHS/BESSD agency's main objective in the CMS project was to improve the citizen experience, improve data quality, provide an optimized 360° view of cases across all the branches, and manage more efficiently an increasing number of cases from citizens requesting assistance without adding additional support staff. They had a clear vision in that they wanted to be able to work cases documents from any of the 34 branch locations.

Business Drivers

- **Increase operational efficiency** - hard paper produced misfiling opportunities and inconsistencies in procedures and processing, and case handling, leading to delays in benefits disbursement. Each branch location had its own manual process for tracking, indexing and reporting.
- **Reduce paper handling** - routing and approval of hard documents were time-consuming, inefficient, and sometimes resulted in document loss. Additionally, storage for paper files and documentation was limited and in some case the branches were not able to file the paper securely.
- **Workflow improvement** - DHS/BESSD experienced difficulty meeting federal service level agreements (SLAs). With the existing application, there was no way to automate the tracking of SLAs, only manual tracking. Once again, each remote office had its own process for handling and tracking SLAs.

THE KEY INNOVATIONS

4.1 Business

State of Hawaii's DHS/BESSD agency now engages its constituents more efficiently with the new CMS application. The CMS has demonstrated that citizen cases are now handled more efficiently with zero loss of information and misfiling. The CMS application has dramatically increased accuracy of data collection and procedure enforcement, providing automated audit control, and real time tracking to ensure federal SLAs can be achieved. The implementation of the new CMS has eliminated the need to fax documents from branch to branch, reduced inter-branch mail, and provided better customer service to the Hawaii citizens with timelier benefits distribution.

4.2 Case Handling

Prior to the CMS implementation, case documentation was centralized to specific branch location based on a citizen's place of residence. Tracking and organizing case documents were a manual process. The documents were only available to the branch where they were collected. Upon request, citizens would provide documentation either via mail and would bring them into the branch of their choice where they were copied and dropped into a paper case folder.

When compliance audits were requested, the paper files were manually assembled and shipped offsite. Case workers were not able to access those files during that time, resulting in potential disruption of service to citizens. Once the files were returned to the branch, staff would have to manually re-file them for use. The business case for the CMS was based upon improving case processing efficiency, providing a consistent framework for working cases, and providing visibility to all the content captured at any of the 34 branch offices across the islands.

The new CMS application allows workers at any branch to view case documents and work a case.

Although every case can be different, the following diagram outlines a general flow for the solution relative to benefits applications:

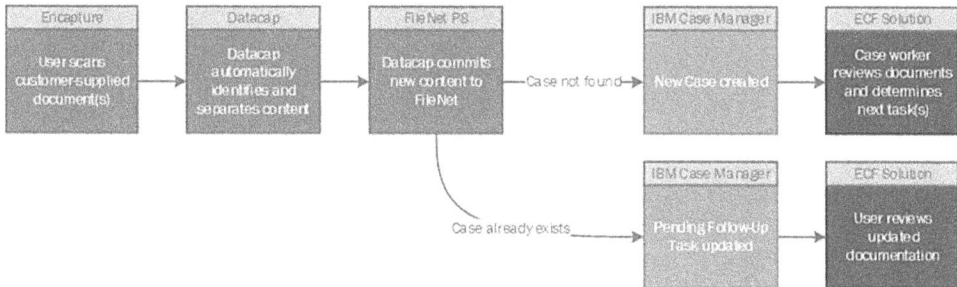

The benefits application process typically begins when a user hand-delivers or mails a benefits application to one of the State of Hawaii's 34 processing centers. A case worker will generally meet with the applicant (if they are present) and gather some key information up front. They then scan any documentation provided into the system.

Once the case worker has scanned the documents, the case application will automatically process the documentation. If the documentation is one of those the application has been trained to recognize it will automatically apply document type information and (depending on the type) extract key business from the document. All other documents are given a generic document type, which prompts users later on to review for manual classification.

When done processing a batch, the case application will commit the documents to the back end repository.

From there, if the documentation corresponds to a new application, the case application will create a case in the system and file the documentation. This will spawn a new task to prompt the case worker to review the incoming documentation for completeness. If the case worker finds that one or more pieces of substantiating documentation are needed, he or she can log a request by filling out a simple e-form, as shown below:

Log New Pending/Processing Item

Case Number:	08765432 - Jones, Jeannie (05/13/1980)
Location:*	190 Waipahu Unit
Type of Work:	SNAP
Expedited:	• Yes
	No
Due Date:*	04/02/2014

Documents Needed

Type	Description
Permanent Records	Birth Certificate - Jeanne Jones
Permanent Records	Birth Certificate - John Jones

Add

Cancel   OK

The form was designed to provide some flexibility in identifying which document(s) are needed to satisfy an application. Case workers select an entry from a list of predefined document types, but they can also enter additional descriptive information for each document being requested.

The process of tracking down missing or deficient documentation was one of the key tasks modeled as part of the overall solution. As the following Case Manager Process Map illustrates, the process allows eligibility workers to log pending requests and then revisit to them when other events (such as the arrival of a new document) occur. Additional functionality allowed for escalation of pending document tasks when the expiration date was approaching, so that customer follow-up and outreach tasks could be performed.

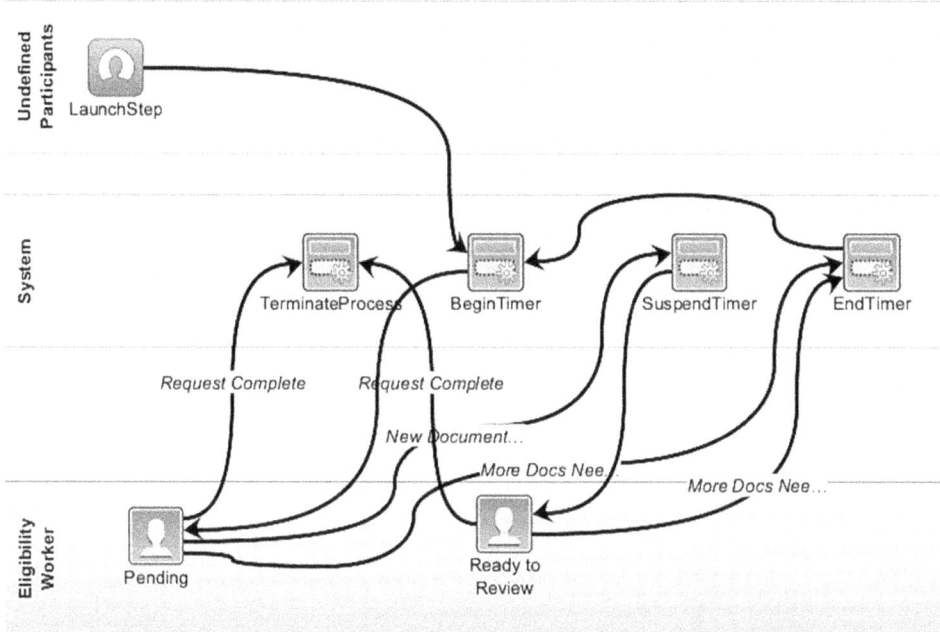

Once a pending task has been created, it is displayed in a summary tab below the contents of the case folder. At any time, a case worker can open the task and review details related to that request.

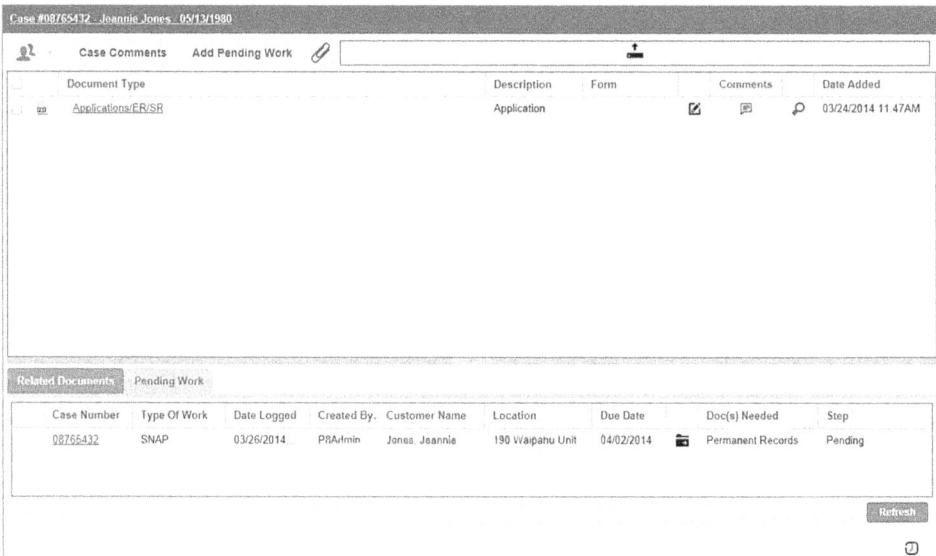

When new documentation corresponds to an existing case is received, the case application will locate the case and add the documentation to the case folder. It will then locate any existing pending documentation follow-up tasks and move them to a state indicating they are ready for review, as shown below. This frees case workers from having to manually follow-up on each open case, allowing them to focus on just those cases warranting further review.

Electronic Case Folder | Pending/Processing Work | Missing Case Numbers

Pending (1) | Ready (2) | Expired (1) | Due Today (0)

Case Number	Type Of Work	Date Logged	Created By	Customer Name	Location	Due Date		Doc(s) Needed
08765432	SNAP	03/26/2014 12:24PM	P8Admin	Jones, Jeannie	190 Waipahu Unit	04/02/2014		Permanent Records
08765432		03/24/2014 11:51AM	P8Admin	Jones, Jeannie	190 Waipahu Unit	03/31/2014		Assets, Expenses

Opening up the task allows the case worker to view the newly received document against the list of needed documents. They can quickly indicate which required documents have been received; if all docs have been received, the task will terminate, otherwise it will go back into a pending status.

Ready to Review

Case Number: 08765432

Name / DOB: Jones, Jeannie (05/13/1980)

Type of Work:	SNAP
Expedited	Yes
Due Date:	04/02/2014

Indicate which document requests have been satisfied

	Type	Description		
✓	Permanent Records	Birth Certificate - Jeanne Jones	✕	🔗

Add

Newly Received Documents

Document Type	Description	
Permanent Records	Birth Certificate - Jeanne Jones	✎

Other Pending Work Items

Work Type	Location	Step	Due Date	Doc(s) Needed..
	190 Waipahu...	Ready to Re...	03/31/2014	Assets, Expe...

Close

Complete

There are a total of 490 authorized users of the system. Three key roles have been identified to interface with the CMS and ECF, which has led to increase collaboration among the workers and enabled them to be more empowered to handle the cases efficiently and accurately:

- **Eligibility Worker** – regardless of whether or not they are supervisors, these individuals have the ability to review content, re-index that content (as needed), and add comments relative to a particular document or the overall case.

- **Clerical Workers** - these hands-on users are predominantly responsible for adding content to the system, but they may also play a role in reviewing, commenting and working in captured documents and/or cases.

- **"Read-only" Support** – this role was recently introduced to help support both agency executives and quality control workers. These users have the ability to view content throughout the entire system whenever necessary.

4.3 Organization & Social

A staged implementation helped to minimize the impact of the new CMS application.

4. HURDLES OVERCOME

Organization Adoption

The staff was set in their ways, accustomed to the existing manual paper processes causing was a level of uncertainty resulting in user apprehension and some resistance. Another challenge with the staff was limited technical skill set. The team addressed the staff concerned by staging the application rollout with hands-on training at each location which would range from less than a day to multiple days.

Management

Due the level of uncertainty with the staff, the management team adopted more of a marketing perspective by bringing the staff in as part of the development process. The knowledge workers actually became part of the process of defining tasks, sequences, and selections.

Business

To better face challenges of implementing the new CMS application the agency facilitated a test pilot program. Originally, citizens would provide documentation to be scanned upon entry of the branch office. This caused significant bottle neck, leaving citizens waiting in long lines to access the scanner causing major delays in service. Soon into the pilot program the agency realized that they would need more of a fundamental shift in the new business process, and adapted the solution to more efficiently meet the citizens' needs and provide a better experience. Once the test pilot program proved to be successful, the staged rollout began, providing the hands-on training and oversight necessary to minimize any further issues.

5. BENEFITS

Following are some key metrics relative to volume; all figures cited are monthly averages based on December 2013 through February 2014:

- Financial Assistance Cases:
  - o Current caseload: 8,961
  - o Applications per month: 1,242
  - o Approvals per month: 556 (45%)
- SNAP (Food Stamps) Cases:
  - o Current caseload: 98,528
  - o Applications per month: 5,758
  - o Approvals per month: 4,564 (79%)

With regards to document storage, in the first four months of usage:
- Nearly 300,000 documents have been added to the system
- Each case references an average of 9 documents
- Nearly 1900 batches are scanned daily using Encapture
- Over 5000 documents are being committed each day

6.1 Cost Savings / Time Reductions

- Staff spent an average 15 minutes per day either looking for the documents or for the actual file itself, and then returning it to a specific location. Documents are now available at their fingertips with just a few clicks.
- Policy has been set to destroy documents after 30 days from the date of scan. This reduces the amount of paper that the agency kept on hand in storage, thereby reducing the need for additional file cabinets and space. Many of the branch offices have very limited storage space.

- Case reviews can be conducted from any location that has access to ECF. This reduces travel time to go to a location to view a case and eliminates the need to transport case files from one location to another (while minimizing shipping costs).
- Documents that have been digitized can easily be sent to other agencies via email attachments immediately instead of having to locate the case file, then locate the document, make a copy or fax, eliminating the need to extract and re-file the document(s) and/or case file.
- Client contact times have been reduced as the worker can access their documents or case file while on the phone with them instead of putting them on hold or calling them back to resume the conversation once they locate the document or file. The CMS application allows worker to be more efficient when working with documents and files.
- Fraud investigations are handled much more efficiently, and more completely, now that the digitized content is easily accessible from one location. There is no longer need to transport case files nor is there a need for assembling files where in some cases files may be located in more than one branch. Additionally, the CMS triggers a web service that calls the Eligibility System which tracks duplicate requests for benefits, again, helping to minimize the time spent locating files and investigating fraudulent requests.

6.2 Increased Revenues

The CMS application allowed the agency to more efficiently manage an increase number of cases without adding additional staff helping costs to remain constant.

6.3 Quality Improvements

- The CMS application has reduced the need for filing cabinets to house all case files, and offices can configure their space differently. Citizen documentation is now securely stored.
- The CMS eliminates injuries that can occur when handling thick case files.
- The CMS application minimizes the frustration in trying to locate documents and case files which helped improve staff morale. Working in files is no longer a cumbersome, time consuming process.

BEST PRACTICES, LEARNING POINTS AND PITFALLS

7.1 Best Practices and Learning Points

- ✓ *Keep it simple. It is better to have many smaller focused, straightforward tasks vs. fewer comprehensive tasks.*
- ✓ *Keep the customer in mind. Offload decision making to the system vs. the customer wherever possible.*
- ✓ *Keep your users in mind. Let the knowledge workers drive the priority of tasks, selections, and sequence based on their first-hand experience of working with and delivering benefits to citizens'.*

7.2 Pitfalls

- ✘ *Do not assume that every case will be handled the same way. Each citizen case is dynamic, requiring unique selections (documentation) and sequence of tasks based on the type of assistance required.*

7. COMPETITIVE ADVANTAGES

Applying the strengths of the CMS application to improve how the DHS/BESSD agency provides services to citizens was the central focus. Given the inherently document-intensive nature of how these services are delivered, the integration of "transactional capture" features into the application provides an ideal extension of the case platform to the first "point of touch" with the citizen. Additionally, this CMS application was built from the ground up to support a complex array of document management requirements and business rules, and can scale easily to meet expanded requirements and/or demand for services.

8. TECHNOLOGY

The **Electronic Case Folder** (ECF) application is a front-end application through which case workers access both the content to be viewed and the tasks to be performed for each benefits recipient. The ECF application uses IBM's rich set of Application Programing Interfaces (APIs) to interact with both FileNet P8 (for content) and IBM Case Manager (for accessing cases and tasks).

The Electronic Case Folder solution is built upon the following core components:

- **The solution** uses Imagine Solutions' Encapture to remotely capture documentation at each of the 34 processing centers located throughout the State of Hawaii. Workers use a combination of workstation-attached scanners and network-attached multi-function devices to scan relevant case-related documentation. Encapture's ability to provide centralized administration and support a wide variety of capture devices were key factors in its selection for this solution.

- **IBM Datacap** is an advanced document capture platform. The ECF solution leverages Datacap's advanced document recognition functionality to automatically classify 15 of the most common document types received in conjunction with benefits applications. Additionally, the solution uses Datacap's data extraction capabilities to extract key business data (such as due dates) from certain documents; this information is used to drive downstream case management tasks.

- **IBM FileNet P8** is the core Enterprise Content Management platform used by the State of Hawaii. The State of Hawaii required that as part of the solution, all case-related content would be stored in a single enterprise-class repository. Moving from paper to electronic files provides users with greater efficiencies for working with information, and allows the State of Hawaii to ensure that document retention and destruction policies can be enforced consistently and automatically.

- **IBM Case Manager** works in conjunction with FileNet P8 to offer robust case management services. Case Manager forms the heart of the ECF solution, and is used to manage the various tasks involved with reviewing initial applications and following up on additional documentation that is required for a decision to be made. IBM Case Manager's robust set of APIs and easy-to-use case modeling tools made it a natural choice for this solution.

- **HAWI** is a host-based application that is used by the BESSD staff for a variety of activities related to processing benefits. Developers associated with the State of Hawaii built a web service interface to HAWI that allowed both Encapture and the ECF application to access key case information and leverage it for indexing purposes, thus ensuring that content and processes were kept in sync across multiple systems.

9. THE TECHNOLOGY AND SERVICE PROVIDERS

About Imagine Solutions

Imagine Solutions provides innovative enterprise content management (ECM) technology solutions that bring new levels of automation and agility to document–intensive business processes. From our flexible capture platform - *Encapture*, to our complete range of ECM services, leveraging our skilled ECM consultants, we help clients substantially improve information quality, increase operational effectiveness and mitigate compliance risk.

Imagine Solutions has quickly become an ECM leader within some of North America's leading financial institutions and government services organizations. Imagine Solutions, an IBM Premier Business Partner, recently received IBM's Partner Achievement Award 2013 for innovation and excellence in ECM.

For more information, visit www.ImagineSolutions.com.

About IBM

The primary solution software for this adaptive case management solution was provided by the IBM Enterprise Content Management (ECM) software division http://www-03.ibm.com/software/products/en/casemana.

The software solution is known as the IBM Case Manager. It is a comprehensive advanced case management solution which also integrates with a document management repository and capture components.

State of Maine, USA

Nominated by Pegasystems, USA

1. EXECUTIVE SUMMARY / ABSTRACT

Under the directive of its CIO, Jim Smith, the State of Maine launched a transformation into a digital enterprise built on top of a BPM solution. The goal – create an organization with the agility to adapt to market changes and provide superior customer services, replicating the operations of market-leading commercial organizations. This philosophy is unique to state government. Supporting the State of Maine's emergence as a BPM thought leader, is the establishment of an Enterprise BPM Center of Excellence, to ensure the state continually evolves and expands its operations through the use of BPM.

The State of Maine's successful first rollout was an application to bridge the State's unemployment insurance benefits and tax systems. The state then began to deploy this model into other internal functions, operations and initiatives including licensing. This was all built to increase efficiency using BPM, CRM, and case management combined in a single platform.

"Deploying BPM has been truly transformational," says Smith. "It has been the foundation for the delivery of services that rivals the private sector and offer new services responsive to ever changing mandates and requirements."

Key to Maine's decision was the ability to deploy via a secure and reliable cloud platform including the ability to easily and safely move applications and/or data to and from the cloud while maintaining security, privacy, regulatory and compliance requirements. Maine's visionary approach sets the standard for government and private sector alike.

2. OVERVIEW

The State of Maine was looking to modernize and upgrade both its operations and internal infrastructure to enable the state to keep pace with rapid changes impacting all businesses and governments nationwide, to become more efficient and to continually provide better service to its constituency.

While the state had already begun to go through the exercise of establishing a lean value stream mapping process to improve internal processes, they did not have the software infrastructure to support the development; in fact it was not available as the state needed. Under the leadership of CIO Jim Smith, the state began to search for an infrastructure that enable the state to achieve its goals, while providing the flexibility to adapt as changes continue to shape the market in the future. To that end, Mr. Smith selected an infrastructure that incorporated a secure, cloud-based infrastructure featuring BPM, CRM and case management on one single platform.

The biggest benefits and challenges in achieving this goal centered on internal cultural transformation. As the State of Maine was at the beginning of a transformational journey that required a change in awareness of about how to reach its goals, the benefits and challenges facing this project was more about cultural change than technology infrastructure and methodology. The technology, methodology and goals were agreed upon, in place and ready to move forward.

Cultural benefits were achieved as the business leaders took an "out-of-the-box" approach to building business processes around how to work more efficiently, using the benefits of technology to reach their goals. Additionally, for every business process recreated, the business leaders can reuse the assets to apply to other areas of government, capitalizing on already successful methodologies. From an end user standpoint, the transformation was easier, as once they became familiar with the system; they quickly realized how much more efficiently they could accomplish their work.

3. BUSINESS CONTEXT

It's well known that government organizations – federal, state and local – are continually facing the challenges of rapidly changing environments that include new regulations, increased demands and costs, while being required to watch budgets more closely. As such, state governments are constantly looking toward operating more efficiently, and the State of Maine is no different than its 49 brethren.

As standard operating procedure for state governments - federal mandates imposed upon states with no lead time that require immediate action – has developed a culture at the government of the State of Maine, to react quickly to change. The business has always been focused and ready to change, however, the processes available have transformed over the course of the state's innovative transformation through using technology.

Because of this culture at the State of Maine, the adoption of Pegasystems was easy, as the system enhanced the state's ability to change quickly, and enable them to achieve more, more quickly, more efficiently and effectively … truly transformational.

4. THE KEY INNOVATIONS

4.1 Business

The project involved the processing of blocked unemployment claims, a process that had numerous manual steps to reach the state of completion for each claim. Blocked claims could result in eligibility verification for a place of employment (such as a place of business did not keep appropriate records), which impacted the ability to verify wages, social security numbers … and ultimately led to claims unemployment benefits going unpaid as the case was resolved. Ultimately, if employment wage records cannot be matched to a claimant's work history, the UI benefit goes unpaid until the reconciliation can be determined. This process was largely automated and streamlined through case management.

The new system provided complete visibility for all claims, a unified data base of information accessible when needed, and resulted in a number of benefits that included more timely in paying constituents for their claims, and better upfront fraud detection of fraudulent claims. In fact, before the initiative, the average processing time to pay an unemployment claim was 42 days, with the new system the target was 21 days, and it wound up being reduced to less than one week.

4.2 Case Handling

As referenced above, the State of Maine previously went through an exercise of lean value stream mapping, to improve efficiency of overall operations. However, despite the benefits of that exercise, the state did not have a tool at its disposal that enabled the state to build the right application to achieve their goals. CIO Jim Smith undertook the initiative to utilize BPM technology to capitalize on the results of the lean value stream mapping exercise, following along the lines of the exercise to build an application that also used Pegasystems for its model driven methodology to achieve its goal.

The key roles

Overall, the roles, responsibilities and assignments within the organization stayed the same. The only change, which is a significant change, is transparency into workloads of staff members, ultimately providing more effective processing and better workloads for the end users.

The main business entities

The project supports and unifies a wide array of departments/functions with the unemployment claims process. Each department has real time access and complete visibility to all information supporting each claim, and the system supports departments across the organization. This includes customer service representatives in the call centre group when dealing with claimants, having the ability to update the system of record in real time. This in turn supports field auditors who can gain access to information as necessary, when working with customers/claimants in supporting their claims processing. Overall it has been a huge boost to the customer service provided to customers/constituents/claimants submitting claims, while ensuring compliance with any new regulations that may arise.

The case template in the system has been a huge benefit for the overall efficiency for the organization. Each template has a multitude of reusable assets that make the overall processes more efficient with greater agility as new issues arise. Reusable assets include document imaging and a variety of other functions. The case templates create more efficiency in the stages of intake determination for each unemployment claim, and the overall final adjudication very consistent across departments within the agency, and other agencies using the same framework for their operations.

Overall, the initiative has realized a 20 percent reduction in development costs through reusability, of which this project has contributed to.

4.3 Organization & Social

A major impact has been less work for the employees, and their workload has become easier to manage because they have complete visibility into their workload, and the status of each case, and many of the manual steps previously required are now automated and managed electronically. This includes having the ability to electronically tag the required data within each case, save it, and eliminate the need to manually make copies of documents, storing the data electronically so it's available as needed and reducing the number of lost information and ultimately reducing stress. Their jobs have become easier to accomplish the tasks with the new initiative.

An enterprise-wide Center Of Excellence has been developed by the State of Maine to define the class structure and reusability of assets across the organization. The state had the focus and expertise to build a system to establish a reliable and smooth running system that manages complex processes. Also, they are able to deliver assets that are easy for the end user to deploy and use enterprise wide, ultimately reducing the cost of each asset the more it is used.

5. HURDLES OVERCOME

The hurdles came more from the business/executive sponsorship, than from an IT perspective. The existing culture was filled with people used to writing IT requirements and essentially throwing them over the wall to the IT department in the hopes that the IT department could deliver on the requests. CIO Jim Smith and his team overcame the challenge to get people to work more collaboratively to create a system and technology infrastructure that met their needs more efficiently and effectively. At first there was strong opposition to this practice, however, once the individuals realized how they could benefit from this new process, they quickly joined the collaboration.

From the overall organizational adoption, the process and initiative has been very well received. End users are experiencing a better working relationship with customers/constituents, reducing the stress on their job functions, and the overall operations organization wide have been improving.

The strategies and experience driving organizational adoption.

Ultimately there was no choice other than receiving full organizational adoption. It was a state mandate and once all parties realized the benefits that the initiative provided, there was no push back. This came through open communication for all parties involved, providing demonstrations and training to make the transition more fluid and grounded.

6. BENEFITS

6.1 Cost Savings / Time Reductions

While some of the cost savings and time reductions are still being determined, top line reductions include reducing the amount of time required to process unemployment claims down from 42 days to less than one week. To date the larger organizational initiative has realized a cost reduction of 20 percent, of which this project has contributed savings to.

6.2 Increased Revenues

Top-line growth is still being determined as the grants from the federal funds earmarked for these types of state programs, in which each state unemployment administration process is based on overall performance, is awaiting feedback from the federal government.

6.3 Quality Improvements

As the project was built on one, centralized system that provides real-time visibility into all cases being worked on, when someone leaves a department or the agency overall, the details of that specific case are easily accessible to complete the specific case. Also, there are no more lost cases that may have been held up for one reason or another, as all cases are in the system and kept active by the system. All information is captured and visible.

7. BEST PRACTICES, LEARNING POINTS AND PITFALLS

7.1 Best Practices and Learning Points

✓ *Think about modularity and reusability early in the process, before launching the initiative.*

✓ *Ensure that your processes are good before you start building out the initiative. For the State of Maine, the value stream mapping exercise that was started and served as the blueprint for the technological and methodological process to make the initiative a success was critical.*

✓ *Early and active engagement from all key business departments/leaders involved in the project from the ground floor. Only through managing the process in that manner, was the project successful in building the system to meet their needs.*

7.2 *Pitfalls*

* ✗ *Avoid the opposite of everything highlighted in best practices above – avoid diving blindly without developing a strong plan, without securing/achieving buy-in from all parties involved, etc.*
* ✗ *Don't start with a project too big or too complex; start small and focused, build upon the success and reuse the successful assets to avoid log jams and downfalls. Think modularity early on.*

8. COMPETITIVE ADVANTAGES

Competitive advantages take on a different meaning for public sector organizations, as we are not in the same competitive environment when dealing with our state constituents as a telephone provider will face over services and fees. We want to always provide the best service and fees, as efficiently and effectively as we can.

This in turn plays into the State of Maine's ability to improve reimbursement by the federal government for grants based on improved performance. Reusability is enhanced in this environment and establishes a better foundation for dealing with the federal government for grants.

9. TECHNOLOGY

Pegasystems software, the PegaCloud, which easily integrated with the State of Maine's security backbone in an Oracle database. Pega also integrated easily with systems such as document management and document imaging systems that are homegrown within the State of Maine's infrastructure.

As referenced above, the biggest benefit is the focus on reusability and refactoring, building assets that are highly reusable and that was the focus when the State of Maine launched its initiative and implemented Pegasystems.

10. THE TECHNOLOGY AND SERVICE PROVIDERS

Pegasystems Build for Change® Platform is the heart of Better Business Software®. It delivers business agility and empowers leading organizations to rapidly close execution gaps and seize new opportunities. Pegasystems leverages its recognized leadership in Business Process Management (BPM), Multi-Channel Customer Relationship Management (CRM), Business Rules, and Adaptive Analytics to uniquely give its clients the power to engage customers, simplify operations and Build For Change®. For more information, please visit us at www.pega.com.

The Antwerp Port Authority, Belgium

Award: Judges' Choice, Best Entry

1. Overview

This personal story is written with a holistic perspective in mind: it's not just about case management, it's a case on knowledge management, information management, lean work organisation, performance management, internal communications, team management. Adaptive case management has shown itself as a major supportive methodology - or even better: philosophy for the organisation of our work. I strongly believe that adaptive case management is one of the pieces of the puzzle that forms our 21st century way of working, though, we do not see the whole yet.

We suspect adaptive case management thinking to be a revolution for today's knowledge company. At least, it made us conscious that in fact *any* problem-solving act can be perceived as *a case*, where intuition, trial and error is necessary to bring it to a good end. To see the agile process being developed around the information in a dialectic way, was for us the discovery of the natural, intuitive way that completely fits knowledge work; mirroring how knowledge production works.

It is not about the introduction of case management in one particular business unit, supporting one specific process. It is about the central Information Management department that takes the initiative to introduce case management thinking with knowledge workers in the whole company, and the externalisation of this will differ from team to team. We promote tools, practices, habits and help teams to fit these into their daily practices.

The tangible environment where we developed our adaptive case management is a wiki-like, team-collaboration software, with basic task management functionality. And with the seamless integration of an issue and project management application, we even please managers and project managers who really demand structured data and reports about the cases. With case management in this application we realized for the first time that *"lean* information and knowledge management" is possible.

A case about a central department promoting and implementing company-wide adaptive case management as a new work organisation philosophy, linking this to lean thinking, will contain most probably more than other cases general reflections and theoretical contemplations. We hope that these may add some new knowledge to the domain of adaptive case management.

Business Context

The 1,650 employees of the Antwerp Port Authority play an important role in the day-to-day operation of the port. They make sure the port is able to function and work on a sustainable future for the Port of Antwerp to ensure it can continue playing a leading role as an international seaport.

The Port Authority, as an organisation, is responsible for the exploitation of the port of Antwerp as a domain. It manages and maintains the docks, bridges, locks, quay walls and land. It is also responsible for the efficient passage and safety of the shipping traffic in the Antwerp port area. It provides tugs and cranes, carries out dredging work and promotes the port in Belgium and abroad. Though you can imagine lots of physical labour is involved, 60% of its 1,650 staff members are knowledge and information workers, and this will only grow.

With the blueprints for a new and prestigious administrative building, a major change project was set up in 2009: *"Overstag"* (*"Tacking our sailboat"*) that aims for the introduction of a new culture, a new way of working, cooperative working, digital working. At the end of 2010, the Archives Department got a refocus towards an Information Management Department, as digital information had grown so much in importance, also in the perspective of the Overstag project. Alfresco got implemented as ECM software application.

In 2013 information management got linked to knowledge management which made the scope on information richer and more practical. We started screening and walking the first processes, and from the perspective of head of the information management department, it was astonishing to see that many of these softwares had been conceived and implemented from the perspective of managers who need and want to be reported on things. Despite the richness and multitude of software applications, none of them really helps the "masses" of knowledge and information workers doing their work more efficiently. On the contrary: many of these softwares are fed manually with data that also exist in other applications, and these data mainly come from individually managed Excel-files, lists, Word-documents. We intentionally wanted to have our main focus on the unexplored working domain of the information worker, where Word-files, e-mails, Excel files, Evernotes, fly around to become meaningful, of which many in vain, while politically strongly positioned applications kept absorbing structured data, generating the necessary reports.

Main challenge: lean information management in support of efficient knowledge work

In 2013, the mission of the Information Management Department was linked to knowledge management. Though we use the term KM in this case explicitly, at home - in Belgium - we are more modest. In Continental Europe, 'generic' knowledge managers are not as densely employed compared to *Anglospheric* companies; the domain of KM in short seems not as popular. At this moment we find KM dispersed over and interwoven with the domain of HR (mainly learning and development, and performance management), information management, internal communications (that has become very active in the KM domain of collaboration due to the introduction of social media), quality management (continuous improvement), business intelligence (with a KM variant that is more focused on structured data), process management.

It might be helpful to explain what we mean by knowledge management in this case, from the perspective of information management. In short, we want to rethink how information management can help the organisation be a more intelligent organisation. If we measure the intelligence of a company on the speed, agility and quality of their problem solving processes, the quality of their decisions taken and on the task performance that effectively supports the execution of these decisions, then it certainly is our ambition to provide the management and knowledge workers with information management tools, processes and habits that support these ambitions.

Deduction, induction and abduction

We want to enrich knowledge work and problem solving contexts by having the three modes of logical reasoning supported: deduction, induction and abduction. I give examples of 'information contexts' that support, enable and foster each of these modes.

Deduction (general rule > particular case) is supported by the presence and proximity of taxonomies, record management centers, lessons learnt, knowledge repositories, sets of masterdata and metadata, information governance, intellectual property management, knowledge sharing, ...

Induction (individual cases > general rule) will profit from environments that foster easy information retrieval, expertise finding, help structuring unstructured information, modelling, hyperlinking, content curation, codification, wayfinding, rich context....

A*bduction,* where hypotheses are formulated, profits from bringing together several personal information repositories, dialogue and conversation, draft management, freestyling, idea management, creativity, discovery and serendipity stimulation, brainstorming, social drafting, 'related information' algorithms, recall, unstructured information...

All three modes are normally used in what we call *semiosis:* the dynamic process of meaning creation. Software applications that are used to automate knowledge workflows are deductive by nature: we can only create particular cases that meet generally stated criteria. Involving induction in these softwares is less frequently noticed; abduction gets no chance at all. Abduction and induction mainly start from non-structured information arenas.

Lean

When we speak about *value creation, speed, and efficiency*, we cannot but set up *lean* ambitions for our information and knowledge management projects. Lean principles applied on information management [1]will generically be translated as 1) the focus on creating *value* for and by the knowledge worker, 2) the elimination of *waste* in knowledge work 3) the creation of *flow* in knowledge work 4) the involvement of *pull* mechanisms (- this is where *agility* pops up) and 5) *continuous improvement.*

User Experience

When we apply lean principles to the design of processes, applications, interfaces, websites, then, by definition, we care about the user experience. How logical and soundly built your application, processes and interfaces might be, if they do not lead your user physically and mentally in the shortest and easiest way towards his goal, then you can and should do better - which means: getting rid of waste with a complete focus on creating value.

2. THE KEY INNOVATIONS

A holistic view: our ambitions about tools, processes and culture get realized

Focusing on efficient, effective, fast and agile institutional and the aligned team and personal problem solving, we surely want to provide tools and processes
- *that support a sound and efficient task and project management*
- *that support lean and agile information management*
- *that foster abduction and induction and deduction*
- *that foster learning in any step we take so that we can do better next time*

Now we realize that there were two important moments that were tipping points in the realisation of our success:

---

[1] *For a list of examples of the wastes in information management, see addendum in the digital version of this book*

1. the introduction of a wiki-like, team-collaboration software, with basic task management functionality; this made us conscious that "lean information and knowledge management" is possible.
2. the introduction of case management as central idea for our information management in support of knowledge management; it made us conscious that in fact *any* problem-solving act can be perceived as *a case*, where intuition and freedom is necessary to bring it to a good end. To see the agile process being developed around the information in a dialectic way, was for us the discovery of the natural, intuitive way that completely fits knowledge work - mirroring how knowledge production works.

We managed in bringing the two together, working out case management in the collaborative wiki environment (see below). And we won a bonus. Knowledge workers heavily involved in project management, mainly from the management side of the projects, asked for more structured data and reports than what we could offer with the wiki.

The issue and project management application from the same developer as the wiki got seamlessly integrated in our wiki-application (and vice versa) so that parties preferring structured data, unstructured and semi-structured information all experience a huge profit in this consistent system.

We sum up the main innovations of which we think our project is different from other initiatives.

The introduction of 'Lean' for information management in support of knowledge management

As a matter of fact, there is not much relevant literature on lean information management. Either it's quite superficial or it completely misses the point (e.g. "how to apply 5S to your mailbox"). Lean is in the first place about value creation.

Information is for action, not for storage.

- Starting up a new case, case templates in our projects always ask the user to complete a section on the problem to be solved in this particular case , and what the aimed at result is. All information, notes, ideas, discussions, plans, tasks, files, that will become part of this case, will pass this gateway and focal point, getting confronted with the necessity to serve this final aim *or they shall not be part of this case at all*. The path to that result is not or only vaguely stated; it's up to the knowledge worker to walk his iterative journey.
- It's not document management, it's problem-solving related information management. That's a huge difference. Do we just classify files in folders, leaving the most interesting information in the heads of our knowledge workers, or do we really process information to solve a problem?
- Case related tasks are not put in one or other silo, but they form an integral part of the content in the case itself. Tasks are defined and assigned wherever they pop up, amidst the content that is relevant to the execution of this task. (Macros enable us to generate ordered task lists though.) And more relevant information will be added to bring the task to a good end. There is an interesting information dialectics between task and case, creating positive feedback loops.
- Cases must show the blood, tears and sweat (and joy) that accompany the wrought-through product. Fierce discussions, dead ends, rework, mistakes, problems, failure must be logged in the case - these are the real lessons learnt. Apart from the refined comment and discussion functions

our wiki offers, we also provide templates to explicitly add problems identified, lessons learnt, retrospectives. In case teams, we ask to have the role of knowledge manager identified in one or more persons involved. They are asked to be alert towards this information (see below: roles).

- Cases must live in environments that are at the edge of hyperkinetics: as the message is the dynamics of semiosis, the medium should be this message. We find this in the freedom that a wiki offers its users, in the activity streams, in the personalized dashboards, in the interaction of sharing and pulling, commenting and replying. Case teams need a community manager who makes you enthusiastic and wild, but the team also needs an information manager who calls for order, as semiosis must end in a sign.

When information is used for and in action, its potential as knowledge is realized and value is created.

Your knowledge and information world must be one: integration creating consistency and a good user experience will create flow and happiness

Some knowledge workers live in their e-mail application, others in Word, and I met one who fixes everything with Excel - magic, but doubtful, and certainly not lean.

The home that we provide to our knowledge workers is the wiki.

- It's not a separate place for his case management. It's the place where he constantly is - even if he's abroad, in meetings, or working at home. It's a place that creates proximity. It's the place where the team posts its internal messages, where pregnancies are announced, it's the place where meetings are prepared, happen and followed up, it's the place where we co-edit texts, where I get notified about changes and replies to my input, where I define my tasks or get tasks assigned, where I check them as completed, it's the place where regular feedback on my and your performance is posted and commented, maybe disputed, and so on.
It's the richest content arena they have ever been at, without even moving from one application to another. Now that we also succeeded in integrating the project and issue management application seamlessly, even the structured-data-profiles do not need to leave their home. This creates flow, almost literally: you see complete lifecycles of cases and content, and not a mere selection of records moments. Knowledge managers profit from this, as they certainly identify tacit knowledge in these contexts.
- This does not only create flow, but it also creates a mass of dynamics and interaction that you need to reach the necessary tipping point to make your house a lively home, something all social media platforms need to survive. Empty platforms are doomed to stay empty forever.
- You offer an integrated platform that fosters abduction (fostered by the wiki freedom, the activity streams and notifications, the hyperlinks that lead you to surprising places, "related content", the collaboration arena, ...), induction (with its semi-structuredness, its manual sorting of pages and notes linked to overview pages, with streams of excerpted content, with the links and labels creating unity of dispersed information...) and deduction (eg. with the templates and workflows).
- This is also the necessary breeding ground for fostering interrelationships between content elements. If we see the easiness with which the wiki makes you link information to other information, cases to other related cases, at that moment you become aware of the very poor environment

you always worked in with your Word files, your shared drives or your BPM Softwares.

Keep it simple, and make trust one of your values.

After all, our case management system is about simple pages and simpler pages, that are sorted and linked. Even lay-out cannot be made complex: less is more. Easy made templates make it even simpler, as they guide you with predefined content through the process. Checklists remind you of necessary steps. You never need to rush gathering information from several silos: it's all at one single place. Notification mails pull you to the page. Activity streams tell you what's going on. Macros might be the most difficult element in the system, though, these macros are still much easier to configure than macros in Excel.

Using soft workflows, steered by people, *invites* participants to *cooperate,* they are not forced by anonymous workflow forces and automatic and unnatural system reminders. You truly collaborate in this environment. For page titles and excerpts (see below) you are asked to use your brain in summarizing the most relevant information of a note or a mail: you are a content curator, we rely on your wisdom. And the system will not fail or break because of you filling a field with invalidated data, you get the freedom as a knowledge worker to use predefined content in templates or not, or you can choose to add new 'empty' pages, that you will fill with the content that you find relevant and important at this moment.

Again, the medium is the message. And as the wiki by nature is an open and transparent system, you support and foster an open and transparent culture, where trust and respect can be true values.

Lean search

I attended the knowledge management summit *KM World 2013* in Washington, where I focused on the *search challenge* in information management. It was a relief to hear several cases from professionals and experts who stressed the importance of humans creating wayfinding instead of purely counting on the miracle search machine.

That's exactly where lean search enters the scene. Through working out loud our work, much process information floats on top, as cream on milk. That's meta-information. With the right attitude and sound and simple processes, team members are more pushed on the meta-level, being confronted with complexity, lack of contextual information, lack of unity, lack of consistency, lack of relations, lack of proximity. That's where they need to act, on the meta-level by adding meta-information and meta-data. They categorize, they hyperlink, they create navigation screens, they summarize, they order and sort, they clean out the mess - this is the true 5S in information management.

At these moments they work to improve findability, they support wayfinding in their world of information. This is the human brain. This is culture. But, you need to integrate information and knowledge work in a system that supports flow and consistency - that's the clue.

Working out loud

John Stepper (Managing Director Social Media and Collaboration at *Deutsche Bank*), has an interesting blog on this topic. Following Bryce Williams, he coined the term *"working out loud"* and defined it *as "creating/ modifying/ storing your work in places that others can see it, follow it, and contribute to it IN PROCESS."*

Working out loud is all about communication-in-the-process, and most probably, this will be one of the positively changing aspects in knowledge work: we're moving away from a non-communicative work context to a job where constant communication about your work is the standard.

And of course, this is made possible through the use of our wiki. Activity streams, 'naked' content (instead of closed files), notifications, sharing content, following content and persons, dashboards, version histories, comments and replies create full transparency and openness. Working out loud is of course interesting for knowledge managers, as thought processes are externalized in discussion lines, draft texts, mistakes, disagreements etc.

The role of knowledge manager in the case team is necessary to valorize this (see below: roles), and it would be ideal that every case manager adapts to this role. This is not easy, but a central department can help in stimulating this attentiveness, building local knowledge management awareness and skills.

But also the role of *community manager* is important. In our practice we stimulate team leaders to take up this role. They need to motivate the team members (and quite often with light pressure) to participate in these transparent dynamics.

It's also interesting for us (the information management department) at a meta-level to see what happens. Certainly in the beginning, we watch the activity of new teams, interfering 'live' in comments with tips and tricks.

We are at the beginning of a very interesting decade now: for the very first time it looks as if software (i.e. social media, enterprise social networks, enterprise content management systems) truly enables enterprise collaboration and knowledge sharing. Today's software is not only situated much more 'in-the-flow' of the knowledge worker's job, is has also grown tremendously in its 'usability' and user experience.

Meetings 2.0

Personally I cannot say that I like the genre 'meeting', although it is the preferred instrument to discuss blockers and progress of the open and planned cases in the team or organisation. Too many people gather for too much time around too many diverse cases. It's a huge loss of time, in many cases ending in unclear follow up.

Adaptive case management being "worked out loud" does not need those hours of group therapy. Profit from the pull mechanism: think 'just in time'. First of all, through working out loud, others can react immediately. Do you need to discuss one specific topic? Why waiting until we physically gather in one room? Just start the discussion online, and invite colleagues to provide input, when they have time, and feel best to do so. I always feel sympathetic towards people feeling so tired in meetings.

We advise team leaders to stimulate written discussions for several reasons:
- it forces you to think, analyse and synthesize before you write - there is more guarantee that it is to the point than in oral discussions
- people get time to answer and are less under pressure than in oral situations, where they need to reply instantly
- answers can be prepared better; you look up what's unclear or unknown
- information can be checked when it's doubtful
- there is less rhetoric and political power exerted in written discussions than in oral discussions
- it externalizes and stores thoughts and process information
- it enables asynchronous communication: people participate when it suits them best

Of course, my team leaders are sceptic that we question live meetings - we don't do this at all. We question unprepared, long meetings with too many participants for whom not all items are relevant. We do support short, focused meetings as "meta case moments", with those for whom the topic is relevant, and guaranteeing that the outcome is a clear commitment to action. That's why our meetings always have produced new tasks assigned to the team members.

We neither copy files in special "meeting folders". We just create, with a template, a meeting page. Discussion topics link to the cases in the wiki. Comments and tasks are added in the case, but these are linked back to the meeting page. Light meetings with light minutes, but providing all necessary and relevant information we need to get the things done.

And the more official the platform of the meeting is, the more complex the process gets, the longer the minutes, and the more complex softwares and workflows enter the scene.

My current IT department is preparing an update of their e-decision platform (i.e. meeting notes management, decisions management). They calculated 900 mythical man days for this job. After we reviewed the decision process, they recalculated it to 650 days. Now, with our wiki and project management applications entering the scene, I can do them a proposal of 70 days. I won't as we all adhere peace.

Active and conscious information management

It almost sounds too good to be true, but we see a more active participation in information management.

One reason is certainly the case perspective: a case groups all relevant information around a problem solving action at this moment. Each letter, each mail, each telephone call containing business information fits in a case. When the case does not exist, it must be started up. A new request? A new challenge? A case must be set up, using the correct template for that specific case type. The process owner gets notified automatically; he can interfere if necessary.

And from then on, each piece of information, content that is relevant to the case, will generate a new page in that case, using suggested templates. Each page type has its own labels, codes in the page title, that makes it easy to sort them, find them, or generate overview lists with macros. By default, the pages are sorted chronologically, but users can change the order. As a matter of fact, this is easy, natural and intuitive information management.

Take into account the freedom you get as a user in the wiki, and you can easily create chaos. The wiki certainly is prone to chaos. But activity floats as cream on milk. That's why case team members notice this and react to tendencies to chaos by adding meta-comments to notes about bad page titles, or bad excerpt information, or about bad page orders. They discuss openly about their information management, mainly how to improve it. They also discuss improvements of templates, of the composition of their case types etcetera.

It is not only because they are in an initial stage, and still see themselves as learners. It is because the experience of flexibility, dynamics, the strength and power to interfere in the system.

Mind that we always advise case teams to identify the role of information manager in their team. Somebody needs to systematically keep an eye on order in the information arena (see below).

Case management introduction in teams; Case handling

When a team contacts us to get introduced in case management in the wiki, we start by isolating one or two processes to start with. We 'walk' the process and do a short analysis of its workflow, milestones and information artefacts. With this information we work out some templates, and introductory pages, after which some case team members move some open cases to the wiki. For different roles (see below), we set up relevant overview pages. Normally, the team gets a short introduction. According to their role, this lasts for 1 hour, but there is also peer support on the wiki itself. We have a public space where any wiki user can post his questions.

The case management implementation based on the wiki and project management application is seen as an iterative process. We introduce team after team in the new environment, but each individual team also grows in the complexity, integration and features we offer. Teams normally start their case management in the new environment sorting and ordering their information using templates, and creating interesting overview pages that offer them and their managers a clear view on the progress and status. In many cases they still use other applications e.g. to store files.

Next steps can be that they set up more complex templates or, that they start using the integrated tasks, linked to their content. Team communication is also one of these things that grow. Soft workflow (passing through information, sharing, assigning tasks) might grow to a more solid and hard workflow, using step by step instructions, templates, tasks that need to be checked off. The ultimate integration, that we only see realized in one team at this moment, is an environment that integrates the complete team internal communication, content management, task management, case management, project management.

The Case elements

Annotations:
- My personal task list
- share with groups or individuals
- get notified of changes
- breadcrumbs and case title
- 4 buttons to add 4 types of case notes, each one based on a template with predefined structure, contents, labels, name format...
- Case basic information:
- Problem ID
- Expected results
- Tasks, anywhere you want to put them.
- related cases
- labels
- title of the subpage (case note), semi-coded
- Dossiernotities: Overview, here chronologically sorted.
- cases and subcases
- click your case and it opens in this pane
- comments and discussions
- 1 Reactie
- Extra information, added by the knowledge worker ("excerpts")

A page and its subpages

To create content, you create pages. where you can add all content you want: text, tables, diagrams, images, video, attachments, screenshots, links, mails, macros (see below).

As a user you add as few or as much structure to the page as you like, through adding sections (in columns and rows) and headings.

You can easily import your notes from the cloud (e.g. Evernote), issues/tasks from your project management system, Word files...

Attached multi-page pdf-files, MS Office files can be 'shown' in the page as browsable documents, without needing to open them. Attached MS Office files can easily be edited.

Pages have a name. Naming conventions are important, as names of pages are shown in "children pages overviews". These overview lists will provide you with important and relevant information about the status of the case. Apart from some predefined codes in the title, this 'important' information is manually typed by the knowledge worker. This is an important meta moment where the knowledge worker must be empathetic enough towards other stakeholders in this case that he succeeds in translating to them the content, relevance and importance of the added note in 1 condensed line.

By structuring pages and sub(sub)pages, you create hierarchy and unity: browsable case *files* are formed.

The hyperlink

It might be unnecessary to mention such evident things, but the easiness to link content to other content in and outside the wiki makes it a very dynamic and rich information arena. This is where we say goodbye to the book metaphor that we have always used to base our information management on. We are able to jump in 3 dimensions to all relevant information we need.

These hyperlinks are essential in wayfinding, so the users are stimulated to take that step in linking relevant information. When adding a page to a case, or, when starting up a new case, we always provide a section in a page asking for links to other cases or pages. We explicitly ask case administrators, owners and actors to invest in these wayfinding sections. This is not experienced as an annoying manual task, but it is an important moment that creates recall, that reminds case starters of precedents or possibly interesting knowledge for the execution of his case.

Macros

Macros are very powerful means to generate dynamic content and activity streams (*recently changed items, lists of added pages, tasks, mentions, content by labels...*), to format content, to create wayfinding pages (*table of contents, indices, anchors, children pages, page tree overviews, ...*) , to echo content that has been produced elsewhere, to manage your wiki (*statistics, label lists, changes, orphaned pages, lists of new spaces, lists of new pages, ...*), to create new content (*buttons to create new spaces, new pages from templates, new blogs, ...*). These macros can be put anywhere on a page, and they are easily configurable by all those who have edit-rights on that page. In your personal space, you can build your own relevant overviews using all available macros.

Templates

You can create new pages by using templates. Anyone with space admin rights can add templates or edit them. A template is started up as a normal page, adding all content types as mentioned above, but you can also add instructional text - that is only shown in edit mode - and fields with variables.

When you add macros such as "*create new page by template*", you not only help users start up easily a new case, but you can also guide the user in executing each step of the process in the right order by providing him with these buttons, if you want, combined with checklist buttons, in the right order. He can check these as finished when accomplished.

If templates are defined this way, process owners can get alerted that a new case has been started up. Also other tasks, even assigned to concrete users, can be pre-defined in templates. They become active once the page is generated and saved, then the assignee gets notified.

Adding a new page to a case is an important meta moment: you need to choose the correct page type, refine the name, add excerpts, add labels, manual labels, tasks, and invest in wayfinding. This is necessary knowledge work, that is partially manual, partially automated through choosing the correct template.

When having a new intake meeting with a team, looking into their processes for which they want to set up case management in the wiki, we walk through the process, after which we do suggestions on templates. Normally my department prepares the space and templates, after which they can start. In most cases, during practicing the first cases, these templates are fine-tuned either by us (on their request) or by themselves. As the central department also has at least one admin in each space, we can 'watch' the space in the beginning to get notified how they start up. Normally then, we give advice through comments with some tips, extra advice on leaner practices than what's has been done in the space.

Restrictions

At application level, admins can define which groups and users (linked to the Active Directory) can use the wiki, create new spaces, add/invite new users.

At space level, user rights are focused on what one can do with pages, blogs, comments, attachments, and the space as a whole (admin, export). E.g. for page operations, users are allowed or not to restrict pages.

At page level, users can restrict a single page in two clicks, arranging who (individuals or groups) can see and/or edit this page. All existing and future child pages inherit these restrictions. In a few clicks, you can remove these restrictions.

Tasks

Tasks can easily be defined anywhere on a page, though, in templates we provide a separate section on the page.

The assignee gets a notification mail, and the task also appears in his "workbox" in his profile corner. Clicking on the task will pull him to the concerned page in the case.

With macros you can create task lists and queries based on a combination of parameters: spaces, pages, labels, assignee, creator, creation date, status, completion date.

Labels

Through folksonomies users can tag their pages and attachments. Labelling influences higher rankings in search results, makes it possible to click a label and find all related pages, or to find related labels (i.e. labels that are often combined with this label at one page). But the most potential is found in using the macro "*content by label*', which enables you to show dynamic content overviews on pages. We advise teams to agree upon their *teamonomy*. The macro *'label list'* shows all used labels in their spaces. The information manager of the team can keep an eye on the consistency in the use and growth of this set. He does some scaffolding and gardening, merging labels, correcting them, and notifying users about his actions. In templates we can use the "*choose label*' macro, offering the creator of a new page a subset of labels to choose from.

Workflow

The system logs everything what happens on a page: who did what when. So you can always reconstruct a realized workflow post factum. If you want to define a proactive workflow, you can visualize or summarize this soft workflow through the use of a template; you can add procedural checklists if you want.

One step further in making the workflow stricter is through assigning tasks to individuals, who need to check for completion. This generates notification mails to anybody who's watching the page. Anywhere you like, you can generate dynamic task report lists.

At last, the most rigid possibility is the use of a workflow plugin, though this is not practiced at the moment. The teams concerned prefer the simple soft workflow procedure.

In cases where case owners want to use the integration with the project management software, they are provided with a technical room, a cockpit, that enables them to act as a real project manager, defining tasks with all possible parameters known in project management, starting workflows.

Collaboration

We profit from all advantages that wikis offer: true collaboration on content (not files!): group edits, discussions (forums), version history, task assignments, share, pull, mentions, ... The blog enables internal communication for teams and also meta-case information gets blogged, so that the team is aware of progress, problems, etc. The information manager also posts blogs on changes in label sets, naming conventions for pages etc.

Profiles of users (providing *activity overviews, status updates and history, "about me"*, and a link to the personal space) enable knowledge workers to find relevant expertise, skills, knowledge contained in humans. You can "follow" people, watch spaces and pages. But page authors can also assign people as watchers, so that they are kept notified of changes. You can share pages with an accompanying message (sent as a mail), mention people, assign tasks to people, to explicitly pull them to the content, in order to act.

A last interesting item I want to share concerning collaboration, is the possibility to use a plug-in to add annotated screenshots to pages. Adding deixis in these screenshots, they act as laser-pointers in a live presentations. In an a-synchronic way, case team members can discuss images or detailed data sets, and "point" at relevant parts of it.

Roles

The case-related roles are negotiated with the process owner.

Case manager

This is the responsible knowledge worker; he/she

- owns the case, is business savvy, is responsible for realizing the objectives for the case. Delegates tasks and does the follow-ups, reminds people of doing things in time.
- is responsible for flow of action, involvement of partners necessary for the execution, responsible for meeting objectives taking deadlines into consideration, decides in discussions, identification of problems or noise, reports statuses of the case
- can mark the case as 'done', based on the agreed upon criteria.
- is very interested in the "daily changes report" that the system generates automatically.

Case administrator

Supports case manager and information manager

Workflow actors

They are expected to act in the workflow to continue the process. Some need to provide the case with information, others need to come together in a meeting to agree upon things or reach a consensus, others need to approve or reject the results of a certain workflow step, still others need to perform certain actions etc.

Information manager

Maintains the lean 5S method in cases and spaces:
- Sorts out (separates) what is irrelevant (delete, archive, …)
- Sorts what's relevant (add and manage metadata, labels and user rights, set up wayfinding pages (eg. providing the coloured lines that guide visitors in hospitals)) (guards the case management structure at macro, meso, micro level)
- Shines (keep tidy) (syntheses of discussion lines, re-ordering, blogs with 'news', orphaned pages management, restricted pages management, …, find causes of noise, inefficiencies, mistakes)
- Standardizes (setting up methods, models, instruments) (rules for names of pages, tagging, documentation, training, …)
- Sustains (audits, checklists, evaluations, advice)

Through the 'Labels list macro', he guards good use of labels. He checks 'Orphaned pages', Restricted pages overview and publishes statistics: views, edits, pages, comments, users.

After the case is closed, the information manager will archive the case. It will disappear from case overviews, and it will not be included in search results.

For long term archiving, we can export a whole case (including comments and attachments) as an xml-file which is a good format for long term digital preservation.

Community manager

Keeps the drive and dynamics in the case, in discussions, he teases the members, asks for alternatives, pulls members to discussions and tasks, asks questions, posts requests.

Knowledge broker

Works on a meta-level, is interested in opportunities for process improvement, has a problem/solution focus, walks the process, has a learning focus, identifies waste, extracts 'interesting' process information, suggests new templates or adjustment of existing ones. He will evaluate the case with the team from the perspective of 'case management' to generate lessons learnt. Therefore we have a template for "restrospectives".

The manager

Is interested in reports on the progress and status of cases.

3. HURDLES OVERCOME

Management

- Questioned the introduction of yet another application; steered case management towards other politically strong BPM software applications (for e.g. asset management, ERP).
- The CIO needed to accept that even recent ECM implementations did not meet the needs of the knowledge worker
  - We arranged a case management test and pilot project, that could be easily set up, and fast. The BPMS application managers can never act that fast to offer their alternative in time.
  - We could easily show that we created value, by confronting the management with the positive reactions of the users involved.
- The management is not familiar with user experience, that is also important in the design of processes. They mainly are risk avoiding in their process designs and wishes. This is not lean, neither agile. Their risk aversion is also translated in their favouring BPM Softwares and not semi-structured systems. Managers must also understand the reality of many of the BPM Softwares that mainly help them in generating interesting reports, but not really helping the knowledge worker who walks the process.
  - Each time we have the opportunity, we 'preach' about UX. We show them the value of investing in it, through the voice of the user. We show them the sometimes minute differences and explain why some applications are not popular, and others are.
  - With the wiki, we use the metaphor of the "wiki oil stain": it spreads and we cannot hold it. Through word of mouth, teams contact us after hearing about positive experiences with the wiki from other teams. This queue of waiting teams to get introduced in our adaptive case management is of course also visible for our management; if not, we show them.
- Three of the 7 senior managers are in our Enterprise Information Management committee. We have time to discuss such hurdles with them and clarify things with sound arguments. They easily convince the other managers.

Business

- "Yet another tool! What with the other information management tools?": We provided teams with a simple scheme that shows the importance of the several applications, and what can best be used for what aim.
- Teams need to change their culture towards an open, communicative team, working out loud. This is not evident, but with a well-chosen community manager in the team, and with support of the team leader (who preferably acts as the community manager), this can be successful.
- The team needs to invest in the information role from the beginning, so that agreements on how they run their processes are clear, shared and met. From a central perspective, we watch new teams in what they do in their space. We actively interfere with comments and blog posts, suggesting a better or other information management. Team leaders are contacted with the explicit request to appoint somebody for this role.

Organization

It's still too early to say that through these applications that generate dynamics, openness, collaboration, we also change the culture of the company.

We have proof of at least one team that intensely used the applications, and that effectively changed completely their way of working together. But we do believe that the medium is the message, and that these collaboration enabling tools do influence the corporate culture.

Benefits

- At this time, we must say that benefits are mainly measured on a qualitative level.
- We have surveys with the users and team leaders and thanks to the very positive results and feedback, it was easy to broaden the implementation of the case management solution towards the whole company. With the tests and pilot projects, we were limited to 100 users. Since some months, we have the 500 user license, after the management was not only convinced through the very positive quantitative results of the evaluation surveys, but also from direct feedback from their departmental managers who expressed a wow concerning the easiness of sharing information, collaboration on content, transparency about statuses and content overviews, more efficient meetings etc.
- Other teams report us on how easily they find their information, not because of a splendid search engine, but because of the adaptive case management perspective on information.
- The information management department sees evidence of conscious information management (see above).
- Compared to previous practices, I can certainly say that I see many cases of 'leaner' information work and knowledge sharing.
- All teams that step into the adaptive case management methodology, report that the quality of their cases has enormously increased and that is much easier for them to report to their managers about the progress of cases.

4. BEST PRACTICES, LEARNING POINTS AND PITFALLS

Best Practices and Learning Points

- ✓ *try to fit your actions into a holistic view, it makes the implementation easier and more sustainable; your solution is perceived as more authentic, and it's easier to create some passion about the project and to walk the talk.*
- ✓ *aim for consistency in the integration of different applications to create flow in knowledge work: preferably, make the case platform part of the complete knowledge and information system, so that you profit from positive feedback loop dynamics*
- ✓ *refocus information management (case management is part of it) towards action, not storage*
- ✓ *keep it simple and think lean; you will automatically create value*

Pitfalls

- ✗ *think at the level of the user, and try to introduce a +1 level, even if you see the light and benefits of a +3 level; do it step by step.*
- ✗ *do not think from your desk, but go to the gemba and act: visit teams, talk with field knowledge workers, let them show how they work, have your team develop a mini-solution to demo them, and it's sold.*

- ✗ *if the application is not intuitive, serving a splendid user experience and flow, give it back to the reseller.*
- ✗ *don't use the words 'lean' and 'knowledge management' on the floor - this is bizarre jargon.*
- ✗ *never be complacent, believe that anything can be done (at least somewhat) better*

5. TECHNOLOGY

There is a wiki application and an issue and project management software with a licence for 500 users installed on our own servers, after we had tested it in the cloud. Several plug-ins are installed that provide extra functionality.

The application manager is member of the Information Management department.

Both applications have a desktop interface and a mobile (leaner) interface. The mobile interface is more focused on workflow events (tasks, mentions), while for instance, editing is only possible in the desktop interface. The desktop interface offers all functionality, and also works satisfactory on tablets.

Unified Communications: we use a separate application for VOIP calling, video conferencing, screen sharing, that is not integrated with our wiki. This is not experienced as a disadvantage.

6. THE TECHNOLOGY AND SERVICE PROVIDERS

The technology used is Confluence (the wiki-core) and JIRA (for issue and project management) from Atlassian, an Australian software company. As both are products from the same company, there is a full integration of the semi-structured world with the structured world, from both sides. In JIRA, one can create and link Confluence pages, and in Confluence you easily start a new JIRA issue. In Confluence you also generate all kinds of lists with relevant subsets of issues, linked to your content.

We start testing JIRA Agile, an add-on to JIRA, that enables teams in their ambitions for a scrum methodology and an agile culture. JIRA Servicedesk can be considered to offer a portal to case stakeholders for all case information.

http://www.atlassian.com

We use Screensnipe from Spartez to easily integrate and annotate screenshots directly in pages.

Draw.io and Gliffy for the integration of diagrams and process visualisations.

http://www.spartez.com/screensnipe

http://www.gliffy.com/

http://www.draw.io

We tested Hipchat from Atlassian, but in the end Lync (from Microsoft) got implemented as unified communication tool, as Hipchat, at the moment of testing, was not a mature UC tool yet

http://www.hipchat.com

http://office.microsoft.com/en-001/lync/

For refined exports to pdf and Word, we use the Scroll Exporter plugin from K15t.

http://www.k15t.com/software/scroll-pdf-exporter/overview

To meet the demand to link to people's individual and personal notes, we installed the Evernote plug-in that can easily import Evernote notes as pages in the cases.

http://stiltsoft.com/evernote/

We tested a Workflow plugin from Comalatech but did not implement it. At this moment there is no need identified within teams for this, but we do not exclude this in future practices.

http://www.adhocworkflows.com/

Records are stored in Alfresco One, and we plan pilots with Fred (from Xenit), an Alfresco Desktop interface that increases the usability of the document libraries in Alfresco. With Fred we are ready to have teams move their files from shared drives to Alfresco.

http://www.alfresco.com

http://www.xenit.eu/fred

We have tested a plugin from Appfusions that integrates Alfresco folder views in Confluence pages; this has not been implemented (yet).

http://www.appfusions.com/display/CONFALF/Home

*This chapter was assembled and authored by **Filip Callewaert, Head of Information Management, Antwerp Port Authority, Belgium.** Bio is available in the Author Appendix.*

TIAA-CREF, USA

Nominated by IBM, USA

1. EXECUTIVE SUMMARY / ABSTRACT

TIAA was the vision of the philanthropist Andrew Carnegie and founded in 1918 (nearly 100 years ago) through his Carnegie Corporation of New York and the Carnegie Foundation with the goal of supporting the financial well-being of college teachers through a pioneering system of annuities and low-cost life insurance. CREF was established in 1952.

The organization now employs 9,000 employees in more than 90 local offices with $564 billion assets under the management as of May 2014. TIAA-CREF is currently serving 4.8 million individuals overall.

TIAA-CREF has diversified product portfolio offerings, including retirement, IRA, brokerage, insurance, mutual funds, management of 529 college savings plans, trust and banking services, which, by virtue of their complexity, require a great deal of synergy and collaboration within and across the business lines.

TIAA-CREF has implemented solutions to their stakeholders across diversified businesses, empowering them to collaborate and achieve a highly efficient and low-cost business model, mitigating operational risks, adhering to regulatory controls and enhancing customer satisfaction and case worker competence.

With the case management end-to-end solution, TIAA-CREF case processes can now be consistent across all channels (web, phone and paper), achieving and optimizing a 360-degree case view. The solution enables all correspondence from all channels to be stored within the case folder and available to all necessary parties.

To provide a comprehensive granular view of the case, TIAA-CREF provides an extensive set of case assets, which includes, but is not limited to, documents, subject matter expert/real-time correspondence and email, voice footages, tasks, timelines and actions, unique case notes and in-line productivity views. TIAA-CREF leverages advanced analytics capabilities to provide adaptive and dynamic work queue management, providing case visibility to all stakeholders, and manages productivity to optimize case outcomes. The roll out of the case management solution has resulted in major benefits: speed to market, with a simple and shortened effort cycle; reduced costs, by extending this solution to new/additional related business processes with an incremental cost savings of 80%; increased revenues, due to shorter and error-free client servicing cycles, reducing operational dollars spent; and, quality improvements, with enhanced quality client servicing resulting in a reduction in the need for complaint handling.

2. OVERVIEW

TIAA-CREF has implemented Advanced Case Management solutions across multiple business areas and product lines, such as Institutional Onboarding, Plan and Fund-lineup Management Services, Pension Distributions, Survivor Benefits Compliance Management Services, Brokerage Client Onboarding and Cash Management Services.

One such project was scoped to automate Pension Distribution request processing. Clients (Participants) enrolled and contributing to pension plans administered by TIAA-CREF on behalf of their employers can request withdrawals/distributions out of their accumulated contract balances based on various plan rules due to a personal hardship or required minimum distributions to fulfill their tax obligations. Clients have multiple choice options to take their withdrawal/distribution as a cash payment, external rollover, internal rollover or direct transfer to an alternate carrier of the plan.

The business process was previously extremely complex involving eligibility determination and requiring wet-signed supplemental documents verification, plan sponsor approvals, term date verifications and random quality checks before making payments. Additionally, when requested, TIAA-CREF had to provide options to clients for setting up recurring payments for various payment frequencies and allowing modification of payment terms and conditions over the cycle of scheduled payments.

We encountered various complex challenges in this initiative ranging from defining the target state case processing flow accommodating all of the business processing issues, blending the case management design into TIAA-CREF's complex application topology and bringing about case management awareness among the identified case workers.

Our efforts resulted in successful delivery of an end-to-end solution offering a gamut of benefits in the form of:

    a.   Channel consistent Case Processing;
    b.   Automation of feasible process activities;
    c.   Implementation of process controls;
    d.   Empowering cross team collaboration on human interactions;
    e.   Audit trail of processed activities; and
    f.   Optimal 360-degree case visibility to all stakeholders – clients, front, middle and back-office operational teams.

3. BUSINESS CONTEXT

Following the implementation of the Advanced Case Management solution, the business process operations in the retirement business area:

    a.   Are more automated and less manual intensive;
    b.   Are more efficient, with quicker processing times;
    c.   Have robust monitoring of regulatory controls;
    d.   Mitigated exposure to operational risks;
    e.   Include end-to-end visibility on the back-end processing to various stakeholders (clients, front, middle and back-office operations);
    f.   Facilitate cross team collaboration on tasks requiring cross departmental interventions;
    g.   Included an application/solution topology with a fewer multiple home-grown workflow and content management systems processing discretely.

4. THE KEY INNOVATIONS

With the successful implementation of case processing solutions, our retirement business sponsors received a low cost and highly efficient operating case management solution for processing the pension distributions/withdrawals.

4.1 Business

The solution delivered satisfied its stakeholders (clients, front, middle and back-office operational teams) in terms of:

    1.   Speed and Efficiency in processing distributions/withdrawals with shorter turnaround times greatly enhanced our client experience;

2. Cross department collaboration and visibility on the case assets for Case Workers increased their competency levels and empowered them to take quicker and better-informed decisions optimizing outcomes;
3. Implementation of process controls and audit trails satisfied our regulatory requirements;
4. 360-degree view and case analytics empowered our management to monitor for the optimized outcomes and identify cross/up-selling opportunities.

4.2 Case Handling

Prior to implementation of the case processing solution, each request from the client was handled through a chain of independent tasks in a disparate workflow and content management solution with no provision for tethering them from end-to-end visibility, controls, audit trail and cross team collaboration perspectives. Post implementation, a case folder was created for each request and a streamlined case execution was filed of all the case artifacts/assets fulfilled to ensure a satisfactory solution.

We had defined a universal case template of reusable case artifacts such as:

- Case Properties
- Case & Task Types
- Documents
- Role(s) & Profile(s)
- Caddy Widgets; packaged into ONE solution box and successfully deployed across a multitude of business processes in the payout/distribution business area.

The following diagram showcases a skeleton view of the universal case processing solution rolled out to our payout/distributions business users.

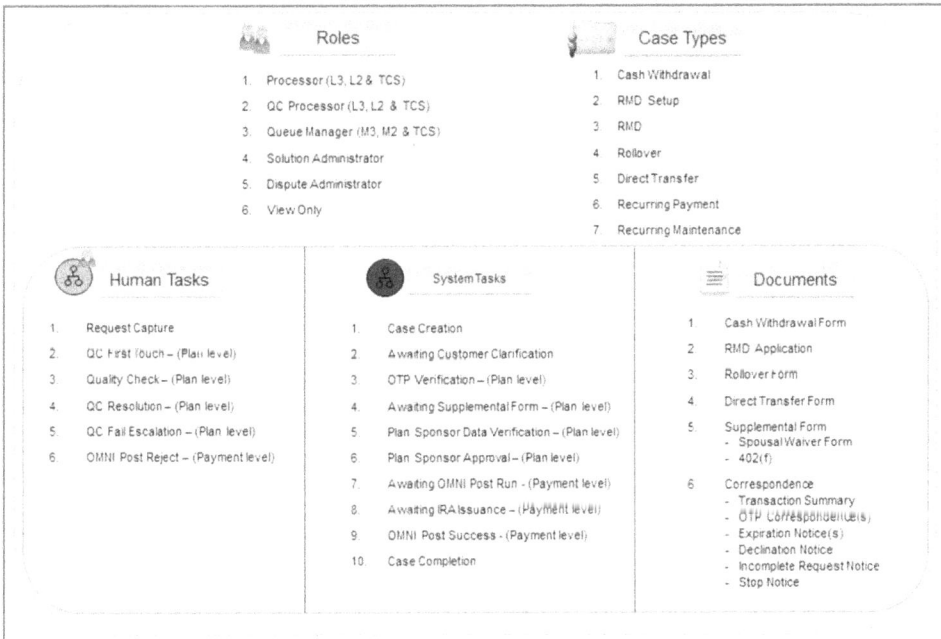

Roles
1. Processor (L3, L2 & TCS)
2. QC Processor (L3, L2 & TCS)
3. Queue Manager (M3, M2 & TCS)
4. Solution Administrator
5. Dispute Administrator
6. View Only

Case Types
1. Cash Withdrawal
2. RMD Setup
3. RMD
4. Rollover
5. Direct Transfer
6. Recurring Payment
7. Recurring Maintenance

Human Tasks
1. Request Capture
2. QC First Touch – (Plan level)
3. Quality Check – (Plan level)
4. QC Resolution – (Plan level)
5. QC Fail Escalation – (Plan level)
6. OMNI Post Reject – (Payment level)

System Tasks
1. Case Creation
2. Awaiting Customer Clarification
3. OTP Verification – (Plan level)
4. Awaiting Supplemental Form – (Plan level)
5. Plan Sponsor Data Verification – (Plan level)
6. Plan Sponsor Approval – (Plan level)
7. Awaiting OMNI Post Run - (Payment level)
8. Awaiting IRA Issuance – (Payment level)
9. OMNI Post Success - (Payment level)
10. Case Completion

Documents
1. Cash Withdrawal Form
2. RMD Application
3. Rollover Form
4. Direct Transfer Form
5. Supplemental Form
   - Spousal Waiver Form
   - 402(f)
6. Correspondence
   - Transaction Summary
   - OTP Correspondence(s)
   - Expiration Notice(s)
   - Declination Notice
   - Incomplete Request Notice
   - Stop Notice

Universal Payout & Distributions Case Template

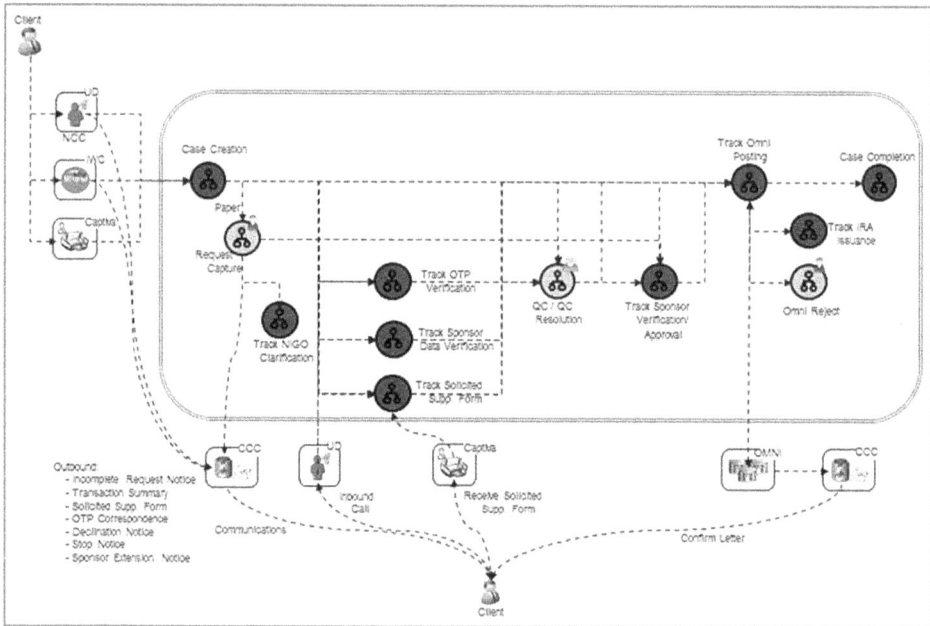

Channel Consistent Use Case

Unique Case Handling Functions

A short summary on some of the unique case handling functions implemented through Case Manager follows:

- **Adaptive Processing –** The solution implemented fulfilled adaptive case processing requirements with the following reusable artifacts:

Role(s) & Associated Human Tasks

a. **Processor Role –** This is a universal role object designed and implemented for all of the middle/back-office processing solutions in Case Manager. The paradigm it follows is "Once a Processor, always a Processor". Irrespective of the multiple organizational departments performing first level case processing on the various human tasks, the case workers are all mapped into a common "Processor" role, which enables standardization of role and queue configurations and work management among the workers. The tasks performed by the case workers belonging to this role are also designed in the solution based on the nature of processing functions such as:

   i. **Request Capture Task –** This is a universal task template for any case type involving "Paper" as a channel of entry into back-office and requires the case worker mapped to the Processor Role to perform data entry functions on the case.

   ii. **QC Resolution Task –** This is a collaborative task created on-demand by a case worker (QC Processor) as part of performing the Quality Check task processing. This is a universal task template for any case type wherein the case worker mapped to the Processor Role requires resolving the data entry errors identified as part of the quality check task processing.

iii. **Omni Post Reject Task** - This is a universal task template for any case type requiring the case worker mapped to the Processor Role to fix platform processing rejects by the system of records on a transaction processed within a case.

b. **QC Processor Role** – This is a universal role object designed and implemented for all of the middle/back-office processing solutions in Case Manager. Irrespective of the multiple organizational departments performing oversight (Quality Check) processing on the various cases in-progress, the case workers are all mapped into a common "QC Processor" role, which enables standardization of role and queue configurations and work management among the workers. The tasks performed by the case workers belonging to this role are also designed in the solution based on nature of processing functions such as:

  i. **Quality Check Task** – This is a collaborative task created on-demand based on a business rule validation of a pre-defined QC criterion for a case worker (QC Processor) to perform an oversight process on the case data.

c. **Queue Manager Role** – This is a universal role object designed and implemented for all of the middle/back-office processing solutions in Case Manager. This role is primarily assigned to process owners to perform queue management and work assign/re-assign functions among the various case workers in the context of their case processes.

d. **Solution Administrator Role** – This is a universal role object designed and implemented for all of the middle/back-office processing solutions in Case Manager. This role is primarily assigned to solution administrators to perform administrative functions on the case solution and support the case workers in effective and efficient processing.

Tasks Tracking System Activities/Events Performed in External Applications

In order to provide a 360-degree view of the case processing status, the case solution required to track system activities and/or events performed in external applications (record keeping, partner institutions, CRM systems etc.), we have defined generic/universal tasks processing system steps exclusively to track and monitor such activities and events providing visibility to the case workers and other stakeholders reviewing a case and its status. Some of such common system activities/events performed by outside applications and yet tracked on the case view are:

a. **Awaiting Supplemental Forms** – A universal system task template to track the event of waiting for secondary forms to be received from the client before releasing the transaction for processing in system of records. Upon receipt of the associated forms through the imaging business process, the case is systematically updated with the form images, and a dynamic human task is assigned to a case worker to review the form. The content of this task is adaptive to the type of form being received and is required to be reviewed by the case worker.

b. **OTP Verification** – A universal system task template to track the event of waiting for clients to authenticate the OTP (One Time Passcode) issued as a security control before processing key case transactions with monetary involvement.

c. **Plan Sponsor Approval** - A universal system task template to track the event of Plan Sponsor (Institution Partner) approving key Client (Institution Employee) case transactions with monetary involvement.

d. **Awaiting Omni Post Run** - A universal system task template to track the system activity performed in OMNI (TIAA-CREF Record Keeping Application) for case transactions released for final processing.

• **Business Analytics & Metrics**

The following snapshot showcases a few of the analytics being retrieved from the case processing data:

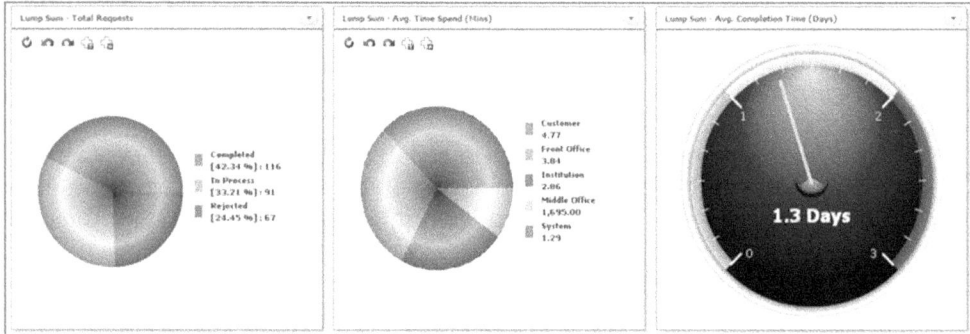

Metrics and Analytics

• **Business Rules**

We have externalized all of our business rules into a Rules Engine to provide us channel consistent processing experience and quick/easy maintenance.

4.3 Organization & Social

Prior to implementation of the case management solution, each request split into disparate workflow tasks and was processed by different departments, which often lacked awareness or knowledge of the status of the request once it left their boundaries. Collaboration was manual and teams lacked skillsets outside of their routine job duties. Post implementation, the teams got an opportunity to break their boundaries and get visibility on the end-to-end request through their association to all the case artifacts/assets from a single folder. This also presented them with an opportunity to enrich their awareness/competency levels on case processing activities performed beyond their team boundaries in order to successfully fulfill/deliver clients' servicing requirements.

Due to early identified success, retirement business sponsors have formed a Case Management Delivery team with primary responsibility to identify potential business process candidates requiring implementation of the Case Management solution leveraging all of the benefits realized so far.

The following diagram showcases a comprehensive view of the organization's Business Process Vision 2020 map for Case Management implementation.

Customer Experience, Collaboration, Operational Efficiency & Visibility and Compliance

Retirement	Brokerage	Banking	Insurance	Trust
• Enrolments	• Enrolments	• Account Opening	• Policy Enrolments	• Account Opening
• Allocations & Contributions	• Transfers	• Deposits & Withdrawals	• Underwriting	• Asset Allocations
• Transfer (Internal)	• Trading	• Transfers	• Claims Processing	• Investment Policies
• Asset Takeovers	• Asset Takeovers	• Loans	• Policy Administration	• Planned Giving
• Loans	• Cash Management	• Mortgages	• Participant Maintenance	• Endowments
• Withdrawals	• Participant Maintenance	• Credit Cards		• Custodian Services
• Distributions	• Wealth Management	• Participant Maintenance		• Participant Maintenance
• Participant Maintenance		• Wealth Management		
• Wealth Management				

Operational Synergy in Motion through Case Management

5. CHALLENGES OVERCOME

Management

Challenges from a management perspective primarily were how to infuse confidence on making a final go decision on adopting the case management methodology and solution as the optimum model for achieving all of the business and technology goals laid out in the organization's business and IT road map.

We successfully overcame this challenge through conceptualization and presentation of a blueprint of the futuristic case map. We built a quick win proof of concept showcasing the tangible benefits of a full-blown operational-model solution.

Business

As part of the management approval, we were required to get a consensus from our business partners on the need for adopting Case Management solutions. We worked through this objective by conducting awareness sessions with key business stakeholders through concept presentations and building a small scale prototype solution for one of their key challenging business processes showcasing conceptual benefits when implemented on a large scale. The business was quick and adaptive to visualize the case management strategy and its benefits in the long run to meet all of their key business goals in TIAA-CREF Vision 2020.

Organization Adoption

Upon receiving the buy-in and commitment from our management and business stakeholders, our next project goal was to socialize the case management methodology and tools across the pilot project stakeholders of our organization – End Users (case workers) of the solution, IT partners, audit and compliance managers and others. This was fulfilled through IT Expo shows wherein we demonstrated the solution delivered for the Pilot Release. In addition, we organized scheduled demos to multiple groups of case workers, educating them on the tools, concepts and benefits to be reaped when effectively implemented.

6. BENEFITS

The successful rollout of the case management solution to our retirement business partners for automating the payout/distribution business processes has provided organizational benefits in the form of:

a) Channel consistent case processing – Clients have a consistent and pleasant experience irrespective of any channels they choose to submit and get visibility on the case processing status;

b) Automation of feasible process activities – A sizeable number of human centric activities performed on the withdrawal/distribution request in the middle-office were automated yet maintained case visibility;

c) Flexible and ad-hoc tasks – Case workers have been empowered to create and assign on-demand tasks in the context of the case processing as needed;

d) Empowering cross team collaboration on human interactions – Case workers can now cross collaborate with each other in the context of the case and share their knowledge or seek clarifications as needed to make well-informed case decisions;

e) Audit trail of processed activities – A comprehensive case diary is filed, tracking and providing visibility into the process audit trail;

f) Implementation of process controls – Key Process Controls like SLAs and Random Quality Checks have been implemented;

g) Optimal 360-degree case visibility to all stakeholders – clients, front, middle and back-office operational teams;

h) Metrics and analytics are being pulled out for case monitoring and cross/up-sell opportunities.

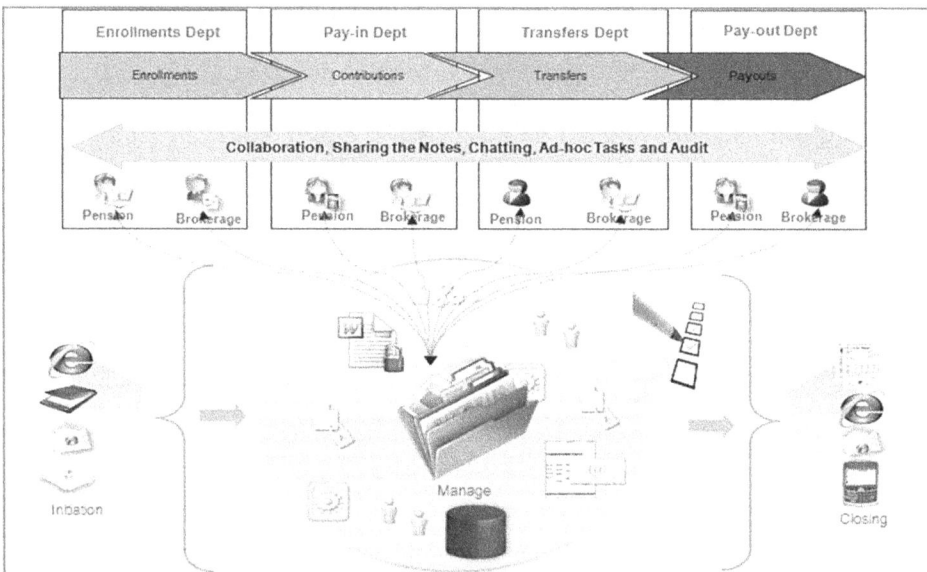

360-degree Case View – Collaboration, Ad-hoc tasks & Audit

6.1 Cost Savings / Time Reductions

The design and roll-out of a universal case management solution across all of the varied payout/distribution transactions have resulted in the following benefits:

- Speed to Market – As more payout-related transactions are identified for automation, extending the case management solution to them has been a simple and shortened effort cycle.
- Reduced Costs – We have been successfully extending this solution to new/additional related business processes with an incremental cost, resulting in savings of 80% of what we would have spent otherwise.

6.2 Increased Revenues

Our stakeholders (front, middle, back-office, regulatory and compliance teams) now have first-hand insight into case information in a single view tethered together end-to-end, resulting in shorter and error-free client servicing cycles, thereby reducing the operational dollars spent.

The solution delivered has optimal automation of human centric activities minimizing human touch points on a case, thereby allowing our case workers to focus on complex transactions exclusively. With the time and effort saved in their routine job duties, the case workers are now available to service other business transactions/additional volumes without any incremental operational costs.

6.3 Quality Improvements

The automated case controls have greatly reduced have enhanced the quality of case processing, resulting in satisfied clients and regulators. The enhanced quality of our client servicing has benefitted us with a reduction in complaint handling.

7. BEST PRACTICES, LEARNING POINTS AND PITFALLS

7.1 Best Practices and Learning Points

- ✓ Start with defining a target state case model encompassing the case assets required to be built as part of the solution template;
- ✓ Organize the case artifacts with generic and reusable case and task skeletons to extend the solution to futuristic related transaction processing;
- ✓ Define an organized document folder structure (inbound vs. outbound content) so to have an optimized federated lookup across the consumers;
- ✓ Define Solution Role(s) by grouping by similar case functions performed rather than by departments;
- ✓ Always take a back-up of the TOS – target object store and DOS – design object store before any solution deployments so as to allow easy and quick restoration to original state prior to deployment;
- ✓ Always build your own wrapper services on top of the out-of-the-box provided Case/CMIS REST Services when there is a need to aggregate logical yet multiple functions fulfilled by individual services;
- ✓ Create a global solution template housing the case properties and documents that are required to be used globally across multiple solution(s); and
- ✓ In order to benefit from optimized case processing, avoid using content and human BPM for orchestrating the case tasks with external applications and instead leverage system BPM.

  Below is a conceptual view on leveraging heterogeneous BPM approach for Optimized Case Management benefits

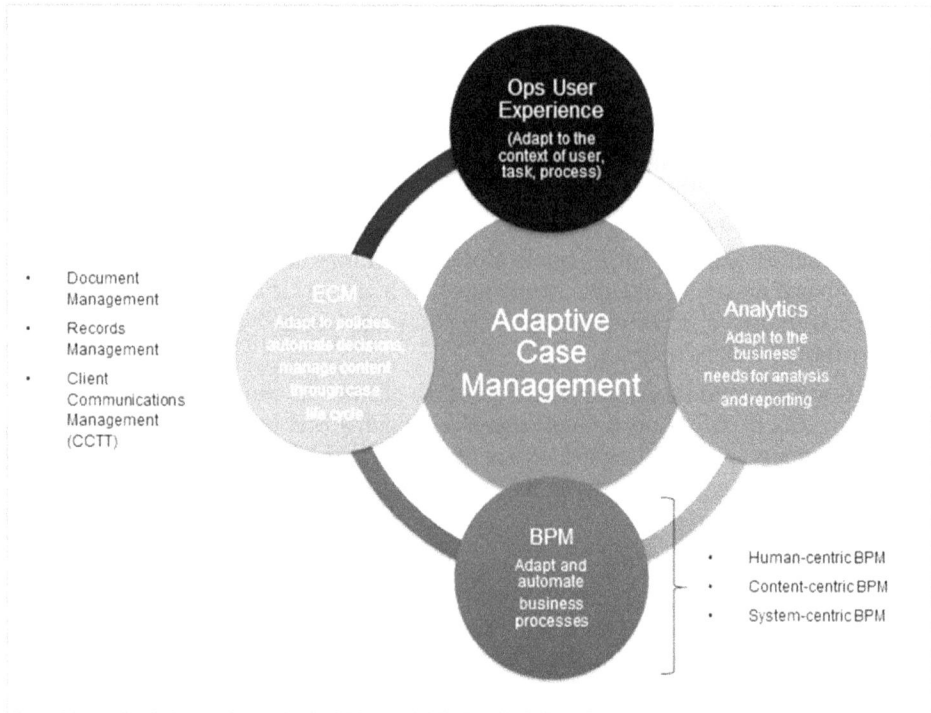

8. COMPETITIVE ADVANTAGES

TIAA-CREF is the among the first financial services providers to begin implementing the Advanced Case Management across its enterprise, including multiple business areas in the retirement, IRA and brokerage services.

We are also among the top organizations in the Industry to implement case management solutions leveraging system, content and human management process paradigms to automate business processes involving multiple application integrations.

We have a core business and technology team in place to extend the case management footprint across all of the critical business processes in the organization's Vision 2020 process map.

9. TECHNOLOGY

The following diagram showcases a comprehensive view of the technology infrastructure leveraged from IBM's FileNet & Advanced Case Management (IBM Case Manager) components used to implement case management solutions.

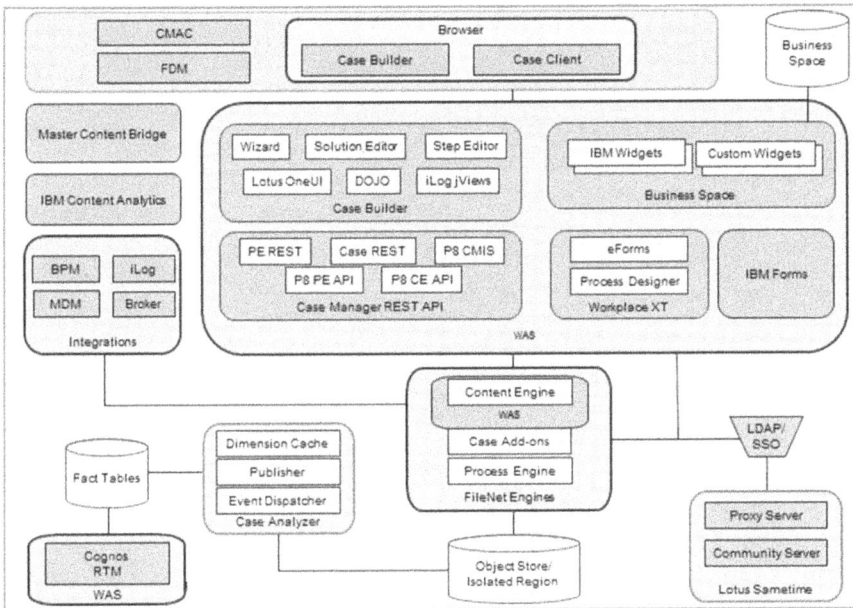

10. THE TECHNOLOGY AND SERVICE PROVIDERS

The primary solution software for this adaptive case management solution was provided by the IBM Enterprise Content Management (ECM) software division http://www-03.ibm.com/software/products/en/casemana. The software solution is known as the IBM Case Manager. It is a comprehensive advanced case management solution, which also integrates with a document management repository and capture components.

WESTMED Practice Partners, USA

Nominated by Hyland, creator of OnBase®, USA

1. EXECUTIVE SUMMARY / ABSTRACT

Providing high-quality services through cutting-edge technology is the longtime mission of WESTMED Practice Partners (WPP). However, with thousands of policies and procedures supporting its multispecialty practice facility clients, WPP was challenged to effectively manage all processes.

Searching for a solution to these challenges, Dr. Simeon Schwartz, WPP's Chairman and CEO, found inspiration in a checklist approach to healthcare – as well-documented in Atul Gawande's book *The Checklist Manifesto*[1]. This led WPP to look for a software solution that would help WPP build checklist-style applications to improve process quality, consistency and outcomes, both for the organization itself and its hospital system clients.

WPP partnered with its enterprise content management (ECM) vendor to implement these applications using its comprehensive case management platform. WPP used the flexible platform to design and deploy a wide variety of applications supporting processes enterprise-wide. These range from more standard case-based applications to unique checklist-driven applications for process control in areas like IT help desk, labs and medical testing, front desk, patient billing, new site openings, human resources and physician compensation.

More than 2,000 policies and procedures were incrementally incorporated into WPP's process control application, leveraging a flexible checklist framework that allows staff to track process completion, flag steps for review and communicate issues or opportunities to managers. The application also provides supervisors with increased visibility into process status via dashboard views and accessible feedback loops.

In addition to organization-wide checklist process control, WPP used the same case management platform to build a variety of other case-driven applications, including provider credentialing, incident tracking and HIPAA violation tracking. By building several applications on one core platform, WPP has a single place to control security and manage all data and documents that support its key processes.

2. OVERVIEW

Before implementing a case management platform, WPP faced challenges of managing thousands of processes throughout the organization and for its health system clients. Different departments and individuals were handling and tracking processes in different ways, including shared spreadsheets, individual checklists and e-mail communications – limiting both consistency, visibility and creating too much opportunity for error.

To improve process quality, consistency and outcomes, WPP's Chairman and CEO Dr. Simeon Schwartz turned to a checklist approach, an idea well documented in Atul Gawande's book *The Checklist Manifesto*. WPP searched for a software solution that would help it build checklist-style applications to support and improve processes for WPP and its hospital system clients.

---

[1] Gawande, Atul. The Checklist Manifesto: How to Get Things Right. New York: Metropolitan Books, 2010. Print.

By partnering with its existing ECM vendor, WPP leveraged its comprehensive case management platform to design and deploy a variety of applications. The platform supports processes across the organization, ranging from more standard case-based applications to unique checklist-driven applications for process control in areas like IT help desk, labs and medical testing, front desk, patient billing, new site openings, human resources and physician compensation.

WPP's process control application was a major element of the implementation, incorporating more than 2,000 of WPP's policies and procedures spanning a variety of departments and types of work. Leveraging a flexible checklist framework, the application allows staff to track process completion, flag process steps for review and communicate issues or opportunities to managers. The process control application also provides process owners and managers with increased visibility into process status via detailed dashboard views and easily accessible feedback loops. Additionally, by prominently displaying process dashboards on large TV monitors across the organization, WPP allows employees to see the status of daily processes and understand how they are contributing to the bottom line. This increases transparency, accountability and employee engagement.

In 2013, WPP's process control system generated more than 40,000 checklists, which were completed by more than 700 employees. Of those generated, a number of checklists required some level of management review, either because an issue was flagged or the process itself requires sign-off. The application allows for reviews to occur quickly and efficiently, notifying those responsible of required reviews and surfacing any feedback from employees. Since implementation, use of the system has grown rapidly. WPP generated close to 40,000 checklists in the first quarter of 2014 alone.

In addition to organization-wide checklist process control, WPP leveraged the same case management platform to build a variety of other case management applications. These include provider credentialing and incident and HIPAA violation tracking. WPP is in the process of finalizing a contract management application. The provider credentialing application is proving especially valuable. WPP plans to greatly increase its number of providers in the next few years, and the application supports the different information and activities required for the different types of providers, streamlining the credentialing process.

By building several applications on one core platform, WPP has a single place to control security and manage all data and documents that support its key processes. Overall, the enterprise case management platform helps WPP further its commitment to technology and innovation, and to achieve its goal of delivering high-quality services in a consistent and transparent manner. The number of processes that have been streamlined and automated – and the degree to which employees have been equipped to consistently handle knowledge-driven tasks – have allowed WPP to become leaner and more efficient. Additionally, WPP better serves its health-system clients by using the platform to manage processes on their behalf, including physician credentialing and billing.

Throughout the ultimately successful implementation process, WPP overcame various challenges, including training, adaptation and incomplete checklists. The organization revised its training curriculum and created classes focused solely on how to develop proper checklists that effectively support functional policies. Additionally, WPP requires managers to approve checklists for their departments, making them accountable not only for creating checklists, but also for the checklist content. With a dedication to transparency and accountability, WPP was able to focus all stakeholders on providing quality content for their checklists and motivate them to regularly create and complete those checklists. For example, the TV dashboards provide real-time statistics on who has and has not completed their checklists. Additionally, every Monday morning, WPP's executive team receives analytics data on processes scheduled for completion that were not completed. As a result of these practices, 97% of WPP's checklists are completed on time.

3. BUSINESS CONTEXT

Before implementation, WPP had many different departments and individuals tracking what needed to be done, but each one did it his/her own way. This included thousands of Excel spreadsheets, notes in e-mails from managers to employees, SharePoint checklists and scattered file shares. These methods resulted in inconsistencies and little visibility for managers into what was truly being done, such as issues that arose but were buried in spreadsheets or lived in workers' minds. WPP also lacked an alert functionality that would notify individuals of work to be done, new actions to take or concerns that surfaced.

WPP realized it had a tremendous opportunity to get the whole company rallied around a consistent format for doing process-related activities. That's when the organization decided to implement a solution that would help unify and standardize processes while improving visibility, quality and, ultimately, patient service.

4. THE KEY INNOVATIONS

Overall, the case management project has had a tremendous impact in several areas. By leveraging the platform to rapidly deploy applications, WPP continues to work toward its goal of unified, consistent and efficient processes organization-wide. With applications built on the same platform, WPP evaluates processes and activities, standardizes certain steps, and reviews outcomes for continuous improvement. With each application, WPP takes an innovative approach to process improvement by capturing information first, then identifying relationships, related tasks and steps that can be automated to increase efficiency.

Since implementing the case management platform, WPP has developed a comprehensive, organization-wide vision of how to improve quality. Virtually every manager is engaged in making sure that processes are completed correctly. Consistent with its mission to enhance the health of its community, WPP will continue to add more and more clinical workflows to directly impact quality and patient care in addition to the administrative improvements already made. With enterprise-wide dashboard views, both management and the rest of the workforce enjoy increased visibility, improved decision-making, increased accountability and enhanced employee engagement.

WPP also benefits from continuous improvement initiatives by putting processes and checklists through a "clean up" process to reevaluate how work is getting done. Feedback from employees – submitted within the process control system itself – is essential for the continuous redesign of processes and checklists.

4.1 Business

WPP provides a turnkey solution for its hospital system clients looking to build free-standing, comprehensive ambulatory centers offering a full range of primary, specialty and ancillary services. WPP manages certain services on behalf of its clients, including credentialing and billing. By helping manage these processes, the case management platform and specialized applications ensure that all processes are structured, consistent and transparent for client organizations.

The case management platform also easily scales to meet changing business needs and priorities. For example, WPP experienced 35% growth in 2013 and anticipates a similar significant growth over the next few years. WPP's case management platform – specifically the provider credentialing application – will help the organization handle this rapid growth and ensure that all steps are taken to properly credential all new providers.

4.2 Case Handling

Pre- and Post-Implementation

Before the solution implementation, employees typically completed processes using checklists on spreadsheets, which resulted in thousands of spreadsheet files. This made it extremely difficult to find required information and provided little to no visibility into who completed the tasks or when they were completed. It also made it very challenging for supervisors to determine whether steps were done correctly or to identify any issues that emerged. Additionally, whenever a process was updated, it was difficult to ensure that individuals were following the most up-to-date process. In some cases, employees were using outdated spreadsheets with processes that were no longer deemed appropriate.

Post-implementation, WPP can effectively manage over a thousand different processes by having process checklists generated and delivered to the right person at the right time. A percentage of these checklists are flagged as exceptions – either because the process requires additional scrutiny or the person completing the checklist encountered a problem that required management review. Those with oversight responsibilities no longer have to rely on someone telling them about an issue because the system automatically alerts them through e-mail notifications and management dashboards. Every checklist that requires management review is reviewed because none are lost, forgotten or buried in scattered files in some network location. The staff working on the checklists are empowered with the knowledge that their concerns and suggestions for improvement go directly to those individuals responsible for process oversight.

System Architecture

WPP's enterprise case management platform has allowed it to conceptualize, configure and deploy a number of specialized applications, including process control applications and a physician credentialing application. WPP is also actively working on a case-based contracts solution that will be put into production within the next few months. All of these applications are built upon the same comprehensive platform.

WPP's case templates (and checklists) were defined through performing extensive discovery with process owners and other stakeholders; understanding their policies, procedures and business requirements; and configuring templates that met those specific needs.

WPP's extensive process control application is also fully integrated into the ECM platform. All checklist-related data (when they were generated, who worked on them, status, noted exceptions, etc.) is stored within a central database that is part of the ECM database. The software used to create the application automatically connects any part of the ECM system to the checklists, if needed. For example, if a checklist is generated to handle the clean-up of a chemical spill, one of the steps an employee needs to do is read through the appropriate Material Safety Data Sheet. This document can be attached to the checklist manually or automatically, providing the responsible employee with the correct steps and supporting information to complete the tasks safely.

The database is connected to one or more application servers, which allows the entire organization to take advantage of the process control application and all other applications built on this platform – even in geographically separate locations. This is key for WPP, which operates multiple sites within a metropolitan area. The application servers connect to WPP's e-mail services, allowing notifications and calendar reminders to be automatically sent to stakeholders involved in the process.

The templates used to define the checklists are configured so that process owners (not the IT department) have control over changes to the process. Templates can be configured to have checklists generated automatically according to a schedule or generated on demand. Process owners add the "who, what, where, when and why" to each template to fully describe the process. The process control engine takes that information and ensures that the right person gets the right checklist at the right time.

Key Roles

Key roles in WPP's enterprise case management solution vary based on the process/application being managed. For example, in the provider credentialing application, key roles are the credentialing staff, supervisor and managerial users (i.e. CMO). In the contract management application, key roles include contract requestor, approvers, legal staff, executives and management.

With the process control application, there are essentially three main roles: process owners (who design the process), process workers (who complete the checklists) and managers/supervisors (who review/approve processes and have oversight responsibility). Each template has drop-down list fields that allow the checklist owner to select individuals from these various roles. The template is saved with the individual's information, and every checklist that is generated from the template inherits that individual assigned. Whenever there is a personnel change, the system provides an easy way for WPP to reassign all incomplete checklists to another individual. The system also provides the ability to easily change any of the other roles on the template.

Business Entities, Maintenance and Lifecycles

The common thread among WPP's case management applications is that they're all maintained through a common configuration. This allows case-related information, data attributes and documents to all be automatically connected and easily accessible to employees.

The business users who use the process control application include the IT department, facilities management, human resources, laboratories, testing and billing. Checklist templates are stored in the central database, but the system automatically checks each template to determine whether it needs to go for an annual review to ensure the process is still appropriate. Checklists that have exceptions or issues also automatically go through a review process. The application notifies key stakeholders that a problem exists and that a review is required. When those individuals log into the system, it presents the appropriate checklists and templates to the user, who can spend the time reviewing the information and taking appropriate actions. Each template contains information about where the checklists are used, and the system automatically sorts checklists so that the right people see the right ones.

In the template lifecycle, templates start with a status of "under development" until they are fully promulgated by review groups and approved for use. Once activated, a template will generate checklists and deliver them to the right person. Over time, as a process needs to change, the template allows WPP to make enhancements. All changes are maintained in the history of the template, so an audit can be performed, showing who made the change and when. When a template is no longer needed, the checklist owner can mark the template as retired, which takes it out of circulation yet still preserves it for historical purposes.

Other specific application entity examples include:

Physician Credentialing:	Contracts Management:
Providers	Contract
Delineations	External Clients (Vendor, Provider, etc.)
Entities	
Educational History	Approvers
Tasks, Notes, and Diaries	Notes

Case Template Adaptation

Based on the specific application, how the case can be adapted is subject to change. In the process control application, each template used to generate checklists contains the "who, what, where, when and why" for the process it supports. When any checklist is generated from the template, it is automatically delivered to the right person at the right time for completion. That person can add information to the checklist, which process owners will use to improve the process. This could include identifying better ways to complete the process, identifying problems or exceptions, or even adding a step that doesn't yet exist but was required based on user judgment. This allows WPP to respond to changes as they occur. The template automatically collects information and presents it to reviewers so they can immediately see where a process needs to be changed. Each template maintains a version history so that changes are recorded. This is an important step for WPP, as it can analyze the data from the checklists to see if any changes to the process resulted in improved outcomes.

In the physician credentialing application, credentialing power users have the ability to define credentialing task lists. Based on the entity, hospital and specialty of the doctor being credentialed, the end user is displayed with different tasks. Tasks can vary from verifying a doctor's state board is valid to ensuring a specific document is in the file. These templates can be modified from run-time configuration rather than design-time configuration. Therefore, when something changes on a template, a business analyst or trained administrator can make changes to the solution without having to call IT or the vendor.

4.3 Organization & Social

The case management solution has made it much easier for WPP to onboard and off-board employees to specific job functions. Processes are documented in the process control application, reviewed and approved by managers, and deployed to staff for implementation. WPP's culture reflects a strong emphasis on knowledge-sharing and a commitment to a consistent approach with process control as one of the main implementation vehicles.

Employees are also more easily able to provide process feedback directly to managers and supervisors. And, with enterprise-wide dashboard views, the entire workforce has increased visibility into how they are impacting the bottom line, which increases employee engagement.

Finally, by eliminating manual, tedious work, WPP allows staff to focus on higher value activities. For example, by automating its physician compensation formula and putting it into a process control application, WPP was able to transfer a senior accountant who was doing much of that work to a valuable budgeting role.

5. HURDLES OVERCOME

Management

This initiative was sponsored by WPP's President and CEO, and therefore the project benefited from a top-down implementation that quickly garnered the commitment of all management tiers. WPP's biggest challenge was getting everyone to understand how such a system could work and the benefits to their area when fully implemented.

Business

During the initial implementation process, WPP worked with supervisors and staff throughout the organization to create checklists that supported their policies and procedures. However, WPP quickly noticed that the content associated with the checklists was incomplete. The organization revised its training curriculum and created classes focused solely on how to develop proper checklists that effectively support functional policies. Additionally, managers were required to approve checklists for their departments, making them accountable not only for creating checklists, but also for the checklist content.

Organization Adoption

Though the average user was used to working on "tribal knowledge" checklists, ensuring proper documentation and organization of his/her checklists for wide distribution was a major hurdle. With a dedication to transparency and accountability, WPP was able to focus all stakeholders on providing quality content for their checklists and also motivate them to regularly create and complete checklists. For example, the TV dashboards provide real-time statistics on who has and has not completed their checklists. Additionally, every Monday morning WPP's executive team receives analytics data on processes that were scheduled for completion but not completed. As a result of these practices, 97% of WPP's checklists are completed on time.

6. BENEFITS

6.1 Cost Savings / Time Reductions

So far in 2014, WPP has roughly 2,200 unique checklist templates (policies and procedures) in its process control application. The application has generated about 40,000 total checklists, and 97% of these checklists are completed on time. Additionally, with the implementation, IT system uptime has improved from 85% pre-solution to 98% post-solution.

6.2 Quality Improvements

In the spirit of continuous process improvement, WPP uses the process control application to maintain its 99% patient insurance eligibility rate year-over-year. The application assists by providing personnel with the necessary reminders and guidelines to proactively check for and resolve potential conflicts that could negatively impact patient experience and, subsequently, be more expensive to address later on.

Additionally, with 35% growth last year and similar growth expected this year, WPP utilizes the process control, credentialing and other case management applications to consistently meet service-level requirements for onboarding providers and clients.

7. BEST PRACTICES, LEARNING POINTS AND PITFALLS

7.1 Best Practices and Learning Points

✓ *Perform discovery and collect all necessary data up front. Everyone is working off these checklists – not just certain departments. Because this is a company-wide implementation, it pays off to spend the time understanding all the elements, where the data is coming from and what type of decisions are made based on that data.*

✓ *Visibility should go beyond just management. Displaying dashboards throughout the organization increases accountability and engagement.*

✓ *You can't always use traditional workflow to map out these types of "knowledge processes." Instead, you can capture the information first, then start to identify relationships, related tasks and potential steps that can be automated to improve processes.*

7.2 Pitfalls

✗ *Avoid trying to work out the workflow before understanding what the process truly is and all the data elements involved.*

✗ *If you don't take the time to first collect all the data and do a true discovery, you will waste time and effort.*

8. COMPETITIVE ADVANTAGES

WPP's proprietary software and centralized management systems – including the case management applications – combine to help drive its mission of enhancing the health of its community. Leveraging this innovative technology, WPP can control costs while making care delivery more effective and efficient. "At WESTMED," explains Dr. Schwartz, "if a woman has an abnormal mammogram in the morning, we can get her an appointment with a quality breast surgeon the same day, a biopsy by five o'clock, and the results by noon the next day." All of those care-related processes, from imaging to the lab work, are done in-house.[2]

Additionally, by increasing process quality, consistency and efficiency, WPP continues to pursue its self-identified critical success factors, specifically to be: the best place for patients to receive care, the best place for physicians to practice medicine, and the best place for employees to work.

9. TECHNOLOGY

WPP worked with its existing ECM vendor and utilized its flexible enterprise case management platform. Through this partnership, WPP has been able to conceptualize, configure and deploy a number of case management solutions within its organization, including extensive process control applications and a host of comprehensive case management applications, such as physician credentialing.

The process control solution is entirely built on a rapid point-and-click application development platform provided by the company's ECM vendor. This platform combines document management, business process management (BPM) and customer relationship management (CRM) capabilities into a single application. This infrastructure allowed the application to be rapidly developed as it was built on WPP's existing ECM platform, taking advantage of existing inherent functionality, such as security controls, audit trails, document management, dashboards and calendar

---

[2] http://www.westchestermagazine.com/914-INC/Q1-2014/Westchesters-Changing-Healthcare-Landscape

views. All the checklist and case management applications can easily connect to other content (documents, folders and other items) in the repository.

Because they are built on the existing ECM platform, the checklist and case management applications can seamlessly interact with the WPP e-mail and calendar systems. Through this interaction, notifications of checklists are automated and can populate a user's calendar with expected completion dates and times. The individuals using these applications can use the same web client interface and smart client interfaces available with their ECM solution. Both are designed for enterprise use and are built with Microsoft.Net tools such as C#.

10. THE TECHNOLOGY AND SERVICE PROVIDERS

About OnBase by Hyland

OnBase is a flexible and comprehensive enterprise content management (ECM) solution that helps organizations manage documents and data to streamline business operations. Integrating with everyday business applications, OnBase provides instant access to critical information when you need it, wherever you are. OnBase grows with organizations as needs change and business evolves. For more information, please visit OnBase.com.

About Hyland, Creator of OnBase

For over 20 years, Hyland, creator of OnBase, has helped our more than 13,000 lifetime customers by providing real-world solutions to everyday business challenges. That dedication is why 98 percent of our customer base continues to renew our partnership and receive access to the latest product enhancements. Named one of Fortune's Best Companies to Work For® 2014, Hyland continues to thrive and develop one of the most flexible and comprehensive enterprise content management (ECM) solutions available.

For more information, please visit OnBase.com.

Appendix

Author Appendix

ILIA BIDER

Lecturer and researcher at the department of Computer and System Sciences of Stockholm University and co-founder of IbisSoft AB, Sweden

Dr. Ilia Bider is Software Engineer, Business Analyst, IS-researcher and Teacher with long experience in several IT-related fields. He has MS in Electronic Engineering and PhD in Computer and System Sciences, and combined experience of over 30 years of research (in the fields of IS, SE, DB, and computational linguistics), and practical work (business analysis, and software design, coding, sales, and marketing) in five countries (Norway, Russia, Sweden, United Kingdom, and United States). Dr. Bider has published over 50 research papers as well as a considerable number of articles for practitioners. His main specialty is finding research topics in business practice, and testing research results in business practice. Dr. Bider is an inventor of the state-oriented approach to business process modeling and control that is based on the application of the conceptual ideas of the Mathematical system theory to the realm of business processes. This approach has been successfully tested in business analysis and software application development practice of IbisSoft and its partners. Dr. Bider puts a lot of effort in bridging the gap between the academics and practitioners.

WILLIAM BRANTLEY

Adjunct faculty at the University of Maryland, University of Louisville (Kentucky), and George Mason University. Supervisory Human Resources Specialist (Information Systems) at the U.S. Department of Agriculture in Rural Development

Dr. William Brantley is a Certified Information Professional, Human Resources Information Professional, EMC2 Data Science Associate, and Project Management Professional. His Ph.D. is in Public Policy and Administration, and he has worked in state and Federal government for over twenty years. Dr. Brantley's focus is in improving how government works, and that is why he was attracted to adaptive case management. Public administration is shifting from purely transactional work to knowledge work and needs new methods and training for government employees to best serve citizens. In recent research, Dr. Brantley has merged human-centered design, Lean Startup methodology, and agile project management to better manage government projects. Dr. Brantley is also doing research on agile policy making where data science techniques are merged with organizational health and network health concepts to aid government policy makers create and implement better government policies. Adaptive case management is a key component of agile policy making.

FILIP CALLEWAERT

Head of Information Management, Antwerp Port Authority, Belgium

Peter Drucker's assertion that "making knowledge workers productive is the biggest of the 21st century management challenges" is the inspiration for Filip's professional life. Filip believes we're only at the very beginning of this huge project, as we do not have 'the big data' yet about the black box processes these workers perform to solve their problems. Yet we have started unveiling these processes in new and user-friendly collaboration platforms and the future of the New World of Work is promising.

Filip is by nature and education a linguist and is especially interested in how the medium, form, structure determine contents and messages. He prefers to use concepts from semiotics to understand this issue and applies it to the question of *authentic* knowledge work.

In his professional problem-solving cases, most often in the context of the New World of Work projects, Filip's responsibility *adaptively* combines many disciplines: information management, internal communications, organizational development, leadership, performance management, community management, knowledge management, process management, project management, business intelligence, IT, and even workplace ergonomics.

He worked as a teacher in secondary education, was knowledge manager for the Doctoral Schools at the Vrije Universiteit Brussel, after which he led the International Relations Department there; he was responsible for the information and knowledge management at the Social Welfare service at the city of Roeselare (Belgium), and now he performs that function at the Port of Antwerp (Belgium).

STEINAR CARLSEN
Chief Engineer, Computas AS, Norway

Dr. Steinar Carlsen is a recognized Norwegian expert within business processes and workflow technology. He is a senior advisor specializing in adaptive case management, business process management, knowledge management, social technologies, with more than 20 years of experience in different approaches to the modelling of work processes. His focus is on realizing work support systems, as well as baselining "organizational implementation/enactment". Steinar has a background from applied research within business process modelling, enterprise modelling, enterprise architecture and requirements engineering. Steinar is the product owner of FrameSolutions™ - Computas AS' framework for realizing operational ACM solutions.

GUNNAR JOHN COLL
Senior Advisor, VP, Computas AS

Gunnar John Coll represents a behavioural approach to technology, organization and knowledge. He assists customers in corporate process initiatives, including knowledge management and organizational learning. His main area of work is where business process and human competence meet with new technology, to answer the need for change. He provides perspectives, facilitates and manages initiatives in close cooperation with customer's key personnel. Gunnar has more than 25 years of experience in IT projects related to organizational processes. Due to his combined background as a psychologist and an IT professional, he provides a complementary perspective on system development and organizational adoption.

LLOYD DUGAN
Chief Architect, BPM, Inc.

Lloyd Dugan is the Chief Architect for BPM, Inc., and is a widely recognized expert and thought leader in the development and use of leading modeling languages, methodologies, and tools, covering from the level of Enterprise Architecture (EA) and Business Architecture (BA) through Business Process Management (BPM) and Service-Oriented Architecture (SOA).

He specializes in the use of the standard language for describing business processes, the Business Process Model & Notation (BPMN) language from the

Object Management Group (OMG), having developed and delivered BPM and BPMN training to the Department of Defense (DoD) and contractors from several IT consulting companies, presented on it at national and international conferences, and co-authored the seminal BPMN 2.0 Handbook, chapter on Making a BPMN 2.0 Model Executable, sponsored by the Workflow Management Coalition.

He is also an Advisory Board Member of the Business Architecture Guild. In addition, he is a Co-founder of Semantic BPMN, which is dedicated to proving the proposition that realizing BPMN's full potential lies in leveraging semantic technologies to address BPMN model data.

LAYNA FISCHER
Publisher, Future Strategies Inc., USA

Ms Fischer is Editor-in-Chief and Publisher at Future Strategies Inc., the official publishers to WfMC.org. She was also Executive Director of WfMC and BPMI (now merged with OMG) and continues to work closely with these organizations to promote industry awareness of BPM and Workflow.

Future Strategies Inc. (www.FutStrat.com) publishes unique books and papers on business process management and workflow, specializing in dissemination of information about BPM and workflow technology and electronic commerce. As such, the company contracts and works closely with individual authors and corporations worldwide and also manages the renowned annual Global Awards for Excellence in BPM and Workflow and the new annual Adaptive Case Management Awards.

Future Strategies Inc., is the publisher of the business book series *New Tools for New Times*, the annual *Excellence in Practice* series of award-winning case studies and the annual *BPM and Workflow Handbook* series, published in collaboration with the WfMC. Ms. Fischer was a senior editor of a leading international computer publication for four years and has been involved in international computer journalism and publishing for over 20 years.

JÜRGEN KRESS
EMEA Alliances and Channels, Oracle

An expert in middleware, Jürgen currently works at Oracle EMEA Alliances and Channels and is responsible for Oracle's EMEA fusion middleware partner business. He is the founder of the Oracle SOA & BPM, WebLogic Partner Communities, and the global Oracle Partner Advisory Councils. The Fusion Middleware Partner Community is home to over 5,000 members internationally as Oracle's most active and successful community, which Jürgen manages with monthly newsletters, Webcasts, and conferences. He also hosts the annual Fusion Middleware Partner Community Forums and Fusion Middleware Summer Camps, where more than 200 partners receive product updates, roadmap insights, and hands-on training supplemented by a variety of Web 2.0 tools like Twitter, discussion forums, online communities, blogs, and wikis.

Jürgen is also a member of the steering board of the International SOA, Cloud + Service Technology Symposium, and is a frequent speaker at conferences that include the SOA & BPM Integration Days, JAX, UKOUG, OUGN, and OOP. More information about Jürgen Kress is available at https://soacommunity.wordpress.com.

JOHN T. MATTHIAS, J.D., PMP
Principal Court Management Consultant, National Center for State Courts

Mr. Matthias has worked as a management consultant and business analyst in courts and justice agencies in 35 states, as a city prosecutor, and as program manager of a commercial case management system product. His experience in 80 projects spans caseflow management, CMS needs assessment, requirements definition, performance measurement, and business process redesign. He has contributed to *Trends in State Courts,* and a variety of his reports and publications are available at www.ncsc.org and courttechbulletin.blogspot.com (search Matthias).

HAJO NORMANN
SOA & BPM Community of Practice Lead, Accenture

Hajo Normann works for Accenture in the role of SOA & BPM Community of Practice Lead in ASG. Hajo is responsible for the architecture and solution design of SOA/BPM projects, mostly acting as the interface between business and the IT sides. He enjoys tackling organizational and technical challenges and motivates solutions in customer workshops, conferences, and publications. Hajo leads together with Torsten Winterberg the DOAG SIG Middleware and is an Oracle ACE Director and an active member of a global network within Accenture, as well as in regular contact with SOA/BPM architects from around the world.

NATHANIEL PALMER
Vice President and CTO, BPM, Inc.

Rated as the #1 Most Influential Thought Leader in Business Process Management (BPM) by independent research, Nathaniel is recognized as one of the early originators of BPM, and has the led the design for some of the industry's largest-scale and most complex projects involving investments of $200 Million or more. Today he is the Editor-in-Chief of BPM.com, as well as the Executive Director of the Workflow Management Coalition, as well as VP and CTO of BPM, Inc.

Previously he had been the BPM Practice Director of SRA International, and prior to that Director, Business Consulting for Perot Systems Corp, as well as spent over a decade with Delphi Group serving as VP and CTO. He frequently tops the lists of the most recognized names in his field, and was the first individual named as Laureate in Workflow. Nathaniel has authored or co-authored a dozen books on process innovation and business transformation, including "Intelligent BPM" (2013), "How Knowledge Workers Get Things Done" (2012), "Social BPM" (2011), "Mastering the Unpredictable" (2008) which reached #2 on the Amazon.com Best Seller's List, "Excellence in Practice" (2007), "Encyclopedia of Database Systems" (2007) and "The X-Economy" (2001).

He has been featured in numerous media ranging from Fortune to The New York Times to National Public Radio. Nathaniel holds a DISCO Secret Clearance as well as a Position of Trust with in the U.S. federal government.

SURENDRA REDDY
CEO, Quantiply Corporation

Surendra Reddy is the founder and CEO of Quantiply Corporation, an emerging predictive business process intelligence company, being incubated at PARC. Prior to Quantiply, Surendra was the CTO of Cloud and Big Data futures where he was responsible for the applied technology research, business strategy and strategic partnerships for cloud, high performance analytics and big data futures across PARC. Prior to PARC, Surendra served as the General Manager and CTO for SIOS Technology group companies, where he was responsible for defining global cloud strategy and guiding the 200+ strong engineering organization with the technology direction and innovation programs. Before this, he was Vice President of Virtualization and Cloud R&D at Yahoo!, developing a company-wide cloud strategy to increase the operational efficiencies of data centers and reduce operational cost by 20 percent in first two years and up to 50 percent in the third year. Prior to joining Yahoo, he was the CTO and VP of Engineering at Amitive, first cloud based platform for document-driven process automation. Amitive was acquired by GXS and became part of their trading platform. Surendra was also the founder and CTO of Optena Corporation, a pioneer in data center automation and grid computing. He also spent more than seven years as Director of Engineering in Server Technologies at Oracle.

Surendra co-authored RFC 5323, contributed to RFC 3648. He founded the Big Data Foundry, a global initiative to promote the applied research in process intelligence and big data analytics and is an active researcher on business process intelligence, process mining, systems thinking, customer behavioral patterns, case based reasoning, large data sets and data access, security, and integrity issues.

Surendra received his MBA from the Kellogg School of Management at Northwestern University and his Bachelor of Technology in Electronics and Communication Engineering from Jawaharlal Nehru Technological University, India.

DR ALEXANDER SAMARIN
SAMARIN.BIZ

Alexander Samarin wrote his first software program in 1973. He obtained a PhD (in computer graphics) in 1986. He has worked for a variety of international clients in Switzerland, the UK, France, Australia and Africa. He specialises in architecture, implementation and evolution of enterprise-wide solutions with the holistic use of enterprise architecture, business architecture, BPM, SOA, ECM, IT governance, information security and IT strategy. In October 2009 he published a book "Improving enterprise business process management systems". Since August 2013 he has been working as a consulting enterprise architect for achieving the synergy between strategy, business best practices and disruptive digital technologies.

HELLE FRISAK SEM
Chief Architect, Computas AS, Norway

Dr. Helle Frisak Sem is a Chief Architect in Computas, specializing in solution architecture and requirements engineering. With more than 20 years of experience, Helle leads functional teams towards the realization of operational ACM solutions, in collaboration with customer and user. She is a senior advisor in knowledge management, work process support, enterprise modelling, estimation of software projects and user interface design. From a background in research and education, Helle combines deep technical knowledge with experience on how customers' problems may be met by an operational solution. Helle is the functional architect behind several award winning ACM solutions, and over the last 20 years she has been a main contributor to FrameSolutions™ Computas AS' framework for realizing operational ACM solutions.

KEITH SWENSON
Vice President of R&D, Fujitsu America Inc., USA

Keith Swenson is Vice President of Research and Development at Fujitsu America Inc. and is the Chief Software Architect for the Interstage family of products. He is known for having been a pioneer in collaboration software and web services, and has helped the development of many workflow and BPM standards. He is currently the Chairman of the Workflow Management Coalition. In the past, he led development of collaboration software MS2, Netscape, Ashton Tate and Fujitsu. In 2004 he was awarded the Marvin L. Manheim Award for outstanding contributions in the field of workflow. His blog is at http://social-biz.org/.

CLEMENS UTSCHIG-UTSCHIG
Chief Architect Marketing & Sales IT, Boehringer Ingelheim Pharma GmbH & Co KG, Germany

Clemens Utschig-Utschig works for Boehringer Ingelheim, one of the leading researching Pharmaceutical companies in the world at its corporate headquarter in Ingelheim, Germany. Currently he heads up the global Architecture team for Marketing and Sales IT – driving the implementation of the digital revolution and global consolidation efforts towards a single platform.

Prior he ran the Global Master Data Management Program, starting at development of global standard processes, through implementation at the network sites, to providing global transactional data maintenance services from BI's Shared Service Center, Global Business Services. Before joining Boehringer Ingelheim, Clemens worked for a decade at Oracle as Platform Architect on the SOA / BPM development team in Redwood Shores, CA, helping customers to establish enterprise wide SOA. He also drove the development of several platform components such as the Weblogic SCA container and the Spring Service Engine.

Clemens can be reached through clemens.utschig@gmail.com

TORSTEN WINTERBERG
OPITZ CONSULTING

Torsten Winterberg is active in several roles at OPITZ CONSULTING all with a strong focus on delivering value to the customer: Being part of the business development & innovation department he searches and evaluates emerging trends and technologies to deliver innovative and differentiating solutions to customers. As a director of the competence center for integration and business process solutions he follows his passion to build the best delivery unit for customer solutions in the area of SOA and BPM. Torsten has long-time experience as developer, coach and architect in the area of building complex mission critical Java EE applications. His competence and passion lies in the design and architecture of complex IT systems with regard to BPMN, BPEL, ESB, BAM and service oriented architecture in general. He is a known speaker in the German Java and Oracle communities and has written numerous articles on SOA/BPM related topics. Torsten is part of the Oracle ACE director team (ACE=Acknowledged Community Expert) and leads the DOAG middleware community.

Award-winning Case Studies

COGNOCARE, AN ACM-BASED SYSTEM FOR ONCOLOGY US
Contact: Cognocare, USA

Nominated by: IActive US Corp
Contact: Luis Castillo, Chief Technology Officer
luis.castillo@iactiveit.com
Website: http://www.iactiveit.com/

CRAWFORD & COMPANY
Contact: Brian Flynn, Crawford & Company, USA, Global CIO & Executive Vice President
Website: http://us.crawfordandcompany.com/

Nominated by: Appian
Contact: Michael Ingrisano, Media Relations Manager
michael.ingrisano@appian.com
Website: www.appian.com

INFOSYS MCCAMISH SYSTEMS LLC
Contact: Sai Sindhe, Infosys McCamish Systems LLC, USA, Head of Product Delivery
Website: www.infosys.com

Nominated by: Pegasystems
Contact: Andy Dear, Sr. Manager Public Relations
andy.dear@pega.com
Website: www.pegasystems.com

JURISHARE - CONTRACT GENERATION SYSTEM
Contact: Marcelo Vicentini Marchetti, Camargo Correa S.A., Brazil
Website: www.camargocorrea.com

Nominated by: Mind Services
Contact: Mauricio Amarante, Contracts Manager
mauricio.amarante@mindservices.com.br
Website: http://www.mindservices.com.br

NATIONAL POLICE IMMIGRATION SERVICES (NPIS)
Contact: Eirik Aarre, National Police Immigration Services (NPIS), Norway, Senior Advisor
Website: www.politiet.no

Nominated by: Computas AS
Contact: Steinar Carlsen, Chief engineer
sca@computas.com
Website: www.computas.com

OFFICE OF THE SECRETARY TO GOVERNMENT OF FEDERATION NIGERIA (OSGF)
Contact: Office of the Secretary to Government of Federation (OSGF), Nigeria

Nominated by: Newgen
Contact: Ankita Sinha, Senior Executive – Products & Solutions
ankita@newgen.co.in
Website: http://www.newgen.com

PERSHING LLC, A BNY MELLON COMPANY
Contact: Regina DeGennaro, Pershing LLC, a BNY Mellon company, USA
Website: www.pershing.com

Nominated by: Pershing LLC, a BNY Mellon company

Contact: Kate Henry, Vice President, Global Marketing
kate.henry@pershing.com
Website: www.pershing.com

STATE OF HAWAII DEPARTMENT OF HUMAN SERVICES
Contact: Pankaj Bhanot, Department of Human Services, State of Hawaii, USA, Systems Operations & Requirements Office
Website: http://humanservices.hawaii.gov/

Nominated by: Imagine Solutions
Contact: Jayne Metz, Senior Project Manager
jayne.metz@imaginesolutions.com
Website: www.imaginesolutions.com

STATE OF MAINE
Contact: Jim Smith, State of Maine, USA, CIO, Office of Information Technology
Website: www.maine.gov

Nominated by: Pegasystems
Contact: Andy Dear, Sr. Manager Public Relations
andy.dear@pega.com
Website: www.pegasystems.com

THE PORT OF ANTWERP
Contact: Filip Callewaert, Port of Antwerp, Belgium, Head of Information Management
Website: http://www.portofantwerp.com/

Nominated by: Port of Antwerp
Contact: Filip Callewaert,
filip.callewaert@portofantwerp.com
Website: http://www.portofantwerp.com/

TIAA CREF
Contact: Ravi Modukuri, TIAA CREF, USA, Manager, Business Transaction Management
Website: www.tiaa-cref.org

Nominated by: IBM
Contact: William Mills, Senior Marketing Manager
wdocmills@us.ibm.com
Website: http://www.ibm.com/

WESTMED
Contact: William Saint-Louis, WESTMED, USA
Website: www.westmedgroup.com

Nominated by: Hyland, creator of OnBase
Contact: Ashley Topping, Solutions Program Marketing, IT
Ashley.Topping@onbase.com
Website: www.onbase.com

WfMC Structure and Membership Information

The Workflow Management Coalition (WfMC), founded in August 1993, is a non-profit, international organization of BPM and workflow vendors, users, analysts and university/research groups. The Coalition's mission is to promote and develop the use of collaborative technologies such as workflow, BPM and case management through the establishment of standards for software terminology, interoperability and connectivity among products and to publicize successful use cases.

WORKFLOW STANDARDS FRAMEWORK

The Coalition has developed a framework for the establishment of workflow standards. This framework includes five categories of interoperability and communication standards that will allow multiple collaboration products to coexist and interoperate within a user's environment. Technical details are included in the white paper entitled, "The Work of the Coalition," available at www.wfmc.org.

ACHIEVEMENTS

The initial work of the Coalition focused on publishing the Reference Model and Glossary, defining a common architecture and terminology for the industry. A major milestone was achieved with the publication of the first versions of the Workflow API (WAPI) specification, covering the Workflow Client Application Interface, and the Workflow Interoperability specification.

In addition to a series of successful tutorials industry wide, the WfMC invested many person-years over the past 20 years helping to drive awareness, understanding and adoption of XPDL, now the standard means for business process definition in over 80 BPM products. As a result, it has been cited as the most deployed BPM standard by a number of industry analysts, and continues to receive a growing amount of media attention.

Workflow Reference Model

The Workflow Reference Model was published first in 1995 and still forms the basis of most BPM and workflow software systems in use today. It was developed from the generic workflow application structure by identifying the interfaces which enable products to interoperate at a variety of levels. All workflow systems contain a number of generic components which interact in a defined set of ways; different products will typically exhibit different levels of capability within each of these generic components. To achieve interoperability between workflow products a standardized set of interfaces and data interchange formats between such components is necessary. A number of distinct interoperability scenarios can then be constructed by reference to such interfaces, identifying different levels of functional conformance as appropriate to the range of products in the market.

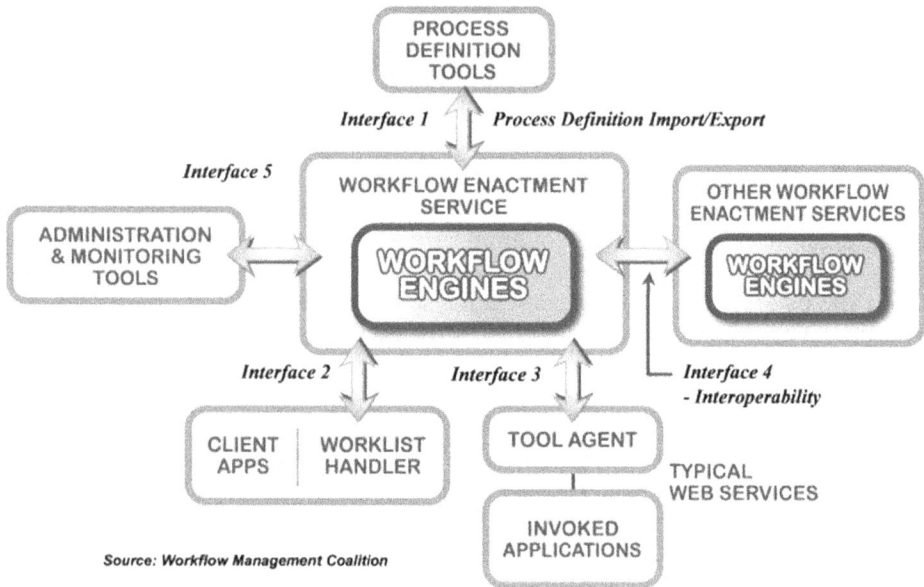

WORKFLOW REFERENCE MODEL DIAGRAM

XPDL (XML Process Definition Language)

An XML based language for describing a process definition, developed by the WfMC. Version 1.0 was released in 2002. Version 2.0 was released in Oct 2005. The goal of XPDL is to store and exchange the process diagram, to allow one tool to model a process diagram, and another to read the diagram and edit, another to "run" the process model on an XPDL-compliant BPM engine, and so on. For this reason, XPDL is not an executable programming language like BPEL, but specifically a process design format that literally represents the "drawing" of the process definition. Thus it has 'XY' or vector coordinates, including lines and points that define process flows. This allows an XPDL to store a one-to-one representation of a BPMN process diagram. For this reason, XPDL is effectively the file format or "serialization" of BPMN, as well as any non-BPMN design method or process model which use in their underlying definition the XPDL meta-model (there are presently about 60 tools which use XPDL for storing process models.)

In spring 2012, the WfMC completed XPDL 2.2 as the *fifth* revision of this specification. XPDL 2.2 builds on version 2.1 by introducing support for the process modeling extensions added to BPMN 2.0.

BPSim

The Business Process Simulation (BPSim) framework is a standardized specification that allows business process models captured in either BPMN or XPDL to be augmented with information in support of rigorous methods of analysis. It defines the parameterization and interchange of process analysis data allowing structural and capacity analysis of process models. BPSim is meant to support both pre-execution and post-execution optimization of said process models. The BPSim specification consists of an underlying computer-interpretable representation (meta-model) and an accompanying electronic file format to ease the safeguard and transfer of this data between different tools (interchange format).

Wf-XML

Wf-XML is designed and implemented as an extension to the OASIS Asynchronous Service Access Protocol (ASAP). ASAP provides a standardized way that a program can start and monitor a program that might take a long time to complete. It provides the capability to monitor the running service, and be informed of changes in its status. Wf-XML extends this by providing additional standard web service operations that allow sending and retrieving the "program" or definition of the service which is provided. A process engine has this behavior of providing a service that lasts a long time, and also being programmable by being able to install process definitions.

Awards

The Workflow Management Coalition sponsors three annual award programs.

1. The **Global Awards for Excellence in BPM & Workflow**[1] recognizes organizations that have implemented particularly innovative workflow solutions. Every year between 10 and 15 BPM and workflow solutions are recognized in this manner. WfMC publishes the case studies in the annual Excellence in Practice series.

2. WfMC inaugurated a Global Awards program in 2011 for **Excellence in Case Management**[2] case studies to recognize and focus upon successful use cases for coordinating unpredictable work patterns. Awards are given in the category of Production Case Management and in Adaptive Case Management which are both new technological approaches to supporting knowledge work in today's leading edge organizations. These awards are designed to highlight the best examples of technology to support knowledge workers. In 2013, WfMC updated the program to "WfMC Awards for Excellence in Case Management" to recognize the growing deployment of Production Case Management.

3. The **Marvin L. Manheim Award For Significant Contributions** in the Field of Workflow is given to one person every year in recognition of individual contributions to workflow and BPM standards. This award commemorates Marvin Manheim who played a key motivational role in the founding of the WfMC.

The Workflow Management Coalition gives you the unique opportunity to participate in the creation of standards for the workflow industry as they are developing. Your contributions to our community ensure that progress continues in the adoption of royalty-free workflow and process standards.

The Secretariat

Workflow Management Coalition (WfMC.org)

Nathaniel Palmer, Executive Director

---

[1] www.BPMF.org

[2] www.adaptivecasemanagement.org

Index

More Reading and Resources

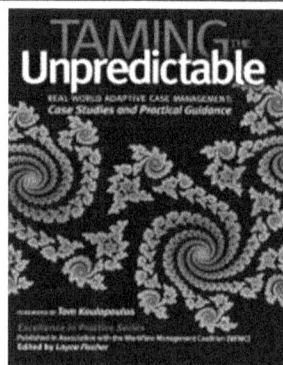

How Knowledge Workers Get Things Done

http://www.futstrat.com/books/HowKnowledgeWorkers.php

How Knowledge Workers Get Things Done describes the work of managers, decision makers, executives, doctors, lawyers, campaign managers, emergency responders, strategist, and many others who have to think for a living. These are people who figure out what needs to be done, at the same time that they do it, and there is a new approach to support this presents the logical starting point for understanding how to take advantage of ACM.
Retail $49.95 (see discount offer on website)

Delivering BPM Excellence

http://futstrat.com/books/Delivering_BPM.php

Business Process Management in Practice

The companies whose case studies are featured in this book have proven excellence in their creative and successful deployment of advanced BPM concepts. These companies focused on excelling in *innovation, implementation* and *impact* when installing BPM and workflow technologies. The positive impact includes increased revenues, more productive and satisfied employees, product enhancements, better customer service and quality improvements.
$39.95 (see discount on website)

Delivering the Customer-Centric Organization

http://futstrat.com/books/Customer-Centric.php
The ability to successfully manage the customer value chain across the life cycle of a customer is the key to the survival of any company today. Business processes must react to changing and diverse customer needs and interactions to ensure efficient and effective outcomes.

This important book looks at the shifting nature of consumers and the workplace, and how BPM and associated emergent technologies will play a part in shaping the companies of the future. **Retail $39.95**

BPMN 2.0 Handbook SECOND EDITION

(see two-BPM book bundle offer on website: get BPMN Reference Guide Free)
http://futstrat.com/books/bpmnhandbook2.php

Updated and expanded with exciting new content!

Authored by members of WfMC, OMG and other key participants in the development of BPMN 2.0, the BPMN 2.0 Handbook brings together worldwide thought-leaders and experts in this space. Exclusive and unique contributions examine a variety of aspects that start with an introduction of what's new in BPMN 2.0, and look closely at interchange, analytics, conformance, optimization, simulation and more.
Retail $75.00

www.ingramcontent.com/pod-product-compliance
Lightning Source LLC
Chambersburg PA
CBHW080720220326
41520CB00056B/7155